Backroad Mapbook

Welcome to the third edition of the Backroad Mapbook for the Kamloops/ Okanagan Region of British Columbia

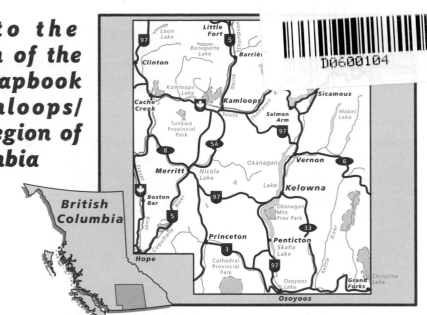

The Backroad Mapbooks have had a history of doing substantial changes and updates to the book and we are very confident you will be astounded by the improvements found within this book.

The first part of the book is devoted solely to the reference section. It is easy to see that this section has been expanded. People will find more lakes and streams to fish, more parks to visit, more areas to paddle and even places to look for wildlife.

In addition to the writing, followers of the Backroad Mapbooks will be impressed with the new look of the maps. The first thing that will jump out at you is the relief shading. This amazing feature will help people visualize the dramatic topography found in the Southern Interior of BC. Another prominent feature is the clarification of paved roads. Now people with RV's and cars will know which roads they will find much smoother to travel on. We have also spent countless hours updating the road and trail systems as well as adding new recreational features such as new provincial parks and wildlife viewing areas.

The Kamloops/Okanagan is a backroaders paradise. The rolling hillsides, open fields, and hot climate make

this region of BC truly unique. We cover a large area and offer a lifetime of things to do and see in the outdoors. From Hope and Clinton in the west to Grand Forks and Revelstoke in the east, from the US border north of the Bonaparte Plateau and Shuswap Lake, the recreational opportunities are endless.

The Backroad Mapbook is much more than a set of maps; it is an explorer's guide. The maps and writing will let you dream of places not so far away, so sit back and enjoy what we have to offer.

Backroad Mapbooks

DIRECTORS
Russell Mussio
Wesley Mussio
Penny Stainton-Mussio

COVER DESIGN & LAYOUT
Farnaz Faghihi

PRODUCTION
Adrian Brugge
Alfred Burger
Shawn Caswell
Farnaz Faghihi
Brett Firth
Dale Tober
Grace Teo
Heather Yetman

SALES /MARKETING
Shawn Caswell
Jason Marleau

WRITERS
Russell Mussio
Wesley Mussio
Trent Ernst

National Library of Canada Cataloguing in Publication Data

Mussio, Russell, 1969-
Mussio Venture presents Backroad mapbook. --
3rd ed.

Includes indexes.
Cover title.
Prepared by Russell and Wesley Mussio; vol. 3 by
Russell Mussio,
Wesley Mussio and Trent Ernst.
Incomplete contents: Vol. 1. Southwestern B.C.
-- v. 2. Vancouver
Island and the Gulf Islands. -- v. 3. Kamloops/
Okanagan.
ISBN 0-9697877-0-7 (v. 1). -- ISBN 1-894556-
10-0 (v. 2). -- ISBN 1-894556-21-6 (v. 3).

1. Recreation areas--British Columbia--Maps. 2.
British Columbia--Maps. I. Mussio, Wesley, 1964-
II. Ernst, Trent, 1970- III.
Title. IV. Title: Backroad mapbook.
G1170.B23 1998   912.711   C99-002459-8

Published by:

**Backroad
Mapbooks**
232 Anthony Court
New Westminster, B.C. V3L 5T5
P. (604) 438-3474   F. (604) 438-3470
E-mail: info@backroadmapbooks.com
www.backroadmapbooks.com
Copyright © 2003 Mussio Ventures Ltd.

Acknowledgements

This book could not have been compiled without the relentless effort of Trent Ernst.
He headed the research and writing effort and did a fabulous job of digging up countless
recreational opportunities and describing them in a creative, yet appealing way.
Combined with the talented people at Mussio Ventures Ltd., Adrian Brugge, Alfred
Burger, Shawn Caswell, Farnaz Faghihi, Brett Firth, Dale Tober, Grace Teo and
Heather Yetman, we were able to produce the most comprehensive guidebook for a
wonderful region of British Columbia.

Books like this are an exercise in research, not only by us, but also by the many people
who we can turn to for answers and information. Some are paid to know what they
know (recreation officers, forest rangers, etc.), some, like us, are just passionate about
the outdoors, and have spent their lives learning all they can about their neck of the
woods. Some of the people whose knowledge we leaned upon for this update were:
the Forest Service Recreation Officers like Jennifer Eastwood (Kamloops), Werner
Baliko (Boundary), Dave McIntosh (Vernon), Pierre Rossouw (Salmon Arm) Geordie
Patterson (100 Mile house), Roger Venables (Penticton) and Noelle Kekula (Merritt)
who did their best to answer questions about which sites are currently open and
which ones are closed. Other extremely helpful map providers such as Walter Hayashi
at the Boundary Forest District, Marlon Dosch and Rob MacLaren at the Merritt
Forest District, Dave Anderson at the Penticton Forest District as well as Hans
Svendsen from Riverside Forest Products in Kelowna. This is not to discount the
many other helpful people at all the Ministry of Highway district offices, and the
fine folks at Pope and Talbot in Midway and the several Weyerhaeuser Canada
locations throughout the region.

Thank you also to all the people who sent us emails to tell us updated information on
their favourite areas, be it road deactivations, new trails, or species of fish that can't be
found in certain lakes. We could not have done this without you all, and your help is
invaluable. Thanks to Penny Gubbels from the Friends of the South Slopes in Kelowna,
Mary Baily and all the others (Verner, Randy, Larry, Stephane, just to name a few)
for your input and gentle corrections. Thanks to all the BC Parks people who gave
us information on new parks, and set us straight on some errors that slipped through
the last time. And to all of you who we may have forgotten to mention, but who have
provided input into making this the best mapbook on the market, we are grateful
for your help and support.

Finally we would like to thank Allison, Devon, Nancy, Madison and Penny Mussio
for their continued support of the Backroad Mapbook Series. As our family grows,
it is becoming more and more challenging to break away from it all to explore our
beautiful country.

Help Us Help You

A comprehensive resource such as **Backroad Mapbooks** for Kamloops/Okanagan
could not be put together without a great deal of help and support. Despite our best
efforts to ensure that everything is accurate, errors do occur. If you see any errors or
omissions, please continue to let us know.

Please contact us at:
Mussio Ventures Ltd.
5811 Beresford St
Burnaby, B.C. V5J 1K1

Email: updates@backroadmapbooks.com

Call (604) 438-3474 or toll free 1-877-520-5670
Fax 1-604-438-3470

All updates will be posted on our web site:
www.backroadmapbooks.com

Disclaimer

Mussio Ventures Ltd. does not warrant that the backroads and trails indicated in this Mapbook are
passable nor does it claim that the Mapbook is completely accurate. Therefore, please be careful
when using this or any source to plan and carry out your outdoor recreation activity.

Please note that traveling on logging roads, river routes and trails is inherently dangerous,
and without limiting the generality of the foregoing, you may encounter poor road conditions,
unexpected traffic, poor visibility, and low or no road/trail maintenance. Please use extreme caution
when traveling logging roads and trails.

Please refer to the Fishing and Hunting Regulations for closures and restrictions. It is your
responsibility to know when and where closures and restrictions apply.

Table of Contents

Outdoor Recreation Reference Section

Map Section

Backroad Mapbooks

www.backroadmapbooks.com

Distributed by **Gordon Soules Book Publishers Ltd.**
1359 Ambleside Lane, West Vancouver, BC Canada V7T 2Y9
PMB 620, 1916 Pike Place #12, Seattle, WA 98101-1097, US
Web site: www.gordonsoules.com E-mail: books@gordonsoules.com
604-922-6588 Fax: 604-688-5442

Foreword

The Backroad Mapbook is truly a unique product. No other source covers the Southern Interior of BC with as much detail or information on all types of outdoor recreation activities.

The Backroad Mapbook is simple to use. There are two sections in the book, the reference section and the maps. If you know the activity you are planning, simply turn to that reference section and find the area that you are interested in. If you are planning a trip to a specific area, you should consult the index to find the appropriate map(s) and look for the various recreational opportunities highlighted in green and red.

The reference section found in the guide includes information on freshwater fishing, paddling routes, parks and wilderness camping (recreational sites), multi-use trails (hiking/biking, and off road trails), wildlife viewing and winter recreation. Countless hours have been spent in researching this book, making it the most complete compilation of outdoor recreation information you will find on the region anywhere. This information can be enjoyed by anyone who spends time in the great outdoors.

Our maps have been developed and updated using a wide variety of sources including the current forestry and logging road maps. Therefore, our maps are very detailed as they show a myriad of logging roads in addition to the various trail systems available. We provide a map legend at the start of the maps to illustrate the region we cover as well as how to decipher the various grades of roads and symbols used on the maps.

New to the maps is relief shading. It should be pointed out that this relief is included to give readers a general idea of topography. The accuracy is 25 metres (82 feet) with a sun angle of NW & SW. We have also included UTM Grids (datum NAD 1983; projection Albers Equal Area) and Longitude and Latitude reference points for GPS users. We must emphasis that these are for reference only. We cannot guarantee the accuracy of all sources we use to update the maps.

Although the Backroad Mapbook is the most detailed and up-to-date resource available to recreationists, it must be noted that it is only a planning and access guide. We have gone to great lengths to ensure the accuracy of the book. However, over time, road and trail conditions change. Always be prepared and please respect private property!

Russell and Wesley Mussio: Founders of Backroad Mapbooks

Backroad Travel

The Southern Interior is blessed with a good combination of highways and logging road. In fact, outside of a few notable exceptions, there are few areas in this region that are not accessible by some sort of motorized vehicle. This makes getting to the backcountry lake or hidden trailhead all that much easier.

Cars or RVs can travel many of the secondary roads, most of which are paved or hard packed gravel. The paved roads are shown on the maps as thicker black lines with a white fill. Thicker black lines mark the better gravel or main roads. Branching from the main roads are side roads and trails of all shapes and sizes. These routes, marked by thinner black lines and dashed lines on our maps, should be left to the off-road enthusiasts and trail users.

Although we have done our best to classify the road systems on our maps, road and trail conditions can change very quickly. Weather, the status of road systems and the degree of maintenance can all affect the road systems. During logging hours (6am to 6pm) or at times of extreme fire hazard, logging and rural roads may be closed to the public. Other roads may be gated to protect equipment in the area. Further, with the change in the Forest Practices Code, more and more roads are being deactivated. This can result in bridges and culverts being removed, making the road virtually impassable. Be sure to pay attention to road signs and always watch for logging trucks. Please contact the nearest Forest District Office for information on specific road conditions.

It is currently a period of great upheaval in the provincial recreation system. The Forest Service will no longer be looking after Forest Recreation Sites and many forest service roads (FSR) will not be maintained. This is going to restrict access to many of the recreational areas, and people without access to a four-wheel drive or an ATV may find it more difficult to access the backcountry.

The road systems that lead to active logging, mining or other industry sites will continue to see maintenance; as will those roads leading to remote communities. But it is the roads that are classified as Wilderness Use Roads that will not be graded or brushed. These roads will remain open, as long as they are safe, or if they are important for forest fire access. In the Southern Interior, as with other areas of the province, most of these roads that will be turned into Wilderness Use Roads are the ones that lead to really interesting destinations. Add in the overzealous cross-ditching practices of the 90's and backroaders will need a lot of patience when they get off of the main roads. So slow down and allow a bit of extra time to get to your destination.

While this is an accurate picture of outdoor recreation in the Southern Interior at the time it was written, we cannot vouch that it will be by the time you read this. If possible, check with someone in the know before you go. Our website www.backroadmapbooks.com has updates on access issues, as well as any new or changed information. If you try to go somewhere and find that things have changed from what we've written, please send us an email and let us know.

As always, we encourage comments, stories and pictures from our readers. Please drop us a line.

Backroad Mapbooks

www.backroadmapbooks.com

Freshwater Fishing

(Lake, River and Stream Fishing)

Lake Fishing

Some of the best lake fishing in the province is found in the Kamloops/Okanagan region. This region offers an amazing selection of lakes and is home to the world famous Kamloops Rainbow Trout. We have over 465 lakes written up, and there are still a few out there that we haven't mentioned (the others are mostly poor producers or are really, really small). The abundance of nutrient rich alkaline waters in the region means that fish are faster growing and achieve larger sizes than other lakes in the province. Big fish, combined with a wide variety of lakes—from huge valley-bottom lakes, like Okanagan and Shuswap Lakes, to tiny, high elevation lakes—provide anglers with a wide variety of opportunities.

In this region, seasonal water temperatures usually determine the quality of fishing. After the ice melts in the spring (April-May), fish can be found feeding near the surface and are the easiest to catch. As summer approaches, the fish retreat to deeper waters to avoid the algae bloom and the warmer waters, and the quality of fishing takes a corresponding drop. By fall, the water temperature starts to drop again and both the fish and the fishing quality start to rise. The lakes start to ice over in December. Winter is not usually as cold here as in other areas of the Interior, and ice fishing is limited.

Because of the number of lakes in the area, we have classified the lakes into fishing regions that match the Provincial Freshwater Fishing Regulations. For anglers looking for more detailed information, including depth charts and fishing tips, it is well advised to pick up a matching copy of the FISHING BC Series. These books cover many of the better fishing holes in each region (including the Thompson/Nicola and Okanagan Regions) and are the perfect complement to the Backroad Mapbook.

Please note *there are regulations imposed for many of the lakes in order to preserve the quality resource. Some of the regulations include bait bans, artificial fly only lakes, boating restrictions, catch and release, and closures. Check the Freshwater Fishing Regulations before fishing!*

Thompson/Nicola Region Lakes

There are many prime fishing lakes in the proximity of Merritt and Kamloops. This is because the lakes tend to be alkaline, nutrient rich waters ideal for insect populations; the mainstay of the rainbow diet. Fly fishing is extremely popular as this is home to the famous Kamloops Rainbow Trout.

Abbott Lake (Map 24/C3)
Abbott Lake is a 15 hectare lake with reasonable fishing for rainbow trout to 1 kg (2 lbs) throughout the ice free season. The lake is stocked annually with rainbow trout, which are best caught by spincasting, bait fishing or fly fishing. The high elevation (1,220 metres/3,965 feet) lake is found on a 4wd spur road east of Highway 8 and offers a small forest service site with a cartop boat launch.

Adams Lake (Maps 43, 51, 52)
This large 12,800 hectare, deep lake is easily accessed by a main haul logging road (except the remote southeast stretches). In the late spring (May and June) fishing is at its best as fish are actively feeding near the surface on salmon fry. To take advantage of the feed, it is best to troll a Silver Bucktail or Silver Spoon quickly on the surface. Often times, the salmon fry hold up in small bays and fly fishing or spincasting in these areas is very effective. By the summertime, the rainbow creep to the depths as the water warms and it is best to troll with a downrigger at 10–25 metres (30-90 feet) using a plug, Apex or Flatfish. The lake contains rainbow trout that average 3 kg (6+ lbs) as well as some larger lake trout and dolly varden (to 10 kg/22 lbs). Kokanee fishing can be effective in August through October. For the larger fish, try trolling a spoon, plug or Apex. For kokanee, a willow leaf meets with success. If you catch one kokanee, chances are you have found a school of kokanee so it is best to troll over the same area continuously for best results. The lake, at 405 metres (1,316 feet) in elevation, has boat launches at Skwaam Bay and Momich River. Several campsites line the lake.

Akehurst Lake (Map 49/E3)
A large 220 hectare lake located north of Bonaparte Lake on a 2wd/4wd road, this high elevation (1,275 metres/4,144 feet) lake has rainbow that reach 2 kg (4.5 lbs). The best time to fish is in the spring or fall by fly fishing (chironomids, damsel flies or leeches) or trolling. There is a resort on the lake.

Allan Lake (Map 49/G6)
Allan Lake is a 149 hectare lake accessed by a 2wd logging road off Highway 5 west of Barriere. The lake sees heavy fishing pressure throughout the ice free season for rainbow to 1 kg (2 lbs) and whitefish with trolling and fly fishing being the most popular methods. At the east end of the lake is a forest service site with a cartop boat launch and camping facilities. The lake elevation is 1,183 metres (3,883 feet) above sea level.

Alleyne Lake (Map 17/C3)
Part of the Kentucky-Alleyne Rec Area, this lake is a popular destination in the open water season with picnicking, boat launch facilities and camping. The 55 hectare lake is found 976 m (3,200 ft) above sea level and offers rainbow to 2 kg (4.5 lbs). The lake is often trolled but you can achieve success by fly fishing (shrimp and chironomids) the many marshy areas that ring the lake.

Antler Lake (Map 24/E1)
Located on a 4wd spur road north of Chataway Lake, this lake is reasonably good for rainbow trout to 1.5 kg (3 lbs) best caught on a fly. The lake is at a fairly high elevation (1,235 metres/4,014 feet), but still warms up in the summer. The sedge hatch begins in late June and is usually the best time to fly fish. There is a forest service site on the lake that offers camping as well as an opportunity to launch small boats.

Arthur Lake (Map 36/A5)
Found off the Bolean Lake Road (good 2wd access), Arthur Lake has a forest service site complete with a cartop boat launch. The 75 hectare lake is found at 1,465 m (4,806 ft) in elevation and offers good fishing for rainbow through the summer. The best time to fish the lake is in early June on a fly.

Badger and Spooney Lakes (Map 42/D3)
Badger and **Spooney Lakes** are separated by a narrow channel and stocked regularly with rainbow. The lakes, given their bait and ice fishing ban, are best fished in the spring and fall by fly fishing or spincasting. For fly fishermen, the sedge hatch in mid-June and the spring mayfly hatch are goods times to fish. Later in the spring and into the fall, try a caddisfly or dragonfly pattern. Also, try casting towards one of the many shoals that line the dark lakes. The lakes are at around 1,100 metres (3,575 feet) in elevation, and there is a forest service site at Badger Lake. The lakes are best accessed off Knouff Lake Road, a good road (most of the time), which leads from Highway 5 north of Heffley Creek. **Little Badger** is a 7 hectare lake, located to the northeast of Badger Lake. The lake offers slow fishing for rainbow that can reach 1 kg (2 lbs) in size.

Bare Lake (Map 49/D6)

Bare Lake is a large (230 hectare), remote lake reached by a 6 km (3.6 mile) hike along the Heller Lake Trail. The lake offers good fishing throughout the ice free season for rainbow to 1.5 kg (3 lbs) in size primarily by fly fishing or spincasting. Fly fishermen should try using chironomids, mayflies, sedges and leeches around the many shoals. The lake is at 1,340 metres (4,355 feet) in elevation and has a resort.

Barnes Lake (Map 31/F1)

Barnes Lake is easily accessed off Highway 97C on the Barnes Lake Road. The lake has a forest service site complete with a nice campground and a cartop boat launch. The lake covers 55 hectares, and is located at 700 metres (2,275 feet) in elevation. It is stocked annually with rainbow trout and provides reasonably good fishing for rainbow trout to 1 kg (2 lbs) by trolling or fly fishing. It is possible to cast a line from shore; especially in the summer when the lake suffers from draw down and the shoreline expands.

Big Ok (Island) Lake (Map 32/A6)

Often referred to as Island Lake, Big Ok is managed as a catch-and-release, fly fishing only lake (check the regulations for other restrictions). As a result, some big trout (up to 5 kg (10 lbs) are caught annually. Chironomid, caddisfly and mayflies are the preferred patterns but don't rule out leeches. The 24 hectare lake is found at 1,524 m (4,999 ft) in elevation and offers a popular forest service campsite and boat launch. Casting from a float tube towards the weeds and sunken island can be very effective.

Billy Lake (Map 32/E7)

Billy Lake is located on a 4wd road north of Chataway Lake. It is possible to catch a rainbow in the 2–3 kg (4.5–6+ lb) category but most of the fish are significantly smaller. The nutrient rich lake covers 24 hectares and usually produces well throughout the summer months for small rainbow on a fly or by spincasting. For the fly fishermen, try a shrimp, dragonfly or leech pattern for best results. Camping and a cartop boat launch are provided at the small forest service site.

Birch Lake (Map 49/E1)

Southeast of Lac des Roches and Highway 24, Birch Lake covers 240 hectares in size and found at 1,113 metres (3,651 feet) in elevation. The lake is best fished by fly fishing or trolling throughout the ice free season for rainbow that reach 2 kg (4.5 lbs) in size. There is also a fishery for burbot. Effective fly patterns include chironomids, mayflies, damsel flies, sedges and leeches. The lake has cartop boat launch facilities as well as a resort. Rainbow are stocked annually.

Black Lake (Map 34/C6)

See Roche Lake Group.

Blackwell Lake (Map 26/E1)

Blackwell Lake is reached by a 3 km (1.8 mile) hike from the Pratt Lake Forest Service Site. Set below Mt Bulman, the scenic lake has a rustic forest service site and offers good fly fishing or spincasting for rainbow that can grow to 1 kg (2 lbs). The waters are quite nutrient-rich and as a result the insects thrive. Matching the mayfly, caddisfly and chironomid hatches can result in great fishing for stocked rainbow. Fishing remains active throughout the summer months.

Bleeker Lake (Map 34/C6)

Bleeker Lake is a shallow, 40 hectare lake located north of Roche Lake along a 4wd road. The murky, nutrient-rich waters allow rainbow to grow to 3 kg (6+ lbs) as long as the lake is not exposed to winterkill, a problem in cold, long winters. At 1,044 m (3,425 ft), the lake is best fly fished using a shrimp, leech or dragonfly pattern in the early spring or late fall. The lake is used for irrigation so draw down and the warm days really affect fishing in the summer.

Blue Earth Lake (Map 31/B3)

This 115 hectare lake is located south of Upper Hat Creek on the Earth Lake Road (2wd access). The lake is not overly popular despite its scenic surroundings, crystal clear water and prominent shoals. It offers a good fishery for rainbow trout to 1 kg (2 lbs) by fly fishing (shrimp, dragonfly and damselfly patterns) or trolling (gang troll). A forest service site at the lake provides boat launching facilities and a small campsite. The lake is found at 1,370 metres (4,453 feet) in elevation and is stocked periodically with rainbow.

Blue Lakes (Map 26/B4)

Renowned for having good-sized rainbow (to 2 kg/4.5 lbs), **Blue Lake** is also notoriously difficult to fish. Your best bet is to cast a sinking line towards one of the shoals or into the deep section of the lake (towards the middle). Chironomid patterns in the spring, sedge patterns in early July and water boatman patterns in the fall are the most productive. The 12 hectare lake is stocked annually with rainbow and is an artificial fly only lake with no ice fishing allowed. Rustic camping and a cartop boat launch are available at the lake, which is accessed off of Lauder Road east of Glimpse Lake. The high elevation (1,220 metres/3,965 feet) water body remains active throughout the summer. Nearby **Little Blue Lake** grows some pretty big fish, with rainbow that can reach 1.5 kg (3 lbs). The difficult 4wd access discourages fishermen but there is a place to launch cartop boats or even camp next to the lake. The 7 hectare lake is stocked annually with rainbow.

Bob's Lake (Map 17/G3)

The 10 hectare lake has a forest service site with a cartop boat launch, picnicking and a camping area. The lake provides good fishing for small rainbow that can reach 1 kg (2 lbs) in size by fly fishing, bait fishing or spincasting.

Bogmar Lake (Map 49/G5)

Bogmar Lake is located to the east of Mayson Lake off the Jamieson Creek Road. A short hike is required to reach the 15 hectare lake, which is at 1,220m (4,000 ft) in elevation. The lake contains rainbow trout to 1 kg (2 lbs) in size that are best caught in the spring or fall.

Bolean Lake (Map 35/G5)

With a resort, campground, cabins and rentals, this 78 hectare lake certainly sees its share of anglers. As a result, the rainbow rarely grow over 1 kg (2 lbs) in size and can be a bit more challenging to hook. The tea coloured lake is at 1,437 metres (4,715 feet) in elevation and best worked near the deeper northwest end. Attractor type fly patterns or lures with bait can be effective.

Bonaparte Lake (Map 49/C5)

Bonaparte Lake is the largest lake on the Bonaparte Plateau north of Kamloops. The lake is high enough (1,169 metres/3,834 feet) and deep enough to stay cool through summer, meaning that fishing is good throughout the open water season. Bonaparte is also a good ice fishing lake. There are a number of resorts on the lake, as well as a forest service site with a cartop boat launch and camping. Fishing can be very slow, but the big rainbow (over 5 kg/10 lbs) make the wait well worth it. Trolling is the mainstay of the lake with plugs and Crocodile lures working the best when your gear is trolled deep. There is also a good number of small kokanee that can be taken by trolling.

Boot Lake (Map 17/G3)

Boot Lake is a high elevation (1,500 metres/4,875 feet) lake, which offers a good fishery for rainbow trout to 1 kg (2 lbs) throughout the summer months. The access into the 30 hectare lake is a little rough but there is a rustic forest service site offering camping and a cartop boat launch.

Bose Lake (Map 32/B3)

Bose Lake is located north of Highway 97C on a 4wd road (Bose Lake Road). The high elevation (1,280 metres/4,160 feet) lake offers good fishing for rainbow trout to 1 kg (2 lbs) in size on a fly. The lake has a small forest service site complete with camping and a cartop boat launch. Rainbow are stocked annually at the 30 hectare lake.

Boulder Lake (Map 18/A4)

Boulder Lake is a hike-in lake north of the Okanagan Connector (Hwy 97C) offering reasonably good fishing for small rainbow on a fly, using bait or by spincasting. The lake is 20 hectares in size, and offers fishing throughout the summer months because of its high elevation (1,465 metres/4,761 feet).

Bryden and Pement Lake (Map 35/G1)

Bryden and Pement Lakes are accessed by a trail off the China Valley Road. The lakes total 16 hectares and are best fished for the small rainbow using a bobber and bait or by fly fishing. For fly fishermen, try a Doc Spratley or Woolly Bugger. Fishing remains fairly good from June to September as the number of fish in both lakes is very good. The lakes have camping and are at 1,340 metres (4,355 feet) in elevation.

Calling Lake (Map 32/A7)

Calling Lake is a 30 hectare, high elevation (1,560 metres/5,070 feet) lake, which suffers from both winterkill and summer draw down. Still, the lake still produces well for rainbow trout to 1 kg (2 lbs) in size throughout the spring and fall by trolling (gang troll or leech pattern) or by fly fishing (shrimp pattern). The lake is comprised of dark, nutrient rich waters and is stocked periodically. There is no camping at the lake but there is an opportunity to launch small boats.

Campbell Lake (Map 34/D5)

Campbell Lake covers 110 hectares, and is considered a great fly fishing lake for the skilled angler, especially in the late spring during the caddisfly hatch. This lake suffers from an algae bloom in the summer due to its shallow, dark and nutrient-rich waters. Winds also play havoc to boaters. Campbell Lake offers a forest service site near the southwest end that must be accessed from the west as the north end of the lake is private property. The stocked rainbow trout can reach 5 kg (10 lbs) in size but average 1.5 kg (3 lbs).

Caverhill Lake (Map 49/F3)

Caverhill Lake has rainbow to 1 kg (2 lbs) best caught by trolling (flies or gang troll), fly fishing (chironomids, mayflies, sedges or leeches) or spincasting (small lures) throughout the ice free season. Despite its size, the 542 hectare lake has many bays and islands that are ideal for casting a line. A boat access resort on the lake provides the ideal getaway including hiking trails and rentals.

Chapperon Lake (Map 26/E5)

Found in the heart of the Douglas Lake Ranch, this is a private lake that offers very good fly fishing for rainbow to 2 kg (4.5 lbs). The 393 hectare lake is quite shallow and subject to winterkill.

Chataway Lake (Map 24/E1)

Chataway Lake is a popular high elevation (1,500 metres/4,875 feet) lake that serves as the hub of several small mountain lakes (including Antler, Billy, Dot, Gypsum and Gump Lakes). Despite the heavy fishing pressure, it consistently produces small rainbow with some reaching 2 kg (4.5 lbs). The 15 hectare lake is best trolled, although fly fishing is popular. The most productive fly patterns are attractor type patterns like a woolly bugger or a Doc Spratley. There is a nice fishing resort as well as camping facilities and a boat launch at the lake.

Community Lake (Map 42/E4)

Community Lake is located on a good road off the Knouff Lake Road. The high elevation (1,375 metre/4,469 feet) allows fishing to remain good throughout the summer months, although draw down in some years may limit summer fishing. Since there is a bait and ice fishing ban, your best bet is to fly fish or spincast for the rainbow that reach 1.5 kg (3+ lbs). The sedge hatch in mid-June and the spring chironomid hatch are the best times to fly fish. Outside these hatches, fly fishermen can produce with caddis fly, damselfly or dragonfly patterns. It is best to try around the islands or the shoals, especially at dusk with sedge flies. The 40 hectare lake is stocked annually with rainbow and has a forest service site with a cartop boat launch and camping facilities.

Corbett Lake (Map 17/B1)

This 29 hectare lake is located right next to the Okanagan Connector (Hwy 97C) at the junction with the Kane Valley Road. It is a private, fly fishing only lake and there is a charge to fish for visitors not staying at the inn. The lake is stocked annually with rainbow to ensure reasonable success for the fishermen. The lake, at 1,042 metres (3,418 feet) in elevation, is quite shallow and contains clear water, which allows you to see the drop-offs.

Courtney Lake (Map 17/B1)

Located alongside Highway 97C, the 74 hectare Courtney Lake contains redside shiners (much to the dismay of most anglers) and stocked rainbow. Despite its close proximity to the highway, the good sized trout (to 1.5 kg/3 lbs) and large shoals, Courtney is often overlooked as a fly fishing destination. Check the regulations for restrictions.

Crater Lake (Map 17/C3)

This lake, at 1,000 metres (3,250 feet) in elevation, offers surprisingly good fishing for smaller rainbow that can reach 2 kg (4.5 lbs) in size. Trolling is the mainstay of the 20 hectare lake.

Crystal Lake (Maps 48/G1, 49/A1)

Located on the North Bonaparte Lake Road (2wd) southwest of Bridge Lake and Highway 24, this 138 hectare lake offers reasonably good fishing for rainbow trout. The fish average just under 1 kg (2 lbs) but can reach 2 kg (4.5 lbs) in size. In addition to a guest ranch, there is a forest service site on the west side of the lake. The lake is stocked annually and can be fished throughout the ice free season by trolling or fly fishing as well as during the winter by bait fishing. The lake is at 1,159 metres (3,81 feet) in elevation.

Cultus Lake (Map 40/B6)

This 48 hectare lake is easily accessed of the Deadman-Cache Creek Road and offers fair fishing for small rainbow. At 838 m (2,750 ft) in elevation, the shallow lake does suffer from the summer doldrums.

Cummins Lake (Map 45/F6)

Cummins Lake is a mountain lake located off the Yard Creek FSR (4wd access) and then a short trail. The lake can be fished from July to August for rainbow reaching 1 kg (2 lbs). Try a bobber and bait, fly fishing or spincasting. It is possible to camp at the lake.

Dagger Lake (Map 49/F7)

This remote 49 hectare lake is only accessed by trail or by the horse drawn car service of Skitchine Lodge. As a result, the lake sees few anglers and can be very good fishing for stocked rainbow trout. Due to the elevation (1,458 m/4,783 ft), the fishing remains good in the summer months.

Dairy Lake (Map 33/A3)

This 25 hectare lake is located along a 2wd road to the east of Greenstone Mountain and is found at 1,460 metres (4,745 feet) in elevation. The lake is subject to winterkill, and draw down in the summer, but an aggressive stocking program helps maintain the fishery. The lake is best fished by trolling, although fly fishing can be effective at times. There is a cartop boat launch at the forest service site on the northeast shore.

Dardanelles Lake (Map 26/C1)

Dardanelles Lake has very good fly fishing for rainbow to 1.5 kg (3 lbs). In the spring, there is a good caddisfly and chironomid hatch to imitate, while a strong sedge hatch occurs in mid-June. In the fall, water boatmen patterns can be effective. At other times of the year, slowly trolling a leech pattern will produce. Watch for the single barbless hook restriction and bait ban.

Deadman Lake (Map 48/F7)

Deadman Lake is located off the Deadman Vidette Road (rough in sections), which runs southward from Vidette to Highway 1 west of Kamloops Lake. The 49 hectare lake has reasonably good fishing for rainbow and kokanee that reach 1 kg (2 lbs) in size that are best caught by fly fishing or trolling. The lake has a forest service site on the eastern shore.

Dennis Lake (Map 43/B7)

This 6 hectare lake is subject to winterkill but can be fairly productive in good years for rainbow that reach 1 kg (2 lbs). To offset the winterkill, the lake is stocked periodically. There is a small forest service site and a cartop boat launch on the lake, which may require a 4wd vehicle to reach. The lake is 1,220 metres (3,965 feet) in elevation.

Desmond Lake (Map 33/B7)

Desmond Lake is located on the rough Surrey Lake FSR just south of the Meadow Creek Road west of Highway 5. The 25 hectare lake has spotty fishing for rainbow trout to 1 kg (2 lbs), with three distinct holes to work.

Dixon Lake (Map 50/G7)

This small 13 hectare lake is located on the Dixon Creek Road and provides good fishing for small rainbow by fly fishing or spincasting. Most attractor type flies or small lures work on the easily caught rainbow. The lake is at 980 metres (3,185 feet) in elevation.

Dominic Lake (Map 33/A4)

The 35 hectare Dominic Lake is located north of Face Lake on the Paska Lake Road (4wd recommended). The lake offers good fishing for rainbow to 1 kg (2 lbs) best caught by fly fishing (attractor patterns) or trolling (gang troll). There is an undeveloped campsite on the east end of the lake as well as a resort with camping facilities. The lake is subject to draw down but given its high elevation (1,540 metres/5,005 feet), it still offers reasonable fishing throughout the summer months.

Dot Lake (Map 24/E1)

Dot is a high elevation (1,220 metres/3,965 feet) lake with sporadic rainbow trout that reach 1 kg (2 lbs) in size. Trolling is the best way to locate the fish in this 40 hectare lake. A forest service site offers camping and an opportunity to launch a small boat.

Douglas Lake (Map 26/A6)

Douglas Lake is located along the paved Douglas Lake Road and is at 825 metres (2,681 feet) in elevation. The lake is noted more for cattle ranching than for fishing, but it is possible to catch rainbow to 1 kg (2 lbs), small kokanee and burbot (through the ice). The Douglas Lake Cattle Company offers a campground with a boat launch that can be used for a fee. The lake covers 650 hectares.

Duffy Lake (Map 33/A2)

This 23 hectare lake is located on a 2wd road south of Cherry Creek. The lake is stocked annually with rainbow that can reach 2 kg (4.5 lbs) in size, although the average catch is quite small. Both trolling and fly fishing can be quite effective throughout the spring and fall. For the fly fishermen, try a shrimp, dragonfly or mayfly pattern depending on the hatch. The lake has a small forest service site with camping and boat launch facilities.

Dum Lake (Map 50/A1)

Off a 4wd road west of Little Fort, this small (15 hectare) lake offers good fishing primarily by fly fishing throughout the spring and fall. For best results, try a caddisfly or dragonfly pattern.

Dunn Lake (Map 50/D1)

Located on a 2wd road east of Little Fort, Dunn Lake is a scenic lake set below Mt Fennell. The 131 hectare lake is 451 metres (1,480 feet) in elevation and contains fair numbers of rainbow trout, dolly vardens, lake trout and kokanee best caught by trolling throughout the spring or fall. There is a forest service site at the north end of the lake offering camping and a cartop boat launch as well as a rustic resort on the west end of the lake.

Dunsapie Lake (Map 49/G6)

This 10 hectare lake is located along the Jamieson Creek Road. It has a nice forest service site with camping and a cartop boat launch. The lake is primarily trolled for the fair number of rainbow to 1 kg (2 lbs). The high elevation lake (1,375 metres/4,469 feet) has reasonably good fishing throughout the summer months. Fly fishers will find that spring and fall are the better times to fish.

Eagan Lake (Map 49/A3)

Northwest of Bonaparte Lake along the Egan-Bonaparte Lake FSR, this lake offers fairly good fishing for rainbow that can reach 1 kg (2 lbs) in size. There are also some small kokanee that inhabit the lake. The lake is 1,050 metres (3,413 feet) above sea level, and has a resort on the north end of the lake.

East Barriere Lake (Map 51/B5)

A long narrow lake found on the East Barriere FSR (2wd access), this 1,036 hectare lake is usually trolled. Try working flies or a gang troll near the many shoals for the dolly varden, rainbow trout, lake trout and kokanee that inhabit the lake. The lake is 640 metres (2,100 feet) above sea level and sports an airstrip, a forest service site with camping and a boat launch as well as a resort on the west end of the lake. The Barriere Lakes are good alternatives if you want to get away from the crowds that other lakes in the area see.

Edith Lake (Map 33/G4)

Edith Lake is easily accessed off a 2wd road from Knutsford. The lake covers 27 hectares and has a surprisingly good fishery for brook trout in the early spring and late fall as well as during ice fishing season. The fish are best caught by a small lure with bait during the open water season or bait and hook during ice fishing season. The lake is at 1,020 metres (3,345 feet) in elevation and is rumoured to have a few rainbow that are very hard to catch. Both brook trout and rainbow are stocked annually at the lake to counteract winterkill.

Edna Lake (Map 16/G1)

Edna Lake covers 11 hectares, and is located on a 2wd access road. It is considered a reasonably good lake for fishing small brook trout. The lake, at 1,130 metres (3,673 feet) in elevation, is best fished during the fall or during ice fishing season. It is possible to launch small boats at the lake.

Eileen Lake (Map 42/G7)

Eileen Lake is found on a 2wd access road south of Sun Peaks and provides a reasonably good fishery for small rainbow. The 10 hectare lake is stocked annually allowing some of the trout to reach 1.5 kg (3+ lbs) in size. The lake is at 915 metres (2,974 feet) in elevation and warms in the summer so it is best to fish in the spring or fall. It is possible to launch small boats at the lake.

Elbow Lake (Map 49/C7)
You'll have to hike in to Elbow Lake, along the Heller Lake Trail, but you won't have to carry a tent if you're planning on staying (unless you want to), as there is a resort on the west end of the lake. Elbow offers great fishing for rainbow trout to 1 kg (2 lbs) by fly fishing or spincasting. The lake is high enough (at 1,400 metres/4,550 feet) to stay cool through summer, so the fishing remains fairly active throughout the ice free season. Fly fishermen can try chironomids, mayflies, damsel flies or leeches around the shoals.

Face Lake (Map 33/B5)
Face Lake is located north of Highway 97C on Paska Lake Road (4wd). A nice forest service site lies on the north end of the lake offering a boat launch as well as camping facilities. The 60 hectare lake is best trolled with a Flatfish or other small lure anytime during the spring or fall for rainbow to 1 kg (2 lbs). Although fly fishing is usually difficult at this high elevation (1,310 metres/4,258 feet) lake, attractor type patterns can produce at times.

Fleming Lake (Map 43/G7)
The Skimikin Lake Road provides good access to several lakes. Fleming Lake is a tiny 1.6 hectare lake surrounded by bulrushes making boat launching difficult. The lake does have fairly good numbers of small rainbow but coarse fish do compete heavily for available food. Anglers will find success with a bobber and worm.

Forest Lake (Map 42/G1)
Found next to a main haul logging road, Forest Lake offers reasonable fishing for small rainbow primarily by trolling. The 27 hectare lake is fairly low in elevation, at 600 metres (1,950 feet), so fishing is best in spring and fall. There is a cartop boat launch.

Fred Lake (Map 33/F7)
Fred Lake has stocked rainbow as well as brook trout which both can reach 2 kg (4.5 lbs). The 10 hectare lake is found on a 4wd road east of Lac Le Jeune and has a cartop boat launch but no developed camping. The lake is found at 1,250 metres (4,063 feet) in elevation and is best fished using bait or by spincasting or fly fishing with attractor type patterns. The lake is subject to winterkill.

Frogmoore Lakes (Map 25/C1)
A pair of lakes, covering 80 hectares in total, the Frogmoores have rainbow trout to 2 kg in size. The lakes are 1,140 metres (3,705 feet) above sea level, and tend to get too warm to fish in summer.

Gannett Lake (Map 52/C1)
Found near the 13 km mark of the Gannett Lake FSR, the side road to this lake may require a 4wd vehicle. The rainbow are generally small but there are expansive shallows and weed beds to provide good cover. Fly anglers should work these areas, while trollers should work the deeper parts of the 78 hectare lake. There is a forest service site on the northern shore that offers a cartop boat launch.

Gillis Lake (Map 16/C3)
This popular 15 hectare lake is easily accessed off the Coquihalla Highway. As a result, the forest service site with a cartop boat launch can be busy on weekends. Fishing for rainbow trout to 1.5 kg (3 lbs) in size remains steady due in part to the stocking program. The best time for fishing is during the spring and fall using a fly or by trolling.

Glimpse Lake (Map 26/A4)
Glimpse Lake provides good fishing for rainbow trout to 1 kg (2 lbs). Your best bet is to fly fish or troll any time during the open water season for the stocked rainbow. For fly fishermen, a sedge pattern in the early summer or a damselfly nymph pattern in the spring meet with success. The lake has a cartop boat launch, camping facilities and a resort. The 95 hectare lake is at 1,219 metres (4,000 feet) in elevation and has an electric motor only restriction in effect.

Green Lake (Maps 47/F2-48/B1)
Green Lake is renowned for its beautiful green waters, and as a result, it is a popular recreation lake. A provincial park with several camping/day-use facilities as well as several resorts appeal to the many visitors throughout the summer months. This Cariboo lake is easily accessed and provides fair fishing for kokanee and rainbow trout (to 3 kg/6+ lbs) primarily by trolling.

Gordon Lake (Map 24/C3)
Gordon Lake provides good fishing for rainbow trout to 1.5 kg (3 lbs). The preferred methods of fishing are fly fishing and trolling particularly during the spring or fall. Access to this shallow, high elevation (1,400 metres/4,550 feet) lake is by 4wd road off the Tyner FSR. There is a forest service site with a cartop boat launch and camping at the 30 hectare lake. A stocking program is in effect at the lake.

Gorman Lake (Map 50/A5)
West of Barriere, Gorman Lake covers an area of 20 hectares and is high enough (1,135 metres/4,051 feet) and deep enough to remain cool throughout the summer months. Despite the easy access and forest service site complete with a cartop boat launch and camping facilities, it offers fairly good fishing for stocked rainbow trout that can reach 1 kg (2 lbs) in size. Bait fishing, trolling and fly fishing (chironomids, damsel flies or leeches) all produce throughout the ice free season.

Griffin Lake (Map 46/B4)
Griffin Lake is located next to Highway 1 northwest of Three Valley Gap. The 35 hectare lake has a small population of rainbow trout, lake trout and dollies, which reach 2 kg (4.5 lbs) on occasion. Your best chance for success is to troll a willow leaf, plug or Flatfish.

Grizzly Lake (Map 52/D7)
Once a remote fishing gem, Grizzly Lake has suffered from over fishing ever since an ATV trail was cut into the lake. Now, there is fairly slow fishing for rainbow that can grow to over 1 kg (2 lbs). The lake is at 1,500 metres (4,875 feet) in elevation and is best fished in the early summer or into the fall.

Gump Lake (Map 32/E7)
The 20 hectare Gump Lake contains stocked rainbow that can reach 2 kg (4.5 lbs) in size, but don't expect to catch too many of these cagey fish. The shallow, clear lake is accessed by hiking the deactivated roads from the Witches Brook Road. Fly fishing is the preferred method of fishing with the spring chironomid and mayfly hatches or the mid-June sedge hatch being the best times to fish.

Gwen Lake (Map 16/G1)
Gwen Lake is accessed off the Comstock Road (4wd recommended) and holds rainbow to 2 kg (4.5 lbs). The fishing remains reasonably productive throughout the open water season. There are camping facilities available at the forest service site next to the 20 hectare lake.

Gypsum Lake (Map 24/E2)
The 12 hectare Gypsum Lake provides a fishery for rainbow trout to 1 kg (2 lbs). The best time for fishing is during the spring and fall at which time spincasting and fly fishing can be productive. A cartop boat launch and camping facilities are available at the high elevation (1,430 metres/4,648 feet) lake. Access to the lake is via a 4wd road.

Hamilton Lake (Map 25/B7)
Hamilton Lake is a 22 hectare lake that suffers from winterkill. Brook trout can migrate into the lake and the best time to fish is in the fall just before spawning season. At this time, the fish are taken easily on large fly patterns and lures (Deadly Dicks) with a worm. The lake is at 1,100 metres (3,575 feet) in elevation and is accessed by a 2wd road just off the Highway. There is a place to launch cartop boats.

Hammer Lake (Map 49/A5)
Hammer Lake has a good sedge fly hatch, which means that fly fishing is best in late June and into July. Be forewarned that the lake can be

quite moody especially in the summer when the waters warm due to the shallow depths. The lake contains rainbow in the 1–2 kg (2–4.5 lb) range, although there is the odd fish that reaches 3 kg (6+ lbs). The lake covers 68 hectares, and has a forest service site found along the 3700 Road. There is an electric motor only restriction on the 1,311 metre (4,300 feet) high lake.

Harmon Lakes (Map 17/A2) ⌖
See Kane Valley Lakes.

Harper Lake (Map 35/C1) ⌖
On a secondary road off the Chase-Falkland Road, this 28 hectare lake offers fair fishing for rainbow, which reach 2 kg (4.5 lbs). The preferred method of fishing is by fly as there is a bait ban, single hook restriction and ice fishing ban at the lake. Fly fishermen should have a little patience and a good selection of leeches, shrimp or during the summer, dragonfly patterns. The low elevation lake has a forest service site and opens earlier than many in the area.

Hatheume Lake (Map 18/E2) ⌖
The 134 hectare Hatheume Lake is a catch-and-release fishery for rainbow that are now reaching 1.5 kg (3 lbs) in size. It is ideal for fly fishing with a good spring chironomid hatch and late June sedge hatch. The high elevation (1,395 metres/4,576 feet) lake has a resort as well as a forest service site with camping facilities. There is a single hook restriction, bait ban and ice fishing ban at the lake.

Heffley Lakes (Map 42/E6) ⌖
On the paved Sun Peaks Road, **Heffley Lake** covers 203 hectares, while the nearby **Little Heffley Lake** only covers seven. Heffley Lake has two resorts as well as a forest service site and numerous private homes. Due to their good access, the lakes receive heavy fishing pressure but they do offer some reasonable fishing for rainbow trout to 1.5 kg (3+ lbs) throughout the ice-free season. Most troll the bigger lake but fly fishermen can try the shoals at the west end of the lake during the spring damselfly or mayfly hatch. The stocked lakes are at 943 metres (3,095 feet) in elevation.

Heller Lake (Map 49/B4)
Heller Lake is another hike-in lake, accessed along the Heller Lake Trail, which starts at the south end of the Bonaparte Provincial Park. The lake is high enough (1,220 metres/3,965 feet) to provide very good fishing for rainbow trout to 1.5 kg (3.5 lbs) in size throughout the ice free season.

Helmer Lake (Map 25/A2)
This 15 hectare lake offers some good fishing for small rainbow trout during the spring and fall. Try casting a small lure or an attractor type fly. The lake is accessed off a 2wd road (Helmer Road) from the Coquihalla Highway. There is a small forest service site with camping at the lake. Summer draw down can be a problem since the lake is used for irrigation purposes.

Herman Lake (Map 44/F5)
Although this lake is only 4 hectares, it is worth mentioning because it offers very good fishing for small brook trout, especially in the fall or during ice fishing season. The lake is located on a rough 2wd road and has a forest service site complete with a boat launch and campground. For best results, spincasting the shallows with a Deadly Dick and worm or fly fish with an attractant type fly. The lake is stocked regularly.

Hiahkwah Lake (Map 41/D1)
This lake can be reached by a 4wd road or trail and has a good population of rainbow that can grow to 1 kg (2 lbs). Fly fishing around the shoals with sedge flies at dusk in June and July is quite effective. Chironomids, mayflies and leeches also work. The lake is at 1,325m (4,350 feet) in elevation.

Hihium Lake (Map 40/A1)
This 350 hectare lake is located by 2wd road from Loon Lake or from

the east on the 3400 Road. The lake is known as an excellent fly fishing lake, given its abundant weed beds and rocky shoals, which provides natural cover for the rainbow that reach 2 kg (4.5 lbs). A good chironomid and mayfly hatch as well as the smaller damselfly and sedge (in June and July) hatches are good times to fish. Anglers also try trolling a leech or casting an attractor pattern at other times of the year. The high elevation (1,375 metres/4,469 feet) has two forest service sites and a boat access fish camp on its shores. Restrictions include single hooks and bans on ice fishing and bait use. Wind can be a problem for boaters.

Hoopatatkwa Lake (Map 49/E6) ⌖
Located near the north end of Bonaparte Provincial Park, this lake is accessible only by trail or float plane. The high elevation (1,387 metres/4,550 feet) lake covers 104 hectares, and has good fishing for rainbow trout to 2 kg (4.5 lbs). Fly fishing (chironomids, damsel flies and sedges), bait fishing or spincasting are all effective. There is a resort at the lake.

Hosli Lake (Map 34/C6)
Hosli Lake is stocked annually with rainbow trout that can reach 2 kg (4.5 lbs) in size. There is a bait and ice fishing ban in effect so your best options are to fly fish or spincast in the spring or fall. Casting around the sunken island or near the drop-offs during the June sedge hatch can be great. It is possible to launch cartop boats or even camp at lakeside, but these options are undeveloped. The lake is at 1,175 metres (3,818 feet) in elevation.

Humamilt Lake (Maps 52/G4, 53/A4)
Humamilt Lake is a long narrow lake—actually a chain of three small lakes totaling 465 hectares—which offer fairly good fishing in the spring and fall for small rainbow trout. Trolling and fly fishing are the preferred methods of fishing. There are forest service sites on the west and east ends of the low elevation (580 metres/1,885 feet) lake.

Hunakwa Lake (Map 53/B7)
This remote lake can only be accessed by boat and then on foot from the north end of Anstey Arm of Shuswap Lake. Needless to say, there are few visitors to this 497 hectare lake. Trolling, fly fishing and spincasting can all produce rainbow.

Hyas & Area Lakes (Map 42/G7) ⌖
North of Paul Lake, a series of small mountain lakes offer good fishing. The access to the lakes is via the Hyas Lake Road, which is sometimes passable by 2wd, but you will probably need a 4wd vehicle. The lakes are found around 1,230 m (4,035 ft) and are best fished in the spring and fall:

Hyas Lake is a 64 hectare lake, with fair fishing for rainbow to 2 kg (4.5 lbs). Because the lake has deep, clear water, trolling is the primary fishing method although fly fishing can work. There is a resort and forest service site on the lakeshore.

Hadlow Lake is a small hike-in lake northwest of Hyas Lake, which has small rainbow that can reach 1 kg (2 lbs) in size. The 7 hectare lake is best fished by casting a lure and bait or by fly fishing (the sedge hatch in the spring is the best time to fly fish). The lake is stocked periodically given the fact that the shallowness of the lake makes winterkill a real problem.

Pemberton Lake provides fairly good fishing for stocked rainbow that can reach 1.5 kg (3 lbs). Fly fishing (shrimp and dragonfly patterns) and trolling (gang troll) are the main fishing methods. The 13 hectare lake is subject to draw down during the summer, so it is best to fish in the spring or fall. A small forest service site on the lake provides camping and cartop boat launch facilities.

Warren Lake offers good fishing for rainbow in the 2–3 kg (4.5–6+ lbs) range, although most fish are substantially smaller than that. There are private cabins on the 25 hectare lake, and an option to launch a small boat.

Island Lake (Map 18/A3) 🐟

Island Lake offers small, stocked rainbow that can be caught fairly regularly throughout the ice free season. There is a forest service site next to the 34 hectare lake.

Isobel Lake (Map 41/F6) 🐟

Isobel Lake is a small 14 hectare lake with a good population of stocked brook trout that are best caught in the fall or through the ice. There is a forest service site providing camping and a cartop boat launch at the lake, which is at 976 metres (3,200 feet) in elevation.

Jacko Lake (Map 33/F3)

Promoted as one of the better lakes around Kamloops, Jacko Lake has rainbow that can reach 2 kg (4.5 lbs) in size. Along with chironomids, shrimp and leeches make up the majority of the trout's diet. The 40 hectare lake is one of the first in the area to open up (early April) as it is only 884 m (2,900 ft) in elevation. Shore fishing is possible but a float tube or small boat is an asset. The is a cartop boat launch but ice fishing is banned.

Jackson Lake (Map 18/D1)

Jackson is reached by a short trail from the north end of Pennask Lake or from a slightly longer trail (2 km/1.2 miles) from a logging road north of both lakes. The lake offers good fishing for rainbow trout to 2 kg (4.5 lbs) throughout the ice free season. Try casting a lure with bait or fly (caddisfly, leech or dragonfly pattern).

Janning Lake (Map 50/A4)

This 10 hectare lake provides fishing for rainbow trout to 1 kg (2 lbs), primarily by trolling or fly fishing. The lake is at 1,280 metres (4,160 feet) in elevation.

Jimmy Lake (Map 27/A2)

Jimmy Lake is located on a 2wd road (Jimmy Lake Road) and has a small forest service site with camping and a cartop boat launch. The lake is highly regulated; including the requirement to release any fish under 50 cm (21 inches). As a result, the lake is now producing rainbow to 3 kg (6+ lbs). The trout are pretty tough to catch but are best fished by fly fishing. There is a particularly good sedge hatch beginning in late June. The lake is at 1,350 metres (4,388 feet) in elevation.

Johnson Lake (Map 51/C7) 🐟

Johnson Lake covers an area of 362 hectares, and is easily accessed off the Johnson Lake Road. The lake, at 1,067 metres (3,600 feet) in elevation, is best trolled for rainbow that can reach 2 kg (4.5 lbs). However, fly fishing can still be effective using long, fine leaders at the outflow near the west end of the lake or near one of the numerous shoals and drop-offs. Try a shrimp, dragonfly or caddisfly pattern for best success. There is a resort on the lake offering cabins and campsites as well as a forest service site.

Joyce (Green) Lake (Map 35/E5)

This small 8 hectare lake is located beside the Chase-Falkland Road (good 2wd access) and offers reasonable fishing for rainbow trout that can reach 1 kg (2 lbs) in size. The low elevation (795 metres/2,584 feet) lake is best fished in spring or fall from a boat or shore with a lure or by fly fishing. The lake is stocked regularly and has a forest service site on the north end of the lake.

Kamloops Lake (Maps 33, 42) 🐟

This very large (5,585 hectare), deep lake extends along Highway 1 eastward from Kamloops. It is not particularly great for fishing, although it is possible to catch rainbow (to 1 kg/2 lbs) and small kokanee or dollies (to 2 kg/4.5 lbs) by trolling in the early spring or late fall and even winter. Full facilities are available on the south side of the lake, which is at 343 metres (1,125 feet) in elevation.

Kane Valley Lakes (Map 17/A2) 🐟

The Kane Valley is a popular recreational destination with good access provided by the Kane Valley Road. Within the valley are several lakes around the 1,100 metre (3,575 ft) level. The lakes warm up in the summer leaving spring and fall the best times to fish. Check the regulations for restrictions before heading out:

Chicken Ranch Lake is a tiny 5 hectare lake found northeast of the Kane Lakes. The lake is heavily managed to ensure that a good fishery for small brook trout exists. For best success, it is recommended that you cast your lure or fly towards many of the weed beds that line the shores. There is opportunity to launch a small boat at the lake.

Englishman Lake covers 13 hectares and is being intensively managed so that there is now some reasonably good fly fishing for rainbow trout to 1 kg (2 lbs) in size. For best results, try casting towards the many weed beds.

Kane Lakes are a pair of small lakes that are ideal for fly fishing, with nice shoals that line the lake. Fishing is quite spotty for the stocked rainbow and brook trout that reach 2 kg (4.5 lbs). Your best bet when fly fishing the dark, nutrient rich waters, is to match the caddisfly or mayfly hatch. There is a popular forest service site on the **Lower Kane Lake** as well as several places to launch small boats or float-tubes. The lakes are stocked annually.

Harmon Lake is a very popular lake found in the heart of the Kane Valley. The lake is easily accessed off the Kane Valley Road and there are several forest service sites that surround the 21 hectare lake. Despite the heavy fishing pressure throughout the ice free season, stocked rainbow that reach 1.5 kg (3 lbs) are taken consistently. The lake is usually fly fished at the south end of the lake in the shallows and trolled along the west side of the lake with a gang troll or leech.

Little Harmon Lake is accessed by a short 200 metre trail that runs from the south end of Harmon Lake. It is possible to pack a float tube or a small cartop boat to the tiny 3 hectare lake that offers generally good fishing for small rainbow.

Second Lakes are two small lakes that now provide a good fishery for brook trout to 1 kg (2 lbs) in size. The lakes are best fished in the fall with a small lure and worm or during ice fishing season with bait. Fly fishermen should try a damselfly pattern, leech or dragonfly pattern. The brook trout are stocked annually at both lakes. Despite their good access, they do not receive as much fishing pressure as the other Kane Valley lakes.

Kernaghan Lake (Map 36/A3)

On a 4wd road south of Wallensteen Lake, Kerneghan Lake has good numbers of small rainbow easily taken by trolling a Willow Leaf and worm, small lure or Flatfish. There is a forest service site at the 7 hectare lake, which is at 1,516 metres (4,927 feet) in elevation. Expect to carry your boat to the lake.

Kersey (Five Mile) Lake (Map 39/A2) 🐟

Located next to Highway 97 south of Clinton, this tiny (5 hectare) lake has day-use facilities and a boat launch. At 925 metres (3,006 feet) in elevation, the lake has many small brook trout best caught in the fall or during ice fishing season.

Knight (Echo) Lake (Map 24/C1)

Knight Lake is a small 6 hectare lake accessed by a short trail leading west from **Roscoe Lake**. The lake receives little fishing pressure but offers some very good fishing for smaller rainbow easily taken on a fly or by spincasting. The weed beds to the south end of the lake are the best place to cast your line. Chataway Lake Resort maintains boats for this hike-in lake.

Knouff (Sullivan) Lake (Map 42/D4) 🐟

Knouff Lake offers good fishing for rainbow trout throughout the ice free season by fly fishing or trolling. The rainbow are generally small although some grow to 1.5 kg (3+ lbs) in size. For fly fishermen, try casting a fly near one of the many shoals or sunken islands that are easily seen through the clear water. There is a forest service site at the north end as well as a resort. The 103 hectare lake is found 1,149 metres (3,768 feet) into the mountains along Knouff Lake Road.

Lac Le Jeune (Map 33/E7)

Lac Le Jeune is a popular 149 hectare lake that offers reasonably good fishing throughout the ice free season. Stocked rainbow to 2 kg (4.5 lbs) can be caught on a fly or by trolling. For fly fishermen, the many bays and shoals make ideal casting areas. Try hitting the lake during the caddisfly hatch beginning in late June or during the mayfly and damsel fly hatches. There is a provincial park that offers camping, picnicking and a boat launch as well as a full service resort on the lake. The lake is at 1,184 metres (3,883 feet), and iice fishing is possible.

Leighton Lake (Map 32/E3)

Found within the borders of Tunkwa Provincial Park, Leighton Lake usually provides good fly fishing and trolling for rainbow trout to 2-3 kg (4.5-6+ lbs). Unfortunately, the lake suffers from draw down, winterkill and heavy fishing pressure. Shore fishing is possible and fly fishermen should try the damselfly hatch in June. The 55 hectare lake is stocked annually with rainbow and has a campsite with a boat launch.

Lily Lake (Map 16/D1)

Rainbow trout weighing up to 1.5 kg (3 lbs) are found in this stocked lake. There is a forest service site offering camping and a boat launch.

Little Shuswap Lake (Map 43/E6)

Located right next to the Trans Canada Highway (Hwy 1), this large 1,814 hectare lake is at 347 metres (1,137 feet) in elevation. The Little Shuswap Park offers a boat launch, beach and picnic site. There is private camping along the lake as well. Like the Shuswap Lake, this lake offers reasonable fishing for rainbow to 5 kg (10 lbs) primarily by trolling Bucktails, Apex or a plug near the surface in May to June and October to November. Fishing slows during the summer months and requires a downrigger to fish in the 10-25 m (30-90 ft) range.

Lodgepole Lake (Map 33/D6)

Lodgepole Lake is a high elevation (1,433 metres/4, 017 feet) lake, that offers fair fishing even in the summer. Fly fishing is the mainstay of the lake with dragonfly or shrimp patterns being the most consistent flies. The lake covers 7 hectares, is stocked annually with rainbow and has a forest service site with a cartop boat launch and wharf. There is an electric motor only restriction on the lake.

Logan Lake (Map 32/G6)

Despite the proximity to town, Logan Lake offers good fishing for large rainbow trout. The stocked trout have been known to reach 7 kg (15 lbs) on occasion due in part to the redside shiners that infest the lake. The fishing remains fairly good throughout the spring and fall as well as during ice fishing season (be aware of the aerators installed to prevent winterkill). There is a campground, wharf and boat launch on the 12 hectare lake.

Long Lake (Map 41/F7)

Long Lake is an 80 hectare lake inside Lac Du Bois Grasslands Provincial Park. The lake offers fairly good fishing for rainbow trout

that can reach 2 kg (4.5 lbs) in size. There is a resort and camping facilities at the high elevation (1,310 metres/4,258 feet) lake. An ice fishing ban is in effect.

Loon Lake (Maps 39/E1-47/G7)

Loon Lake is a popular recreational lake easily accessed on the Loon Lake Road. It offers reasonably good trolling for small rainbow trout (to 1.5 kg/3+ lbs) using a lure with bait. Fly fishermen produce using attractor patterns. Despite a relatively low elevation (815 metres/2,649 feet), fishing remains active throughout the ice free season. There is a resort, camping and boat launch at the 970 hectare lake.

Lundbom Lake (Map 25/B7)

Lundbom Lake is 1,130 metres (3,673 feet) above sea level, and provides fair fishing for rainbow trout to 2 kg (4.5 lbs) throughout the spring and fall. The popular 47 hectare lake is stocked annually and offers camping and picnicking facilities at the large forest service site. Trolling is the primary fishing method although fly fishermen do well in late June by matching the sedge hatch or by using a scud or leech pattern in the fall. There are bait and ice fishing restrictions.

Lupin Lakes (Map 49/G4)

Better known for their canoeing than their fishing, this series of mountain lakes strung out along Caverhill Creek offers rainbow to 1 kg (2 lbs) by spincasting or fly fishing. Fishing remains fairly active throughout the ice free season (given that the lakes are at 1150 metres/3738 feet in elevation) although spring and fall are the better times to fish. A paddling route connects the lakes.

Mab Lake (Map 25/C3)

Good fishing for rainbow trout is offered in the spring and fall. The access to this 25 hectare lake is via 2wd road north of Nicola Lake.

Machete Lake (Map 49/C2)

Machete Lake is a popular recreation lake, complete with camping, resorts, picnicking and boat launching facilities. The lake is at 1,100 metres (3,608 feet) above sea level, and is 440 hectares in size. It has fair fishing for stocked rainbow trout and kokanee to 1 kg (2 lbs). The preferred methods of fishing are by trolling (lures or leech patterns) and by ice fishing. Fly fishermen should try attractor type patterns.

Mamit Lake (Map 24/G1)

Fair fishing during the open water season is offered for rainbow trout reaching 2 kg (4.5 lbs). The lake is at 970 metres (3,182 feet) in elevation and covers 165 hectares. Your best bet is to try trolling the lake although fly fishing during the spring mayfly hatch or with an attractor type pattern through the spring or fall can be effective. Winter fishing for burbot is often very good. The lake is accessed by paved road (Highway 97C) between Logan Lake and Merritt and has a cartop boat launch.

Marquart Lake (Map 25/A7)

This 23 hectare lake has big rainbow and brook trout that can be caught any time of the year, including winter. The lake is 1,130 metres (3,673 feet) above sea level and has a forest service site.

McConnell Lake (Map 33/E6)

Next to Lac Le Jeune Road, this high elevation (1,305 metres/4,280 feet) lake has fairly good fishing for rainbow trout to 1 kg (2 lbs) throughout the ice free season. The 38 hectare lake is stocked annually and is best trolled (leech pattern or gang troll) or fly fished (Doc Spratley, Wooley Bugger or dragonfly pattern). A cartop boat launch, day-use facilities and a myriad of trails in the area provide an opportunity alternative activities.

McGillvray Lake (Map 43/A6)

The 90 hectare McGillvray Lake is a high elevation lake (1,375 metres/4,469 feet), with dark, nutrient rich water. As a result, there can be very good fishing for rainbow reaching over 1.5 kg (3 lbs) in size. Fly fisherman can try caddisflies (in early spring), chironomids, May and damsel nymphs and leeches around the shoals. A slow troll with a Deadly Dick or Flatfish can also be effective. The lake sees a lot of traffic as it is has good road access and a forest service site. A bait ban and gear restrictions are in effect on the lake.

McGlashan Lake (Map 34/E6)

This small 10 hectare lake contains stocked brook trout that grow to 2 kg (4.5 lbs). The best time to fish is in the fall and during ice fishing season. Spincasting and trolling are the most productive methods of fishing although expert fly anglers will find success when casting towards one of the many weed beds that line the lake. The lake is accessed by a trail and is at 1,030 metres (3,348 feet) in elevation.

McTaggart Lakes (Map 50/D2) ;

On the Dunn Lake Road, these two small lakes (about 18 hectares in size each) offer some reasonably good fly fishing and spincasting for rainbow trout that can reach 1 kg (2 lbs). The lakes are at 430 metres (1,410 feet) in elevation and best fished in the spring and fall.

Minnie Lake (Map 17/E1)

This 120 hectare lake is managed as a private lake by the resort. A fee is charged for fishing the lake, but it may be worth the expense, as the fishing remains fairly good during the spring and fall. The lake is 1,000 metres (3,250 feet) above sea level.

Momich Lakes (Map 52/B3)

A series of scenic valley lakes have been protected by the creation of the Momich Lakes Park. In addition to camping and boat launches, the park makes a fine canoeing or fishing destination. The main lake is 203 hectare in size and at 472 metres (1,548 feet) in elevation. It is best trolled for the rainbow trout and dolly vardens, which grow to 2 kg (4.5 lbs). The fish are somewhat difficult to catch, especially in the summer. **Little Momich Lake** can be reached by canoe from the main lake, while the **Third Momich Lake** is best reached by road.

Monte Lake (Map 35/A6)

Monte Lake is a 176 hectare lake located next to the quiet stretches of Highway 97. Trolling for the rainbow trout to 2 kg (4.5 lbs) is your best bet. A private campground and undeveloped provincial park with a nice beach will help you enjoy the lake. The lake is at 684 metres (2,245 feet) in elevation.

Moose Lake (Map 49/D7)

This high elevation (1,280 metres/4,160 feet), hike-in lake is also reached by the Heller Lake Trail. It has fair fishing for rainbow trout to 1 kg (2 lbs) in size throughout the spring and fall.

Morrissey Lake (Map 43/A5)

Morrissey Lake is a just down the road from McGillvray Lake but, at 25 hectares, is much smaller. It is also lower in elevation at 1,200 metres (3,900 feet). However, the fishing usually remains good throughout the summer. Morrissey also has dark, nutrient rich waters and produces rainbow up to (and over) 1.5 kg (3 lbs). These fish can be caught by a slow troll or fly fishing. There is a small forest service site as well as a bait ban and gear restrictions on the lake.

Mowich Lake (Map 40/E2)

The 29 hectare Mowich Lake has fair fishing for small rainbow and kokanee best caught by fly fishing or spincasting throughout the spring and fall. There is a resort on the north end of the lake.

Mulholland Lake (Map 50/A3)

This lake is accessed by a short hike, and has rainbow to 1 kg (2 lbs). The preferred methods of fishing are bait and bobber, fly fishing and spincasting throughout the spring or fall. The lake is only at 600 metres (1,950 feet) above sea level, so fishing slows in the summer.

Murray Lake (Map 16/B6)

Murray Lake is easily accessed off the Coquihalla Highway (Hwy 5). There are two forest service campsites and a boat launch on the 35 hectare lake. Trolling and fly fishing with dragonflies, leeches or shrimp patterns are your best bet.

Nicola Lake (Map 25/C5)

Set beneath the grassy slopes of the Nicola Valley at 623m (2,045 ft) in elevation, the large 6,215 hectare lake offers fair fishing for small kokanee and rainbow trout. There are rumours of trout reaching 9 kg (20 lbs). Trolling a small spin'n glo or a Willow Leaf with bait (maggots or worm) in June to mid-July is most effective for the kokanee. In the winter, burbot fishing can be very effective. The lake, which is more of a water sport lake than a fishing lake, is easily accessed by paved road. There are full facilities at the lake.

Niskonlith Lake (Maps 35/B1, 43/B7)

East of the South Thompson River, this lake offers good trolling, bait fishing and fly fishing for small, stocked rainbow and kokanee. For fly fisherman, good hatches are offered in the spring and summer with the best place to fish being around the island. There is boat launching and camping facilities on the west side of the 370 hectare lake, which is easily accessed off the Niskonlith Lake Road. The lake is at 513 metres (1,684 feet) in elevation.

Noble Lake (Map 41/G6)

Noble Lake is located on a 4wd access road off the Dairy Creek Road north of Isobel. It is a small (8 hectare) lake with fairly good fishing for stocked rainbow that can reach 1 kg (2 lbs) in size. For fly fishermen, try a dragonfly pattern, Wooley Bugger or Doc Spratley. It is possible to launch a small boat onto the clear water lake, which is at 1,067 metres (3,500 feet) in elevation.

North Barriere Lake (Map 51/A3)

North Barriere Lake produces large dollies, rainbow and lake trout (to 4 kg/9 lbs) as well as some smaller kokanee, whitefish and ling cod. The preferred method of fishing is trolling with the spring and fall being the best times. At 637 metres (2,090 feet) above sea level, the 637 hectare lake is not high enough to keep the water cool during the summer months, which adversely affects the fishing. There is a forest service site on the north side of the lake.

Nugget Lake (Map 27/A2)

Nugget Lake is managed as a quality fishery. It covers 8 hectares and is located by 4wd road south of Jimmy Lake. The stocked rainbow can grow to over 1.5 kg (3 lbs). Fly fishing is the preferred method of fishing given the bait ban and the single hook restriction.

Paradise Lake (Map 18/A3)

Paradise Lake is the largest lake (at 136 hectares) in a cluster of lakes north of the Okanagan Connector (Hwy 97C). It offers many small rainbow trout easily caught by fly fishing or trolling during the open water season. In fact, the limit of 8 fish attests to how good the fishing can be. The high elevation (1,524 metres/5,000 feet) lake has dark, nutrient rich water making an attractor type lure or fly your best bet. There is a cartop boat launch and a resort on the lake.

Paska Lake (Map 33/A5)

Paska Lake has rainbow to 1 kg (2 lbs) that are caught throughout the spring and fall by trolling a Flatfish or leech pattern or by casting a

damselfly or attractor fly. The 50 hectare lake is 1,320 metres (4,290 feet) above sea level, and has a cartop boat launch and camping facilities at a small forest service site on its northwestern shore.

Pass Lake (Map 41/E6)
Pass Lake is located on the Lac Du Bois Road (2wd) and drains into Watching Creek. Managed as a quality fishery, there are many restrictions that help grow the Kamloops Rainbow Trout to 4 kg (8 lbs). Of course the bigger fish are notoriously hard to catch. The 28 hectare lake is a fly fishing only lake and is best fished in the early season given its elevation (948 metres/3,109 feet) or again in late September to October. Try matching the early spring chironomid or mayfly hatches and casting near the northeastern shoals. Later in the spring or into the fall, leech, dragonfly, sedge or caddisfly patterns work. A forest service site offers a nice place to camp and launch a small boat.

Pasulko Lake (Map 31/A7)
This 20 hectare lake holds stocked rainbow that are easily caught using most methods of fishing during the spring and fall. The lake has a cartop boat launch and is easily accessed.

Patrick Lake (Map 49/G3)
At 1,375 metres (4,469 feet) above sea level, Patrick Lake provides good fishing throughout the summer months for rainbow to 1 kg (2 lbs) by spincasting or fly fishing. The lake covers an area of 15 hectares, and is accessed by an undeveloped trail.

Paul Lake (Map 34/D1)
This large 258 hectare lake offers a provincial park with camping and picnicking facilities as well as a boat launch. The lake is stocked annually with rainbow that can reach 2.5 kg (5 lbs) and are best caught by trolling near the shoals in the spring or fall. It is a renowned mayfly lake but chironomids, caddisflies and even minnow patterns (in August) can produce at other times in the year. Ice fishing is possible.

Pefferle Lake (Map 18/C1)
The 25 hectare Pefferle Lake (don't ask us how to pronounce it), contains rainbow trout that reach 1.5 kg (3 lbs). Access is from the northwestern shore of Pennask Lake (boat access), or along a 4wd spur road off the Pennask Lake FSR. Fishing is usually good in the spring and fall due to the limited access.

Pennask Lake (Map 18/C2)
The largest lake (at 1,041 hectares) in the immediate area, Pennask Lake produces brood stock to help stock many of the lakes in the province with feisty rainbow trout. Fishing on Pennask is limited to fly fishing only but there are a lot of small rainbow in the lake. The most consistent fly patterns seem to be shrimp or mayflies although many others work. The high elevation lake (1,402 metres/4,600 feet) is accessed by rough roads and has a member's only resort as well as primitive camping and boat launch facilities.

Peterhope Lake (Map 25/G3)
Peterhope Lake is known for its good potential for fly fishing given the numerous shoals and sunken islands that hold very large rainbow (to 5 kg/10 lbs). However, you should be prepared for many long hours before you will be able to hook one of these beauties. The 116 hectare is best fished in the spring and fall. The lake is located along the Peter Hope Road (good 2wd road) at 1,112 metres (3,650 feet) in elevation. There is a forest service site as well as a timeshare fish camp at the lake. Watch for the bait and ice fishing bans.

Peterson Lake (Map 18/D2)
Peterson Lake has many small rainbow that are easily caught by spincasting or fly fishing in the spring or fall. The lake covers 42 hectares, and is located off the beaten path leading from the Pennask Lake Road. There is camping at the nearby Pennask Lake Provincial Park.

Phillips Lake (Map 43/G7)
Phillips Lake covers an area of 22 hectares and is found 610 metres (1,983 feet) above sea level. The lake is shallow (up to 15 metres/50 ft) and warms quickly in the summer and the brook trout that can reach 3 kg (6+ lbs) in size are quite difficult to catch then. The best fishing is in the early spring by either trolling a Willow Leaf or Ford Fender with a Flatfish slowly along the lily pads. Fly fishing using a wet line and a nymph or leech pattern is also effective. Alternatively, try through the ice in winter. There is a cartop boat launch at the lake.

Pillar Lake (Map 35/D4)
Named for the dramatic basalt Pillars to the east of the lake, Pillar Lake offers good fly fishing, bait fishing and trolling in May and June for rainbow that can reach 1 kg (2 lbs) in size. Fly fishermen should try casting a damselfly or dragonfly pattern during the spring hatches towards the shoals that are found at the north end of the lake. The 38 hectare lake is 853 metres (2,799 feet) above sea level, and has a private resort as well as a forest service site with a boat launch and camping. The access to the lake is via the Chase-Falkland Road (good 2wd access).

Pimainus Lakes (Map 24/A1)
Rainbow trout to 1 kg (2 lbs) in size are found in this 40 hectare lake. Most fishermen fly fish or troll in the spring or fall. The access to the lake is via 4wd road off the Pimainus Lake Road. When you reach the lake, you will find a cartop boat launch, campground and a resort.

Pinantan Lake (Map 34/F1)
This 68 hectare lake on the Paul Lake Road is surrounded by private homes and has a resort with camping. Regardless, the lake is still fairly good for fishing for rainbow that can reach 2 kg (4.5 lbs). Trolling is the mainstay of the deep lake, which is stocked annually to maintain the fishery. Fly fishing is generally spotty, although it can produce around the shoals in the spring and fall with attractor patterns being the best bet. The lake, at 876 metres (2,873 feet), can be ice fished with reasonable success.

Pinnacle Lake (Map 18/E2)
Pinnacle Lake offers fair fly fishing for rainbow trout to 2 kg (4.5 lbs) with the best time being the spring or fall. Shrimp and dragonfly patterns seem to be consistent producers. The 12 hectare, high elevation lake (at 1,430 metres/4,648 feet) is stocked annually. There is a ban on ice fishing.

Plateau Lake (Map 26/A2)
This 17 hectare lake is found via a 4wd road east of Stump Lake. At 1,220m (3,965 feet), the lake is just high enough to stay cool in the summer. You will find good fishing for rainbow to 2 kg (4.5 lbs) by fly fishing, spincasting or trolling (gang troll or leech patterns). For fly fishermen, the sedge hatch in early July is the best time to cast your line. There is a nice forest service site that offers a cartop boat launch and camping at the lake. An annual stocking program is in effect to offset the winterkill problem. Check the regulations for restrictions.

Pothole Lake (Map 17/C3) ⟨fish⟩

Despite its close proximity to the Coquihalla Connector (Hwy 97C), this small 4.3 hectare lake is rather difficult to access. The lake also supports good insect growth and as a result the fishing is good for rainbow to 1.5 kg (3 lbs).

Pratt Lake (Map 34/C7)

The 30 hectare Pratt Lake is used extensively for irrigation purposes and draw down can be extreme in hot, dry summers. The (1,310 metres/4,258 feet) high lake does hold a fair number of rainbow that reach 1 kg (2 lbs). Casting a fly (leech or caddis fly pattern) or trolling (leech or Willow Leaf) can be effective. The lake has a cartop boat launch and has camping facilities.

Pressy Lake (Map 48/C3) ⟨fish⟩

Located along the North Bonaparte Road, Pressy Lake is a long, thin lake with a forest service site providing camping and a boat launch. The 57 hectare lake offers a good fishery for rainbow trout to 1 kg (2 lbs) in size throughout the spring and fall.

Red Lake (Map 40/G5) ⟨fish⟩

Red Lake is set below Carbine Hill on a forestry road north of Kamloops Lake. It has a fairly good population of brook trout (to 1 kg/2 lbs), which are best fished during the fall or during ice fishing season. Fly fishing, with chironomids papa, shrimp patterns and leeches, slow trolling and spincasting around the shoals can all produce. The lake has an undeveloped boat launch together with a rustic camping area. The lake covers 109 hectares, and is 947 metres (3, 071 feet) above sea level. The water warms significantly in the summer affecting water quality and fishing. The lake is also susceptible to winterkill.

Reservoir Lake (Map 18/B3)

As the name implies, this 45 hectare lake is affected by draw down in the summer. Despite this, the high elevation (1,540 metres/5,005 feet) lake offers good fishing throughout the open water season for rainbow trout to 1 kg (2 lbs). Access leading to the forest service site with a cartop boat launch and camping facilities is by a 4wd road. Leading from the rec site are trails to nearby Skunk and Walker Lakes.

Rey Lake (Map 25/A1)

Good fishing for rainbow trout is offered at this 25 hectare lake. Access to the lake is via a 2wd road east of Mamit Lake. Try trolling or fly fishing for best success.

Ridge Lakes (Map 33/E7)

These two small lakes (they cover a total of 18 hectares) are located on a 4wd road south of Lac Le Jeune. The high elevation (1,480 metres/4,810 feet) lakes offer good rainbow fishing beginning in the early summer and running into the fall. The rainbow are stocked annually and are best caught by fly fishing, bait fishing or spincasting. Since the water in the lakes is dark due to the organic content, leech and other attractor patterns work well for fly-fishermen. There is undeveloped camping and cartop boat launch facilities at both lakes.

Roche Lake Group (Map 34/C7) ⟨fish⟩

The lakes in and around Roche Lake are usually murky and nutrient-rich, and as a result offer very good fishing for fast growing rainbow trout. Most anglers use the resort or campsite on Roche Lake as a base to explore the many lakes in the area:

Black Lake has a misleading name since the lake has crystal clear water. The 20 hectare lake provides a reasonable fishery for brook trout to 2 kg (4.5 lbs), which are stocked annually. The brook trout are best fished in the fall or during ice fishing season using bait or lures but not flies. The lake is 1,040 metres (3,380 feet) above sea level and found east of Roche Lake on a rough road. There is a campsite on the lake.

Bog Lake is a small 6 hectare lake, noted for its large brook trout that come readily to a lure and bait in the fall or bait and hook during ice fishing season. The lake is just east of Roche Lake on a 4wd road.

Bulman Lake produces large insect populations, which in turn feed the reasonably good sized rainbow (to 2 kg/4.5 lbs). The lake, however, is very moody with fly fishing during the sedge hatch in late June or the water boatman hatch in the fall being your best bet. The lake is at 1,190 metres (3,868 feet) in elevation and has a bait and ice fishing ban.

Ernest Lake is a small 28 hectare lake found on a 4wd spur road near the eastern border of Roche Lake Provincial Park. The lake is a moody, fly-only lake with an electric motor only restriction and no ice fishing. The rainbow average 2 kg (4.5 lbs) in size and generally prove to be quite a challenge to catch. For best results, you must closely match the hatch (chironomids in the spring, caddisflies in late June and a water boatmen in the fall). The lake is stocked annually and there is a rustic campground as well as a cartop boat launch.

Frisken Lake is very productive, with rainbow growing to 2 kg (4.5 lbs)…if winterkill does not occur. The lake offers good fly fishing during the chironomid hatch in mid-May and the sedge hatch in late June. There is a cartop boat launch and camping at the 30 hectare lake, which is accessed by 4wd road. The lake is at 1,140 metres (3,705 feet) in elevation and is stocked annually.

Horseshoe Lake has both brook trout and rainbow trout that can grow to 3 kg (6+ lbs) in size. The 12 hectare lake, which is at 1,115 metres (3,624 feet) in elevation, is best fished using bait or by spincasting in the spring or fall. An aerator has been installed to prevent winterkill. Fly fishing using a shrimp, dragonfly or damselfly pattern can be productive at times.

John Frank Lake is located in the heart of Roche Lake Provincial Park on a 4wd road. The lake is best fly fished by casting a leech or dragonfly pattern near the lily pads that line the shallow lake. The 20 hectare lake has dark, nutrient-rich waters, which have been dammed for a Ducks Unlimited irrigation project. The rainbow grow rapidly but only reach 2 kg (4.5 lbs) in size because of winterkill problems. Cartop boat launching facilities are available at the lake, which has a bait and ice-fishing ban in effect.

Rose and Tulip Lakes are two small lakes found next to the popular Roche Lake. They offer good fishing for stocked brook trout to 1 kg (2 lbs) by spincasting or bait fishing. The fish are best caught in the fall before spawning season or during ice fishing season (be wary of the aerators).

Roche Lake is a very popular lake, complete with a resort, campground and good rainbow fishing. Due to the clear waters, most fishermen troll the 134 hectare lake for the rainbow that reach 3 kg (6+ lbs). Die-hard fly fishermen can do very well by casting a line near the drop-offs or near one of the many shoals that line the lake. A good chironomid hatch occurs in the spring, while a smaller sedge hatch begins in early June. The lake is at 1,135 metres (3,723 feet) in elevation, and has a ban on ice fishing as well as other restrictions.

Rock Lake (Map 40/G1)

This tiny 4 hectare lake southeast of Deadman Falls is worth noting because it provides a surprisingly good fishery for small rainbow easily taken by fly fishing or spincasting. The lake requires a hike along an undeveloped trail. Since the lake warms during the summer, it is best to try your luck in the spring.

Roscoe Lake (Map 24/D1)

Roscoe Lake is a small, 25 hectare lake located on a tough to find 2wd road northwest of Chataway Lake. The lake is good for small rainbow in the spring and fall taken by fly fishing or trolling but don't expect any big fish. The lake can be easily fished from shore, as there is a path around the entire lake that also leads to nearby Knight Lake. A cartop boat launch and campground are available at the south end of the lake.

Ross-Moore Lake (Map 33/F7)

This 50 hectare lake has stocked rainbow trout to 2 kg (4.5 lbs), which are caught either by trolling or fly fishing. For best results, hit the chironomid hatch in the spring or try a leech or dragonfly pattern until early summer or again in the fall. The 1,280 metre (4,160 feet) high lake is subject to draw down, which causes mid-summer fishing to suffer. There is a cartop boat launch as well as camping facilities at the lakeshore forest service site. A 4wd vehicle is recommended to access the lake, which has a bait and ice fishing ban.

Sabiston Lake (Map 40/F6)

Sabiston Lake is located along the Sabiston Creek Road (2wd) and provides a good fishery for brook trout to 1 kg (2 lbs) during the fall or during ice fishing season. Try spincasting for best success. The 30 hectare lake is at 1,000 metres (3,250 feet) in elevation and has undeveloped camping facilities and the opportunity to launch small boats. Sabiston Lake is subject to winterkill but the stocking program has helped in ensuring that the fish population is maintained.

Salmon Lake (Map 26/F4) 🐟

You would think that Salmon Lake, a 149 hectare lake found along the Douglas Lake Road would have salmon, wouldn't you? Instead, the lake is a popular fly fishing destination for rainbow trout to 1 kg (2 lbs). Most fly fishermen cast towards the weed beds that line the west side of the lake using a damselfly (green), shrimp or chironomid pattern. Trolling a leech pattern is also fruitful. The lake is quite shallow and awfully silty so it warms significantly in the summer. At 1,184 metres (3,883 feet) in elevation, the lake has a resort as well as a boat launch. No ice fishing is allowed.

Saskum Lake (Map 51/D2) 🐟

Saskum Lake is home to rainbow trout, dollies and kokanee. The fish, which can reach 2 kg (4.5 lbs) in size, are best caught by trolling during the spring or fall. The 115 hectare lake offers a forest service site with a boat launch and campground at the south end.

Saul Lake (Map 41/B5)

This 25 hectare lake is located on the Sawmill Lake FSR (2wd) and has a forest service site with a campground. The popular lake offers good fishing throughout the ice free season for small rainbow that are easily taken on a fly (shrimp or attractor patterns) or by a gang troll. The lake is at 1,330m (4,365 feet) in elevation.

Scot Lakes (Map 48/G5) 🐟

Accessed off the Egan-Bonaparte FSR, **Scot Lake** offers a forest service site with camping and a boat launch. There are nice shoals around the inflow and outflow streams for fly anglers to try their luck for the rainbow trout. Trolling is also possible and can be quite effective near the drop-off in the summer when the fish retreat to the cool, deeper waters. At 1,185 m (3,887 ft) in elevation, this 29 hectare lake can be fished throughout the ice free season. Nearby **Little Scot Lake** (to the northwest) also offers a forest service site with camping. The smaller lake is best fished in the spring and fall for average size rainbow.

Scott Lake (Map 50/A6)

This small (30 hectare), high elevation (1,300 metres/4,225 feet) lake is located on a 2wd road off of the Gorman Lake Road. The lake provides good fishing for rainbow trout to 1 kg (2 lbs) throughout the spring and fall by fly fishing. The lake has a forest service site.

Scuitto Lake (Map 34/C5) 🐟

At 94 hectares, Scuitto Lake is one of the larger, but shallower lakes in the Roche Lake area. The lake provides good fly fishing for rainbow that average under 2 kg (4.5 lbs) in size but can reach 5 kg (10 lbs). The lake has dark, nutrient-rich water, which warms in the summer resulting in an algae bloom and poor fishing. The late spring caddis hatch is the best time to fly fish. Most 2wd vehicles should be able to access the lake from the north.

Sedge Lake (Map 40/E6)

Sedge Lake is a 10 hectare lake, located high in the hills north of Kamloops Lake (at 1,280 metres/4,160 feet), and offers good fishing for rainbow trout throughout the spring and fall by fly fishing and spincasting. The lake is accessed by a 4wd spur road.

Shea Lake (Map 16/G4)

The 25 hectare Shea Lake has a popular forest service site complete with a picnic facility, camping and a cartop boat launch. The lake offers good fishing for rainbow to 1 kg (2 lbs) in size by trolling.

Shelley Lake (Map 41/E1)

Shelley Lake is a small hike in lake along Deadman Trail. The 40 hectare lake offers good fishing for rainbow trout by fly fishing or spin casting, and because it is a high elevation lake (at 1,390 metres/4,518 feet), the fishing remains constant throughout the summer and fall.

Shuswap Lake (Maps 36, 43-45, 53)

In recent years, this large (30,000 hectare), deep lake has seen a dramatic improvement in its fishing for large rainbow given the conservation measures in place. At 350 metres (1,138 feet) in elevation, the best fishing is May–June and October–November by trolling Bucktails, an Apex or a plug near the surface. Fishing slows during the summer months and requires a downrigger to get to depths of 10–25 m (30–90 ft) where the fish are. The rainbow can reach 10 kg (22 lbs) with 2 kg (4 lb) fish being the norm rather than the exception. There is also a fairly good population of kokanee as well as some lake trout (to 10 kg/22 lbs) and dolly vardens. Full facilities are found around the easily accessible parts of the lake.

Skimikin Lake (Map 44/A7) 🐟

This 20 hectare lake can be fairly productive for rainbow reaching 1 kg (2 lbs). Fishing near the inflow or outflow using a bobber and worm or fly will produce best results. The low elevation lake (525 metres/1,722 feet) is quite shallow so it warms in the summer making fishing in the early spring or late fall your best bet. There is a forest service site with a cartop boat launch on the east end.

Skookum Lake (Map 40/F1) 🐟

Because of the relatively low elevation (808 metres/2,650 feet), this 19 hectare lake is best fished in the spring or fall for rainbow and kokanee that can reach 1 kg (2 lbs) in size. The shallow lake has some nice shoals for fly anglers to work, while trollers will want to stick to light gear. It has a forest service site.

Skunk Lake (Map 18/B3)

We are not sure if the name refers to the fishing or the little critters that frequent the area. Regardless, the 40 hectare Skunk Lake is a hike-in lake that is accessed by a 1.5 km trail from the Reservoir Lake Recreation Site. It is stocked annually to counteract the problems with winterkill and the rainbow trout can grow to 1 kg (2 lbs).

Smith Lake (Map 50/A3)

This 20 hectare lake is reached by a short hike north of the Darlington Creek FSR. At 1,280 metres (4,160 feet) in elevation, fishing is still best in the spring or fall for rainbow trout to 1 kg (2 lbs).

Snohoosh Lake (Map 40/E1) 🐟

This long, thin 91 hectare lake has a forest service site at the north end of the lake with a boat launch and camping as well as a private campground at the south end of the lake. The lake contains rainbow trout and kokanee up to 1 kg (2 lbs). The elevation is relatively low (817 m/2,680 ft), meaning the lake warms during the summer, making the spring and fall the best time to fish.

South Barriere Lake (Map 51/B6)

This 65 hectare lake (the smallest of the three Barriere Lakes) contains many rainbow trout caught by fly fishing or trolling throughout the spring or fall. The lake is at 930 metres (3,050 ft) in elevation and has a forest service site complete with a cartop boat launch and camping.

Spa Lake (Map 36/A5)
There is a rustic campground with a cartop boat launch at this 77 hectare lake east of Bolean Lake. Spa Lake offers good fishing from June through August given the elevation (1,525 metres/4,956 feet) with the best method of fishing being fly fishing (wet or dry fly). The rainbow trout can reach 1.5 kg (3 lbs) in size.

Spanish Lake (Map 35/G6)
Spanish Lake is an 8 hectare lake with a fairly good fishery for rainbow trout reaching 1 kg (2 lbs) in size. It is best to fly fish or spincast the shallows anytime during the spring or fall. The lake is located on the Silvernails Road (2wd) at 825 metres (2,681 feet) in elevation. Set below Mt Connaught, it is a scenic destination.

Spectacle Lake (Map 48/F4)
Off the 3700 Road (2wd), Spectacle Lake is a small (12 hectare) lake at 1,000 metres (3,250 feet) in elevation. The lake offers fair fishing for stocked rainbow trout to 1 kg (2 lbs) in size with fly fishing, bait fishing and spincasting being the preferred methods. For fly fishermen, try a shrimp or dragonfly pattern.

Stake Lake (Map 33/E6)
Stake Lake is a 25 hectare lake with a cartop boat launch north of Lac Le Juene. There are fair numbers of rainbow trout that grow to 2 kg (4.5 lbs). The lake has an aerator to guard against winterkill and it is stocked annually. The mainstay of the lake is trolling, although fly fishermen can produce using a caddisfly pattern in late May. For best results, cast near the shoals and drop-offs, which are easily seen through the clear water. The lake is 1,335 metres (4,379 feet) above sea level and usually opens up at the end of April.

Stinking Lake (Map 40/A6)
This shallow 5–10 metre (20–30 feet) lake offers good fishing for brook trout in the spring and fall. Try spincasting with bait and fishing near the bottom. Good access is provided along the Deadman-Cache Creek Road. Brook trout are stocked every two years.

Stukemapten Lake (Map 52/E3)
Easily accessed on the Humamilt Lake Road, this 119 hectare lake is usually trolled for the rainbow trout that reach 2 kg (4.5 lbs). The best time to fish is in the late spring or early fall as the lake warms during the summer. The lake is at 594 metres (1,948 feet) in elevation and given its distance from civilization, usually offers good fishing.

Stump Lake (Map 25/G1)
This large 780 hectare lake is located right next to Highway 5A. Despite easy access, the lake does not receive a lot of fishing pressure. It is known for being extremely difficult to fish because of wily fish and unpredictable winds that can play havoc with boaters. The lake does produce large rainbow (to 5 kg/10 lbs), brook trout (to 2 kg/4.5 lbs) and kokanee (to 1 kg/2 lbs). Since the lake is only 750 metres (2,460 feet) above sea level, and is quite shallow, it tends to warm during the summer. Trolling is the mainstay of the lake although fly fishermen may wish to try their luck at the south and north end of the lakes where the shoals offer good natural habitat for the trout. The lake has picnic facilities, a boat launch and private camping facilities.

Surrey Lake (Map 25/B1)
Surrey Lakes is accessed by the rough Surrey Lake FSR, just off the Coquihalla Highway (Hwy 5). The 55 hectare, high elevation (1,280 metre/4,160 feet) lake has many small rainbow trout that are best caught by fly fishing with an attractor type pattern or by spincasting a small lure during the open water season. Ice fishing is also productive. Surrey Lake has a resort offering cabins and campsites.

Sussex Lake (Map 25/B1)
Sussex Lake is accessed by the Surrey Lake FSR (2wd road), just off the Coquihalla Highway. Like Surrey Lake just up the road (and stream), the 20 hectare Sussex Lake has numerous small trout that rise quickly to a fly. There is a forest service site on the shores of the high elevation (1,370 metres/4,453 feet) lake.

Telfer Lake (Map 52/B1)
Telfer Lake is a remote lake north of Adams Lake that requires a bit of walking to access the shoreline. The lake is 48 hectares in size and offers good fishing for rainbow trout that can reach 1 kg (2 lbs) but average 20-25 cm (8-10 in). The lake is best fly fished in the spring or fall. Spincasting from shore is possible although using a float tube is a better bet.

Three Mile Lake (Map 39/A1)
Found south of Clinton along side Highway 97, this small 15 hectare lake has small brook trout. It is a deep water lake that is best fished through the ice in winter. During the ice-free season, shore fishing is possible.

Three Valley Lake (Map 46/C4)
This lake is known more for its scenery and water sports than fishing. With a bit of effort, it is possible to catch a few rainbow, the odd dolly varden or lake trout or even a kokanee. There is a good boat launch as well a resort and camping available at the roadside lake, which is at 490 metres (1,593 feet) in elevation.

Thuya Lakes (Map 49/G2)
Most anglers use the lodge as a base to explore this chain of lakes, which are found off the 2300 Road south of the Eakin Creek Road. There are a series of ATV accessible trails that connect the lakes, which hold rainbow trout. There is an electric motors only restriction.

Todd Lake (Map 34/E7)
Todd Lake is a narrow 35 hectare lake that lies alongside the 2wd accessible Monte Creek-George FSR, just north of Pratt Lake. The lake holds fair numbers of stocked rainbow trout, which grow to 1 kg (2 lbs). The lake has a cartop boat launch and is best fished in spring and fall due to the elevation (1,280 metres/4,160 feet).

Tranquille Lake (Map 41/C4)
This 58 hectare lake is located on a rough 2wd road north of Kamloops. It is a high elevation lake (at 1,400 metres/4,592 feet) and considered a good option throughout the ice free season for the abundant small rainbow (to 1 kg/2 lbs) and kokanee. Fly fishing (Doc Spratley, leeches or small attractors), trolling (Willow Leaf and maggots) and spincasting (small lures) all work. There is a resort on the lake.

Tsikwustum Lake (Map 52/D1)
This lake is found on the Rock Creek Main and covers an area of 123 hectares. The lake holds rainbow trout to 1 kg (2 lbs) that are best caught by trolling in the early summer or fall. Found at 1,515 metres (4,969 feet) in elevation, it is possible to camp or launch small boats at the lake.

Tsintsunko Lake (Map 41/E2)
This 100 hectare high elevation (1,440 metres/4,680 feet) lake offers reasonable fishing for small rainbow trout on a fly or by trolling throughout the summer months and into the fall. The lake is found along the Tsintsunko Lake Trail, which leads off the 4300 Road.

Tunkwa Lake (Map 32/E3)

Perhaps the most popular fishery in the region, Tunkwa Lake has fair numbers of rainbow trout that can grow to 3 kg (6+ lbs). The 296 hectare lake is stocked regularly and is best fished using a fly or by trolling in the spring or fall since the lake is subject to draw down in the summer. Shore fishing can also be effective. For patient fly fishermen the early June damselfly hatch and the spring chironomid hatch are probably the best times to fish. The lake is at 1,144m (3,752 feet) in elevation and has a resort as well as a campsite complete with a boat launch. Expect a lot of company throughout the summer especially during the long weekends.

Tupper Lake (Map 32/C7)

Tupper Lake is accessed by a 4wd road north of Cathaway Lake and offers good rainbow trout fishing throughout the spring and fall. It is best to fish the 15 hectare lake using a fly (attractor type pattern) or by spincasting a small lure with bait. There is a forest service site complete with a cartop boat launch on the lake.

Twin Lake (Map 49/E6)

Found near the northern border of the Bonaparte Provincial Park, Twin Lake is a hike-in angling destination. Due to the remote access, fishing can be good for rainbow to 2 kg (4.5 lbs). Casting from shore is possible on the 10 hectare lake but a float tube will certainly improve the chances. The lake is at 1,433 m (4,699 ft) in elevation and can be fished throughout the ice free season.

Tyner Lake (Map 24/D3)

Tyner Lake is found along a 2wd road off the Skuhun-Pimainus FSR. It has a forest service site with a cartop boat launch and campground. The 24 hectare, high elevation (1,225 metres/3,981 feet) lake, offers fairly good fishing for rainbow trout to 1.5 kg (3 lbs) in size during the spring and fall. Fly fishing and trolling are the preferred methods of fishing.

Venables Lake (Map 31/D4)

This 40 hectare lake supports rainbow that can reach 1 kg (2 lbs). Trolling in the spring or fall is your best bet. A cartop boat launch is at the lake, which is accessed via the Venables Valley Road (2wd access).

Victor Lake (Map 46/D4)

This small 8 hectare lake is located just off the Trans Canada Highway (Hwy 1) near Eagle Pass. The lake has limited fishing for small rainbow and a few larger dollies and lake trout. The best method of fishing is by bobber and bait or by trolling. Victor Lake Park offers access to the lake and it is possible to hand launch a boat. The lake is at 520 metres (1,690 feet) in elevation.

Vidette Lake (Map 48/E7)

This 35 hectare lake is found at a relatively low elevation (762 metres/2,500 feet). Although this is a deep lake, fishing is still best during spring and fall. The lake is also a popular ice fishing location in winter. Both the small kokanee and average size rainbow are best caught by trolling (try deeper for the trout). There is a resort as well as a forest service site on this popular summer destination lake.

Walker Lake (Map 18/B4)

Walker Lake is a high elevation (1,550 metres/5,038 feet) lake with good fishing for stocked rainbow to 1 kg (2 lbs) throughout the open water season. There is no ice fishing allowed at the 16 hectare lake, which is accessed by a 1 km trail from the Reservoir Lake Recreation Site.

Wallensteen Lake (Map 36/A3)

The high elevation (1,460 metres/4,745 feet) Wallensteen Lake offers good fishing for small rainbow from June to October with August being the best time. Your best bet is to try fly fishing during the evening using a float-tube, although trolling and bait fishing can also be productive. The 10 hectare lake has a forest service site with a campground and boat launch.

Walloper Lake (Map 33/C7)

Walloper Lake is a dark, nutrient rich lake with many small rainbow trout that can easily be caught. It is a popular family lake due to the good shore fishing opportunities and the fact the rainbow are stocked annually. Fly fishermen should try attractor type flies such as a Woolly Bugger or a Doc Spratley. The 43 hectare lake, which is at 1,305 metres (4,284 feet) in elevation is aerated in winter to prevent winterkill. Ice fishing is not recommended. Picnicking, a wharf and boat launch facilities are found at the provincial park.

White Lake (Map 44/D5)

White Lake is a popular 568 hectare recreational lake located off the White Lake Road north of Tappen. The lake offers fair to good fishing for rainbow that can reach 6 kg (13+ lbs) with the primary method of fishing being trolling. In the early spring and late fall, fly fishing is particularly effective because of the many shoals that line the lake. Ice fishing is effective using most bait beginning in December after the ice thickens. There is a provincial park with camping on the north end of the lake as well as a number of private cabins and camping facilities. There is also a picnic area and boat launch near the east end of the lake, which is at 470 metres (1,528 feet) in elevation.

Whitewood Lake (Map 41/G1)

Located along the Jamieson Creek FSR (2wd access), the 15 hectare Whitewood Lake has a forest service site, complete with camping and boat launching facilities. The lake is fairly good for trolling and fly fishing for rainbow that can reach 1 kg (2 lbs) but average 20-25 cm. Fishing is best during the spring and fall, since at 1,100 metres (3,575 feet), the lake is not high enough to remain cool during summer.

Willowgrouse Lake (Map 49/E7)

Willowgrouse provides good fishing for rainbow to 1 kg (2 lbs) by fly fishing or spincasting. The lake is at 1,200 metres (3,900 feet) in elevation and covers an area of 105 hectares. It is best fished in the spring and fall. The lake can be accessed along the Tuwut Lake Canoe Route or by the Masters Sub-Alpine Trek.

Windy Lake (Map 41/F1)

Windy Lake is located just outside of Bonaparte Provincial Park, on the Windy Lake Road (2wd access). The forest service site on the 25 hectare lake is popular with both hikers and fishermen. The lake is not quite high enough (at 1,250 metres/4,063 feet) to sustain summer fishing, but has fair fishing for rainbow to 1 kg (2 lbs) during the spring and fall. The preferred methods are trolling and fly fishing. Fly fishermen can try chironomids, mayflies or leeches.

Woods Lake (Map 27/B1)

A 4wd access road limits visitors to the area but those that venture in will find fair fishing for rainbow that reach 1.5 kg (3 lbs). Trolling and fly fishing near the many shoals and drop-offs can create exciting action. The lake is at 1,1175 m (3,855 ft) and offers a cartop boat launch and camping at the forest service site.

Young Lake (Map 48/D5)

This 252 hectare lake provides reasonably good fishing for rainbow trout to 1 kg (2 lbs) and small kokanee by trolling. The narrow lake is best accessed from the north and is a relatively low (936 metres/3,070 feet) elevation lake. The best times to fish are spring and fall.

Okanagan Region Lakes

The Okanagan is notorious for its big valley bottom lakes. Although the beaches get most of the attention, there is some very good fishing for a variety of species in these large water bodies. In the hills that surround the valleys are hundreds of smaller mountain lakes. Most of these lakes offer excellent fishing for the infamous rainbow trout.

Aberdeen Lake (Map 28/G7, 29/A7)

This 241 hectare man-made lake is dammed for domestic watershed purposes. It offers good fishing for wild rainbow trout to 1 kg (2 lbs). At 1,278 metres (4,193 feet) in elevation, the lake is not quite high enough to maintain a summer fishery. Fly fishing the many bays and small islands is the preferred method of fishing in late spring and fall. The forest service site has been closed but it should still be possible to launch small boats.

Agur Lake (Map 11/A3)

This 5 hectare lake has many small brook trout and rainbow trout easily caught by fly fishing or spincasting. The lake is at 1,160 metres (3,770 feet) in elevation and is stocked regularly to counteract the winterkill problem. Access to the lake is via a 2wd road (Fish Lake Road) and it is possible to camp or launch small boats at lakeside.

Aileen Lake (Map 28/F7)

This tiny 5 hectare lake is subject to both winterkill and summerkill but a stocking program has helped maintain the fishery. You will find good fishing for rainbow trout to 1 kg (2 lbs) (average 15-25 cm) that are best caught in early summer or in the fall. The lake is at 1,375 metres (4,469 feet). The access to the lake is by 4wd road off the Aberdeen Lake Road. A treed forest service site awaits the overnight visitor.

Alaric Lake (Map 10/C2)

Alaric Lake is a secluded hike-in lake with spectacular scenery and good fishing for rainbow that can reach 1 kg (2 lbs). The lake is at 1,465 metres (4,761 feet) in elevation, meaning fishing picks up in early summer (mid July) and lasts until October.

Alex Lake (Map 28/E7)

Alex Lake has good fishing for wild rainbow trout due to its rough access (4wd or hiking). The 8 hectare, high elevation (1,460 metres/4,745 feet) lake does not have any developed facilities. The lake is found off the Dee Lake Road and is best fished in the summer and fall.

Allendale Lake (Map 12/C7)

This 21 hectare lake is located off the Okanagan Falls FSR, 7 km (4.3 miles) north of the junction with Ripperto FSR. Present management strategies are to increase the size of the rainbow by decreasing stocking levels. The lake has a recreation site with a campground and cartop boat launch. There are also rental cabins and boats available at a fishing camp on the high elevation lake (1,524 m/5,000 ft).

Allison Lake (Map 9/B1)

Allison Lake covers 71 hectares and is one of the most popular lakes in the area, due in no small part to the fact that the lake stretches alongside Highway 5A. It features camping and a boat launch at a provincial park on the south end of the lake. Despite its easy access, the lake offers a fairly good summer and winter fishery for rainbow trout that can reach 1 kg (2 lbs) in size. The lake, which is at 853 metres (2,799 feet) in elevation, also has a few small kokanee.

Andy's Lake (Map 16/D7)

This high elevation (1,525 metre/4,956 feet) lake holds good numbers of small rainbow that can be caught using a bobber and bait, by fly fishing or by spincasting from a float tube or shore. Casting towards the many weed beds is your best bet. The 12 hectare lake receives very little fishing pressure.

Arlington Lakes (Map 12/G2)

A trio of lakes located on a 2wd road just west of Highway 33 and next to the Kettle Valley Railway. All three lakes hold fair numbers of small rainbow trout, caught primarily by fly fishing or trolling. There is a recreation site at the southern lake, complete with cartop boat launch and camping facilities. The lakes are between 1,030 and 1,060 metres (3,451 feet) in elevation and best fished in the spring or fall.

Baird Lake (Map 37/E5)

Baird Lake is easily accessed on the Hidden Lake Road just east of Hidden Lake. This small 10 hectare lake has a forest service site with a boat launch as well as camping facilities. The primary method of fishing for the many small rainbow that inhabit the lake is fly fishing. There is an electric motor only restriction on the lake.

Banana Lake (Map 19/A3)

Banana Lake is a tiny 3 hectare lake with spotty fishing for rainbow trout. Why bother coming here? Well, some of those trout can reach 4 kg (9 lbs). The lake is at 1,100 metres (3,575 feet) in elevation and is best fished during the spring and fall. A short hike from the Jackpine FSR is required to reach the lake. A growing shiner population is seriously affecting the rainbow population.

Bardolph Lake (Map 28/G3)

While this 10 hectare lake is not a high elevation lake (at 1,036 metres/3,399 feet), it is deep enough to remain cool during the summer. A small stream runs into the lake near the forest service site at the lake's north end. This is one of the best places to fish for small rainbow that can be caught throughout the open water season, and again during winter. The 4wd access lake is stocked with rainbow.

Barge Lake (Map 20/F7)

This small 5 hectare lake has brook trout and rainbow trout that both grow to 1 kg (2 lbs). The lake offers good fishing throughout the spring and fall primarily due to its hike-in access. The trail/old road is found near the south end of Idabel Lake off the Okanagan Falls FSR.

Barton Lake (Maps 18/G1, 26/G7)

Small rainbow trout are found in this 45 hectare lake. The lake is stocked regularly and is best fished during the spring and fall. The access to this lake is by a long hike/4wd road ensuring little fishing pressure.

Bear (June) Lake (Map 28/F6)

Despite the 4wd/hike-in access, Bear Lake has slow fishing for large rainbow trout (to 2 kg/4 lbs). The lake is not stocked, and the wild rainbow that remain are wily. The lake covers 7 hectares and is best fished using a fly in early summer or the fall. The lake has camping facilities at a forest service site.

Beaver (Swalwell) Lake (Map 20/E1)

Whether you call it Beaver or Swalwell Lake, the fact remains the same; this is a very popular fishing destination. The rustic resort and forest service site help attract attention to the lake. Despite its popularity, the 306 hectare lake still produces extremely well for rainbow trout to 2 kg (4.5 lbs) by trolling or fly fishing throughout the early summer or fall. Ice fishing is also common. The lake is at 1,348 metres (4,423 feet) in elevation and is stocked annually.

Becker Lake (Map 28/F4) 🐟

Becker Lake is a 9 hectare fishing lake east of Vernon. The lake is not quite high enough (at 1,234 metres/4,0498 feet) to keep cool in the summer, making spring, fall and winter (after the ice forms) the best times to fish. The lake is stocked annually with brook trout that grow to 1 kg (2 lbs). Access to the lake is the 2wd Becker Road and there is a forest service site with cartop boat launch and campground.

Big Meadow Lake (Map 12/A1) 🐟

Big Meadow is a 18 hectare lake that once held rainbow trout. Summer draw down has all but wiped out the fishery. The high elevation lake (1,608m/5,273 ft) is accessed by a deactivated road system that also discourages many would be visitors.

Bisson Lake (Map 22/A1)

Rainbow trout to 2 kg (4.5 lbs) are found in this 15 hectare lake. The lake is stocked annually with rainbow and trolling or fly fishing during the early summer or in the fall can be productive. The high elevation lake (1,420 metres/4,615 feet) has a lakeside forest service site. A 4wd spur road off the Kettle River FSR accesses the lake.

Bluey Lake (Map 17/C4)

Bluey Lake is located on a rough 4wd road, which is probably easier to hike than to drive especially in wetter conditions. An intensive stocking program has improved the numbers of rainbow that occasionally reach 2 kg (4.5 lbs) in size. There is a forest service site at the north end that offers camping and a cartop boat launch. Due to the access and the depth, the 30 ha lake is not easily trolled.

Bonneau Lake (Map 29/F6)

Bonneau Lake has stocked rainbow trout to 1.5 kg (3+ lbs) in size best caught during the summer and fall using a fly or by casting a lure. Access to this lake is by bushwhacking off the Denison Lake Trail. This lake is an excellent choice for a secluded fishing experience.

Borgeson Lake (Map 9/B1)

Like the other lakes in the area found beside Highway 5A, the 15 hectare Borgenson Lake receives heavy use. Unlike Allison Lake to the north or Dry Lake to the south, the fishing is not particularly good for the small rainbow and brook trout, as the lake is not as well stocked. Trolling is the most popular method of fishing although fly fishermen and bait fishermen can meet with success. The lake is at 825 metres (2,681 feet) in elevation and has a launching area for small boats.

Boss Lake (Map 16/G4)

Boss Lake offers a good retreat for fisherman that want to enjoy the sunny open rangeland that the Voght Valley has to offer. There is a popular forest service site at the lake, which has camping and cartop boat launch facilities. The 20 hectare lake is often trolled for the stocked rainbow that reach 1 kg (2 lbs) in size, but fly fishing is certainly possible. The lake is at 1,021 metres (3, 503 feet) in elevation.

Bouleau Lakes (Map 27/D3) 🐟

Good fishing for small, but wild rainbow trout is offered at Bouleau Lake. The 67 hectare lake is at 1,386 metres (4,547 feet), which is high enough in elevation to provide good fishing in summer through fall. There is a forest service site with a campground and cartop boat launch that is easily reached via the Bouleau Main. To the west is **Little Bouleau Lake**, a 15 hectare lake that is best reached by a 4wd vehicle. The smaller lake offers some good fishing for small rainbow throughout the early summer and fall.

Brenda Lake (Map 18/E4) 🐟

Brenda Lake offers fair fishing for rainbow trout growing to 2 kg (4.5 lbs). The lake covers 9 hectares, and, at 1,707 metres (5,600 feet), is high enough to remain cool in the summer. Too bad that the shallow lake suffers from draw down at that time. Camping facilities are available at a forest service site.

Brook Lake (Map 16/D7)

Brook Lake is accessed off the Brook Creek Road but will require a short hike given the deteriorating road conditions. The 15 hectare lake, like neighbouring Andy's Lake, offers a secluded experience where you are likely to catch a number of small rainbow using bait, flies or a lure. The lake is 1,525 metres (4,956 feet) above sea level.

Browne (Island) Lake (Map 20/E6)

Browne Lake is one of the better fishing lakes in the area and is blessed with a forest service campsite and boat launch. The 25 hectare lake contains good numbers of rainbow trout growing to 2 kg (4.5 lbs) in size. The lake is at 1,280 metres (4,160 feet) in elevation and best fished is in the spring and fall. It is a fly fishing only lake.

Brunette Lake (Map 28/F7)

This high elevation (1,375 metres/4,469 feet) lake supports a good population of large rainbow trout. The reason for the large fish is the hike-in access and the limited stocking program. The 10 hectare lake is best fished during the summer and fall.

Buck Lake (Map 13/B4)

Buck Lake is a fairly difficult lake to get to. The road to the lake is a rugged 4wd road that most people hike or ATV in. Because there isn't heavy fishing pressure, the 25 hectare lake produces very well for rainbow to 2 kg (4.5 lbs). At 1,390 metres (4,518 feet), the lake is high enough to remain cool over summer (meaning the fishing stays hot) and sports a recreation site, complete with cartop boat launch. The lake is best fished with a fly rod from a float tube or by trolling.

Burnell (Sawmill) Lake (Map 26/G2)

Locally known as Burnell Lake, this is a popular catch-and-release fishery east of the Douglas Lake Road. The restrictions, along with a new aerator to help combat winterkill, have helped turn this lake into a quality fishery with stocked rainbow trout that can grow to 2.5 kg (5+ lbs) in size. At 730 metres (2,372 feet) in elevation, the lake is best fished in the spring and fall by trolling.

Cameo Lake (Map 19/A2)

This high elevation (1,460 metre/4,745 feet) lake has many small rainbow trout easily caught by trolling or fly fishing in the spring or fall. The lake is located along a good mainline logging road (Bear Creek Main) and sports a forest service site.

Canyon Lake (Map 12/C1)

Rainbow trout can be caught by fly fishing or trolling during the summer and fall at this 18 hectare lake. The lake is at 1,550 metres (5,038 feet) in elevation and is accessed by a 4wd forestry road.

Caribou Lake (Map 46/A5)

Found off a short trail from the end of the rough Yard Creek FSR (4wd access), this small lake offers good fishing throughout July and August. The small rainbow trout can be caught on a float and worm, fly or small lure. The lake has a rustic area for camping.

Cathedral Park Lakes (Maps 1, 2)

Cathedral Park offers a truly rugged mountain experience. Within the park are a number of small alpine lakes at about 2,000 metres (6,500 feet) in elevation, four of which were stocked back in the 1930s with rainbow and/or cutthroat, and now have a self-supporting population. The trout are caught easily by fly fishing, bait fishing or spincasting. The turquoise-coloured lakes and the spectacular scenery will add to the enjoyable fishing experience. Given the high elevation, fishing is best in late July through October. Most of the fishing happens in the core lakes—**Quiniscoe, Pyramid, Ladyslipper** and **Lake of the Woods**—but there is also fish in Haystack Lakes. Access is on foot; although the Cathedral Lakes Lodge jeep service (for a fee) is certainly easier, especially if hauling a float tube.

Chain Lake (Map 10/A1)

This 42 hectare lake has very good fishing for small, stocked rainbow that can reach 3 kg (6+ lbs) in size. Trolling is the most popular method of fishing although fly fishing and spincasting can produce. The lake has a forest service site with a campground and a boat launch. It is at 1,036 metres (3,399 feet) in elevation and suffers from an algae bloom in the summer. No ice fishing is allowed.

Chapman Lake (Map 18/E6)

This small 8 hectare lake has small rainbow trout best fished in the spring or fall using a fly or by spincasting. Access is by a long trail (along an old road), which should ensure that you will be the only one at the lake when you get there.

Christie Lake (Map 27/E7)

This 3 hectare lake is unique because it's best fishing is during the winter when the brook trout to 1 kg (2 lbs) come readily to a hook and bait. Which is even odder, because, at 1,340 metres (4,355 feet), the lake is subject to winterkill. It is stocked annually.

Christina Lake (Map 6/G5)

Christina Lake is a large 2,549 hectare recreational lake found alongside Highway 3. The lake is a popular place to swim and boat in summer since the low elevation (457 m/1,499 ft) lake gets quite warm in summer. The lake contains large rainbow (to 3 kg/6+ lbs), small kokanee, smallmouth bass and whitefish. Spincasting or fly fishing for the smallmouth bass (during summer) and rainbow (in the spring and fall) in shallow bays and at the creek mouths can be effective. The southern end of the lake has a number of private resorts and campgrounds to accommodate the visitor. The less developed northern end has a number of boat access campsites to enjoy.

Chute Lake (Map 11/F1)

There is a 10 hp maximum engine restriction on this well known lake between Penticton and Kelowna. At 1,160 metres (3,770 feet) in elevation, it still gets a little warm in the heart of summer so fishing is best in the spring and fall. The 40 hectare lake has good fishing for small wild rainbow trout despite consistent use from visitors to the forest service site and the popular resort.

Clark Lake (Map 13/B3)

Clark Lake is a small hike-in lake to the south of Joan Lake. It offers very good fishing for its small rainbow trout primarily by fly fishing or using a float with bait. The lake is 1,280 metres (4,160 feet) above sea level and produces well during the summer months. The lake sports a small recreation site.

Clifford Lake (Map 16/G7)

This small 9 hectare lake is found west of the much more popular Thalia Lake. Similar to most lakes in the area, it has a forest service site and is stocked with rainbow trout. The marshy area surrounding the lake helps produce plenty of insects for the fish and mosquitoes for the campers.

Collier Lakes (Map 13/C4)

Collier Lake is a small 12 hectare lake that can be accessed by a 3 km (1.5 mile) trail from the Sago Creek Recreation Site on the Beaverdell-State Creek FSR. There is a forest service site (little more than a clearing for a tent or two) on the north shore of the high elevation (1,173 metres/3,848 feet) lake, which contains stocked rainbow. The best spot to fish is near a stream inlet on the eastern shores of the lake. Due to the murky waters, fly patterns should have some sort of attractant on them.

Upper Collier Lake is an 8 hectare lake that requires a hike from either Collier Lake or from the 4wd road along Dear Creek. The smaller lake contains stocked rainbow to 30 cm (12 inches), which are fairly aggressive in spring, and possibly some cutthroat. The lake has a forest service site on its eastern shore.

Conkle (Fish) Lake (Map 4/G4)

This 124 hectare lake is accessed by rough 2wd road from Highway 3 or from Highway 33. The lake is home to a beautiful provincial park that offers a boat launch, camping and hiking trails. The lake has pretty good fishing for stocked rainbow trout that reach 2 kg (4.5 lbs) in size, with trolling being the popular fishing method. The lake is at 1,052 metres (3,451 feet) in elevation and can be fished through the ice in winter. There is an electric motor only restriction on the lake.

Copperkettle Lake (Map 13/E1)

It is a 3 km hike from the Christian Valley Road to Copperkettle Lake. The 20 hectare lake is 1,143 metres (3,750 feet) above sea level and fishing slows during the summer. But in the spring and fall the lake provides good fly fishing (no bait or spinners allowed) for rainbow to 1 kg (2 lbs). A rustic campground adds to the remote wilderness setting.

Coquihalla Lakes (Map 8/B2)

The 10 hectare Coquihalla Lakes receives very little fishing pressure, despite the fact that it lies alongside a major highway and has a quaint resort. Even more surprising, the lake offers good fishing for rainbow trout to 1 kg (2 lbs) by trolling. The fishing season, given the 2,000 metres (6,500 feet) elevation, begins in early summer and lasts to the fall. The resort offers cabins and camping.

Crescent Lake (Map 18/D6)

This 30 hectare lake has rainbow trout to 2 kg (4.5 lbs) that average much smaller. There is camping and a cartop boat launch at the lakeshore forest service site. Fishing holds throughout the summer as the lake is at 1,370 metres (4,453 feet) in elevation.

Cup Lake (Map 13/C3)

Cup Lake is a scenic lake that is easily accessed via the Lassie Lake Road. It is 9 hectares in size and is 1,295 metres (4,249 feet) above sea level. Most of the stocked rainbow remain small, although some reach 1 kg (2 lbs) in size. Trolling or fly fishing from a float tube is very effective. A forest service site is located at the north end of the lake where you will find a cartop boat launch for electric motors only.

Curtis Lake (Map 29/A7)

Curtis Lake has an abundance of small rainbow trout that offer fast fishing during the spring or fall with bobber and bait or by fly fishing. The lake is accessed by a 4wd road off the Hadoo Main and is found at 1,280 metres (4,160 feet) in elevation.

Damer (Round) Lake (Map 28/D6)

This 7 hectare lake is accessed by a 4wd road off Oyama Lake Road. The lake is at 950 metres (3088 feet) in elevation and has camping and a rough boat launch at the lakeshore forest service site. Since the lake is subject to summer draw down, the rainbow trout are best caught throughout the spring and fall using a fly or by trolling.

Darke (Fish) Lake (Maps 11/A1, 19/A7)

Brook and rainbow trout are stocked regularly in this 40 hectare lake. The fish, which can reach 2 kg (4.5 lbs) in size, are best caught in the spring or fall as the lake is subject to severe draw down in summer. Located in Darke Lake Provincial Park, the lake is accessed by 2wd road and has camping and boat launching facilities.

Davis Lake (Map 16/G5) 🐟

This 23 hectare lake holds stocked rainbow to 2 kg (4.5 lbs) that are best caught by trolling, although fly fishing or bait and bobber can be effective. The very popular lake has a forest service site offering camping and a cartop boat launch. The lake has good 2wd access, and as a result receives heavy fishing pressure throughout the summer months.

Deadman Lake (Map 17/B7)

A small 6 hectare lake that is accessed by a 4wd road, Deadman Lake has stocked rainbow that are caught by using a bobber and bait, by spincasting or by fly fishing. There is a forest service site with a campground at the lake, which is 1,035 metres (3,364 feet) above sea level. Fishing is best if you bring a small boat but shore fishing is still possible. For trollers, an orange Flatfish or a gang troll seem to work the best. For the fly fishermen, try a dragonfly nymph, leech or shrimp pattern throughout the year. Mayfly, chironomid and damselfly patterns during the spring hatches are also very effective.

Dee Lakes (Map 28/F7) 🐟

This string of lakes is comprised of four interconnecting lakes (**Crooked Lake, Deer Lake, Dee Lake and Island Lake**) are accessed off the Dee Lake Road (2wd). The lakes are fairly similar in quality of fishing and elevation (1,350 metres/4,430 feet). They offer good fishing for small rainbow caught by either fly fishing or trolling. Dee Lake is known to produce the largest rainbow in the series (up to 2 kg/4.5 lbs), while Deer and Island Lakes are more difficult to access. Facilities include a forest service site and boat launch on Island Lake as well as a boat launch and rustic resort on Dee Lake. Since Crooked Lake is dammed, the water level tends to fluctuate in the summer.

Deep Lake (Map 28/E5)

Deep Lake is a tiny 5 hectare lake with hike-in access from Kalamalka Lake Provincial Park. The lake contains stocked rainbow trout, which don't see many hooks so usually take readily to flies; especially during the spring hatches.

Deninson Lake (Map 29/E6)

The high elevation (1,460 metres/4,745 feet) Deninson Lake is accessed by a 2 km (1.2 mile) trail off the Bonneau FSR. The 6 hectare lake has rainbow trout growing to 2 kg (4.5 lbs) that are best fished by fly fishing or spincasting in the spring or fall.

Divide Lake (Map 19/E7)

One of two small lakes (this one covers just four hectares) in Okanagan Mountain Park worth fishing, Divide Lake has lots of small rainbow. To catch some, try using a fly or try spincasting anytime during the early summer or fall. The trail access (hike, bike or horse) lake is 1,375 metres (4,469 feet) above sea level.

Dobbin Lake (Map 19/A2)

This 10 hectare lake is stocked regularly with brook trout, and wild rainbow trout. The high elevation lake (1,470 metres/4,778 feet) offers fair trolling or fly fishing in the early summer and fall. The lake is accessed by a 2wd road and has a cartop boat launch.

Doreen Lake (Map 28/F7)

Doreen Lake is located off the Dee Lake Road (2wd) and has a large forest service site with camping and a cartop boat launch. The 40 hectare lake is a fly fishing only lake and holds good numbers of rainbow in the 2 kg (4.5 lbs) range. Although there are many fish to entice the angler, the rainbow tend to be extremely moody. If you want any chance of success, then it is best to match the hatch.

Dry Lake (Map 9/B1) 🐟

Dry Lake is at 838 metres (2,749 feet) in elevation and has a resort, camping facilities as well as a beach and boat launch. Rainbow are stocked annually at the 35 hectare lake and some of them grow to be 2 kg (4.5 lbs) in size although most are quite small given the heavy fishing pressure. There are also some brook trout available at the lake. Trolling (electric motors only) is the mainstay of the lake.

Duo Via Lake (Map 27/D7)

This 5 hectare lake has a decent population of stocked brook trout growing to 1 kg (2 lbs) in size. These fish are best caught in the fall by casting a small lure or fly.

Eastmere Lake (Map 18/B7)

Eastmere is a small, remote mountain lake located at 1,465 metres (4,761 feet) in elevation. The lake is reached by a 4 km (2.4 mile) trail/old road from the (former) Osprey Lake Recreation Site. As a result, the lake is a great place to go for a secluded fly fishing or spincasting experience with a good possibility of catching small rainbow.

Echo (Lumby) Lake (Map 29/F5) 🐟

Echo Lake is home to a nice resort and an undeveloped provincial park. The 75 hectare lake has good numbers of rainbow trout that grow to 4 kg (9 lbs) as well as a few large kokanee and some lake trout that grow to 5 kg (11 lbs). The lake is at a relatively low elevation (843 metres/2,765 feet), so spring and fall are the best times for fishing. Ice fishing can also be great at times. Trolling is the preferred method of fishing, but the lake can be fly fished with some success; particularly at the shoals at the western end of the lake. The lake has a large shrimp population, which in turn leads to the large fish. The lake does receive heavy fishing pressure.

Eileen Lake (Map 19/A1)

Rainbow trout to 2 kg (4.5 lbs) in size are found in this 10 hectare lake, which is accessed via a 2wd road. The lake is at 1,460 metres (4,745 feet) and is best fished during the early summer or fall.

Elinor Lake (Map 11/F1) 🐟

Many small rainbow trout can be caught in this 1,280 metres (4,199 foot) high lake. The lake is only 8 hectares in size and best accessed from Chute Lake to the north. The best time for fishing is during the early summer or fall since the lake is subject to draw down.

Eneas Lakes (Map 18/G7)

The Eneas Lakes are comprised of a trio of lakes: **Island Lake, Eneas Lake** and **Tsuh Lake** that total 18 hectare in size. All three are found in Eneas Lakes Provincial Park and have fair numbers of rainbow trout that are caught using a fly or by spincasting anytime during the open water season. At 1,525 metres (4,956 feet) in elevation, they make a fine summer fishing retreat. Eneas Lake has a cartop boat launch and is accessed by the Eneas Lake Road (2wd). Island Lake requires a short hike, while Tsuh Lake is along a 4wd road (you can hike the road to the lake) and also has a place to launch small boats.

Ern Lake (Map 20/E6)

Ern Lake is stocked regularly with brook trout which average 20–30 cm (8-12 in) in size. Try bait fishing or spincasting in the spring or fall for best results. The lake is at 1,280 metres (4,160 feet) above sea level in elevation and found just northeast of Hydraulic Lake.

Esperon Lake (Map 27/B7)

The 20 hectare Esperon Lake has rainbow that tend to be small and rather scarce. There is a place to launch small boats and a snowmobile cabin on the lake. The high elevation (1,650 metres/5,363 feet) lake is not ice free until June.

Falls Lake (Map 8/A2)

Located west of the Coquihalla Toll Booth, Falls Lake is accessed by a gentle 2 km (1.2 mile) trail from Exit 221 on Highway 5. Not many anglers venture into this scenic mountain lake, which provides fast action for small rainbow on a fly or by spincasting.

Fish Hawk Lake (Map 21/D1)

This 40 hectare lake has rainbow trout to 1 kg (2 lbs) in size caught in the summer and early fall with bait, by spincasting or by fly fishing. A high elevation lake, at 1,800 metres (5,850 feet) above sea level, Fish Hawk has a forest service site with camping and a cartop boat launch. The lake is accessed by the Graystokes Road, which is best travelled by a 4wd or mountain bike.

Fish Lake (Map 20/E6)

Connected to Browne Lake by a short channel, Fish Lake is beginning to see more and more catches of rainbow, although brook trout are the dominant species. Spincasting and fly fishing in the spring or fall meets with success. The 15 hectare lake is at 1,310 metres (4,258 feet) in elevation.

Five O'Clock Lake (Map 13/C3)

While this lake is known officially by the identifier 00796KETL, it is known unofficially as Five O'Clock Lake. The 8 hectare lake is home to small numbers of stocked rainbow that can reach up to 1 kg (2 lbs). Because the lake is located off the Lassie Lake Road via a 1 km trail, it doesn't see as much pressure as many of the roadside lakes in the area. There is a small walk-in forest service site on the lakeshore.

Flyfish Lakes (Map 28/F7)

These two lakes are restricted to fly fishing only. The stocked lakes offer good fishing for rainbow to 1.5 kg (3+ lbs). A 1 km hike accesses the smaller lake (Flyfish 1), whereas the larger lake (Flyfish 2) can be accessed by a 2wd road off the mainline. There are forest service sites at both lakes, which are found at 1,340 metres (4,355 feet) in elevation.

Galena Lake (Map 18/A6)

Galena Lake is located on a 4wd spur road off the Whitehead Lake Road and doesn't get as much fishing pressure as many of the lakes in the area. The lake covers an area of 20 hectares and offers fairly good fishing for rainbow by trolling or fly fishing.

Gardom Lake (Map 36/E4)

Just off Highway 97B, Gardom Lake has an area of 75 hectares and offers fishing for brook trout and rainbow (to 2 kg/4.5 lbs) primarily by fly fishing. Perch have been illegally introduced into the lake and are thriving in the heavy vegetation. Gardom Lake Park, on the west side of the lake, offers picnicking and a boat launch. The low elevation lake (540 metres/1,755 feet) lake warms during the summer.

Garnet Lake (Map 11/B1)

Garnet Lake has good fishing for both rainbow trout and brook trout that can reach 1 kg (2 lbs) in size. The fishing success holds throughout the summer for the rainbow and there are ice fishing possibilities for the brook trout in the winter. The lake is at 630 metres (2,067 feet) in elevation and covers 40 hectares. The Garnet Valley Road is restricted access. You will have to scramble down the steep bank near the south end of the lake. People still haul in small boats (electric motors only).

Garrison Lakes (Map 1/A3)

Accessed by a steep 4 km (2 mile) trail from the Sunday Summit FSR, these two lakes provide good fly fishing for rainbow that average 1.5 kg (3 lbs). The crystal clear waters are best fished using an attractor pattern or by spincasting a small lure with bait. Fishing holds throughout the summer months as the elevation is 1,400 metres (4,550 feet).

Gellately Lake (Map 19/A3)

This is a tiny lake just west of Jackpine Lake. It suffers from winterkill but can still produce some large rainbow if there is a series of warm winters. The fish are difficult to catch, however.

Gladstone Lake (Map 17/A7)

Another in a series of small (this one covers 9 hectares) lakes next to Highway 5A, this one produces well for stocked rainbow to 1 kg (2 lbs) in both the summer and winter. Although trolling is the most popular method of catching fish, fly fishing or spincasting are certainly an option. The lake has a cartop boat launch as well as picnic facilities. It is found at 1,006m (3,300 ft) in elevation.

Glen Lake (Map 18/F6)

Glen Lake is a small 11 hectare lake, with fair fishing for brook trout that can grow to 1.5 kg (3+ lbs) in size. Try bait fishing or spincasting during the spring and fall for best results. The lake is 1,160 metres (3,806 feet) above sea level, and is accessed by a 2wd road.

Goat Mountain Lake (Map 29/B7)

This lake is found along a 2wd forestry road and offers good fishing for small rainbow trout. Fly fishing is the preferred method of fishing with the spring and fall being the best time to fish. The 1,375 metre (4,469 feet) high lake has camping facilities and a boat launch at a small lakeshore forest service site.

Goose Lake (Map 16/G7)

Goose Lake receives heavy use, but the fishing still remains fairly good for small rainbow taken by trolling or fly fishing likely due to the extensive stocking program in effect. There are forest service sites at both ends of the 30 hectare lake but the southern location is much better for accessing the lake. The lake is at 1,035 metres (3,364 feet) in elevation. Some rainbow can reach 1.5 kg (3+ lbs) in size.

Goose Lake (Map 28/C3)

Easily accessed from Vernon, this lake should receive more attention than it does. Although the brook trout are testy, they do grow to some nice sizes. Fly anglers should try trolling a leech or Muddler Minnow to find bigger fish. At 472 metres (1,549 feet) in elevation, the fishing slows considerably in the summer.

Graystoke Lake (Map 21/D2)

This area northeast of Kelowna is a high elevation plateau known as the Graystokes. The 46 hectare lake is accessed by the Graystokes Road, which is best travelled by a 4wd. There is a forest service site and fishing for rainbow in the summer and early fall.

Green Lake (Map 3/CF1)

Rainbow trout to 2 kg (4.5 lbs) in size are found in this 18 hectare lake. Fishing is hit-n-miss, with spring and fall being the best time to fish by trolling, spincasting or fly fishing. The access to the lake is by a good 2wd road (Green Lake Road) south of Okanagan Falls. The lake is at 490 metres (1,608 feet) in elevation.

Green Lake (Map 17/A7)

In good years, the tiny 3 hectare Green Lake has been known to produce large rainbow to 2 kg/4.5 lbs by fly fishing or spincasting. However, the lake is susceptible to winterkill and there is now a program to stock brook trout in the lake in hopes to ensure a continuous fishery. The lake is 1,051 metres (3,448 feet) in elevation. Try a dragonfly nymph, leech or shrimp pattern throughout the year. Mayfly, chironomid and damselfly patterns are also very effective.

Greenbush Lake (Map 46/E7) 🐟
Greenbush Lake is accessed after a long drive up the sometimes rough North Shuswap FSR. Depending on the vehicle you bring, it may be a short hike into the lake. The 172 hectare lake offers good fishing for rainbow to 1 kg (2 lbs) and dolly vardens to 3 kg (6+ lbs) primarily in the spring or fall. Found at 1,021 metres (3,350 feet) above sea level, the lake has a cartop boat launch and camping facilities.

Greyback Lake (Map 12/A2)
The access to Greyback Lake is by a good 2wd road (Greyback Road) east of Okanagan Lake. There is a picnic area as well as a boat launch on the lake, which is stocked annually. Fishing for the many small rainbow trout is best by trolling in the early summer or fall. The lake is at 1,585 metres (5,151 feet) in elevation and covers 125 hectares.

Grizzly Lake (Map 28/G7)
Grizzly Lake used to offer fishing for large rainbow trout but the quality of fishing has declined over the years since the dam went in (1978). The lake still offers fish to 45 cm (18 inches). The reservoir covers 138 hectares and is best fished in the spring or fall by trolling. The lake has two places to launch boats and rustic camping opportunities.

Gulliford Lake (Map 17/A6)
This 6 hectare lake, at 915 metres (2,974 feet) in elevation, is located west of Highway 5A. The lake can be productive during the spring or fall for small rainbow, which can reach 1 kg (2 lbs) in size. Bobber and bait, fly fishing or spincasting are the preferred methods of catching the rainbow. There is a cartop boat launch at the lake.

Haddo Lake (Map 28/G7)
This 80 hectare lake has rainbow trout to 2 kg (4.5 lbs) (average 20-25 cm) best caught by trolling or fly fishing in the spring and fall. It is accessed by good 2wd road (Haddo Main) and has a resort together with a forest service site with camping and a cartop boat launch. The lake is used for domestic watershed purposes, so summer draw down is a problem.

Harry Lake (Map 2/G7)
This small 4 hectare lake is set below Snowy Mountain at the 2,195 metre (7,134 foot) mark. Needless to say, the fishing can be dynamite for small rainbow in the late summer and early fall. The downside? In order to reach the lake, you will need strong mountaineering skills to bushwhack in from the Snowy Mountain Trail, or along a rough route from **Joe Lake**.

Harvey Hall Lake (Map 17/A7) 🐟
The 8 hectare Harvey Hall Lake produces fairly well for stocked brook trout and rainbow to 1 kg (2 lbs) in size. Fishing is only really possible from either a float tube or small boat using similar flies as mentioned with nearby **Deadman Lake**. The lake is at 1,143 metres (3,750 feet) in elevation and has a cartop boat launch.

Hastings Lake (Map 17/A6)
This 30 hectare lake offers reasonable fishing for rainbow, with the best option being a bobber or spinner with bait (worms). There is an undeveloped campground on the lake, which is fished throughout the summer months with reasonable success.

Haynes Lake (Map 20/F7)
This 55 hectare lake has stocked rainbow trout, which grow to 2 kg (4.5 lbs) in size. The lake is 1,225 metres (3,981 feet) above sea level and has a good trail system for shore access. It is also possible to launch small boats.

Headwater Lakes (Map 18/F6) 🐟
This series of four lakes receive heavy fishing pressure throughout the open water season. However, you can still expect decent fishing for small rainbow trout and brook trout that can reach 1.5 kg (3+ lbs) in size. The fish are best caught by trolling, although fly fishing the many peat shoals or weed beds that line the lakes can produce well, too. The lakes are located at the crossroads of several main haul logging roads so the access is very good. A nice resort and forest service site are available for visitors. The lakes are at 1,250 metres (4,100 feet) in elevation and in total, cover an area of 130 hectares. Do not be surprised by the floating islands (with trees) on **Headwater 1**. This was created when sections of the peat broke free when dams raised the water level.

Hidden Lake (Map 28/E7)
This 10 hectare lake is reached by way of a rough 2wd road and then a hike. This reduces the fishing pressure and results in good fishing for small rainbow trout. The lake is 1,375 metres (4,469 feet) above sea level. The best time for fishing is during the early summer and fall by spincasting or fly fishing.

Hidden Lake (Map 37/D5) 🐟
Hidden Lake offers good trolling for stocked rainbow that can reach 3 kg (6+ lbs). At just 655 metres (2,150 feet) in elevation, the 130 hectare lake is best fished in the spring and fall. There are also possibilities to fly fish the outlet stream at the north end of the lake as well as the creek estuaries at the south end of the lake.

High Lake (Map 28/D6)
It's only a short hike in to the 12 hectare High Lake from Oyama Lake Road, but it's enough to discourage most would be visitors. Fishing pressure has historically been light for the stocked rainbow trout that can reach 1 kg (2 lbs). The lake is best fished with bait, a fly or a lure throughout the early summer and into the fall. Despite the name, High Lake is only 1,300 metres (4,225 feet) above sea level and has a rustic camping area.

Holiday Lake (Map 37/F2)
This 5 hectare lake has a scenic forest service site, which offers camping and a cartop boat launch. The lake has many small rainbow that are best caught by fly fishing or spincasting.

Holmes Lake (Map 30/F7)
Holmes Lake is accessed by trail/4wd road so it is a good choice for a secluded fishing trip. The Kootenay lake has a good population of small rainbow trout and brook trout that can grow to 1 kg (2 lbs). The lake is found at 1,370 metres (4,453 feet) in elevation and covers 35 hectares. Spincasting, fly fishing and trolling all work throughout the early summer and into the fall. The lake offers camping and a cartop boat launch at the lakeside forest service site.

Holstein Lake (Map 29/G2) 🐟
Holstein is a small, secluded, 11 hectare lake that has a fair population of small stocked rainbow that can be caught anytime during the open water season. The high elevation (1,539 metres/5,049 feet) lake has camping facilities at a small forest service site. The marshy shoreline restricts shore fishing.

Hoodoo Lake (Map 13/B7) 🐟
Hoodoo Lake is located on a deteriorating road and offers fairly good fishing for small, stocked rainbow by trolling or fly fishing. A small forest service site offers a cartop boat launch and camping facilities. The 15 hectare lake is at 1,219 metres (4,000 feet) in elevation and is best fished in the spring or fall.

Hook Lake (Map 17/C6) 🐟
This hook-like lake is found on a 2wd road off the Ketchan Lake FSR and offers fair fishing for some large rainbow (to 2 kg/4.5 lbs). There are also brook trout in the lake, which is at 1,265 metres (4,150 feet) in elevation. The lake has two forest service sites complete with a cartop boat launch and campground. Hook Lake is stocked regularly with rainbow.

Horseshoe Lakes (Map 19/A2) 🐟
Islaht Lake forms the hub of this trio of lakes, which are found on a spur road north of the Bear Creek Main. This 31 hectare, high elevation

(1,500 metre/4,920 feet) lake offers reasonable fishing for rainbow trout to 1 kg (2 lbs) in size. The lake also holds brook trout and can be fished with success anytime during the open water season by spincasting or by fly fishing. Due to an aggressive rainbow stocking program, nearby **Dobbin Lake** offers the better fishing for both rainbow and brook trout. Dobbin is only 12 hectares in size and similar to Islaht, fishing slows in the summer as both lakes are affected by draw down. **West Lake** is too shallow to hold fish.

Howard Lake (Map 12/B3)
This small 7 hectare lake is another hike-in lake, which offers pretty good fishing for small rainbow trout in the summer and fall. The high elevation (1,825 metre/5,931 feet) lake is reached by trail off the Greyback Road.

Hudson Bay Lake (Map 27/C5)
Although fishing can be slow, rainbow trout and brook trout to 2 kg (4.5 lbs) are found in this small 5 hectare lake. It is best fished anytime in the spring and fall by fly fishing. Fly fishermen should try a leech or damselfly nymph pattern whereas spincasters should try a Panther Martin or Deadly Dick. The lake is accessed by a 2wd spur road south of Whiteman Creek FSR.

Hydraulic Lake (McCulloch Reservoir) (Map 20/E7)
This 260 hectare man-made lake has rainbow trout that reach 2 kg (4.5 lbs) in size. The lake is home to the McCulloch Lake Resort, a popular destination with anglers as well as cyclists on the Kettle Valley Railway. The lake also has forest service site with a campground and boat launch and is best fished in the spring or fall by trolling. You can also try fly fishing or spincasting one of the many bays and islands.

Idabel (Cariboo) Lake (Map 20/E7)
Idabel has a healthy population of freshwater shrimp, which means good fishing for large rainbow and stocked brook trout particularly in the spring and fall by fly fishing or trolling. The lake covers an area of 46 hectares and has a scenic resort and private cabins as well as a boat launch. The lake is at 1,250 metres (4,101 feet) in elevation.

Ideal (Belgo) Lake (Map 20/G1)
This is indeed an ideal family lake that offers good fishing for small, stocked rainbow that average 20–30 cm (8-12 in) in size. The 145 hectare lake, at 1,310 metres (4,258 feet) in elevation, is best fished in the spring or fall by trolling or fly fishing since summer draw down is a problem. For fly fishermen, there is a prominent June damselfly hatch as well as a good spring caddisfly hatch. Try casting near the small island or the shallow bay. Accessed by a 2wd road, there is a lakeside forest service site offering camping and a boat launch.

Idleback Lake (Map 12/C5)
Next to the Okanagan Falls FSR (good 2wd access), Idleback Lake covers 14 hectares and has rainbow that can reach 3 kg (6+ lbs). This high elevation lake (1,430 metres/4,692 feet), offers a fly fishing-only experience. There are also restrictions on ice fishing (not allowed), and boat motors (electric only). The lake is best fished in the early summer or fall when the hatches are at their peak. A cartop boat launch is found at the forest service site on the lake's north shore.

Isintok Lake (Map 10/F4)
Camping and a cartop boat launch at the lakeshore forest service site help you enjoy this 40 hectare lake. The decent fishing for stocked rainbow trout that grow to 1.5 kg (3+ lbs) in size also attracts visitors. The high elevation (1,650 metres/5,363 feet) lake is accessed by 2wd road (Bathfield Road). Draw down affects the summer fishery.

Islaht Lake (Map 19/A2)
See Horseshoe Lakes.

Issitz Lake (Map 9/G6)
Located just west of **Wolfe Lake**, the 16 hectare Issitz Lake is found at 701 metres (2,300 feet) in elevation. The fishing for the small rainbow that inhabit the lake is quite good in the early spring by trolling.

Jackpine Lake (Map 19/A3)
Jackpine Lake is a popular recreation lake with good 2wd access, a resort, camping and boat launch facilities. The lake has reasonable fishing for rainbow trout to 2 kg (4.5 lbs) that are best caught in the spring or fall by trolling or fly fishing. The lake is at 1,311 metres (4,301 feet) in elevation, covers 44 hectares, and is stocked annually. There is an electric motor only restriction.

James (Trapper) Lake (Map 20/D3)
This 55 hectare lake has good fishing for small rainbow trout that can be caught any time during the open water season by trolling or fly fishing. The lake is also a good ice fishing destination. The lake is at 1,375 metres (4,469 feet) in elevation and has a forest service site on the south end. Access to this lake is via a 2wd road.

Jamieson Lake (Map 9/E7)
Jamieson Lake is reached by a short hike off of the often gated Darcy Mine Road. Because of the tough access, the 20 hectare lake is fairly good for small rainbow by bait fishing or fly fishing. It is best fished during the late spring or early fall because, at 915 metres (2,974 feet) in elevation, the lake warms up in summer.

Jewel Lake (Map 6/A4)
In the past, Jewel Lake was famous for it's unbelievably large trout. The largest, rumour has it, was 25 kg (56 lbs). But then, minnows were introduced here, and the dynamics of the lake totally changed. The rainbow have started to rebound, and you can find rainbow up to 3 kg (6+ lbs). The 72 hectare lake is long and narrow, stretching over 2 km (1.2 miles) and has a provincial park at the north end of the lake, and a boat launch at the south. Trolling works well here, as does fly fishing. For fly fisherman, using a wet fly such as a dragonfly pattern or other nymph patterns is effective. A dry fly in the evening when the fish are rising can be a lot of fun. The lake is at 1,143 metres (3,750 feet), and does not warm excessively in the summer.

Joan Lake (Map 13/B2)
This 50 hectare, high elevation (1,300 metres/4,225 feet) lake is accessed by a short hike off a short spur road, which in turn is off the Lassie Lake Road. The lake offers very good fishing for small rainbow in the spring and fall from a float-tube. There is a forest service site on the eastern shores of the lake, as well as a hike-in site in the southwest corner of the lake.

Joe Lake (Map 2/G6)
Your shortest point of access to this small sub-alpine lake is from the end of Susap Creek FSR. It still means hiking a couple kilometres. The lake is at 2,100 metres (6,825 feet) in elevation and has exceptional fishing for small rainbow and cutthroat, which can be caught on just about anything. This lake is a wonderful destination if you want a remote backpacking experience and are willing to put the legwork in to get there. A cabin is available by the lake.

Johnny Lake (Map 16/G7)
Access into this 10 hectare lake can be a little rough but the forest service site with camping and a cartop boat launch still remains busy. The lake is very productive for small, stocked rainbow that come readily to a fly, bait or a lure.

Kalamalka Lake (Map 28/B7-D5)
In the heart of the Okanagan Valley, this big lake is known more for water skiing than fishing. There are a few lake trout and rainbow trout both growing to 8 kg (18 lbs) as well as a few small kokanee. The low elevation (391 metres/ 1,283 feet) lake is best fished by trolling in the early spring or late fall. It covers 2,574 hectares and has full facilities and numerous access points.

Kate Lake (Map 38/D7)
Kate Lake is reached by a 3 km (1.8 mile) trail off the Sugar Mountain Road (4wd access). The 25 hectare lake offers very good fishing for small rainbow that can reach 1 kg (2 lbs) in size. Your best option is to cast a fly from a float-tube. A rustic camping is found at the lake.

Kathy Lake (Map 29/F2)

This 5 hectare lake has good fishing for small rainbow trout and brook trout. It is best fished by casting a lure, bait or fly in the early summer or fall. The high elevation (1,370 metres/4,453 feet) lake is stocked annually and offers camping and a cartop boat launch at the forest service site on the east side.

Keefer Lake (Map 30/E7)

The 69 hectare Keefer Lake provides good fishing for small rainbow trout and brook trout to 1 kg (2 lbs) in size throughout the open water season. The lake is at 1,372 metres (4,501 feet) in elevation and easily accessed off the Keefer Lake Road (2wd road). Visitors will find a nice resort with boat launch and camping facilities.

Kentucky Lake (Map 17/C4)

Part of the Kentucky-Alleyne Rec Area, this is a popular destination in the open water season. There is camping on the lake as well as a trail around the lake providing good shore access. The 36 hectare lake is found 991 m (3,251 ft) above sea level and offers rainbow to 2 kg (4.5 lbs). Anglers should be prepared for spotty fishing by trolling and fly fishing (shrimp and chironomids).

Ketchan Lake (Map 17/C6)

Best accessed from the north, Ketchan Lake is a moody lake that is best fished earlier in the year. The shallow 26 hectare lake is found at 1,250 m (4,101 ft) in elevation and offers rainbow trout on the fly or by spincasting.

Kidd Lake (Map 17/B3)

Found next to Highway 5A south of Aspen Grove, you wouldn't expect to find 5 kg (10+ lb) fish in this 19 hectare lake. But the lake has been managed as a catch-n-release fishery and now produces some of BC's biggest trout. Rainbow trout are stocked annually.

Kidney & Liver Lakes (Map 37/G1)

Located on a rough 2wd spur road off the Three Valley-Mabel FSR, **Kidney Lake** offers fairly good fishing for rainbow that can reach 2 kg (4.5 lbs). The best way to fish the lake is to use a float tube and fly fish the many shallows. A forest service site with a campground and cartop boat launch is available at the lake, which covers 25 hectares, and is 855 metres (2,779 feet) above sea level. Just to the north of Kidney is the tiny 3 hectare **Liver Lake**. The lake has many small rainbow primarily caught by fly fishing. Both lakes are currently being managed to decrease stocks, which will ultimately increase the size of fish.

Kilpoola Lake (Map 3/F7)

This lake is accessed by a gated road (please close it as this is ranchland) off Highway 3 west of Osoyoos and is found at 820 metres (2,690 feet) in elevation. It has fair fishing for rainbow and brook trout that can grow to 1 kg (2 lbs). The lake covers an area of 17 hectares, and is stocked regularly because the lake is susceptible to winterkill. There is an undeveloped boat launch at the lake.

King Edward Lake (Map 28/E6)

Summer draw down can transform this 30 hectare lake from a jewel in the rough to an unsightly mud pit. If you time it right, fishing for rainbow trout to 1.5 kg (3+ lbs) can be good. Trolling or fly fishing in the spring or fall should meet with success. The high elevation (1,375 metres/4,469 feet) lake has a lakeshore forest service site.

Kump Lake (Map 17/A7)

Also known as Lost Lake, Kump Lake offers a popular forest service site that provides good access to the lake. This 17 hectare lake is managed as a trophy lake for rainbow, which can be taken by fly fishing only. The fishing is spotty and does suffer from the summer doldrums but the stocked rainbow grow up to 2.5 kg (5 lbs) make this a fine fishing destination.

Lacoma Lake (Map 19/A3)

Lacoma is a small 5 hectare hike-in lake with good fly fishing and spincasting in the spring and fall. The lake is at 1,000 metres (3,250 feet) in elevation and contains rainbow trout to 1 kg (2 lbs) in size.

Laird Lake (Map 9/B2)

Laird Lake receives heavy fishing pressure given its proximity to Highway 5A but still offers good numbers of small rainbow and brook trout caught by trolling, fly fishing or spincasting. The 27 hectare lake is at 808 metres (2,651 feet) in elevation and is best fished in the spring or fall. A cartop boat launch is available at the lake, which is stocked regularly with rainbow.

Lambly (Bear) Lake (Map 19/C3)

Despite easy access (and the resulting heavy pressure) to this 75 hectare lake, the lake still produces well for small rainbow trout throughout the spring or fall by trolling or fly fishing. Perch have been illegally introduced and compete heavily with the stocked trout for available food. The lake is at 1,138 metres (3,800 feet) in elevation and has a resort, campground and boat launch.

Lassie Lake (Map 13/C2)

This Christian Valley lake is a popular place for area anglers interested in good fishing and a scenic place to visit. The 37 hectare lake is well stocked with rainbow that can grow up to 1 kg (2 lbs) or more. The lake is easily accessed by the Lassie Lake Road and not surprisingly, has a forest service site on its southern shore. There is a boat launch and hiking trails in the area. The high elevation lake (1,295 metres/4,249 feet) is deep enough to be trolled, but fly fishing around the inflow of an unnamed creek on its northern shores, or the outflow of Sandrift Creek on its east, are also good bets.

Linden Lake (Map 21/D4)

The rough access (4wd only) prevents some fishermen from enjoying the scenic mountain 12 hectare lake that is set below Mr. Moore. Despite the elevation (1,750 metres/5,688 feet), the fishing slows in summer. Spring or fall are the best times to fly fish or spincast for the rainbow trout growing to 1 kg (2 lbs) in size.

Link Lake (Map 10/A1)

This 15 hectare lake has a nice forest service site with camping and a cartop boat launch. Despite easy access, the lake still provides a reasonable fishery for rainbow that can reach 2 kg (4.5 lbs) in size. The lake is 1,113 metres (3,652 feet) above sea level and is plagued by winterkill. An annual stocking program helps maintain the fishery.

Loch Drinkle (Map 27/D7)

This 17 hectare lake's claim to fame (other than the amusing name) is that it is home to some surprisingly large rainbow trout. The high elevation (1,400 metres/4,550 feet) lake is stocked regularly and receives light fishing pressure due to its hike-in access (about 2 km/1.2 miles if you can make it to the end of the rough logging road). The fishing success can remain fairly good throughout the ice-free season.

Lodestone Lake (Map 8/E5)

Lodestone is a lovely little lake located at the end of the Lodestone FSR (as well as by foot or horse along the Hope Brigade Trail). The high elevation (1,830 metres/5,948 feet) lake offers fast fishing for small rainbow on a fly or by spincasting beginning in early July through to October. A forest service site at the lake has a cartop boat launch and camping for your enjoyment.

Lodwick Lake (Map 16/G7)

Found in an area riddled with fine fishing lakes, Lodwick Lake is also blessed with a forest service campsite. Access into the 19 hectare lake is rough but fishing can be good for trout to 1 kg (2 lbs). The islands and prominent drop-off make fly fishing and spincasting a viable option on this long, narrow lake. The lake is at 1,143 m (3,750 ft) in elevation and is stocked with rainbow.

Loon Lake (Map 28/F7)

Loon Lake receives steady fishing pressure due to its easy access and general popularity. The 10 hectare lake holds fair numbers of rainbow trout to 2 kg (4.5 lbs) that are caught primarily by fly fishing or trolling. The high elevation (1,375 metres/4,469 feet) lake is stocked regularly and is best fished during the early summer and fall. Camping facilities are available at a small treed forest service site.

Loosemore Lake (Map 17/B7)

This small 5 hectare lake is found east of Highway 5A and provides fair fishing for small, stocked rainbow trout. The lake has a day-use facility and a cartop boat launch and can be fished effectively by using similar gear as Deadman Lake to the north.

Lorne Lake (Map 9/F7)

This 40 hectare hike-in lake has reasonably good fishing for rainbow that average 20–25 cm (8–10 inches). The rainbow are caught by spincasting, by fly fishing or with bait.

Lost Lake (Map 28/E7)

This 15 hectare, high elevation (1,300 metres/4,225 feet) lake has fair numbers of rainbow trout that average 20-25 cm (8-10 in) in size. The lake is best fished by fly fishing or trolling.

MacDonald Lake (Map 18/E4)

MacDonald Lake has a good population of small rainbow trout, which are stocked regularly. The high elevation (1,700 metres/5,525 feet) lake can be fished with success any time during the ice free season with bait, a fly or spinner. The 5 hectare lake is found next to Brenda Lake and a lakeshore forest service site.

Mabel Lake (Maps 37/E7-38/A1)

This large 5,986 hectare lake is found east of Enderby and is easily accessed by paved Mabel Lake Road. Mabel Lake is primarily a trolling lake for the large rainbow, which reach 4 kg (9 lbs) as well as the small kokanee, large lake trout (to 7kg/15+ lbs) and large dolly varden (to 4 kg/9 lbs). It is also possible to fly fish or spincast the creek mouths for rainbow and dollies primarily in the spring. For the lake trout, it is best to troll a plug or lure in the depths of the lake. The lake is 393 metres (1,289 feet) above sea level and has full facilities including several forest service sites with boat launches and a nice resort. A provincial park is located at the south end of the lake.

Madden Lake (Map 3/E3)

Madden Lake has a fair population of stocked rainbow trout to 2 kg (4.5 lbs) and a few brook trout. The 11 hectare lake is best fished in the spring or fall by trolling or fly fishing. The lake is at 830 metres (2,723 feet) in elevation and has camping and cartop boat launch facilities at a forest service site. Access to this lake is by 2wd road (Fairview Road) northwest of Oliver.

Maloney Lake (Map 13/C3)

Maloney Lake is a hike-in only high elevation (1,280 metres/4,160 feet) lake in the ever-popular Christian Valley. This beautiful lake requires a 3.5 km hike from Cup Lake that can be extended to loop past Clark Lake to the road southwest of Lassie Lake. Maloney Lake has a forest service site, and reasonably good fishing for rainbow averaging 20–25 cm (8–10 inches). The lake is best fished from a float tube using flies, although spincasting also works.

Mara Lake (Maps 36/G1, 37/A1, 45/A7)

Mara Lake is more of a recreational lake than a fishing lake although it does offer rainbow, lake trout and dolly varden that reach 2 kg (4.5 lbs). At 346 metres (1,135 feet) in elevation, the lake is best trolled in May–June and again in November when the fish are feeding near the surface. It is also effective to troll plugs or lures at 10–25 metres (30–90 feet) during the summer months. Kokanee fishing can be fairly good from July to October. The lake offers full facilities including a resort and a provincial park. It is easily accessed by Highway 97A south of Sicamous.

Marshall Lake (Map 6/A6)

Marshall Lake is a tiny 3 hectare man-made lake created by Grandby Mines. The lake has a forest service site with a cartop boat launch and camping facilities. The area has a maze of cross-country ski trails and is quite popular with gold seekers. The high elevation (1,370 metres/4,453 feet) lake also has a reasonably good population of small rainbow, which can be caught by fly fishing, by casting a float and bait or by spincasting.

Martin's Lake (Map 9/D5)

Martin's Lake is a tiny 3 hectare lake found just north of Princeton. It produces a few rainbow in the 3 kg (6+ lbs) category and also has a small forest service site with a boat launch. The lake is a relatively low elevation lake (610 metres/1,983 feet) in elevation and is best fished in the early spring or fall. Bait fishing is possible although fly fishing and spincasting work better.

Mathews Lake (Map 5/D5)

Mathews Lake is a small 5 hectare mountain lake, set beneath Mt Davis. The lake offers fairly good fishing for small rainbow, primarily by fly fishing, bait fishing or spincasting. There is a quiet forest service site on the lakeshore that can be accessed by a 2wd forestry road

McCaffery Lake (Map 9/C3)

This small 6 hectare lake offers a surprisingly good fishery for small rainbow and given its easy access, it is a good choice for a family outing. The lake also produces well during ice fishing season for the brook trout that inhabit the lake. An undeveloped boat launch and picnic area is available at the lake, which is stocked annually with rainbow. The lake is at 808 metres (2,651 feet) in elevation and can be fished from a float tube or shore.

Min Lake (Map 28/F6)

A small lake with fair fishing for small rainbow, the 5 hectare Min Lake is accessed by a 2wd road off the Dee Lake Road. As with most lakes in the area, it is best fished in the spring or fall with bait, fly or lures all producing results.

Minnow Lake (Map 20/F7)

Minnow Lake is a small 15 hectare lake sandwiched between and connected to Haynes and Hydraulic Lakes. The 1,225 metre high (3,981 feet) lake has rainbow trout to 1 kg (2 lbs) in size best caught by trolling or fly fishing in the spring or fall. The lake is stocked regularly and is accessed by a good 2wd road or trail.

Missezula Lake (Map 17/C6)

Missezula is a large 241 hectare lake that can be accessed from the Coquihalla Connector (Hwy 97C) or Highway 5A. Either way, the access is good which results in heavy fishing pressure. The lake, which is at 1,052 metres (3,451 feet) in elevation, contains stocked rainbow and brook trout to 2 kg (4.5 lbs) as well as some kokanee. The predominant fishing method is trolling and there is a forest service site at the north end of the lake.

Mission Lake (Map 21/D1)

Mission Lake is a 30 hectare, high elevation (1,750 metres/5,688 feet) lake that is accessed by a long trail. It is 6 km (3.6 miles) from Fish Hawk Lake, which in turn requires a 4wd vehicle to access, so the fishing is fairly good for rainbow trout to 1.5 kg (3+ lbs) (average 25-35) in size.

Moore Lake (Map 20/D1)

Moore Lake is 25 hectares in size and is found at the 1,340 metre (4,355 foot) high mark north of Postill Lake. The stocked lake produces well for small rainbow trout during the early summer and into the fall despite the draw down and winterkill problems. The lake has a lakeside forest service site.

Munro Lake (Map 18/G7)

Munro Lake has fairly good fishing for rainbow trout that can reach 1 kg. The 14 hectare lake is stocked annually and is best fished by trolling or with a fly in the spring or fall. The 4wd access limits pressure.

Murphy Lakes (Map 8/D3)

A short 1 km hike off the Lawson-Britton Creek FSR leads to these popular mountain lakes at 1,204 metres (3,950 feet) in elevation. Both lakes are about 8 hectares in size and contain rainbow and brook trout that can grow to 1.5 kg (3+ lbs) in size. The lakes are stocked regularly with rainbow and receive heavy fishing pressure. The eastern lake has larger fish. Campsites are found at both lakes.

Naramata Lake (Map 11/F1)

Located in the hills above Naramata along the deactivated Elinor Lake FSR, this small 14 hectare lake is stocked annually with rainbow trout. Most anglers access this lake from the north.

Nevertouch Lake (Map 21/E6)

On a 2wd secondary road off the Kettle River Main, Nevertouch Lake is 52 hectares in size and offers good fly fishing for rainbow that can reach 1 kg (2 lbs). Although most of the fish are quite small, fishing remains reasonably good throughout the summer at this high elevation (1,295 metre/4,249 feet) lake. The lake has a forest service site.

Nickel Plate Lake (Map 10/F7)

This 80 hectare lake is located below Apex Mountain. Nickel Plate Park provides opportunities for camping as well as cross-country skiing, biking and hiking and, of course, fishing. The lake is fairly good for small rainbow throughout the summer months. Adventurous anglers may be interested in the small lake, which is about a 15 minute walk to the north. This lake holds small (15-25 cm/6-10 in) rainbow that readily take most offerings.

Nicklen Lake (Map 29/A6) Fishing BC

This 89 hectare lake has wild rainbow to 2 kg (4.5 lbs). The high elevation (1,306 metres/4,285 feet) lake is best trolled with the spring or fall being the best times to fish. In summer the lake suffers from draw down. The lake is found along a good 2wd road and offers camping and a cartop boat launch at the forest service site.

Noreen Lake (Map 37/F2)

This 5 hectare lake is located on a 4wd road east of Mabel Lake. The lake has a forest service site with a campground and cartop boat launch and is best fished in the spring or fall. Fly fishing and spincasting often produce small rainbow.

Norman Lake (Map 19/E7)

One of two small lakes in Okanagan Mountain Park worth fishing, the 10 hectare Norman Lake offers good fishing for rainbow trout to 1 kg (2 lbs) throughout the spring and fall. The lake is best fished using bait, a fly or a lure. This is a hike-in lake found north of Baker Lake.

Okanagan Lake (Maps 11, 19, 20, 27, 28)

In the heart of the Okanagan, this huge (35,008 hectare) recreational lake is over 118 km (72 miles) long. Known more for its water sports than the fishing, the lake does hold quite a few rainbow and kokanee. Anglers looking for the bigger trout that on occasion reach over 5 kg (11 lbs) will find better luck in October to March using a plug, spoon or Bucktail. The best areas are near Fintry, Okanagan Mountain Park, Okanagan Centre or Rattlesnake Island. During the summer, smaller trout and kokanee can be caught on gang trolls. There is no shortage of places to access the lake as several resorts, campsites and provincial parks line the lake. Be sure to check the regulations for current limits.

Osoyoos Lake (Maps 3/G6-4/A7)

This is Canada's warmest lake with average summer temperatures at around 24°C. Needless to say, it is a popular water sport lake but it does offer a variety of fishing alternatives. In the spring, trolling can often be successful for large rainbow trout (to 5 kg/11 lbs), which are primarily caught by trolling. For the rest of the year, there is an opportunity to spincast for largemouth or smallmouth bass as well as black crappie or perch. In fact, the BC record largemouth bass was caught in this lake. The bass, perch and black crappie are best caught in the shallow bays that line the lake or in the river channel at the north end of the lake. There is also a population of small kokanee.

Osprey Lake (Map 18/B7)

Osprey Lake is the heart of the three lakes area, and offers a reasonably good fishery for rainbow that can grow to 2 kg (4.5 lbs) in size. A former forest service site offers access to the 48 hectare lake. The lake is best trolled, although fishing from shore can be productive.

Otter Lake (Map 8/G3)

This lake is a popular recreation lake with private cabins, camping as well as a boat launch and a beach at the Otter Lake Provincial Park. A good 2wd skirts the west side of the lake, while the Kettle Valley Railway runs along the east side. Recent stocking attempts have increased the number of rainbow and brook trout in the lake but fishing still remains fairly spotty. There are also some lake trout, kokanee and whitefish available. The best method of fishing is trolling during the early spring or late fall as the lake warms due to the low elevation.

Otter Lake (Map 28/D1)

Found north of Vernon, this lake is easily accessed off the Otter Lake Road. Although fishing for the rainbow and dolly varden is spotty, some big fish can be caught here.

Oyama Lake (Map 28/D7)

Oyama Lake is a 364 hectare lake with surprisingly large rainbow trout reaching 3 kg (6+ lbs). The lake is accessed by a 4wd road and is best fished in the spring or fall with fly fishing around the many islands being the preferred method. The spring caddisfly hatch is the best time. The lake is at 1,358 metres (4,445 feet) in elevation and has a forest service site as well as a resort. Summer draw down is a problem.

Park Lakes (Map 28/E7)

These two small lakes total 7 hectares and have a few small rainbow trout best caught by casting a fly or lure. The lakes warm during the summer and as a result, fishing suffers during that time.

Peachland Lake (Map 18/F5)

This popular lake experiences heavy fishing pressure, resulting in slow fishing for generally small rainbow trout. A stocking program is in effect to help increase the population of rainbow and counteract the coarse fish problem. The 110 hectare lake is found at 1,250 metres (4,063 feet) in elevation along a good 2wd road (Peachland FSR). Your best bet is to troll the lake in the spring or fall as draw down is a problem in the summer. A large open forest service site lines the lake.

Pear Lake (Map 20/F7)

This 14 hectare lake is found next to Haynes Lake, but is slightly higher, at the 1,280 metre mark (4,160 feet). The lake is stocked regularly to ensure good fishing for small rainbow, which are best fished in the spring or fall by spincasting or fly fishing.

Pete Lake (Map 5/B1)

Pete Lake is a small 12 hectare lake with a pretty forest service site at the south end of the lake. Most visitors to the lake enjoy reasonably good fishing for the small rainbow, which are usually caught by trolling or fly fishing.

Pinaus & Area Lakes (Map 35/F7) ⌐

Pinaus Lake is a popular fishing lake with camping facilities and a resort. The 162 hectare lake is accessed by the Pinaus Lake Road, which is rather rough to travel in wet weather. The lake has good fishing for rainbow trout in the 1 kg (2 lbs) size category on a troll or by fly fishing. With a little skill, it is possible to catch a 2-3 kg (6+ lbs) rainbow. The lake is 1,006 metres (3,300 feet) above sea level and infested with perch. Nearby lakes include:

Lady King Lake is a small 5 hectare lake just west of Pinaus Lake. This lake is a good alternative for fly fisherman since it holds good numbers of rainbow in the 1 kg (2 lbs) category. There is an ice fishing ban on the lake to help preserve the resource.

Little Pinaus Lake is a 20 hectare lake east of Pinaus Lake proper that has rainbow to 1 kg (2 lbs) in size. The fish are somewhat hard to catch due to the heavy fishing pressure. The lake has a forest service site.

Square Lake offers good fishing for rainbow trout to 1 kg (2 lbs). The 10 hectare lake has camping at the forest service site and is stocked annually. Fly fishing is your best bet throughout the spring or fall months.

Placer Lake (Map 1/D5)

This small sub-alpine (1,646 metres/5,349 feet) lake is located in the Placer Mountain Motorized Regulated Area and can be accessed by trail. The remote access results in very good fly fishing for small wild rainbow. The forest service site provides access to the 7 hectare lake.

Postill & Area Lakes (Map 20/E2)

Postill Lake forms the hub of a popular fishing destination northeast of Kelowna. Overnight visitors will find good access to the forest service site and the resort. The high elevation (1,375 metres/4,469 feet) lake covers 90 hectares and is stocked annually. The mixed population of brook trout and rainbow are best caught in the spring or fall by trolling or spincasting. Also in the area are several hike-in lakes to explore:

Hereron Lake is a 10 hectare lake that has good fishing for small rainbow trout during the spring or fall. The lake sees fewer visitors than many lakes in the area because of the 3 km hike-in.

Meadow Lake has good numbers of rainbow to 2 kg (4.5 lbs) frequently taken by fly fishing or spincasting. The hike-in access certainly prevents heavy fishing pressure. There is a ban on ice fishing.

South Lake is a short 500 metre hike from Postill Lake. The 25 hectare offers steady fishing for rainbow to 2 kg (4.5 lbs) that can be fished with success throughout the ice free season. There is an artificial fly only restriction at the lake.

Procter Lake (Map 28/F1)

Procter Lake is found on a 4wd road south of Armstrong and offers decent fishing for rainbow trout that can grow to 1 kg (2 lbs). The lake is at 1,460 metres (4,745 feet) in elevation and has an undeveloped campground. For best results, try in the early summer or fall with a fly or small spinner.

Prosser Lake (Map 17/B7)

Prosser Lake is located near Deadman Lake just east of Highway 5A. Despite the closeness to the highway, the access is by 4wd vehicle, which results in light fishing pressure. It offers good fishing for small, stocked rainbow. The 5 hectare lake is found at 1,065 metres (3,461 feet) in elevation.

Rampart Lake (Map 9/D1) ⌐

Rampart Lake is an isolated, 15 hectare lake located on logging road off the Summers Creek Road. At 1,356 metres (4,449 feet) in elevation, the forest service site at the lake is seldom used. The lake is stocked regularly with scrappy rainbow that can grow to 2 kg (4.5 lbs). It is a fly fishing only lake, with a good chironomid hatch in the spring.

Ratnip Lake (Map 19/G7)

Ratnip Lake is found via a short hike off Chute Lake Road. There are lots of small rainbow trout at the 20 hectare lake, and it shouldn't be too hard to hook one or two. The best time for fishing is during the spring and fall since the lake warms in the summer.

Raymer Lake (Map 19/A2)

Accessed by a 4wd road off the Bear Creek Main, this 35 hectare lake has rainbow trout to 1 kg (2 lbs). The high elevation (1,465 metres/4,761 feet) lake is best fished in the early summer or fall by bait fishing, spincasting or fly fishing.

Rickey Lake (Map 16/G7)

Rickey Lake is reached by a 2wd spur road off the Tulameen-Otter Valley Road and offers a forest service campsite. The small rainbow that inhabit the 4 hectare lake are subject to winterkill but the stocking program in effect usually ensures a steady population. The marshy area surrounding the lake helps produce plenty of insects for the fish and mosquitoes for the campers. The lake is at 1,100 metres (3,575 feet) in elevation and can be fished during the winter and early spring or fall.

Ripley Lake (Map 3/E2) ⌐

Ripley Lake is located north of Madden Lake on a spur road. The 6 hectare lake is fairly good for rainbow to 1 kg (2 lbs) by fly fishing or trolling. It is stocked annually with rainbow and is subject to draw down. A small forest service site offers camping and a cartop boat launch.

Robertson Lake (Map 17/A7)

This 9 hectare lake is located by 4wd road to the west of Highway 5A. The lake is best fished during ice fishing season, although there is decent fly fishing or trolling fishery for rainbow to 1 kg (2 lbs) during the spring and fall. It is located 1,070 metres (3,478 feet) in elevation and offers a forest service campsite.

Rod Lake (Map 28/F7)

Rod Lake is a tiny 5 hectare lake with so-so fishing for rainbow trout despite its hike-in access. The high elevation (1,400 metre/4,550 feet) lake is stocked annually and is best fly fished in the spring or early summer.

Rose Valley Lake (Map 19/F4) ⌐

This 42 hectare lake has some good fishing for rainbow trout to 1 kg (2 lbs), primarily in the spring on a fly or by trolling. Ice fishing with bait also works effectively. The lake is at 600 metres (1,968 feet) in elevation and is stocked regularly. The lake, given its proximity to Kelowna, is very popular. Road access into the lake has recently been closed to the public.

Rosemond Lake (Map 36/G2)

Situated at the south end of Mara Lake, this small lake is also known by locals as Mud Lake. The road heading west then north off the Rosemond Lake Road crosses private property and is closed to the public. To access the forestry rec site, you will need to take the longer route that switchbacks east from the Rosemond Branch Forestry Road. Or you can take a canoe or rowboat under the railway trestle from Mara Lake; motorboats are not allowed. Fishing here is similar to Mara Lake, as a short channel connects the two. You'll find rainbow, lake trout and dolly varden to 2 kg (4.5 lbs).

Round Lake (Map 36/C7)

Round Lake isn't really round. The 27 hectare, low elevation (426 metres/1,398 feet) lake is easily accessed off a good road just east of Highway 97. The lake has a few rainbow that can reach 2 kg (4.5 lbs) in size and is best fished by trolling or fly fishing. Spring and fall are the best times to fish the lake.

Ruth Lake (Map 28/F7)

Ruth Lake has good fishing for rainbow trout to 2 kg (4.5 lbs), best caught in the spring or fall on a fly, with bait or on a lure. The 10 hectare lake is stocked annually and has camping at a rustic, user-maintained forest service site. Access to this lake is by hiking from the Flyfish #2 Lake.

Sandrift Lakes (Map 13/D2)

Sandrift Lakes are a trio of small lakes located along the State Lake Road (2wd access). They all offer good fishing for small rainbow with the preferred method of fishing being fly fishing. The lakes are at around 1,250 metres (4,063 feet) in elevation and are best fished in the late spring or fall. There is a small forest service site on the shores of the southwestern-most lake.

Saunier Lake (Map 12/F7)

On the Tuzo-Eugene FSR (good 2wd), this 5 hectare lake is located at 1,100 metres (3,575 feet) in elevation. A small forest service site with a cartop boat launch is located on the shores of the lake. Fly fishing and bait fishing for small rainbow can be productive during the spring and fall.

Sawmill (Burnell) Lake (Map 26/G2)

See Burnell Lake.

Seidner Lake (Map 29/C1)

This 6 hectare lake is accessed by a short hike off the Trinity Valley Road. The lake offers fairly good fishing for small brook trout (averaging 25 cm/10 inches). At 800 metres (2,600 feet) in elevation, the lake is best fished in the fall by spincasting or using a bobber and worm or flies.

Shannon Lake (Map 19/E5)

This 25 hectare lake, just northeast of Westbank, is known for its largemouth bass and perch fishery. The lake is at 520 metres (1,690 feet) in elevation and is subject to warm waters that are preferred by these species. The lake is accessed by a good 2wd road (Shannon Lake Road)

and has a nice park to enjoy.

Sigalet Lake (Map 29/G1)

Off the Silver Hills FSR, this 25 hectare lake has a few rainbow primarily caught by fly fishing. There is also a small population of kokanee that occasionally are caught by trolling. There is no ice fishing allowed at the lake but there is a forest service site with a campground and cartop boat launch available.

Silver Lake (Map 19/A5)

Silver lake is stocked with rainbow trout, so it generally has good fishing for trout that grow to 1 kg (2 lbs) in size. The 10 hectare lake is not high enough (at 1,075 metres/3,494 feet) to stay cool during summer, so the best fishing is during the spring and fall by fly fishing or trolling. The lake is accessed by a good 2wd road and has a small forest service site with a cartop boat launch and campground, in addition to a private forestry lodge. There is an electric motor only restriction on the lake.

Siwash Lake (Map 17/G5)

This 35 hectare lake has hit-n-miss fishing for rainbow trout to 1 kg (2 lbs) with fly fishing, spincasting or trolling in the spring or fall being your best bet. The high elevation (1,465 metres/4,761 feet) lake has resort facilities and is stocked regularly. Access to this lake is by a 4wd road off the Whitehead Lake Road.

Skaha Lake (Maps 3/F1-11/E6)

Located in the arid terrain of the southern Okanagan, this large (2,010 hectare) lake is better for water sports than fishing. The lake is easily accessed by Highway 97 and has full facilities including resorts, camping and beaches. The lake is best trolled for the kokanee and rainbow trout (to 5 kg/11 lbs) that are occasionally caught. There are also good numbers of smallmouth bass, burbot and carp that can be caught by spincasting the shallow bays. The low elevation (339 metres/1,112 feet) lake is best fished in spring and fall.

Solco Lake (Map 12/D7)

Solco Lake is a good choice if you want to try your luck at a high elevation (1,555 metre/5,054 feet) fly fishing lake. The rainbow trout are usually small (20-25 cm/8-10 inch). The lake covers 8 hectares, and is located along the Solco Lake Road (2wd access). Fishing, given the high elevation, usually remains steady throughout the summer months.

Spec Lakes (Map 28/G7)

This trio of lakes just west of Grizzly Lake cover an area of 37 hectares and are found at 1,300 metres (4,225 feet) in elevation. The remote lakes are considered a good option if you have a canoe or pontoon boat to maneuver around in. The southernmost lake is very good for small wild rainbow on a fly or by spincasting. The middle lake holds the largest fish, which reach 1 kg (2 lbs). The northernmost lake sees the most action as it is home to a forest service campsite. Access to the lakes is by a rough, narrow 2wd road south from Aberdeen Lake.

Spectrum Lake (Map 38/F6)

This 35 hectare mountain lake is found in the Monashee Provincial Park and is accessed by a long hike on the Rainbow Falls Trail. Once you reach the lake, you should expect some good fishing for rainbow trout on a fly or by spincasting. The lake is best fished in the early summer or fall for the rainbow, which reach 1 kg (2 lbs) on occasion. Spectrum is also a popular base camp for exploring further into the park.

Spring Lake (Map 19/A6)

Spring Lake has a healthy population of stocked brook trout. Access into the lake can be rough when it is wet. As the name indicates, the best time to fish here is spring, followed closely by early fall. The 900 metre (2,925 feet) high lake is best fished by spincasting or bait fishing.

Spukunne Lake (Map 9/G1)

This small lake offers some large trout (1 kg/2lb fish are common) since the access is somewhat difficult and there is a one fish limit on the lake. Access is limited by the washed out bridge on the Siwash Creek Road (at 8 km).

St. Margaret Lake (Map 21/D3)

Set below Jubilee Mountain, this scenic 25 hectare lake has rainbow trout to 1 kg (2 lbs). The high elevation (2,000 metres/6,500 feet) lake is best fished in the summer and fall using a fly or small lure.

State Lake (Map 13/D3)

State Lake is a secluded, hike-in lake, tailor-made for fly-fishers. In fact, the lake is designated fly fishing only. Check the regulations for other restrictions. The lake contains rainbow to 1 kg (2 lbs), and at 1,174 metres (3, 528 feet) above sea level, it is best fished in the early summer and in the fall. The trail to the lake begins at the State Lake Road Recreation Site and leads downhill to the lake (it is an uphill grunt back to the road).

Stoney Lake (Map 17/A7)

This small 4 hectare lake has surprisingly good fishing for small rainbow by bait fishing, fly fishing or spincasting. The lake, at 1,220 metres (3,965 feet) in elevation, is a good choice if you want to try your luck at a small lake off the beaten path. The lake is stocked regularly with rainbow.

Streak Lake (Map 28/D6)

This 22 hectare lake is a long narrow lake with spotty fishing for stocked rainbow trout that average 20–30 cm (8–12 inches). The lake is accessed off the King Edward Lake Road and is best fished in the spring or fall by trolling or fly fishing. The lake is 911 metres (2,989 feet) above sea level and offers a campground and cartop boat launch at the lakeshore forest service site.

Stringer Lake (Map 9/C1)

This 8 hectare lake is located on a steep 4wd road that winds up the grassy slopes to the east of Allison Lake. The lake has stocked rainbow trout that can grow to 1.5 kg (3+lbs) in size and offers camping at a small forest service site. The lake is at 1,525 metres (4,956 feet) in elevation and fishing remains active throughout the summer.

Sugar Lake (Maps 30/B1, 38/B7)

Sugar Lake is a large (2,080 hectare) lake found at 594 metres (1,949 feet) in elevation. The lake has dollies that usually average 2–4 kg (4–9 lbs) as well as Gerrard-strain rainbow that reach similar sizes. These fish are best caught by trolling the lake, although fly fishing can be successful if you concentrate on the river channel at the north end of the lake or the other creek/river inlets. The lake also has a plentiful supply of large whitefish and some kokanee and burbot. There are several forest service sites on the lake offering camping and boat launch facilities as well as a resort.

Summit Lake (Map 17/A7)

Found next to Highway 5A, this tiny 3 hectare lake is a good choice for a family since the stocked trout take readily to a bobber and bait.

Sunset Lake (Map 18/C4)

This small 10 hectare lake offers good fishing for rainbow trout that can grow to 1 kg (2 lbs). The lake is reached by a well-developed trail, which allows you to pack a canoe into the lake. A trail also leads around the lake providing shore fishing opportunities particularly on the western shores. It is best fished during the spring or fall by spincasting or fly fishing.

Swan Lake (Map 28/D2)

Stocked brook trout and rainbow trout are found in this 410 hectare lake. The fishing is generally slow with the best results being by trolling in the spring or fall or by ice fishing. The lake is accessed by a paved road (Highway 97) and is at 389 metres (1,276 feet) in elevation. There is a commercial RV site and resort at the lake.

Tahla Lake (Map 16/G4)

The 13 hectare Tahla Lake is a good choice for a family outing because of its nice forest service site with a cartop boat launch and camping. The lake can be quite busy and most of the stocked rainbow don't get very big. The lake is usually trolled but spin casting, fly fishing or bobber and bait can produce results as well. The lake is at 1,021 m (3,350 ft) in elevation.

Taurus (Bull) Lake (Map 5/A1)

Despite the name, there are no bull trout in Taurus Lake. Instead, the lake is stocked with rainbow, which can get to 1 kg (2 lbs), but average half that. Trolling and fly fishing both work on the 21 hectare lake, which is at 1,174 metres (3,852 feet) above sea level. Access to the lake is along the rough 2wd Taurus Lake FSR. There are two forest service sites on the lake, and the one on the northwest corner has a cartop boat launch.

Taylor Lake (Map 3/D3)

This small 6 hectare lake, set below Orofino Mountain, is best fished by spincasting or fly fishing for the many small rainbow and brook trout that inhabit the lake. The lake is accessed by a rough 4wd road off the Twin Lake Road and is at 975 metres (3,196 feet) in elevation. The lake suffers from draw down in the summer so the spring and fall are the best times to fish. There is also excellent ice fishing for brook trout beginning in mid-December.

Teepee Lakes (Map 18/A6)

The Teepee Lakes, which comprise **Friday, Saturday** and **Sunday Lakes**, are a good choice if you want to stay at a rustic fishing resort and sample three good fishing lakes. The lakes usually produce small rainbow throughout the spring and into the early summer by fly fishing. The lakes total 50 hectares and are stocked annually. They are at 1,430 metres (4,648 feet) in elevation and have an electric motor only restriction. No ice fishing is permitted at the lake. A hike is required to reach Saturday and Sunday Lakes. A private road from Osprey Lake leads to Friday Lake from the south.

Thalia Lake (Map 16/G7)

A 20 hectare lake found on a 4wd road off of Highway 5A, this lake is one of the more popular lakes in the area. Perhaps it is the rumours of a 10 kg (22 lb) trophy being landed or maybe it is the fact that the lake holds good numbers of rainbow to 1 kg (2 lbs) in size. Regardless, trolling and fly fishing (dragonfly nymph, leech or shrimp patterns) can be quite effective throughout the year. The lake is at 1,052 m (3,451 ft) in elevation and has a forest service site with a cartop boat launch and campground.

Thirsk Lake (Map 10/C1–18/C7)

This 60 hectare, man-made lake offers fair fishing for small rainbow trout, primarily by trolling in the spring or fall. The lake is at 1,040 metres (3380 feet) in elevation, has an electric motor only restriction and offers a forest service site with camping facilities. There are plans to raise the lake levels in the near future, which will likely flood the camping areas. Draw down is a problem in the summer.

Thone Lake (Map 13/E6)

This 10 hectare lake, located on a secondary road off the Christian Valley Road, is a good fly fishing lake for small, stocked rainbow throughout the summer months. The occasional rainbow weighs in at up to 1 kg (2 lbs), but most are about half that. The smaller fish are often very aggressive, and will chase anything you throw at them. Thone is a high elevation lake, at 1,174 metres (3,852 ft), and has a forest service site with a cartop boat launch on its western shores. Fly anglers can have a lot of fun during the late spring caddisfly hatch.

Trapper Lake (Map 1/E7)

Trapper Lake is a great place to go if you want to try your luck at a small mountain lake. The challenging hike-in takes you through some rugged, yet beautiful mountain country. The 30 hectare, high elevation (2,000 metres/6,500 feet) lake has many small rainbow that don't see much action.

Trout (Lusk) Lake (Map 3/C1)

This small 5 hectare lake is right next to Highway 3A. It is intensively stocked with brook trout, and just about as intensively fished. The lake is at 800 metres (2,600 feet) in elevation and is best fished in the late spring or early fall by spincasting or with bait. There is an electric motor only restriction.

Tuc-El-Nuit Lake (Map 3/F3)

In the southern Okanagan, this warm water low elevation (320 metre/1,040 feet) lake has good fishing for bass. The 20 hectare lake is easily accessed by a good 2wd road and has an electric motor only restriction.

Turtle Lake (Map 20/C4)

A small (8 hectare) lake with fair numbers of small brook trout that are best fished in the spring or early fall by casting small lures and bait. The lake is accessed by a trail southwest of McCulloch Reservoir.

Twin Lakes (Map 3/C1)

Easily accessed off Highway 3A on the Twin Lake Road, this pair of lakes offer a decent fishery for brook trout to 1.5 kg (3+ lbs) (average 30-35 cm) as well as a few rainbow and carp. The lakes are stocked regularly with rainbow and brook trout and are best trolled or spincast. There is a resort and boat launch at **Nipit Lake**, while an electric motor only restriction applies to both lakes.

Vaseux Lake (Map 3/G2)

No powerboats are allowed on this 241 hectare lake on the Okanagan River south of Okanagan Falls. The lake is home to many species of fish, including kokanee, smallmouth and largemouth bass, rainbow trout and perch. In fact, it is arguably the best bass fishing lake in the province. The scenic lake lies next to Highway 97 and offers a provincial park for camping.

Vinson Lake (Map 17/E6)

The 20 hectare Vinson Lake is stocked annually with rainbow trout and has special restrictions (check the current regulations). Accessed off the Siwash Creek Forest Service Road, there is a forest service site offering camping.

Wap Lake (Map 46/A6)

Wap Lake is accessed by a good 2wd road south of Three Valley Gap. The 36 hectare lake, at 550 metres (1,788 feet) in elevation, is set in a scenic valley below the Monashee Mountains. The lake is best trolled for rainbow to 2 kg (4.5 lbs) and dolly varden averaging 2–3 kg (4.5–6+ lbs). For the dollies, it is best to fish in the fall, trolling a Krocodile or Flatfish. Casting from the old railbed next to the lake can also be successful. The lake offers a forest service site with a cartop boat launch.

Wells Lake (Map 8/D7)

To reach this tiny 3 hectare remote mountain lake, requires a long hike along the Whatcom Trail or a high clearance 4wd vehicle. When you reach the lake, you will be rewarded with very good fishing for small rainbow on a fly or by spincasting. The lake is at a high enough elevation (1,590 metres/5,168 feet) to remain cool enough to fish in the summer. A very rustic forest service site offers camping at the lake.

Westmere Lake (Map 18/B7)

Located just west of **Eastmere Lake**, this 45 hectare lake is accessed by a 4 km (2 mile) hike from the former Osprey Lake Forest Service Site. The elevation is enough to keep the waters cool in summer (at 1,400 metres/4,550 feet), and fishing usually starts to get good in late June and lasts until October. Rainbow to 1 kg (2 lbs) are best caught by fly fishing or spincasting.

Whitehead Lake (Map 18/B6)

Despite the less-than-tasteful name, the fishing here is pretty good for rainbow trout that can reach 1 kg (2 lbs). The high elevation lake (1,430 metres/4,648 feet), the lake is best trolled or fly fished in the early summer, due to draw down in the summer. The 50 hectare lake is stocked annually, and has a forest service site with camping and boat launch facilities.

Wilgress Lake (Map 6/B3)

This small 17 hectare lake is very popular, mostly because it lays right alongside Highway 3. Despite constant fishing pressure throughout the entire year, the lake still produces well for small rainbow and brook trout by trolling or fly fishing. Ice fishing can be productive at times. The lake is at 991 metres (3,251 feet) in elevation and has a rest stop with picnic tables and a boat launch. Rainbow are stocked annually.

Williamson Lake (Map 5/E1)

Williamson Lake is a small 23 hectare lake found alongside a 4wd spur road off the Christian Valley Road. It offers good fly fishing, bait fishing and trolling for stocked rainbow that can reach 2 kg (4.5 lbs) in size. This is a high elevation lake, at 1,356 metres (4,449 feet), and, like most of the lakes in and around the Christian Valley, has a forest service site, complete with cartop boat launch.

Wilma Lake (Map 28/F7)

Wilma is a small 11 hectare lake, located on a short trail off the Dee Lake Road. At 1,350 metres (4,429 feet), the lake is high enough to support fair fishing for small rainbow trout throughout the ice-free season.

Wolfe Lake (Map 9/D6)

The 28 hectare Wolfe Lake is located 1 km to the west of Highway 3 on a 2wd road that leads through the Indian Reserve. The lake is at 610 metres (2,001 feet) in elevation and offers a good early spring fishery for rainbow to 1 kg (2 lbs).

Wood Lake (Maps 20/A1, 28/A7)

Wood Lake is located in the Okanagan Valley south of Kalamalka Lake at 393 metres (1,289 feet) in elevation. Highway 97 runs along the lake's western shore, and the lake has full facilities (camping, resorts, stores, boat launch) available for the visitor. The 916 hectare lake is best trolled in the early spring or late fall for the rainbow trout and kokanee that grow to 2 kg (4.5 lbs) in size. Fishing is usually very slow.

Xenia Lake (Map 6/F3)

On the Miller Creek FSR, this 15 hectare lake is accessed by 4wd vehicle or trail from **Christina Lake**. The lake has a scenic forest service site with a cartop boat launch and campground and offers good fly fishing for rainbow that average 20–25 cm (8–10 inches). Fishing remains generally productive throughout the summer months given the high elevation of the lake (at 1,219 metres/4,000 feet). The remoteness of the lake and the decent fishing for the stocked rainbow make this lake a good choice.

Yellow Lake (Map 3/B1)

Fair numbers of rainbow and brook trout are found at this 35 hectare lake which is next to Highway 3A. The lake is stocked regularly and is best fished in the early spring or late fall by trolling or fly fishing for rainbow and brook trout. At 760 metres (2,493 feet) in elevation, the lake suffers from algae bloom in summer and is also infested with perch. There are picnic facilities as well as an aeration system.

Stream Fishing

With so many great fishing lakes in this area, stream fishing is often ignored. Too bad, as the Kamloops/Okanagan Region provides many rivers and streams offering very good fishing for small, wild rainbow, brook trout or dolly varden. A few streams also offer runs of Pacific Salmon and steelhead. Since these streams and rivers provide an important spawning and rearing area for wild rainbow and char (brook trout and dollies), strict regulations have been imposed to prevent over fishing. For example, there is a catch-and-release fishery for dollies in Region 3 (Thompson/Nicola) from August 1 to October 31 and for all dollies in Region 8 (Okanagan) year round. Also, there are gear restrictions in place (e.g. single barbless hooks for all streams in Region 8 and Region 3). Further, Region 8 has a fishing ban from April 1 to June 30 and Region 3 has a fishing ban from January 1 to June 30. In addition to these Region wide restrictions, many streams have specific restrictions as well. While these regulations have been in place for a few years now, they are subject to change, so check the regulations before venturing out.

For the smaller streams, bait (worm or grasshopper) with a hook and small weight is the best method of fishing. In the rivers, small lures, fly fishing or a bobber with bait or a fly can produce some big fish.

We have described some of the most popular and productive creeks and rivers of the Kamloops/Okanagan area below.

Adams River (Map 43/E5)

The Adams is known worldwide for its incredible sockeye salmon run every fall. Also found in this 11 km (7 mile) long stream are rainbow trout, dolly varden, whitefish, as well as chinook, chum and coho salmon. Unfortunately, this river is one that is easier to look at than fish. Guided trips for trout are offered by the First Nations (out of Quaaout Lodge) near the source, while the lower portions are protected by Roderick Haig Park.

Allison Creek (Maps 17/C6-9/D6)

Allison Creek offers fair fishing for small rainbow trout that can be caught by bait fishing or by fly fishing the larger pools. The creek runs for 48.5 km (29.6 miles), but is best accessed below Allison Lake, as it parallels Highway 5A all the way from the lake to where it flows into the Similkameen River just east of Princeton.

Almond Creek (Map 6/B1)

Almond Creek is a small creek flowing into the Granby River and accessed by the 2wd Almond Creek FSR. The creek is considered fairly good for small rainbow taken on the fly or by bait fishing.

American Creek (Map 7/A6)

American Creek is a small creek that crosses The Trans-Canada Highway (Hwy 1) approximately 8 km (5 miles) north of Hope. The best fishing occurs during June and July (after spring run-off) for small rainbow trout as well as chinook salmon at the mouth.

Anstey River (Map 53/D6)

Draining into the north end of the Anstey Arm of Shuswap Lake, this small river offers a catch and release fishery for small rainbow and dolly varden. It is a remote river that has some fabulous pools for those willing to bushwhack their way in.

Ashnola River (Maps 1/D7-2/F3)

This river lines the north end of Cathedral Lakes Park and is easily accessed along a good 2wd road (Ashnola River Road). The river has many pools that offer good fishing for small rainbow on a fly, by spin casting or by bait fishing. The spring closure does not apply to this river.

Asp (China) Creek (Map 9/B4)

Asp Creek can be accessed off the Snowpatch Road or the logging roads on the east side of the creek. The creek is located north of Princeton and offers good fishing for small rainbow using bait and hook in the many small pools along the length of the creek. The spring closure does not apply to this creek.

Belgo Creek (Map 20/G3)

Belgo Creek drains into Mission Creek to the east of Kelowna and is best accessed by the Philpot Road (good 2wd access) along its entire length. The creek is very small but provides good fishing for small rainbow using bait and hook.

Bonaparte River (Maps 31, 39, 47-49)

The Bonaparte is a salmon-bearing river, but, like a lot of the rivers this far upstream, there is no salmon fishing allowed. Instead, you can try your luck for the wild rainbow, which are plentiful (but no fishing is allowed below the falls at the fishway). It is a small shallow river with clear water that flows 145 km (88.5 miles) from Bonaparte Lake to the Thompson River through open country with stands of ponderosa pine, Lodgepole pine, fir, and some spruce and aspen. The river is heavily regulated, and these rules include no fish under 25 cm (10 inches), with a daily limit of two that can only be taken on a single barbless hook with no bait.

Bouleau Creek (Map 27/E4)

Bouleau Creek drains into Whiteman Creek and ultimately into the Okanagan Lake. It offers a good choice if you wish to try a small creek for tiny rainbow that come readily to a bait and hook. The creek drains the Little Bouleau Lake and is easily accessed on the Bouleau Main.

Boundary Creek (Maps 13/G7-5/F7)

Boundary Creek is a medium size creek that is easily accessed along Highway 3 and then along the Boundary Creek Road north of Greenwood. The creek sees heavy fishing pressure from travellers on Highway 3 but is still fairly good for rainbow and brook trout that can reach 1 kg (2 lbs) in size. The trout are usually smaller and fly fishing is possible, although bait fishing is the preferred method.

Burrell Creek (Maps 22/F7-14/D7)

This large creek is easily accessed on the Burrell Creek FSR and offers reasonably good fishing for small rainbow and whitefish by bait fishing or fly fishing after the high water has subsided. In recent times; however, landslides have caused a severe reduction in the numbers of rainbow, making the fishing quite poor.

Cherry Creek (Map 30/B4)

Cherry Creek is a large creek to the east of Cherryville. It provides a good option for small dollies and rainbow trout by spincasting tiny lures or by bait fishing. The creek is easily accessed along the North Fork FSR from Cherryville.

Coldwater River (Maps 7, 16, 24)

Coldwater River runs along the Coquihalla Highway (Hwy 5) north of the toll booth and provides spotty fishing for small rainbow and larger dollies. The best fishing being in the lower reaches of the river, closer to Merritt. The river is large enough that fly fishing and casting small lures can be effective. Check the regulations for special restrictions.

Copper Creek (Map 1/A4)

The lower reaches of Copper Creek are accessed on the Copper Creek FSR off of Highway 3, while the upper reaches are accessed by 4wd vehicle on the Sunday Summit FSR. The creek is quite small but still produces well for small rainbow by bait fishing.

Copperkettle Creek (Map 13/E2)

Most of the lower reaches of the Copperkettle Creek are inaccessible unless you are willing to bushwhack up the creek. Therefore, fishing tends to be quite good for small rainbow by bait fishing.

Coquihalla River (Maps 8/B2-7/B7)

The Coquihalla is a medium sized river flowing into the Fraser River at Hope. Access to lower reaches is via Kawakawa Lake Road east of Hope; further upstream access is found off Highway 5. Dolly varden are available all year throughout the system and a small run of winter steelhead are present in the lower reaches from February through March. A bigger run of summer steelhead occurs from June through

September, while a few coho also show up in the lower reaches in October and November. Check the regulations for restrictions, including closures around the infamous railway tunnels.

Creighton Creek (Map 29/D5)
This creek is easily accessed on the Creighton Valley Road east of Lumby and provides a good choice if you want to try bait fishing for small rainbow.

Deadman River (Maps 32, 40, 48, 49)
The Deadman has two distinct sections. Above the impressive Deadman Falls, it is a wild, beautiful river offering good fishing for rainbow to 35 cm (14 in) fly or bait fishing. Below the falls, the river flows through dry ranch country and the trout fishing is marginal. Although steelhead, coho and chinook salmon run the lower reaches, these fragile runs are closed to fishing.

Emory Creek (Map 7/A4)
Emory Creek crosses Highway 1 about 18 km (9 mi) north of Hope and offers a provincial park campsite near its confluence with the Fraser River. The best fishing is during late spring and fall for dollies or in the summer for rainbow trout. The creek also has chinook salmon, which are best caught near the mouth in June and July, and a fall run of coho. A few steelhead are known to show up in late winter.

Eneas Creek (Maps 19/A7-11/D3)
This 19 km (11.5 mile) long creek flows through Garnet Lake and under Highway 97 before flowing into Okanagan Lake. Access to Eneas Creek is best along Garnet Valley Road, or off the aforementioned Highway 97. The creek contains brook and rainbow trout. Kokanee can also be seen spawning in late summer.

Fraser River (Maps 7, 15, 23)
The Fraser is the mightiest of BC rivers, flowing from Mount Robson Provincial Park in the north to the Pacific Ocean in the south. Along the way, it passes through the western edge of this region. North of Hope, the Fraser is a wild, dangerous river. Although the Trans-Canada Highway (Hwy 1) follows it for the entire length that our maps cover, it can be difficult to access. Some of the best places to access the river are the Flood Bar and the Silverhope Creek Bar, both west of Hope, or the Coquihalla Bar, at the mouth of the Coquihalla River. The river is not suitable for spring fishing due to high water but a range of sportfish can be found at other times of the year. Cutthroat trout are best caught in winter months, spring salmon run from May to July, sockeye salmon run from July to September, and coho and steelhead run from November through March. See the regulations for closure and restrictions.

Gable Creek (Maps 13/G6-14/C7)
Gable Creek is found in the Granby River Valley and is another small creek that can provide fairly good fishing for small rainbow. These small trout are best caught by bait fishing after the high water season. The creek is easily accessed by the Gable Creek FSR along its entire length.

Granby River (Maps 6, 14, 22)
Although the headwaters of this river are protected inside Granby Provincial Park, the mid and lower reaches of the river are easily accessed by the Granby River Road. It is a popular river with many large pools to cast a lure, fly or even sink some bait. The river contains small rainbow and brook trout as well as a population of whitefish and can be productive anytime during the summer. Check the regulations as the river may be closed.

Hayes Creek (Maps 10/A1-9/F6)
The upper reaches of Hayes Creek are easily accessed along the Princeton-Summerland Road, whereas the lower reaches require bushwhacking to get into the good pools. The creek, which drains into the Similkameen River to the east of Princeton, provides reasonably good fishing for small rainbow best caught by bait fishing.

Jewel Creek (Map 6/A5)
Jewel Creek is a short (4.7 km/2.9 mile) creek that flows from Jewel Lake into Eholt Creek east of Greenwood. The first 1.5 km (0.9 miles) of the creek below Jewel Lake is closed to fishing. The creek contains rainbow trout.

Keremeos Creek (Maps 3, 10, 11)
Keremeos Creek runs from the Apex Mountain Recreation Area to Keremeos and eventually into the Similkameen River. The creek is easily accessed along Highway 3A, Green Mountain Road and the Keremeos Creek FSR and provides spotty fishing for small rainbow best taken by bait fishing.

Kettle River (Maps 5, 6, 13, 21, 22, 30)
The Kettle River is a large river that borders Highway 33 and Highway 3, eventually entering the United States to the south of Midway. It makes a brief re-entry into BC west of Grand Forks. The river is approximately 150 km (92 miles) in length and offers a number of forest service sites where you can camp. The river is large enough that spincasting and fly fishing is possible. Small rainbow are the mainstay of the fishery although there are brook trout and whitefish that take readily to bait and hook. The best time to fish for the rainbow is in early spring before high water, whereas the best time to fish whitefish is during the winter season. There is a bait ban in effect between April 1 and October 31.

Lawless Creek (Map 8/D2)
Lawless Creek drains the slopes of Mt Thynne towards Tulameen where it flows into the Tulameen River. The creek is accessed along most of its lower reaches by the Lawless Creek FSR, but access to the upper reaches is by bushwhacking. As a result, there can be good fishing for small rainbow trout by bait fishing or fly fishing.

McNutty Creek (Map 10/C6)
This medium size creek drains southward into Hedley Creek north of Hedley. This small creek is noted for its particularly good fishing for small rainbow best caught by using bait in the many small pools that line the creek. Most of the creek is reached by the Stemwinder Mountain FSR system.

Miller Creek (Map 6/E3)
Miller Creek is a short creek that flows westward from Xenia Lake into the Granby River. The creek is easily accessed on the Miller Creek FSR and provides fair fishing for small rainbow from July to October.

Mission Creek (Maps 21/D1-19/G3)
Mission Creek flows 74 km (45 miles) from Mission Lake into Okanagan Lake. Access to the creek is relatively easy for most of the lower reaches, as the creek flows alongside Highway 33 and through Kelowna. However, the stream is closed to fishing below the Gallagher Canyon Falls on the outskirts of Kelowna. The upper reaches of the creek are accessed off the Mission Creek FSR or the Graystokes FSR. The creek contains a number of sportfish, including rainbow and brook trout. Kokanee can also be seen spawning in late summer below the Gallagher Canyon Falls.

Myers Creek (Map 5/B7)

Myers Creek flows from the United States northward eventually draining into the Kettle River west of Midway. The creek is particularly good for small rainbow and brook trout best taken by fly fishing or bait fishing.

Nicola River (Maps 23, 24, 25, 31)

Nicola River is a large river draining Nicola Lake before eventually flowing into the Thompson River. The river is easily accessed along its entire course by either Highway 8 or Highway 5A. The river meanders along its length, providing many bends and pools to try spincasting, fly fishing or bait fishing for rainbow, dolly varden, steelhead and a few salmon species. Check the regulations for special fishing restrictions.

North Thompson River (Maps 33, 41, 42, 50)

The North Thompson River is a tame river that starts in the Robson Valley north of this mapbook eventually joining the South Thompson at Kamloops. Highway 5 parallels the river for the most part, providing good access throughout. It is well advised to bring a boat and drift down the river, although shore fishing is certainly possible. Chinook salmon and dolly varden get most of the angling attention. The river is exempt from the spring fishing ban and all trout under 30 cm (12 inches) must be released.

Okanagan River (Map 3/F1-G6)

Most of the Okanagan River flows in the United States but from Okanagan Falls south to Osoyoos Lake there are approximately 30 km (18.3 miles) of fishable waters. The river is easily accessed along Highway 97 and provides slow fishing for rainbow and some bass. Check the regulations before heading out.

Otter Creek (Maps 8, 16, 17)

Otter Creek is a large creek flowing southward along Highway 5A and eventually into the Tulameen River at Tulameen. The creek is easily accessed along the highway and the Tulameen-Otter Valley Road. As a result, it receives a fair amount of fishing pressure and is not particularly great for fishing. It is still possible to catch small rainbow on a fly, by spincasting or with bait throughout the summer months.

Pasayten River (Map 1/B6)

This small river flows north across the border and into the Similkameen River at Similkameen Falls. The lower reaches of the river are accessed by a good forestry road (Pasayten River FSR), while the upper Canadian section is accessed along the Pasayten River Trail. The river offers reasonably good fishing for small rainbow in the summer months by fly fishing, spincasting or bait fishing.

Pass Creek (Map 6/C4)

This small creek drains eastward into the Granby River north of Grand Forks. It is easily accessed by the Pass Creek FSR and offers reasonably good fishing for small rainbow from July to October by bait fishing or fly fishing.

Peachland Creek (Maps 18/G5-19/B7)

Peachland Creek is a small creek leading from Peachland Lake into Okanagan Lake at Peachland. The creek is easily accessed by a series of forestry roads and the paved Brenda Mine Road. Given the proximity to the Okanagan population and the easy access, the creek is heavily fished. It still offers fair fishing for small rainbow.

Placer Creek (Map 1/C5)

Placer Creek leads northeast from Placer Lake into the Similkameen River. The Placer Mountain FSR provides access to the upper reaches of the creek if you have a 4wd vehicle. Because of the difficult access, fishing remains fairly good for small rainbow on a fly or by bait fishing.

Powers Creek (Map 19/C4)

Powers Creek is a small creek that drains into the Okanagan Lake at Westbank. The creek is accessed by the Jackpine FSR to the upper reaches with the middle reaches of the creek being inaccessible

except by a long hike. The creek offers fairly good fishing for small rainbow using bait.

Quilchena Creek (Maps 17/E1-25/D6)

This creek drains into Nicola Lake and is accessed by a good forestry road along its lower reaches. The creek provides good fishing for small rainbow primarily by bait fishing. It is possible to fly fish certain portions of the creek.

Rendell Creek (Maps 13, 21, 22)

Rendell Creek is accessed on its lower reaches by a good forestry road that is gated. The upper reaches require some bushwhacking to find the better holes. Due to its limited access, good fishing for rainbow trout from July to October can be found. Bait fishing and fly fishing are the preferred methods.

Sawmill (Five Mile) Creek (Map 7/A2)

This small creek crosses Highway 1 approximately 6 km (3.6 miles) north of Yale. You will find chinook salmon near the mouth of the river in June and July.

Seymour River (Map 53/B3)

Similar to nearby Anstey River, the Seymour River helps feed Shuswap Lake. The river offers a catch-and-release fishery for small rainbow and dolly varden.

Shingle Creek (Map 11/C5)

Shingle Creek is a small creek leading into the infamous channel between Okanagan Lake and Skaha Lake at Penticton. It provides an opportunity to fish a small creek located in the heart of the Okanagan but don't expect good fishing for the small rainbow that inhabit the creek. The entire length of the creek is easily accessed by either the Green Mountain Road or the Shingle Creek Road.

Shorts Creek (Map 27/E6)

This small creek leads eastward into the Okanagan Lake and offers good fishing for small rainbow by bait fishing. Access is limited but some nice pools are found along the Short Creek Canyon Trail.

Shuswap River (Maps 29, 30, 36, 37, 46)

This large river begins in the mountains near Greenbush Lake and flows into Sugar Lake before looping north into Mabel Lake. West of Mabel, the river drops into farmland where it slows down and eventually enters Shuswap Lake by a channel out of Mara Lake. A combination of highways, paved roads and logging roads provide good access throughout. The river provides fairly good fishing for rainbow, dolly varden and whitefish along its length with spincasting, fly fishing and bait fishing being productive. The river also contains chinook and coho salmon below the Shuswap Falls (29/E3). Check the regulations before setting out on your fishing adventure.

Similkameen River (Maps 1, 2, 9, 10)

The Similkameen River begins near Allison Pass in Manning Park and flows in an easterly direction some 160 km (97 miles) before entering the United States near Osoyoos. Most of the river length is accessed by Highway 3. The river, despite its easy access, still produces well for rainbow on a (dry) fly, by spincasting small lures or by bait fishing. There is a bait ban from April 1 to October 31 as well as a catch and release fishery for rainbow between the Highway 3 bridge at Princeton and 31 km (19 miles) south of Princeton. A good whitefish fishery is offered in the winter season.

Sitcum Creek (Maps 30/E1, 38/G7)

Sitcum Creek flows 16 km (9.8 miles) from Sitcum Lake to Sugar Lake. Access to the lower reaches is from the Kate-Sitcum FSR; access to the higher reaches is via the Sitcum Lake Trail. The creek contains dolly varden, (spawning) kokanee and rainbow trout.

Siwash Creek (Maps 17/E6-9/G1)

Siwash Creek drains into Hayes Creek to the north of Princeton. A washed out bridge prevents vehicle access above the 8 km mark but anglers can access the upper reaches from the Siwash Creek FSR off

of the Okanagan Connector (Hwy 97C). The creek offers good fishing for small rainbow on a fly or by bait fishing.

South Thompson River (Maps 33, 34, 35, 43)

This slow-moving river flows from Little Shuswap Lake to Kamloops. Fishing really heats up near the headwaters when the millions of sockeye salmon pass through on their way to the Adams. At this time, rainbow trout, dolly varden and whitefish, which all feed on the dislodged salmon eggs, can be excellent. Drift fishing is popular on this river.

Spuzzum Creek (Map 7/A1)

Spuzzum Creek is a small creek that crosses Highway 1, 25km (15 miles) north of Yale. Like most of the small creeks that flow into the Fraser, the closer you get to the Fraser, the better the fishing is. The creek has a steelhead fishery in late winter-early spring, Chinook salmon in June and July, and rainbow throughout the year.

Summers Creek (Maps 17/D7-9/C4)

Summers Creek flows southward from Missezula Lake into Allison Creek just north of Princeton. This small creek provides fairly good fishing for small rainbow and brook trout by fly fishing or bait fishing.

Thompson River (Maps 23, 31, 32, 33)

This large river is renowned for its excellent steelhead fishery. However, in recent times (despite conservation measures), the fishing has declined. Regardless, anglers come from around the world to try to hook into one of these mighty trout (some reach 13 kg/30 lbs) during the late fall (October to December). The pools around Spences Bridge are legendary. Overall, the length of the river is approximately 110 km (70 miles) and most of it is fishable. The most popular rainbow trout section of the river is between Kamloops Lake and Ashcroft. This section of river can be drift fished and provides some excellent (dry) fly fishing for rainbow to 1.5 kg (3+ lbs). Other species in the river include several salmon runs, sturgeon, dolly varden and whitefish. There are a number of provincial parks providing camping next to the river. Please check the regulations as the river is closely regulated to help preserve the fishery.

Trepanier Creek (Maps 18/F4-19/C6)

This small creek is found to the east of Okanagan Lake and is easily accessed by a logging road next to the Okanagan Connector. As a result, the creek is not particularly good but does have some small rainbow best caught by bait fishing.

Trout Creek (Maps 10, 11, 18)

Draining the Headwater Lakes, this creek has gained notoriety as forming a scenic backdrop for sections of the Kettle Valley Railway. Most of the creek is easily accessed along the Princeton-Summerland Road, the KVR or along the Trout Creek FSR. The best fishing is in the upper reaches where it is possible to catch good numbers of small rainbow and brook trout by bait fishing. The spring closure does not apply to this creek.

Tulameen River (Maps 8/C7-9/D6)

The Tulameen flows from the Cascade Mountains before arcing past the town of Tulameen and spilling into the Similkameen River at Princeton. The 81 km (49 mile) long river contains a number of species, most notably rainbow and brook trout and mountain whitefish. Although most sections of the river are easily accessed, there are some remote, wild sections that offer excellent fishing.

Wap Creek (Maps 46/F6-38/A1)

This creek has suffered from deforestation at the hands of loggers, which in turn has caused lots of bank erosion and the destruction of fish habitat. The creek is currently undergoing extensive habitat improvement, and is closed to trout fishing from September 1 to June 30 below Frog Falls. No salmon fishing is allowed.

West Kettle River (Maps 4, 5, 12, 20, 21)

For the most part, this large river is easily accessed along Highway 33. It extends approximately 90 km (55 miles) in length from the Big White Mountain area before joining the Kettle River at Westbridge. Despite its good access, the river still provides fairly good fishing for rainbow that can reach 1 kg (2 lbs) in size but are usually quite small. Bait fishing (between November 1 and March 31 only), casting small lures or fly fishing can be a lot of fun. A portion of the creek, between the Beaverdell Station Bridge and the Highway 33 Bridge at Westbridge, is catch and release only for wild rainbows.

Whipsaw Creek (Maps 1/A1-9/C7)

Whipsaw Creek drains northward into the Similkameen River and is easily accessed along the Whipsaw Creek FSR. The creek receives light fishing pressure and is a good option if you want to try a small creek. Bait fishing for the many small rainbow can be very good.

Yale Creek (Map 7/B3)

Yale Creek is just north of Yale on Highway 1. The creek has good fishing for chinook salmon in June and July. The closer you are to where the creek flows into the Fraser, the better the fishing.

Backroad Mapbooks

www.backroadmapbooks.com

Paddling
(River Routes and Lake Circuits)

River Routes

The Southern Interior is blessed with a good mix of whitewater and flat water paddling. Some rivers meander through the arid interior valleys, and are perfect for a scenic canoe ride. Others plunge steeply down into those valleys, and attract both local and international kayakers looking for more of a challenge. The lakes of the southern interior are also fine places to explore. There are several large valley bottom lakes, with seemingly endless shorelines to explore as well as several smaller, quainter mountain lakes to discover.

In this section, we have identified the best of the paddling opportunities in the Southern Interior. For each river, we have included the put-in and take-out locations for the most popular runs on that river. Also included are short descriptions highlighting the route as well as the grading system.

We use a modified version of the international scale to grade rivers. The grade of a run tells you how difficult overall a stretch of river is. Class rates individual rapids, chutes and other features. A run might be rated Grade II overall, but one section might feature a Class IV drop. In most cases, portages have been established to allow less experienced paddlers a chance to avoid the difficult features of any run.

Water flow effects how difficult a run is. Difficulty of grade and class is given at low water and high water. If a run is rated Grade II/III, it means that at low flows the run is Grade II, while at high flows it is Grade III.

Please note *that these descriptions given in this book are limited, and may not contain enough detail to navigate certain rivers safely, especially rivers with higher ratings. We recommend that you check the current conditions with local canoeists/kayakers or local outdoor stores before heading onto a river. It is also essential to scout ahead. River conditions can change daily.*

Adams River (Map 43/D4-F5)

From Adams Lake to Shuswap Lake, the Adams River runs 14 km (10 miles) over the gravel beds where the famous Adams River Sockeye spawn in fall. Most people put-in at the south end of Adams Lake, and take-out at the Squilax-Anglemond Road Bridge (a total of 10 km/6 miles). However, Holding Road parallels the river for its entire length, and you can put-in or take-out wherever you want to. This is a safe, popular, warm river, with a paddling season that runs from April to October. The Adams is a Grade II river that is a great place for beginners to cut their teeth on a bit of whitewater. There are also enough play holes and standing waves to keep experts interested, too. The only section that might cause problems for inexperienced kayakers is the 75 metre long (245 feet) Gorge, or Devil's Door as it is sometimes called. This section is rated Class III-IV.

Barriere River (Map 50/G4-D6)

The Barriere River flows down a steady gradient over small rock beds, and will prove to be challenging to the guided beginner kayaker, or expert canoeist. The river peaks sharply in June, but there is usually enough water in May and July to keep things interesting. From the Barriere Lakes Road Bridge to the bridge on Barriere Town Road, it is a 20 km/12 mile (3 hour) Grade II/IV route. It is possible to put-in farther upstream, at the North Barriere Lake FSR Bride, for an extra 6 km/3.6 miles (1.5 hours) of paddling. This second put-in will take you through a short, but challenging canyon section. Be aware, the river is notorious for sweepers, deadheads, and logjams.

Burrell Creek (Map 14/D7)

From the bridge at the 7 km mark on the Burrell Creek FSR, this Grade II-III paddle offers an exciting and fast route during high water (May-June). Watch for logjams that line the river. The creek joins the Granby River below the 28 Mile Bridge but ruminants of an old dam require paddlers to exit the creek before the bridge.

Coldwater River (Maps 16/B7-24/G7)

Yes, the name is a pretty fair indication of the river, but you'll be wearing a wetsuit, right? The river flows beside and occasionally under, the Coquihalla Highway for 34.5 km (21 miles) from Juliet Creek to Merritt. Access is fairly good along the winding, fast moving Grade II/II+ river with one Class IV drop after the bridge near the 18 km (11 mile) mark. It is possible to break this river up into a number of bite-sized pieces (common put-ins/take-outs are Larson Hill, Coldwater Interchange, and Patchet Road), or to do it in one long run. The first section between Juliet Creek and Larson Hill is easy (Grade I) and is often skipped by kayakers looking for a bit more excitement. Watch for sweepers.

Eagle River (Map 45/F3-A7)

Eagle River and the Trans-Canada Highway play hide and seek as both river and road weave their way from Sicamous to Revelstoke. A popular, easy (Grade I-II) paddle is from the Last Spike Monument (45/F3) to Shuswap Lake (Map 45/A7), a distance of 29 km (17.7 miles). It will take about six hours to travel the full distance, but there are many good access points along the route to shorten the journey.

Fraser River (Maps 7, 15, 23)

The Fraser River provides 1,600km (976 miles) of paddling from Yellowhead Pass to Vancouver ranging from narrow gorges to wide flat water. In this region, the Fraser River passes through the Fraser Canyon and offers extreme paddling and commercial rafting opportunities only. If you want to sample a piece of the mighty Fraser, we recommend you choose one of the many rafting companies operating in and around Yale.

Granby River (Map 14)

Between Eight Mile Flats and the 52 km marker, the Granby is a Grade II route. Beginner and intermediate paddlers do not want to miss this take-out, as below the 52 km marker, the river becomes a Grade IV+ paddle through the canyon. Experts who want to run the canyon can take-out at the Granby-Burrell Forest Service Site.

Kettle River (Maps 5, 6, 13)

Draining the southeast portion of the Okanagan, for the most part, the Kettle River is a gentle giant. It flows quickly down from Keffer Lake in the Monashee Mountains and through the Christian Valley before settling into the farmlands along Highway 3 west of Rock Creek. From Midway to Grand Forks it dips back and forth between Canada and the USA before it eventually joins the Columbia River in Washington State. Below we have described two of the more popular routes on the big river.

Put-in: Canyon Flats Forest Service Site (Map 13/C7)

Take-out: Highway 3 bridge near Midway (Map 5/C7)

The Christian Valley Road parallels the East Kettle River for most of its length, making access on and off this easy (Grade I/II river) river a breeze. It is 59 km (36 miles) from the put-in at the Canyon Flats Forest Service Site to the Highway 3 bridge near Midway, which can be done in one long, hot summer day. It is possible to continue beyond Midway to Grand Forks (see below).

Put-in: Highway 3 bridge near Midway (Map 5/C7)

Take-out: Trans Canada Trail east of Grand Forks (Map 6/G7)

This is an easy 35 km (21.4 mile), daylong paddle from the Highway 3 bridge near Midway, through farmland, across the USA border and back into BC near Grand Forks. This is a warm, easy route that can be done in an open canoe or even with a float tube. The river is Grade I, with a few easy Class II sections. If you want a longer route then you can continue east of our maps towards Christina Lake (see our Kootenay Mapbook or the Trans Canada Trail: BC guidebook), but make sure you take-out before the Cascade Gorge.

Little Shuswap River (Map 43/D3)
This is a short 3 km (30 minute) Grade II route with few features but fast water between the Shuswap and Little Shuswap Lakes. Access is off the Trans-Canada Highway.

Mission Creek (Map 20/A5)
Found in the southeastern reaches of Kelowna, Mission Creek is a popular recreational retreat for local residents. The creek offers paddlers a chance to test their skills in a bit of whitewater during the spring.

Put-in: Scenic Canyon Park (Map 20/B5)

Take-out: Hollywood Bridge (Map 20/A5)

This 8 km/4.8 mile (1.5 hour) Grade III route becomes a Grade II route during lower water. The route takes you from Scenic Canyon Park, through two canyons with fast flowing water, and over several boulder gardens before you reach the take-out at the Hollywood Bridge. The best time to paddle the creek is from April to June.

Put-in: Hollywood Bridge (Map 20/A5)

Take-out: Bridge on KLO Road (Map 20/A5)

Below Hollywood Bridge, Mission Creek is a much easier paddle. This section is a 6 km (1 hour) Grade II urban paddle through the heart of Kelowna. It is best done in April through June as there is not enough water flow during the summer.

Nicola River (Maps 25/A5-23/E1, 31/E7)
The Nicola flows from Nicola Lake west through Merritt and then north until it flows into the Thompson River near Spences Bridge. There are a number of possible routes to explore along the way.

Put-in: Voght Street, across from RV Park (Map 24/G7)

Take-Out: N'Kwala Forest Service Site (Map 24/B6)

The first part of the Nicola is an easy Grade I paddle starting in Merritt. Past the Sunshine Valley East Bridge (a possible put-in/take-out), the river gets a little rougher, although it is still considered a Grade I route with a few Grade II sections.

Put-in: N'Kwala Forest Service Site (Map 24/B6)

Take-out: Chief Joe Anthony Bridge (Map 24/A3)

This 18 km (11 km) run is rated Grade I, with a couple Class II features, including a little headwall and mini canyon. Hazards along this portion of the river include sweepers, tight corners and blind channels. It is possible to take-out early at an informal campsite after the mini canyon. Watch for it on river left. The Chief Joe Anthony Bridge take-out is accessed by turning left on Dot Ranch Cut-Off Road, 11.8 km (7.2 miles) west of N'Kwala Rec Site. The take-out is just across the bridge, about 1 km down the dirt road that is found on the dirt road 1.3 km (0.8 miles) down the ranch road.

Put-in: Chief Joe Anthony Bridge (Map 24/A3)

Take-out: Shackan Campground (Map 23/G3)

This is the shortest run on the Nicola, but also the most exciting. The river races through a Grade II/III canyon that will challenge most kayakers. In fact, many don't go all the way to the Shackan Campground, but take-out one bend after the canyon (watch for poison ivy at this take-out) and do it again. There are orange cones overhead, marking the start of the canyon. Get out here and scout ahead.

Put-in: Shackan Campground (Map 23/G3)

Take-out: Picnic site, 1 km downstream from Nicola confluence with Thompson (Map 31/C7)

This section of the Nicola is worth a visit as the river cuts through a scenic ponderosa pine dry belt. The 27 km/16.5 mile (4 hour) route pours over gravel beds down a steady Grade II/III route. Depending on rainfall, the paddling season can run from April to July and the trickiest section is near the Rattlesnake Bridge right before the confluence with the Thompson. Some people take-out here, others use the picnic area described above. Good access is found along the whole route via the quiet Highway 8.

Pasayton River (Map 1/C7–B5)
The Pasayton River is rated a solid Grade II, and is quite challenging, especially in high water when there are only a few eddies. The put-in is found 20.7 km (12.6 miles) along the Pasayton River Forest Service Road, while the take-out is actually on the Similkameen River. Paddlers should park their second vehicle at the large gravel pull off on Highway 3, 2.5 km (1.5 miles) downriver from the Pasayton River FSR access bridge. You don't want to miss this take-out, as the Similkameen Falls are just around the corner.

Seymour River (Map 53/B3-B5)
The Seymour River provides a secluded wilderness experience and plenty of variety. From the Bridge below Seymour Falls to the bridge to Silver Beach Provincial Park, there is an 8 km/4.9 mile (2 hour) route. The Grade II paddle has a Class III+ canyon that will keep things interesting. The canyon needs advance scouting due to the potential for sweepers and other obstacles. Further upstream, expert kayakers can increase the length and difficulty of the run by starting at the powerline. This run involves shooting a small canyon, which is not always passable. Scouting is essential! You will also have to tackle several Grade IV drops and then portage around Seymour Falls (bring a rope). The season runs from April to August with the best time to paddle being July.

Shuswap River (Map 36/D2–37/F4)
Starting from Mabel Lake, the Shuswap starts out as a fierce river but soon tames as it flows through the farmland around Enderby. At Enderby the river courses north, eventually spilling into Mara Lake,

which is connected to the much larger Shuswap Lake.

Put-in: Kingfisher Creek (Map 37/F4)

Take-out: Three Valley–Mabel Lake Forest Service Road (Map 37/E4)

This section of the Shuswap is known as 'The Chuck'. From Kingfisher Creek the run courses a 3km (1 hour) Grade III (Grade IV at high water) run through boiling water, large waves, some holes and a few whirlpools towards Enderby. Advanced scouting is highly recommended. The season runs from March to October.

Put-in: Three Valley–Mabel Lake Forest Service Road (Map 37/E4)

Take-out: Cooke Creek Road (Map 37/D4)

Having taken out most of its aggression on The Chuck, the Shuswap quickly turns into a meek and mild river. The next 7 km (4.3 miles) of the river are an easy Grade II paddle suitable for canoeists. The season runs from March to October with the best time to paddle the river being after the spring run off.

Put-in: Cooke Creek Campsite (Map 37/D4)

Take-out: Trinity Valley Road Bridge (Map 37/A5)

This section of the river offers a 20 km (3 hour) Grade II–III route with moderately fast water with rocks and boulders showing. The best time to test the waters is in August through September. In high water, the route swells to a Grade III–IV paddle, and should be left to expert paddlers only.

Put-in: Trinity Valley Road Bridge (Map 37/A5)

Take-out: Enderby Bridge (Map 36/F5)

This paddle is 9km (2 hour) in length and is rated Grade I/II route with fairly easy paddling. The best time to paddle this section of the river is in August or September.

Put-in: Enderby Bridge (Map 36/F5)

Take-out: Mara Lake (Map 37/A1)

This final stretch of the Shuswap River involves a 24 km (14.6 mile) easy Grade I–II paddle. This section is better known for its nature viewing. If you don't feel like doing the whole trip (about four hours), you can put-in/take-out at the Grindrod Bridge on Highway 97A, which is about 9 km (5.5 miles) from Mara Lake.

Similkameen River (Maps 1, 2, 3, 9, 10)

The Similkameen begins its long journey through the dry pine forests and rolling hills of the southeast portion of this book in Manning Park. From the park, it courses north to Princeton before looping southeast towards Osoyoos. South of the border, it spills into the south end of Osoyoos Lake. Highway 3 provides good access to most of the river.

Put-in: Bridge on Placer Mountain Road (Map 1/C4)

Take-out: Princeton (Map 9/C6)

Southwest of Similkameen Falls, the river is often too shallow and loaded with debris to paddle properly. For this reason, most kayakers choose to access the Upper Similkameen from the bridge on Placer Mountain Road. This is a long (40 km/24.4 mile) challenging paddle that should only be tried by experts after spring runoff. The best time to run the river is usually in July. The run is rated as Grade III with numerous Grade IV+ technical drops. Also watch for the remains of gold mining in the canyon. The river mellows out towards Princeton after leaving the canyon and becomes a Grade II paddle. The Elk Ridge Outdoors Campsite, on the river side of Highway 3, 14.9 km south of the Princeton Bridge provides an alternate access point to this stretch of the river. The owners of the campground may want a modest parking fee if you don't camp there.

Put-in: Princeton (Map 9/C6)

Take-out: Bromley Rock Campground (Map 10/A7)

This easy 20 km (12.2 mile) paddle is a great place for novices to bone up on their kayaking skills. There is one section of easy Class II rapids near the Bromley Rock. Most novices will enjoy the challenge of running these or take-out before the rapids.

Put-in: Bromley Rock Campground (Map 10/A7)

Take-out: Highway 3 bridge (Map 10/C7)

Easily accessed from Highway 3, this section of the Similkameen River offers a 10 km/6 mile (2 hour) Grade II route. There is a Grade III drop (at the Golden Dawn Cafe), which you may wish to portage around. The river is generally easy to paddle with surfing waves, warm waters (in the summer) and a steady flow. Watch for boulders throughout the route and Indian pictographs on the north bank. The best paddling is from April–July.

Put-in: 12.7 km west of Keremeos (Map 2/F3)

Take-out: Red Bridge (Map 2/G3)

The Lower Similkameen River begins as a Grade III paddle extending 9 km/5.6 miles (2 hours). This route is best paddled in late June to early July after spring runoff. Any later in the summer and the many shallow sections and underwater rock hazards make paddling difficult.

Put-in: Red Bridge (Map 2/G3)

Take-out: Kobau Regional Park (Map 3/B4)

This section extends 6 km/3.7 miles (2 hours) on a Grade III route that leads through Keremeos ending in Kobau Regional Park. The route is best paddled in late June to early July as low water creates many hazards and shallow sections.

Put-in: Kobau Regional Park (Map 3/B4)

Take-out: Chopaka Road Bridge (Map 3/C6)

This Grade II paddle meanders along the Lower Similkameen River for 19 km (11.6 miles) with some rapids to traverse. The best time to paddle this section is late June to early July as the river has shallow sections later in the summer.

Spius Creek (Map 24/B7-B6)

The put-in for Spius Creek is just below Little Box Canyon, about 8 km south of the fish hatchery. Boats must be lowered down the steep bank by rope or driven down by a 4wd vehicle. The twisting, Grade II stream is a challenging paddle with numerous sweepers to watch out for. The biggest rapids are under the wood bridge, and at a large rock studded left bend. Spius Creek flows into the Nicola River, where it is possible to take-out at the N'Kwala Forest Recreation Site.

South Thompson River (Maps 43/C7-36/A2)

Between Chase (put-in on Pine Street) and the Pritchard Bridge, the South Thompson River meanders through farmland, and offers an easy Grade II paddle. Along the way, you have a good chance to view wildlife or fish the larger pools for rainbow or steelhead.

Thompson River (Map 23)

The southwest reaches of the Thompson River are one of the kayaking and commercial rafting hotspots in the province. This is not an area for the inexperienced (unless you are on a guided trip), but it is THE place for some whitewater thrills.

Put-in: Goldpan Campground (Map 23/C1)

Take-out: Nicomen River (Map 23/C3)

This is a 12 km (7.3 mile) Grade II/III route with plenty of turbulence and large waves but few rock obstacles. Through this section, the river is fast flowing and offers a scenic paddle through dry ponderosa pine country. The paddling season extends year round except during peak flows.

Put-in: Nicomen River (Map 23/C3)

Take-out: Lytton (West of Map 23/A3)

As the Thompson River approaches the Fraser River, it becomes more difficult to paddle as the water level and flow of the river increases. Between Nicomen River and Lytton, the river extends 24 km (14.6 miles) through the dry pine country and is rated as a Grade IV expert kayak route. The paddle is not technically difficult but is intimidating due to its large waves, rapids and holes. It is recommended that the route only be tried after a local has shown you the best line to take through the difficult sections. The route can be paddled year round except during peak runoff.

Tulameen River (Maps 8-9)

The Tulameen area is an area rich in history. From the gold mines to the historic Kettle Valley Railway stops, there are many sites and sounds to see along the way. The Hoodoos and rich red clay banks of the river are certain to be a highlight of the trip.

Put-in: Bridge 7 km west of Tulameen (Map 8/E4)

Take-out: Tulameen (Map 8/G4)

This section of the Tulameen flows through the Tulameen Canyon. The first rapid, visible from the put-in, is a Class II+ with rocks, large waves and holes. It is the calling card for the canyon about 200 metres (600 feet) beyond, which is also full of Class II+ features. Past the canyon, the trip to Tulameen mellows to a Grade I or I+ float.

Put-in: Tulameen (Map 8/G4)

Take-out: Coalmont (Map 9/A5)

Between the famed Coalmont Hotel (B.C.'s oldest operating hotel) and Tulameen, the Tulameen River Road provides good access to the river. But most paddlers choose to run this Grade I - I+ stretch of river from town to town.

Put-in: Coalmont (Map 9/A5)

Take-out: Princeton (Map 9/C6)

The Tulameen River route extends 21 km (5 hours) from Coalmont to Princeton and is rated a Grade II paddle. The Tulameenie Falls, which should be portaged through (the portage is through the KVR Tunnel), is a Grade IV+ drop that is particularly dangerous in low water. Below the falls, the river is mostly Grade I, with a few easy Grade II sections. Throughout the route, the river is quite variable with many pools, rock and boulder gardens. Along the way, admire the history of the Kettle Valley Railway, marvel at the hoodoos or stop and relax on the sandy beaches. The best time to paddle the route is in May or June, during spring runoff.

West Kettle River (Maps 4–5, 13, 20, 21)

The lower stretches of the West Kettle River offer a relatively easy, Grade II paddle with some chutes and sweepers. The river is best run in late spring or early summer, as the water levels get too low to paddle later on. There are numerous areas to put-in since Highway 33 parallels the West Kettle for much of it's length. Poor water flow, debris and the lack of any real exciting stretches do not make this river a destination of choice for area paddlers. Instead, most paddlers put-in at Westbridge (Map 5/B4) and follow the Kettle south to Rock Creek and beyond.

Mussio Ventures Staff

Lakes & Lake Circuits

With over 500 lakes found in this region of Southern B.C., there is an endless number of canoeing opportunities. These lakes range from small wilderness lakes to large recreation lakes. Below we have included information on the canoe circuits and a few of the bigger lakes. Of course this is only a fraction of the places to float a boat, but we realize it would double the size of this book to mention them all. With this in mind, we recommend reviewing the Provincial Parks and Wilderness Camping sections later in this book to see lakes that are popular with paddlers and have facilities such as boat launches.

Christina Lake (Map 6/G4)

Although this is a very popular water skiing/boating lake, you can still enjoy a quiet paddle on this beautiful warm lake. There are five marine recreation sites towards the north end of the lake that offer over night camping opportunities. It is best to launch your canoe at the Texas Point Provincial Park.

Emar Lakes Canoe Circuit (Map 49/G1)

Best accessed from the Long Island Lake just off Highway 24 west of Little Fort, most of this circuit falls north of this mapbook and into the Cariboo edition. The rustic route travels in a circuit crossing four water bodies and six portages. Along the way, paddlers will have a good chance to see wildlife or test the waters for some feisty trout. The trip can be done in a day but makes an ideal overnight trip.

Lupin Lake Canoe Route (Map 49/D3)

This canoe route involves a six hour paddle through six small interconnecting wilderness lakes. You will be required to pack your canoe over four short portages, with the last portage being uphill. To access the lake system, portage off the Bonaparte FSR to the south near the Spruce Grove Lodge.

Okanagan Lake (Maps 11, 19, 20, 27, 28)

This large lake is very popular with water sport enthusiasts and usually gets choppy in the afternoon. As a result, it is best to set out early in the morning and enjoy the natural beauty of the area. There are numerous places to launch and an incredible variety of shoreline to explore. One of the more remote stretches on the lake is found north of Naramata (Maps 11/E3-19/C7) around Okanagan Mountain Park. The beautiful scenery, warm water, pictographs and marine access campsites make this an excellent area to explore by canoe.

Shuswap Lake (Maps 36, 43, 44, 45, 53)

When most people think of Shuswap Lake, they think of house boating. Add in the many water sport enthusiasts and you will see why canoeists do not find this lake all that peaceful. But with over 1000 kilometres of shoreline and 26 marine parks to explore, the big lake can be a good place to paddle in a sea kayak. Canoeists still venture out during the early morning and evenings.

Tuwut Lake Canoe Route (Map 49/C3)

While it is possible to cram all ten (or more, depending on your route) lakes of this circuit into one day, most people spread their enjoyment out over two or three days. This is not a developed paddle, and access to Tuwut Lake is through an old clearcut off the Windy Lake Road. The carry down to the lake will take about twenty minutes, and is by far the most difficult portage of the entire journey. There is no established circuit, although there are well-beaten animal/angler trails between the lakes. The close proximity of lakes makes it possible to shorten or lengthen the trip.

Parks

(Provincial Parks and Protected Areas)

From glorious beaches to mountain retreats, the parks of the Southern Interior provide a perfect destination to get away from it all. Over the last few years, the number and variety of parks and protected areas has grown substantially. Many of these new parks are quite remote and offer little in the way of amenities. They are more likely to be enjoyed by recreationists looking for a more primitive and remote venture. The older, more established parks range from full facility roadside campgrounds to rugged wilderness areas. Regardless of your interests, you are certain to find a park that suits your needs.

To make things easier when planning a trip, we have added recreational symbols beside each park name. These symbols will show you some of the more popular activities pursued in the area, while the description will provide you with a good background of the park.

BC Provincial Park Campgrounds generally operate from early spring through fall. Some stay open all year. Most charge a fee for overnight stays. These fees vary according to the facilities and services provided. We have noted the parks that currently offer a call-in reservation system. It is recommended to call Discover Camping at 1-800-689-9025 (604-689-9025 in Greater Vancouver) or visit www.discovercamping.ca to reserve a space at these often busy campgrounds.

Adams Lake Provincial Park (Map 43/C3)

This tiny (56 hectare) provincial park is located on the southwestern shores of Adams Lake at Bush Creek. The site offers rustic camping, hiking trails and access to the lake. There are 32 campsites.

Adams Lake Marine Park (Map 51/F7)

This marine park is made up of two boat access sites on Adams Lake. **Poplar Point** (Map 51/G6) is a tiny (32-hectare) park providing a stopover for boaters on the lake. **Spillman Beach** (Map 51/F7) is one of the nicest beaches on Adams Lake. It is boat access only, with room for a few picnic or overnight groups on the beach.

Albas Provincial Park (Map 53/A6)

Located on the western shores of the Seymour Arm, this small park can be accessed by road or water. There are 5 campsites and pit toilets south of Blueberry Creek, which are only accessible by water. The park also has picnic facilities as well as a beach for sunbathers. A rough, undeveloped trail follows Celesta Creek to a series of waterfalls. Please be careful around the creek as people have fallen in.

Alexandra Bridge Provincial Park (Map 15/C7)

Alexandra Bridge Provincial Park is situated on the Fraser River about two kilometres north of Spuzzum, or 40 km (24 miles) north of Hope. It is a small park (covering 55 hectares), and the centerpiece is the Cariboo Wagon Road Bridge over the Fraser River. You can access the bridge from a trail through the day-use area.

Allison Lake Provincial Park (Map 9/B1)

Located on Highway 5A, 28km (17 miles) north of Princeton, this 23 hectare provincial park is well away from the crowds of the Okanagan. The park is located on the south end of Allison Lake, which is a good fishing and swimming lake. The campground is more rustic than other nearby parks. There are a total of 24 campsites found above the highway while the boat launch and picnic facilities are found next to the lake.

Anarchist Protected Area (Map 4/B7)

Public access is extremely limited to this new 467 hectare protected area, which offers little in the way of recreational opportunities. It was established to protect a number of red and blue listed bird and plant species, and is an environmentally sensitive area.

Anstey-Hunakwa Protected Area (Map 53/B4)

This large (6,587 hectare) protected area extends from the shore of Hunakwa Lake to the peaks of surrounding mountains. The area protects extensive areas of old growth forest. The best access is provided from the north end of Anstey Arm, which is accessible by boat and valued for its recreational opportunities, sandy beaches and salmon habitat.

Apex Mountain Provincial Park (Map 10/D4)

This park offers year-round recreational opportunities. During the winter, it is home to a popular ski resort and cross-country ski area. In the summer, hikers can access any one of a number of mountains in the area for a great view or to enjoy the beautiful wild flowers.

Arrowstone Provincial Park (Maps 39-40/A6)

This 6,203 hectare park is located in the foothills northeast of Cache Creek. The wilderness park preserves the Arrowstone Creek drainage as well as the Cache Creek Hills and offers no facilities or developed trails. The Deadman-Cache Creek Road, Highway 1 and Battle Creek FSR access portions of the provincial park.

Bear Creek Provincial Park (Map 19/G3)

Bear Creek Park is located north of Kelowna on the Westside Road. The 178 hectare park is on the shores of Okanagan Lake and offers a total of 122 vehicle/tent campsites as well as a boat launch, large picnic area, and a developed beach. The park is extremely popular throughout the summer months due in no small part to a broad, sandy beach, nearly half a kilometre long. The longest trail in the park is a 5 km (3 mile) hike or bike along the scenic Bear Creek Canyon. Campers are recommended to make reservations.

Bedard-Aspen Provincial Park (Map 31/A2)

This 173 hectare park is hike-in access only, from both the east and the west. The centerpiece of the park is Bedard Lake, and most people making the hike in also bring fishing gear.

Blue Earth Lake Provincial Lake (Map 31/B4)

This 705 hectare park is best accessed from the Blue Earth Lake FSR to the east. The park encompasses a track of land set below White Mountain and surrounding Blue Earth Lake. The old Blue Lake Recreation Site is located at the east end of the lake and offers camping and cartop boat launch facilities.

Bonaparte Provincial Park (Maps 41/E1, 49/E6)

This 11,811 hectare park encompasses the highlands of the Bonaparte Plateau. The road access into the park is very limited and requires a long drive along logging roads up Jamieson Creek. Instead, most people get into the park by floatplane, horseback, or on foot. Within the park are numerous fishing lakes, including four fly-in fishing resorts, together with several hiking trails and a canoe route. People interested in camping must be self-sufficient.

Boundary Creek Provincial Park (Map 5/G6) 🏕️ 🚴 🐟

Nestled beside Boundary Creek to the south of Greenwood, this provincial park is easily accessed off Highway 3. There are a total of 18 campsites located in a semi-open area, which are primarily used as a stopover by visitors heading for other destinations. The campground is open from April to October and does provide an opportunity to fish the creek or explore the hillsides for remains of old mining activities.

Brent Mountain Protected Area (Maps 10/G5–11/A6) 🐎 🏕️ 🚵 🛶 📍

This new protected area encompasses a 4,344 hectare section of alpine area around Mount Brent. There are a number of established trails in the area, including one to the top of Brent Mountain, and another along Shatford Creek. Hikers, horseback riders and in winter snowmobilers all frequent the area.

Bromley Rock Provincial Park (Map 10/A7) 🏕️ 🏞️ 🚴 🛶 🏊 🐟 ♿

Bromley Rock is a striking rock bluff along the Similkameen River east of Princeton. The park was named after the rock and is found right next to Highway 3. It is open year round (with full services from mid-April to mid-October) and offers 17 rustic camping sites and a separate picnic area. Although the campsites are used primarily by Highway 3 travellers on their way to other destinations, the large picnic site is a popular destination, especially in the summer months. There is good access to the large fishing and swimming holes of the Similkameen River and good paddling in the area. Daredevils can jump off the cliffs to the river below, but this is not recommended. Tubing from here to Stemwinder Provincial Park downstream is a popular pastime.

Buse Lake Protected Area (Map 34/E4) 🥾 📍

Buse Lake is a relatively new, 228 hectare park with no developed facilities. The park encompasses Buse Lake and the northwestern slopes of Buse Hill. There is a hiking trail to the top of Buse Hill, but the park is best known as a great place for birders and naturalists, as birds are attracted to the lake's rich alkaline shoreline. The park is easily accessed on the Barnhartvale Road southwest of Monte Creek.

Cathedral Provincial Park (Maps 1-2) 🏕️ 🛖 🥾 🧗 🛶 🏊 🏕️ 🐟 🛶 📍 ⛷️

This pristine, 33,000 hectare wilderness park is bounded by the Ashnola River to the north and the US border to the south. The park is known for its jagged mountain peaks, turquoise lakes and alpine meadows and you can spend several days exploring the many trails, climbing opportunities and fishing lakes the park has to offer. To access the Core Area, which contains the beautiful Cathedral Lakes, it is a 16 km (9.8 mile) hike from the Lakeview Trailhead (there are two other ways in, both of which are longer). Many prefer to use the Cathedral Lakes Resort 4wd jeep service (250-226-7560) to avoid the long walk in. Camping within the park's core area is restricted to designated sites near Lake of the Woods, Pyramid Lake and Quiniscoe Lake. Alternatively, you can stay at the lodge (250-492-1606). The hiking season runs from early May to mid-October with mid-July to August being the most popular time to visit. In winter, many of the trails are open to cross-country skiers. These routes are marked but not well-defined and should only be attempted by experienced, well-equipped travellers with map-reading and orienteering skills. No dogs or mountain bikes are allowed in the park.

Along the Ashnola River Road, there are some drive-in camping sites. The Lakeview Trailhead Campground is found near the footbridge spanning the Ashnola River, while the Buckhorn Campground is two kilometres further along the Ashnola River. There is no camping fee at either site, but campsites are user-maintained and there are a limited number of picnic tables, fire rings and pit toilets.

Cathedral Protected Area is a new 353 hectare addition to the existing park. It protects the low elevation forests but offers no additional facilities.

Chasm Provincial Park (Map 47/C6) 🐎 🏞️ 🥾 🚵

The Chasm is a dramatic swath that cuts its way through colourful bands of lava where Chasm Creek flows into the Bonaparte River Valley. It is 8 km (4.8 miles) long, 600 metres (1,950 feet) wide and 300 metres (975 feet) deep. The slow process of erosion in the chasm has created a display of red, brown, yellow and purple bands of rock in the canyon. In 1995, the park was enlarged from 141 hectares to 3,067 hectares to protect more of the colourful rock and ponderosa pine forest. This park is a popular place for photographers but outside of pit toilets and an undeveloped day-use area, there are no facilities.

Christie Memorial Provincial Park (Map 3/C1) 🏞️ 🏖️ 🛶 🏊 🐟 ♿

On the south shore of Skaha Lake at the town of Okanagan Falls, this year-round provincial park offers a day-use facility and a beach. It is a popular spot for swimming and picnicking in the summer months.

Cinnemousun Narrows Provincial Park (Map 45/A3) 🔺 🏖️ 🥾 ⚓

This water access only park is extremely popular with the houseboating crowd and offers several floating stores. It is located on the shores of Shuswap Lake where the four arms of the big lake meet. Access to the provincial park is by boat only. There are 28 walk-in campsites on the south side of the Narrows while the north side is generally undeveloped. Both sides have hiking trails and beaches to enjoy.

Coldwater River Provincial Park (Map 16/B7) 🏞️ 🥾 🚵

This is one of the least publicized, least used, and least known about parks in the province. Access to this park is off the Coquihalla Highway, although there are currently no signs showing the turn-off. About the only people who use this pretty site on a regular basis are cyclists doing the Trans Canada Trail.

Conkle Lake Provincial Park (Map 4/G4) 🏕️ 🔺 🏞️ 🏖️ 🛶 🥾 🚵 🏊 🐟 📍

Located on a rough 2wd road (Johnstone Creek West Road or Conkle Lake Road) in the Okanagan Highland east of Osoyoos, this rustic provincial park is best known for its fishing. There are a total of 36 camping spots together with pit toilets, a cartop boat launch and a sandy beach all at the north end of the picturesque lake. A hiking trail circles the lake as well as leads to the west from the campground to the scenic falls. The provincial park is an ideal location for a summer retreat.

Symbols Used in Reference Section

🏕️	Campsite /Trailer Park
🔲	Road Access Recreation Site
🔺	Trail or Boat Access Recreation Site
🏞️	Day-use, Picnic Site
🏖️	Beach
🚤	Boat Launch
🥾	Hiking Trail
🚵	Mountain Biking Trail
🐎	Horseback Riding
⛷️	Cross Country Skiing
🛷	Snowmobiling
🧗	Mountaineering /Rock Climbing
🛶	Paddling (Canoe /Kayak)
🏍️	Motorbiking /ATV
🏊	Swimming
🛖	Cabin /Hut /Resort
📋	Interpretive Brochure
🐟	Fishing
📍	Viewpoint
♿	Wheel Chair Accessible
⛷️	Downhill Skiing
🎿	Snowshoeing
🤿	Diving
🕐	Reservations
$	Enhanced
🔫	Hunt
🍇	Winery

Cornwall Hills Provincial Park (Map 31/C2)

To the west of Ashcroft, this undeveloped park can be accessed by the Cornwall Lookout Road. The summit of Cornwall Hill is a popular launch for hang gliders and offers nice views of the surrounding area. There are also a number of unmarked trails through the meadows and rare Englemann Spruce in the 1,188 hectare park.

Coquihalla Canyon Provincial Park (Map 7/B4)

This recreation area, just east of Hope, was established in 1986 to preserve the area around the dramatic Othello Tunnels, part of the historic Kettle Valley Railway. In the Coquihalla Canyon the river cut a 300-foot-deep channel through solid granite. A straight line of tunnels and bridges was built through the gorge to get the trains through. Now it is a popular sight-seeing/hiking/biking destination. Most visitors only sample the short hike (less than a kilometre) through the spectacular gorge but the Trans Canada Trail continues east and west.

Coquihalla Summit Recreation Area (Maps 7/G3–8 B2)

To the south of the tollbooth, at the summit of the Coquihalla Highway (Hwy 5), is a lovely picnic area for highway travellers. Most visitors will enjoy the incredible views of Zopkius Ridge and Needle Peak before moving on, but the 5,750 hectare park offers much more. It is possible to explore the sub-alpine terrain around the toll booth, fish at Falls Lake or challenge the many surrounding peaks along mountain routes best left to experienced mountaineers.

Darke Lake Provincial Park (Maps 11/A1-19/A7)

This medium size (1,470-hectare) provincial park is located on a 2wd road northeast of Summerland. It provides a backcountry retreat ideal for fishermen that want to try their luck at a mountain lake. Campers will find 5 rustic campsites as well as pit toilets. The park is open year round and is popular with ice fishermen in the winter.

Dunn Peak Provincial Park (Maps 50-51)

This large (19,353 hectare), remote area is extremely rugged but very beautiful. The provincial park preserves the towering Dunn Peak and most of the Dunn Mountain Range. It is a backcountry park, without developed facilities. The main access into the area shown in this book is via the seldom travelled Dunn Peak Trail, east of Little Fort. Although outside of the park, the scenic Baldy Mountain Lookout is an easier destination.

Eakin Creek Canyon Provincial Park (Map 50/B1)

This small 10 hectare park is found north of Little Fort. A short trail on the south side of Highway 24 leads to a scenic waterfall in the canyon.

Echo Lake Provincial Park (Map 29/F5)

Located on the Creighton Valley Road to the east of Lumby, this provincial park has a day-use area ideal for paddlers, fishermen and sunbathers. Given its distance from the population belt, it is not a particularly busy area and is a fine destination for those seeking solitude. A resort is also found on the lake.

Ellison Provincial Park (Map 28/A3)

Southwest of Vernon, this 200 hectare provincial park is comprised of a rocky forested shoreline with two sheltered bays on Okanagan Lake. It is accessed along the Okanagan Landing Road (paved access), and it provides 71 camping spots together with full facilities including a large day-use area, flush toilets, and running water. This provincial park is very popular in the summer because it not only has good fishing opportunities but also Canada's first freshwater underwater diving park. The mooring facilities, developed beaches (including a separate doggie beach), and over 6 km (3.6 miles) of easy hiking trails make this a fine destination park. Campers are recommended to make reservations during the summer months.

Emar Lake Provincial Park (Map 49/G1)

This 1,604 hectare park encompasses a series of small lakes that are easily accessed off Eakin Creek Road to the south. The park is very popular during the spring through fall with anglers and hunters. The lakes can also be strung together into a peaceful canoe circuit (see Paddling Section) and camping is possible at Long Island Lake, which is south of Highway 24 (and north of this book).

Enderby Cliffs Protected Area (Maps 36/G4, 37/A3)

A new 2,277 hectare protected area has been established in the prominent rock cliffs northwest of Enderby. A couple of existing trails lead to the scenic cliffs, one of which runs past Reeves Lake, a popular walk-in fishing destination. Backcountry camping is possible.

Eneas Lakes Provincial Park (Map 18/G7)

Eneas Lakes Provincial Park is well off the beaten track, in the mountains east of Peachland. The four small lakes within the park are ideal for fishing throughout the ice-free season. Although it is possible to launch a boat at the lakes, camp in one of the many clearings or hike/ bike one of the rough trails, there are no developed facilities in the area. The park is accessed by the Eneas Lakes Road, which has been deactivated, and is very rough 4wd road.

Epsom Provincial Park (Map 31/E2)

Located on the west bank of the Thompson River, north of Spences Bridge, this 102 hectare park provides access to the river, mostly for anglers. There is no road access to the park, so anyone wishing to visit must scramble down to the river from Highway 1 along a rough trail. Be careful crossing the railway tracks.

Fintry Provincial Park (Map 27/G6)

North of Kelowna, this park is an extremely popular destination for tourists, due, no doubt, to its prime location on the western shores of Okanagan Lake. The 360 hectare park (and 593 hectare protected area) was developed on the former Fintry Estate Heritage Site. Fintry was a social and economic centre in the 1800s for the Hudson Bay Company. Today, there are a total of 100 camping sites between two locations, along with a day-use area, developed beach, flush toilets and showers. For the hiker, Short Creek Canyon Trail in the hills to the east offers a walk through a steep canyon as well as some historical features (suspension bridge and remains of irrigation and power generation structures).

Gladstone/Texas Creek Provincial Park (Maps 6, 14)

On the north end of Christina Lake, Gladstone encompasses a large chunk of the Selkirk Foothills. Most of the 39,322 hectare park is pristine wilderness, which is seldom visited except where the park can be reached by boat on Christina Lake. The access points to the park include Lynch Creek/Mt Faith Trails to the north, Highway 3 to the south and the Deer Point/Sandner Creek Trails at the north end of Christina Lake. Seven boat access only campsites line Christina Lake providing camping and beach facilities. They are all very popular in the summer. The Texas Creek Campground is the only vehicle access campsite. It is a very busy campground and reservations are recommended. There is a boat launch near the entrance to the campground and Indian Pictographs are found a short paddle north.

Goldpan Provincial Park (Map 23/C1)

Located right next to Highway 1 (and between 2 busy railroads), this provincial park is best used as a stopover for travellers on Highway 1. The day-use area is open year round and is popular with people who wish to explore the Thompson River for fishing or paddling opportunities. In addition, there are 14 campsites. The provincial park is set within the dry sage brush country typical of the Thompson River Valley.

Granby Provincial Park (Maps 14, 22) ▲ 🏕 ⌂ 🚻

This remote provincial park is assessed by the Granby Wilderness Trail to the south or the Mount Scaia Road to the north. The 40,845 hectare park is a pristine area that was established to preserve important Grizzly Bear habitat as well as the headwaters of the Granby River and several adjacent basins. Wilderness camping, fishing and hunting are some of the recreation pursuits available.

Green Lake Provincial Park (Maps 47/G7, 48/A1)
🎿 🚻 ⛴ 🏊 🚶 🐴 🛶 ⛵ ⌂ ♿ ☽

This Mediterranean coloured lake is a popular destination area. There are three campgrounds within the park, which is made up of eleven separate parcels of land around the lake, totaling 347 hectares. **Emerald Bay** has 51 campsites, **Sunset View** has 54 sites and **Arrowhead** has 16 sites. All campgrounds offer lakeshore camping and developed beaches with Sunset View also offering a boat launch. It is recommended to make reservations during the summer months. The park also has two day-use areas called **Blue Spring** and **Little Arrowhead**. Water sports and fishing are the primary attractions to the lake. Please note the long (14 km) lake is often windy.

Greenbush Lake Protected Area (Map 46/E7) ▲ ⌂

This new protected area was established to protect important grizzly and caribou habitat, as well as old growth forests in the area. In total the park covers 2,820 hectares, including the popular fishing and camping destination lake.

Greenstone Mountain Park (Map 33/B3) 🚶 🚵 🐴 🚻

Off the Dominic Lake FSR, this 124 hectare park encompasses Greenstone Mountain and a former forestry lookout. The park also contains Kwilalkwila Lake and many informal trails, which connect to an extensive bike trail system outside the park.

Graystokes Protected Area (Map 21/D2)
▲ 🚶 🚵 🐴 ⛷ ⌂ 🚻

Graystokes Protected Area was established to protect 11,958 hectares of lakes, swamps, meandering streams and meadows that are prime habitat for moose, mule deer and white-tailed deer. The area has been a popular snowmobile destination for years and there are established trails and warming cabins. When the snow clears, the lakes and former forest service campsites make fine fishing destinations. Please note that motorized access is not permitted.

Herald Provincial Park (Map 44/E7)
🎿 ▲ 🚻 ⛴ 🏊 🚶 🛶 ⛵ ⌂ ♿ ☽

This popular 79 hectare park on the Salmon Arm of Shuswap Lake has 119 camp spots as well as an impressive beach, boat launching facilities and large day-use area. A number of trails including the short trail to Margaret Falls are found within the park. Remains of the old homestead owned by the Herald Family, who donated the land for the park, can also be seen. Water sports and fishing are the primary attractions to the very popular park. This park is extremely popular, and reservations for camping are recommended.

Harry Lake Aspen Provincial Park (Map 39/A7)
▲ ⌂ 🚻

Located to the south of Highway 99, 40 km (24 miles) west of Cache Creek, this park preserves 330 hectares of grassland and aspen forest around Harry Lake. Road access is minimal.

Haynes Point Provincial Park (Map 4/A7)

🎿 🚻 ⛴ 🏊 🚶 🚵 🛶 ⛵ ⌂ ♿ ☽

Two kilometres to the south of Osoyoos on Highway 97, this 38 hectare provincial park is located on a narrow sandy spit on Osoyoos Lake. The park has 41 very cozy campsites that are always busy. There are also day-use facilities, a boat launch and even a pet beach. Osoyoos Lake is considered the warmest lake in Canada. As a result, the primary attraction to the park is water sports. Reservations are recommended.

High Lakes Basin Provincial Park (Map 49/F2) ▲ 🚶 ⌂

This remote provincial park lies north of Bonaparte Lake and encompasses three high elevation lakes containing wild trout. There is no access into the park but it is possible to bushwhack in from the logging roads north of Caverhill Lake. There are some rustic, user-maintained camping spots in the 560 hectare park.

Inkaneep Provincial Park (Map 3/F3) 🎿 🚶 🚵 🛶 ⌂

This provincial park is located 6 km (3.6 miles) north of Oliver on Highway 97 next to the Okanagan River. The small (21 hectare) park provides seven rustic camping spots nestled in large cottonwood trees a short walk from the Okanagan River.

Jewel Lake (Map 6/A4) 🎿 🚻 🚶 🛥 🚵 🛶 ⛵ ⌂ ♿ ⛷

This 3 km (1.8 mile) lake is a great rainbow trout fishing lake, and many of the people who come to this park do so to fish. The lake also boasts a nice beach and can make a great camping destination away from the crowds of other more popular parks in the region. A series of ski trails provide year round enjoyment at the south end of the lake near the lodge.

Johnstone Creek Provincial Park (Map 5/A7)
🎿 🚶 🚵 ⌂

This small 38 hectare provincial park is found on Highway 3 just east of the turnoff to Conkle Lake Provincial Park. There are 16 camping spots in a forested creek draw providing plenty of shade in the heat of the summer. The park is used mainly for a stopover for travellers along Highway 3 and features a short 1 km trail.

Juniper Beach Provincial Park (Map 40/A7)
🎿 🚻 🚶 ⛵ 🏊 ⌂ ♿

On Highway 1 between Cache Creek and Kamloops, Juniper Beach has 30 camping spots on the shores of the Thompson River. It is open from February to November and has full facilities including showers, drinking water and a sani-station. The provincial park is mainly used as a stopover for travellers on Highway 1 although it does offer swimming, fishing and paddling opportunities.

Kalamalka Lake Provincial Park (Map 28/D5)
🚻 🚶 🚵 🐴 🏊 ⛵ ⌂ ♿

Located just south of Vernon is a beautiful 978 hectare provincial park on the northeast shore of Kalamalka Lake. Surrounded by grasslands dotted with Ponderosa Pine, the road access into the park is restricted. You will have to hike/bike from the parking lot at the end of Kidston Road along the paved road to the popular beach at Cosens Bay. While most visitors head for the beach, there is an extensive multi-use trail system. Be wary of the heat and the rattlesnakes.

Kalamalka Lake Protected Area (Map 28/C3) 🚻

This new 3,231 hectare protected area was established to protect the higher elevation forests between Kalamalka Lake Provincial Park and the

Cougar Canyon Ecological Reserve. However, there are no developed facilities or trails through the protected area.

Kentucky-Alleyne Provincial Park (Map 17/C3)

This 144 hectare park is located south of the Okanagan Connector. The popularity of the provincial park is steadily increasing, but you are still likely to find one of the 63 vehicle/tent campsites open, except on the busiest of summer weekends. The park is ideal for visitors who wish to explore the rolling grasslands and dry open forests typical of the cattle country of this region. The park is also an ideal place to sample a few mountain lakes for stocked rainbow trout. At the park, you will find a 4 km (3.4 mile) trail that circles Kentucky Lake. The park is more rustic, and does not have as many facilities at this park as compared to others in the Okanagan (no showers, sani-station or flush toilets).

Keremeos Columns Provincial Park (Map 3/A3)

This undeveloped park is an adventure waiting for the select few willing to make the long hike in. The trail crosses through the dry sagebrush country as you climb steeply to the columns, which, strangely enough, are outside of the park boundaries. Please obtain permission to cross the private property en route and ensure you bring water.

Kettle River Recreation Area (Map 5/A6)

To the north of Rock Creek on Highway 33, the Kettle River Recreation Area is an ideal destination for a family retreat. The 179 hectare park has a scenic picnic area that is popular with anglers and swimmers. To the north of the picnic area is a 53-unit campsite, which is set in a semi-open ponderosa pine forest next to the river. The old Kettle River Railbed, now part of the Trans Canada Trail, bisects the area and can be explored by mountain bike or by foot. There is even an old trestle that spans the river. Many people enjoy tubing on the river. Campers are recommended to make reservations during the summer months.

Kickininee Provincial Park (Map 11/D4)

On the western shores of Okanagan Lake 8 km north of Penticton, this small (49 hectare) provincial park provides day-use facilities at three different locations along the lake— Kickininee, Soorimpt and Pyramid. Each site is easily accessed off Highway 97. There is a boat launch at Soorimpt.

Kukuli Bay Provincial Park (Map 28/B3)

This small (57 ha) provincial park is located on the west side of Kalamalka Lake 11km south of Vernon. It is open year-round and provides a sandy beach ideal for day-use.

Lac Du Bois Grasslands Provincial Park (Maps 33, 41)

Lac Du Bois is a land of open grasslands, dry forests, and grand cliffs and canyons. The park is bisected by the Lac du Bois Road and preserves a series of small lakes in addition to the 15,000 hectares of grassland. There are few facilities in the area but there are a variety of trails to explore. Some camping is available at the old Watching Creek Forest Service Site (off the Tranquille-Criss Creek Road).

Lac Le Jeune Provincial Park (Map 33/D6)

Lac Le Jeune Provincial Park is situated not far from the Coquihalla Highway (Hwy 5) south of Kamloops. There are a total of 144 camp spots, which are open from April to October, as well as a large picnic area. The park is extremely popular for boating, swimming and fishing in the summer months and cross-country skiing in the winter months. Campsite reservations are recommended.

Loon Lake Provincial Park (Maps 39, 47)

One of a number of provincial parks across the province that has seen its facilities completely removed, Loon Lake is now open for swimming, boating and angling. The park is located on the northern shores of Loon Lake and is easily accessed on the Loon Lake Road.

Mabel Lake Provincial Park (Map 37/F7)

This 187 hectare provincial park is found on the eastern shores of Mabel Lake off the Mabel Lake FSR. Given its distance from Highway 6, the park does not see the crowds that other parks in the Okanagan do, making it a good choice for those who prefer more solitude. There are a total of 81 vehicle/tent campsites at two locations in the park as well as a large day-use area, a boat launch and a nice sandy beach. Mabel Lake makes an ideal destination for summer camping as well as a good year-round fishing destination.

Mara Provincial Park (Map 45/A7)

This small provincial park is located on the eastern shores of Mara Lake and offers a nice beach for picnickers or sunbathers.

McConnell Lake Provincial Park (Map 33/E5)

McConnell Lake is noted for big rainbow trout, which means it sees a lot of action from anglers. The park is also a good place to hike, bike or cross-country ski.

Momich Lakes Provincial Park (Map 52/B3)

Momich Lakes are located on the eastern slopes of Adams Lake. The park covers 1,648 hectares and marks the northern extension of the larch tree. It is open for camping from May through October with the 24 unit Momich River Campsite, which is found next to Adams Lake being the most popular site. There are also former forest service recreation sites on the east and west end of Momich Lake. The eastern site offers a beach and boat launch. All lakes in the area provide reasonably good fishing and canoeing.

Monashee Prov Park (Map 38/G6)

This remote provincial park, which covers 7,513 hectares of pristine wilderness, plus another 15,207 hectares in the protected area, is the jewel of the Monashee Mountains. There are 24 km (7.4 miles) of multi-use trails that give access to this backcountry haven. From the parking lot area north of Sugar Lake, the Rainbow Falls Trail leads 6 km/3.6 miles (one-way) to Spectrum Lake and the site of the first wilderness campsite. Although most visitors use this campsite as a staging ground for day trips to the surrounding mountains and other lakes, there are a total of ten wilderness campsites as well as six overnight shelters in the park. Peters Lake, Mikes Lake and Fawn Lakes are other popular resting areas. The park terrain is steep and many of the trails should be left to the experienced backpacker.

Monck Provincial Park (Map 25/C5)

Located on the northern shores of Nicola Lake in the heart of cattle country, Monck Park is an extremely popular park. It is open from March to November and contains 71 camping spots as well as a large picnic area and beach. Trails lead up the mountainside to volcanic outcroppings or to the second beach and some Indian Pictographs, but the focus of the park is water sports on Nicola Lake

Monte Creek Provincial Park (Map 34/G3)

Right on Trans Canada Highway just east of the town of Monte Creek, this tiny (1.7 hectare) park is squeezed between Monte Creek and the South Thompson River. The park protects a treed riparian zone on the Thompson, as well as a First Nations archeological site.

Monte Lake Provincial Park (Map 35/A6)

Next to Monte Lake and Highway 97, this provincial park provides access to this fairly popular lake. There are no facilities, but camping is available at a private campground nearby.

Mount Savona Prov Park (Map 32/G2) 🚶 🚵 🐎 🏍 🚻

Encompassing a former forest service lookout, it is possible to drive to the summit along a rough 4wd road. A number of cattle trails can be hiked or ridden and there are cliffs and caves to explore.

Myra-Bellevue Protected Area (Maps 12, 20)
🚶 🚵 🐎 🚻

This 7,829 hectare protected area encompasses the Myra Canyon section of the Kettle Valley Railway, along with a number of other existing trails.

Nickel Plate Provincial Park (Map 10/G7)
⛺ 🚶 🚵 ⛷ 🛶 🏕 🐟

Nickel Plate Provincial Park is located just north of Apex Mountain. The park is known for its backcountry camping, biking, hiking and fishing opportunities. In the winter, there are several kilometres of maintained cross-country ski trails. The park is also a staging ground for the spectacular but rigorous 20 Mile Creek Trail.

Nicolum River Provincial Park (Map 7/C7) 🏕 ⛽ 🐟

Located east of Hope on Highway 3, the 24 hectare Nicolum River Provincial Park is set in dense forest cover next to a small, fast flowing river. There are only nine campsites here and they fill up quickly.

Niskonlith Lake Provincial Park (Map 43/B7) 🏕 🛶 🐟

Located approximately 8 km from Chase on the Niskonlith Lake Road, this 238 hectare provincial park has 30 rustic campsites on the eastern shores of the lake. It is still possible to hand launch boats in order to try your luck fishing in the lake.

Okanagan Falls Provincial Park (Map 3/C1) 🏕 🐟 ♿

Located at the south end of Skaha Lake in the heart of the Okanagan, this tiny (2 hectare) provincial park is found off Highway 97. It provides 25 camp spots used primarily by visitors to the lake. The area is a popular spot for birding, or viewing the fall display of colours.

Okanagan Lake Provincial Park (Map 11/C1)
🌙 🏕 ⛽ 🛶 🏊 🚶 🛶 🐟 ♿

With 168 campsites between two locations, this is an extremely popular summer vacation getaway for locals and tourists. Campers are well advised to make reservations. The 98 hectare park is located on the western shores of Okanagan Lake north of Summerland, in a ponderosa pine/sage brush ecosystem. The campground is open year-round and there is a picnic/day-use area, over 1 km of sandy beaches, hiking trails, sani-station and a boat launch.

Okanagan Mountain Provincial Park (Maps 11/E1,19/E7)
⛺ ⛽ 🚶 🚵 🐎 🛶 🛶 ⚓ 🐟 🚻

Despite its proximity to Kelowna, this wilderness park remains a quiet year-round destination. It covers 10,542 hectares from the lakeshore to the dry pine forest surrounding Okanagan Mountain. With 24 km (14.4 miles) of multi-use trails and numerous backcountry campsites and lakes, the park provides excellent opportunities for mountain biking, horseback riding, hiking and fishing. Alternatively, there are six marine campgrounds set in secluded bays with sandy beaches that are ideal for boaters or canoers exploring Okanagan Lake. Indian pictographs are found at Commando Bay and south of the park.

Oregon Jack Provincial Park (Map 31/B1) 🐟 🚻

Easily accessed on the Hat Creek Road, this undeveloped park preserves the Notch, a limestone canyon and falls on the Oregon Jack Creek drainage. An Indian Pictograph can be seen in the canyon.

Otter Lake Provincial Park (Map 8/D2)
🏕 ⛽ 🛶 🚶 🚵 🛶 🏊 🐟 ♿

In the Tulameen Valley northwest of Princeton, Otter Lake provides two separate areas to visit. The 45 site lakeside camping area is found near the north end of the lake, while the day-use facility, boat launch and developed beach area are found at the south end of the lake. The 51 hectare park is less developed than other provincial parks so you should expect a more rustic camping experience. The lake is certainly the main feature of the park but the area offers ruminants of a proud mining history. Alternatively, why not explore part of the historic Kettle Valley Railway, which is now part of the Trans Canada Trail.

Painted Bluffs Provincial Park (Maps 40/G7, 41/A7)
🚶 🛶 🐟 🚻

Protecting a small, but geologically significant site on the north shore of Kamloops Lake, this park is rarely visited. It is possible to visit by boat or canoe as well as on foot, but most people enjoy the view of the bluffs from the highway viewpoints across Kamloops Lake.

Paul Lake Provincial Park (Map 34/D1)
🏕 ⛽ 🛶 🛶 🚶 🛶 🏊 🐟 ♿

Nestled in a mixed forest just northeast of Kamloops, Paul Lake has a large beach and day-use area, as well as a large campground with 90 sites. There are seven kilometres of hiking trails, including a popular trail to the top of Gibraltar Rock, and plenty of water sports to enjoy. This is a popular getaway for locals who can make it here from Kamloops in about half an hour.

Pennask Lake Prov Park (Map 18/D2) 🏕 🛶 🏊 🐟

Most of the rainbow trout caught in the south-central interior were gleaned from eggs from Pennask Lake, so, as you might expect, this is a great fishing lake. This can be true, however, access to this 244 hectare park is not that easy. The last four kilometres will take about an hour to navigate, and a 4wd vehicle is highly recommended. In addition to the main campsite, there are several canoe access camping areas and many nooks and crannies to explore on the lake.

Porcupine Meadows Prov Park (Map 41/D3) 🚶 🐎 🚻

This park is mostly comprised of wetlands with some patches of old growth forest. The 2,704 hectare area is designated mostly for conservation, and recreation is limited. There is an old pack trail leading past several small lakes to Porcupine Ridge and an old forestry lookout.

Pritchard Provincial Park (Map 35/A2) 🚶 🛶 🐟 🚻

One of the few spots along the Thompson River between Chase and Kamloops that is not under private ownership, this 15 hectare provincial park gives the public access to the foreshore for birding, exploring and canoeing.

Roche Lake Provincial Park (Map 34/C6)
🏕 ⛺ 🛶 🛶 🚶 🚵 🎣 🐎 🏊 ⛵ 🐟 🛶

Roche Lake is the largest of seven world-class fishing lakes in this 2,041 hectare park. Road access is limited but there are many informal multi-use trails and even a rock climbing area. There are rustic, user-maintained, campsites on Black, Horseshoe and Roche Lakes. A boat launch and resort is also found on the bigger lake.

Roderick Haig-Brown Provincial Park (Map 43/E5)
🚶 🚵 ⛷ 🛶 🐟 🚻 ♿

Named after the famous poet/author/fly fisherman, this provincial park protects both sides of the Adams River for 11 km (6.6 miles). The main attraction to the area is the incredible display of spawning sockeye in October (peak years occur every four years beginning in 2006). This is a busy time to visit the park, but during the rest of the year it is a very peaceful place to be. The park also hosts 26 km (15.6 miles) of multi-use trails and is a popular whitewater paddling destination. While in the area, be sure to hike/bike to the Bear Creek Flume.

Shuswap Lake Park (Map 44/A3)
🌙 🏕 ⛽ 🛶 🛶 🚶 🏊 🐟 ♿

While this park is a mere 149 hectares, it is the largest and most popular campground in the Thompson District. There are 260 campsites in addition to facilities such as picnic grounds, a boat launch, showers and rentals of all sorts. It is a great place to bring the whole family as there is a large sand/pebble beach, a play area, trails and even stores just outside the gates. If you have a boat, it is highly recommended that you visit Copper Island, which is part of the provincial park. This island is one of the better areas to fish in the big lake and it has a series of hiking trails in addition to sheltered mooring for day-use. The park is constantly at capacity, so make sure you reserve a spot before heading out.

Shuswap Lake Marine Provincial Parks (Maps 36, 43, 44, 45, 53) ▲ 🏕 🚤 🚶 🏊 ✈ ⚓ 🛥 🚻

Covering over 1,000 kilometres of shoreline, Shuswap Lake is a big lake with beautiful beaches and plenty of room for the many water based recreationists who visit. To help accommodate the boaters (and houseboats), 26 marine sites have been established around the four arms of the lake. In addition to these rustic boat access sites listed below, there are also a number of full-service, road-accessed sites that we have already described (Albas, Herald and Shuswap Lake). Cinnemousun Narrows, which is also a boat access site, is not part of the Marine Park. We have broken the sites down by Arm:

ANSTEY ARM

This is the remote northeast arm of the lake and is only accessible by boat.

Anstey Arm West (Map 45/B1) has no facilities but is an interesting area to explore because of the rocky shoreline with a forested backdrop.

Anstey Beach (Map 53/C7) at the north end of the Arm, has five developed campsites together with a picnic area, toilets and a beach. The park is often used as a staging ground for fishermen that want to try their luck at Wright or Hunakwa Lake.

Anstey View (Map 45/A2) is found on the west side of Anstey Arm and provides picnic tables as well as a short trail through a mixed forest leading to an old homestead. There are five developed campsites together with a nice beach at this park.

Four Mile Creek (Map 45/C1) is set on a small bay with a nice beach for landing a boat. The site has ten developed campsites together with pit toilets and a picnic site.

Rendezvous Picnic Site (Map 45/B1) is located in a small bay and offers a nice beach but no camping facilities.

Roberts Bay (Map 45/A2) is a sheltered beach with a marked swimming area is the prime draw to this bay. Watch for the large rocks offshore at the south end of the bay.

Twin Bays (Map 45/B1) is a small day-use area with nice beaches north and south of the bay.

MAIN ARM

The Main Arm is the most developed section of the lake and stretches from the Adams River east past Anglemont to Cinnemousun Narrows. The North Shore, as it is known locally, is easily accessed by the paved Squilax-Anglemont Road (beyond St Ives the road turns to gravel). The highway and Eagle Bay Road provide good access to the south. As a result, these parks are accessible by boat or by vehicle:

Horseshoe Bay (Map 44/G3) covers 14 hectares and is found within a sheltered bay on the North Shore near St Ives. There are seven undeveloped vehicle campsites together with a boat launch, beach and picnic tables.

St Ives (Map 44/G3) is located just east of Horseshoe Bay Provincial Park on the north shore of the Main Arm. It is open from May to October and has a small boat launch.

SALMON ARM

Salmon Arm forms the busy southeast portion of the lake. Between Tappen and Sicamous there is good road access off Sunnybrae-Canoe Point Road to the north and the Trans-Canada Highway (Hwy 1) to the south. From Sicamous north, it is boat access only; but it remains very busy with houseboats and powerboats. Within the arm are both boat access only sites and vehicle accessible, full facility sites.

Aline Hill (Map 45/A3) is an undeveloped 20 hectare parcel of land on the western shore. It sees few visitors since it is boat access only and offers no facilities.

Hermit Bay (Map 44/G5) is another day-use, boat access only site on the western shores, just south of Tillus Landing. There is a nice beach to the north end of the park.

Hungry Cove (Map 44/G6) is on the eastern shore to the north of Sicamous. The day-use site offers a sandy beach.

Marble Point (Map 45/A5) is another boat access site on the eastern shore, just north of Hungry Cove. It provides 16 developed campsites together with a picnic and day-use facility, beach and hiking trails. The hiking trail leads between the two camping areas over a short distance (less than 1km) and past old mine workings. There are also Indian Pictographs found nearby.

Paradise Point (Map 44/F7) is a day-use site located on the north side of the Salmon Arm, just to the northeast of Herald Provincial Park. There are no facilities except pit toilets but it is a great place to sunbathe.

Shuswap Lake East (Map 45/A3) is a tiny (1.1 hectare) site, which has a small beach area for day-use activities. It is accessed by boat to the east side of Salmon Arm just south of the Narrows.

Tillis Beach (Map 44/G4) is another small (27 hectare) day-use, boat access site located on the western shores of the Salmon Arm. There are no facilities at the park but there is a nice beach.

SEYMOUR ARM

Seymour Arm forms the northern reaches of the lake. Beyond Ruckell Point, the gravel road becomes a little rougher but should be manageable by most cars and RVs. The eastern shore remains mainly boat access only.

Beach Bay (Map 53/B7) is located on the eastern shores of the Seymour Arm. This undeveloped site offers a beach as well as nearby Indian Pictographs.

Cottonwood Beach (Map 45/A1) is located about 1/3 of the way up the east side of Seymour Arm and provides a small beach for visitors to enjoy.

Encounter Point (Map 53/A7) is located on the western shores of the Seymour Arm. There are five camping sites here, as well as a beach and pit toilets.

Fowler Point (Map 53/A6) is located on the western shores of the Seymour Arm, just north of Albas Park. The small site offers a beach and pit toilets.

Nelson Beach (Map 45/A2) is found just north of the popular Cinnemousun Narrows. It offers a quieter beach to visit.

Two Mile Creek (Map 53/A7) is a boat access only park on the western side of the Seymour Arm with five campsites as well as picnicking facilities and a beach.

Woods Landing (Map 44/G2) is located on the western shores of the Seymour Arm, just north of Ruckell Point. There is no beach or

amenities, but nearby pictographs are well worth the visit.

Woods Landing South (Map 44/G2) is located just south of Woods Landing. There are no amenities.

Wright Creek (Map 53/A7) is located on the east side of the arm, across from Encounter Point. This site has pit toilets and a gravel beach.

Silver Beach Park (Map 53/B6)

This 130 hectare provincial park is found at the north end of the Seymour Arm, where once a gold rush town called Ogden City stood. The campground is located next to a beautiful beach on the Seymour River estuary, and has 30 campsites along with a nice picnic area. The park sees heavy usage from houseboaters. If approaching by boat, watch for sandbars in front of the main beach. Approach is safest from the east.

Silver Star Recreation Area (Maps 28/G1, 29/A2)

This year round provincial park is set in the mountains northeast of Vernon and is easily accessed by the Silver Star Road. While the area is best known for the Silver Star Ski Resort, there is also ski trails and snowmobile trails that can be explored in the summer. The fantastic Trinity/Ricardo Trail network continues north from the park towards Salmon Arm.

Skihist Provincial Park (Map 23/A3)

Just northeast of Lytton on Highway 1, this 33 hectare park is mainly used as a stopover for travellers on Highway 1, or by folks heading out rafting on the Thompson. It has 56 campgrounds and full facilities for camping and picnicking. The park is located well above the highway and railway tracks in a dry ponderosa pine forest. A trail leads to the bench above the campsite and offers fine views of the canyon.

Snowy Protected Area (Maps 2–3)

A new protected area next to Cathedral Provincial Park, this area supports a provincially significant herd of California bighorn sheep. This is a remote area with no facilities, and only unmarked and unmaintained trails. The large areas of open grassland make for easy travel on foot or by horse.

South Okanagan Grasslands Protected Area (Maps 3–4)

This protected area consists of four sites covering 9,364 hectares. The area is unique in Canada and protects habitat for a number of rare and endangered birds, mammals, reptiles and amphibians.

Steelhead Provincial Park (Map 32/E1)

Steelhead is located on the southwest shore of Kamloops Lake, near Savona and the mouth of the Thompson River. It is a popular fishing destination with 32 campsites. While it is across the lake from the railway tracks, the sound of trains passing can be jarring at three in the morning.

Stemwinder Provincial Park (Map 10/B4)

This tiny (4 hectare) park is located on Highway 3 just west of Hedley. It has 27 vehicle/tent campsites as well as a picnic facility all on the shores of the Similkameen River.

Sunnybrae Provincial Park (Map 36/D1)

This is a day-use only site, with picnicking facilities and a beach for sunbathers and water sport participants. A short 1.5 km trail leads to the scenic bluffs overlooking Shuswap Lake.

Sun-oka Provincial Park (Map 11/D4)

Boasting one of the silliest names (despite a pseudo-native ring to it, it's actually just a contraction of "Sunny Okanagan"), this provincial park also boasts one of the best beach and day-use facilities in the province. The park is on the western shore of the Okanagan Lake, about 6 km south of Summerland, and it is extremely popular with sunbathers throughout the summer months.

Trepanier Protected Area (Map 18/G4)

This newly designated area protects 2,884 hectares around Trepanier Creek, and parts of its drainage. There is evidence of an old fur trader trail to the Okanagan in the area.

Tsintsunko Lakes Prov Park (Map 41/E2)

Located on the Bonaparte Plateau, this park protects a series of interconnected lakes and wetlands.

Tunkwa Provincial Park (Map 32/E3)

Tunkwa and Leighton Lakes offer some of the best recreational fishing in the province, so this park sees a lot of anglers. But the park offers much more than just fishing. There are 250 campsites spread around both lakes, horseback riding, and, in the winter, cross-country skiing and snowmobiling.

Upper Adams River Prov Park (Map 52/A1)

This park is located at the north end of the Adams Lake and preserves the estuaries of the Upper Adams River. Although logging roads travel along most of the park, access is difficult. It is possible to canoe or kayak down the scenic river if you are prepared for wilderness travel.

Vaseux Lake Provincial Park (Map 3/F1)

This small (12 ha) provincial park is located on the shores of Vaseux Lake to the south of Okanagan Falls. There are 12 campsites, together with a developed beach and wildlife centre at the park. The primary attraction to the area is the wildlife sanctuary, which contains an abundance of waterfowl as well as Canada's largest herd of California bighorn sheep. Sheep can often be seen in the surrounding cliffs of the Vaseux Wildlife Area. The lake provides decent fishing. In the winter, skating and ice fishing are popular.

Victor Lake Provincial Park (Map 46/D4)

Located near Highway 1 to the southwest of Revelstoke, this 15 hectare park has poor access and no developed facilities. It is a beautiful lake found near Eagle Pass that does hold trout. The lake is also popular for canoeists and windsurfers.

Walloper Lake Provincial Park (Map 33/D6)

Accessed off Exit 336 from the Coquihalla Highway (Hwy 5), Walloper Lake Provincial Park provides a day-use area for fishermen and picnickers. There is a fishing wharf, picnic tables, and pit toilets at the 55 hectare park.

White Lake Provincial Park (Map 44/D5)

White Lake is one of the top three fishing lakes in the province (based on amount of time anglers spend here). It is even a popular ice fishing destination. As a result, the campsite can be busy throughout the year.

White Lake Grasslands Protected Area (Map 3/E1)

The primary role of this new 3,751 hectare area is conservation, and camping is prohibited. If you do visit the area, tread lightly, and stick to developed trails, including the White Lake Trail.

Yard Creek Provincial Park (Map 45/E5)

Trails

From the world famous Kettle Valley Railway to the dramatic peaks of Cathedral Park and the Monashee Mountains, trail users in the Southern Interior are blessed with plenty of variety. The rolling grass covered hills of the area are riddled with trails and old roads to explore. There are also destination oriented trails leading to fishing lakes, mountain vistas, waterfalls and more. This incredible variety allows all user groups (from hikers to mountain bikers and ATV's to snowmobiles) plenty of opportunities to explore.

We have included information on over 280 trails and routes in Southern BC. To help you select the trail that best suits your abilities, we have included information on elevation gain, return distance and special features wherever possible. Unless otherwise noted, distances and times are for round trip hikes. Also included in each description is a symbol to indicate what the trail is used for—mountain biking, hiking, horseback riding, ATV, etc.

Hiking trails are usually tagged with one of the following descriptors: An **easy** trail has gentle grades, and is suitable for family excursions. A **moderate** trail can involve a long, steep hill, some scrambling, and is probably enough to tax most users. Just because they're not considered difficult, doesn't mean that they aren't challenging. Don't overestimate your ability, or underestimate the difficulty of the trail. Only experienced trail users should consider **difficult** routes. These trails are often rough and/or unmarked.

Due to the hot dry climate of the area, it is highly recommended to bring along plenty of water. We should also note that higher elevation trails and routes (over 1,000 metres/3,000 feet) might have a limited season due to late season snow. Most of these trails are found around the east, west and north boundaries of the region. Trail users should leave these trails for late summer and early fall (July until October).

Finding the trailhead is sometimes half the fun (and half the work). For this reason, you should refer to the appropriate map in this book to determine where the trail begins. But remember, our maps are designed only as a general access guide not intended to navigate you through a hidden mountain pass or across an expansive ridge network. If you are traveling on unmarked trails, we recommend that you have mountaineering knowledge and are equipped with a topographic map and a compass. A GPS could also be invaluable to help mark the trail you have taken.

The trails are grouped into the following areas.

· Monashee Mountain Trails
· North Okanagan/Shuswap Trails
· Okanagan Valley Trails
· South Okanagan/Boundary Trails
· Thompson/Nicola Area Trails

Monashee Mountain Trails

The spectacular Monashee Mountains offer a number of spectacular hiking trails into the dramatic mountain range. The sub-alpine lakes offer good fishing and rustic backcountry campsites but hikers should be wary of Grizzly Bears. In addition to being bear aware (pepper spray and bear bells are essential) hikers should be experienced in wilderness travel and be prepared with topographic maps and a compass.

Barnes Creek Trail (Map 30/G6) 🚶 🐎 🏕

Barnes Creek Trail extends off the Fife Creek Road some 8 km (4.9 miles) one-way to Vista Pass. The trail leads beyond Vista Pass along the Vista Pass Trail (see below) to the Railroad Creek Drainage. The trail is popular with both hikers and equestrian riders.

Beaven Mountain Trail (Map 30/E4) 🚶 🏕

This steep, difficult trail leads from the South Fork FSR to the summit of Mount Beaven. The trip is 14 km (8.5 miles) return, climbing 700 m (2,275 feet) to the 2,150 m high (6,988 foot high) summit. The trail begins on a well developed path, but there are some rough sections with loose rock and scrambling is required to reach the top.

Deninson Lake Trail (Map 29/F6) 🔺 🚶 🐟

Deninson Lake Trail extends from a branch road of the Bonneau FSR 2 km (1.2 miles) one-way to a small fishing lake. The lake has a rustic campsite and is popular among individuals wanting to visit a quiet secluded fishing lake.

Kate Lake Trail (Map 38/D7) 🔺 🚶 🐎 🐟

The trail to Kate Lake is an extension of the Sugar Mountain Trail, found about 5.5 km along the popular ATV trail. The Kate extension is 2.5 km (1.5 miles) one-way, and climbs steadily uphill through some boggy sections. The trail is well-marked and is often used by horses. Fishing can be very good at the lake.

Mark Berger Traverse (Map 30/G4) 🔺 🚶 🐟 🏕

A difficult 20 km (12.2 mile) route, the Mark Berger Traverse is mostly unmarked and leads along a series of alpine peaks and narrow ridges. The trail connects Twin Lakes and Monashee Lake Trails and can be reached from either the South or North Fork Forest Service Roads. The trail features great panoramic views and the chance to see wildlife including Grizzly Bears.

Monashee Lake Trail (Map 30/G5) 🔺 🚶 🐟 🏕

The Monashee Lake Trail begins near the end of the South Fork FSR and extends 5 km (3 miles) one-way, gaining 700 m (2,275 feet) to a beautiful mountain lake at 1,950 m (6,337 feet). The trail is marked by red diamonds and is best left to the experienced hiker. From the lake, it is possible to make a number of side trips including the Mark Berger Traverse (see above).

Monashee Provincial Park Trails (Map 38/G6)
🔺 🏕 🚶 🚵 🐎 🐟 🏕

This remote provincial park offers 24 km (7.4 miles) of multi-use trails through a pristine wilderness area. From the parking lot area north of Sugar Lake, the easy **Rainbow Falls Trail** leads 12 km/7.2 miles (4-5 hours) one-way to Spectrum Lake and the site of the first wilderness campsite. Many visitors use this campsite as a staging ground for day trips to the surrounding mountains and other lakes. Peters Lake, Mikes Lake and Fawn Lakes are other popular resting areas.

From Spectrum Lake, the trail system gets more difficult as you climb 4 km/ (3+ hours) to **Little Peters Lake** or 6 km to the south end of Peters Lake. There is an elevation gain of about 800 m (2,625 ft) to the bigger lake. From here there are several difficult alpine routes to explore. These trails traverse steep terrain, and should be left to the experienced backpacker only:

Margie Lake is found in the southeast portion of the park (east of our maps), about 8 km/ (2-3 hours) from Peters Lake. The gentle trail is one of the easier to follow in the area.

Mount Fosthall is the prominent peak to the south. To access the mountain requires a 1000 m (3,281 ft) climb over 7-9 km. Allow at least 6 hours since climbing gear is recommended.

South Caribou Pass must be climbed on the first leg of the difficult route to Mount Fosthall. Due to the distance involved, most day hikers enjoy the views from the pass before returning to Peters Lake. The open ridges can easily be extended into a 9-11 km (8-10 hour) route.

Valley of the Moon is another enticing area of Monashee. The trail into the valley climbs 600-700 m (2,000 ft) over 7-9 km. Allow 6-7 hours to complete this moderate route.

Pinnacles Lake Trail (Map 30/G5)

One of several trails extending off the South Fork FSR and into the Pinnacles, you will cover 9 km (5.5 miles) getting to the lake and back. Expect to take about five hours on this difficult hike with an elevation gain of 450 m (1,463 feet) to the lake. The beautiful sub-alpine lake is at 1,900 m (6,175 feet) and is surrounded by slides and steep hills ideal for mountain climbing.

Rainbow Falls Trail (Map 38/D6)

From the north end of Sugar Lake, this trail extends 12 km/7.2 miles (4-5 hours) one-way past Rainbow Falls to Spectrum Lake in Monashee Provincial Park. It is possible to make it to the lake in a day, but it is a trip best spread out over two or three days. The trail leads along Spectrum Creek and is the main access route in to this remote wilderness park. Once you reach the park, many backcountry fishing and camping opportunities await you.

Rottacker Lake Trail (Map 30/E1)

The trail to Rottacker Lake is a rough, poorly maintained 3 km (1.8 miles) one-way slog along Sitkum Creek. At the lake, you will find a rustic campsite and good fishing. The trailhead is at 20 km (12.2 miles) on the Kate-Sitkum FSR.

Sitkum Lake Trail (Maps 30/E1, 38/F7)

The trailhead to this scenic sub-alpine hike is found 12 km (7.3 miles) from the junction of Kate Creek FSR and Sitkum Creek. The trail extends 8 km (4.9 miles) to Twin Peaks Lake and Sitkum Lake with a possible side trip to Goat Mountain. The trail is steep and rocky in places and traverses through Grizzly Bear country.

Sugar Mountain Trail (Map 38/C7)

Sugar Mountain Trail is a steep 14 km/8.5 mile (6 hour) return trek along a 4wd access road. The route is popular with ATV riders and bikers despite the 900 m (2,925 feet) elevation gain to the forestry lookout at 2,200 m (7,150 feet). The distance of hike depends on how far you dare to drive on the deteriorating road. Once you reach the top, you will be rewarded with spectacular views of rugged alpine peaks and forested valley bottoms.

Twin Lakes Trail (Map 30/G3)

The Twin Lakes Trailhead is found on a deteriorating 4wd road off the North Severside FSR. The trail is a steady 6 km (3.7 mile) one-way climb to the lakes at 2,250 m (7,313 feet) gaining 500 m (1,625 feet) along the way. From the lakes, it is possible to hike the Mark Berger Traverse to Monashee Lake and beyond.

Vista Pass Trail (Map 30/G6)

This is a steep, difficult hike along a well-marked trail to the pass found on the South Pinnacles Ridge. You will climb 700 m (2,275 feet) over 6 km (3.7 mile) one-way but there are opportunities to continue south into the Barnes Creek Drainage. The trailhead to Vista Pass is located on a spur road extending along Railroad Creek.

North Okanagan/Shuswap Trails

This section covers the extensive network of trails that surround the Adams and Shuswap Lakes to the north of the Okanagan Valley. Given the varying topography and ecosystems of this region, there are many different types of trails to explore.

Albas (Celesta) Falls Trail (Map 53/A6)

Within Albas Provincial Park, this 3 km (1.8 miles/45 minute) trail leads from the shores of the Shuswap Lake up both sides of Celista Creek past five gorgeous waterfalls as well as a waterwheel and flume. The park is accessed off the Ross Creek FSR or by boat.

Aylmer Lake Trail (Map 43/C7)

From top of the switchback on Neskonlith Lake Road, an old road leads 9.5 km/5.8miles (3 hours) through a dry hillside and then a second growth forest to this Aylmer Lake hike. The marshy lake is not open to fishing, as it is used to rear brown trout for stocking elsewhere. Also in the area are a series of interconnecting cross-country trails through open rolling terrain. During the early summer the Neskonlith Meadows are teaming with wildflowers. Ask permission to cross the Indian Reserve before heading out.

Bastion Cliffs & Mountain Trail (Map 44/D7)

If you are interested in a challenging hike/mountain bike, try this 36 km (22 mile (day+) return trek from the parking lot near the junction of the Sunnybrae-Canoe Point Road and the Bastion Mountain Road. The route takes you along an old logging road then a trail near the top of the mountain for a good view of Shuswap Lake. Hikers often drive/ATV up the road to reduce the length of the hike as well as decrease the 800 m (2,600 feet) of elevation gain. The Bastion Cliffs are a short 1 km (0.6 miles) side trip. A scenic trail leads from the road to the edge of the cliffs for a great view of Shuswap Lake and the surrounding mountains. Be forewarned that the trail may be closed during fire season.

Blind Bay Trail (Map 44/C6)

This multi-use trail begins from the end of Hautala Road near Little White Lake and extends 8 km (4.9 miles/3 hours) to Blind Bay and back. The trail climbs steadily to the crest of the hill before descending sharply down to Blind Bay and Horse Beach.

Boulder Mountain Trails (Map 46/E3)

Best known as a snowmobile destination, the Boulder Mountain trails are becoming popular with mountain bikers during the off-season. The trails are named and marked and there is a warm-up hut for snowmobilers.

Bryden–Pement Lakes Trail (Map 35/G1)

Depending on the distance you can drive up the Charcoal Creek FSR branch road, there are about 7 km/4.3 miles (1.5 hours) of easy trails leading along Blanc Creek to two small lakes. Found in the rolling Ptarmigan Hills, the multi-use trail system makes a fine overnight fishing destination.

Caribou Lake Trail (Map 46/A5)

From the end of the rough Yard Creek FSR (4wd recommended), a 3 km/1.8 mile (45 minute) loop trail takes you past a beautiful sub-alpine lake set in the mountains below Mount Griffin. The trail is popular with hikers, but mountain bikers and horseback riders use the trail on occasion. There are scenic views of Shuswap Lake as well as a chance to cast a line or camp in a remote wilderness setting.

Cinnemousun Narrows (Map 45/A3)

The narrows are a popular gathering spot for houseboaters. People wanting to take an easy stroll along the shores Shuswap Lake can try exploring the undeveloped trails on both sides of the narrows.

Cooke Creek Trail (Map 37/D4) 🚶 📖 🥾

The trailhead to this hike is found along the Enderby-Mabel Lake Road at the Cooke Creek Forest Service Site. It is a 3 km (1.8 mile (1 hour) easy walk along the Shuswap River and Cooke Creek through an interpretive forest and hatchery.

Copper Island Trails (Map 44/A5) 🚶 🥾

This island, which is part of the Shuswap Lake Provincial Park, receives heavy use in the summer by boaters on the big lake. Circling the island is a scenic 2.8 km (4.9 miles) trail. Alternatively, it is possible to climb to the summit (at 488 m/1,586 feet). The attraction to the island is not only the sheltered waters and beaches but also the wide variety of plant life and animals that frequent the island.

Cotton Belt Trail (Map 53/C1) 🚶 🥾

This hard to follow trail gets its name from the old Cotton Belt Mine on Mount Grace. A moderate 12.8 km (7.8 mile (5 hour) trail leads from the valley bottom to the alpine meadows and is best tackled in July–October. At the old mine, you can explore the remains of several mine shafts and old cabins. Further along the alpine meadows are filled with wildflowers and are dotted with small lakes. The trailhead is marked by a sign on a stump together with blue markers in nearby trees. Be cautious of Grizzly Bears thst frequent the area.

Crowfoot Mountain Trail (Map 44/E2)

🚶 🚴 🎿 🛷 👤 🥾

This trail, which is accessed by the Garland Road, leads 16 km (9.7 miles/8 hours) along an old road to the endless alpine meadows of Cottonwood and Mobley Mountains. The trail follows the remains of the road built in the 1800s gaining 1,750 m (5,688 feet) in elevation along the way. The Mag Fire in 1967 helped open the area to off-road vehicles, who along with hikers and mountain bikers enjoy exploring the area in the summer months. In the winter, about 30 km (18 miles) of trails are groomed for snowmobiling and there is a wonderful chalet to help take the winter chill off. The trail network is also accessible via the Ross Creek Road near Magna Bay.

Cummins Lake Trail (Map 45/F6)

🏕 🚶 🐴 🎿 🚴 👤 🎣 🥾 🎿

The trailhead to this easy 4 km/2.4 mile hike is found off the rough southern branch road of the Yard Creek FSR. The trail, which is used by hikers, bikers and horseback riders, leads along a rough road and trail to a shallow sub-alpine lake where fishing and camping is available. From the lake, it is possible to access the Owlhead Snowmobile Club cabin.

Eagle River Nature Park (Map 45/D5) 🚶 🚴 📖 🐟 🥾

Five flat, easy nature trails lead through a beautiful old growth forest along the Eagle River and Yard Creek. In total there are 10 km (6 miles) of trails to explore. The attraction to the park is the wildflowers, giant cedar trees and salmon spawning in the fall.

Eagle Pass Trail (Map 46/A2) 🚶

An old forestry lookout can be accessed along a steep, difficult 5 km/3 mile (3 hour) trail. The trail winds up the timbered slope, eventually breaking out on the seemingly endless alpine. It is possible to follow an undefined route northeast to Mount Copeland (see below). Given the elevation (2,350 m/7,638 feet), the best time to hike the trail is in mid-summer in order to avoid snow. The trailhead is found 8.8 km (5.4 miles) along the Crazy Creek FSR. Beware of Grizzly Bears.

Enderby Cliffs Trail (Maps 36/G4, 37/A3) 🏕 🚶 🥾

Also known as the Brash-Allan Route, a steep strenuous 10 km/6 mile (5 hour) hike starts at the end of Brash-Allan Road. To locate the trailhead, walk to the driveway to the right and walk through the gap in the white fence marked with ribbons. Since this is private property, please ask permission before crossing. An alternative route is to start near the end of McNabb Road next to the old white barn and hike 6 km (3.6 miles/3 hours) to the base of the cliffs. Once at the base of the cliffs, you can scramble to the top of the highest and most spectacular

basalt cliffs in the Okanagan region. In addition to the magnificent view of the Shuswap Valley, the area is home to a beautiful meadow with wildflowers in June. It is also possible to continue on to Reeves Lake where rustic camping is possible.

Estekwalan Mountain Trail (Map 35/E6)

🚶 🐴 🎿 📖 🥾 🎿

From the Falkland Landfill Road, this is a difficult 11 km/10.7 mile (5 hour) trail gaining 550 m (1,788 feet) to the height of land at 1,550 m (5,038 feet). The lower sections of the trail are well developed, but scrambling is required to reach the ridge and open alpine. The route may be longer depending on whether you can drive to the trailhead.

Fly Hill Trails (Map 36/A1) 🚶 🚴 🎿 🥾 🎿

West of Salmon Arm, Fly Hill has over 70 km (42 miles) of snowmobile trails forming three loops along old roads. After the snow is gone, you can take a short walk along the barren ridge to enjoy a view of Salmon Arm and the wildflowers or you can try mountain biking the extensive road network. Access to the hill from Salmon Arm is via the Fly Hill FSR or from the southwest via the Charcoal Creek FSR.

Gorge Creek Trail (Map 45/F3) 🚶 🥾

From the Last Spike Monument off Highway 1, an easy 2 km/1.2 mile (1 hour) trail leads along both sides of Craigflower (Gorge) Creek through an old growth forest and past three small falls. The scenic trail is well-marked and is a good choice for a family outing.

Hiren Creek Trail (Map 46/D1) 🚶 🐴 🚴 🐟 🥾

From the gate on the Copeland Mine Road, it is a 20 km (6-7 hour) moderate hike/bike along an old mine road that accessed the sub-alpine terrain and several mountain lakes. Once you reach the mine site, you can explore the old workings or continue up the pass to Hiren Lakes (north of the maps). From the gate, the route climbs 525 m (1,720 ft).

Hunakwa Lake Trail (Map 53/B7) 🚶 🐟 🥾

From Anstey Beach on the Anstey Arm of Shuswap Lake, it is possible to hike to Hunakwa Lake. The remote trail branches from the Wright Lake Trail (see below) and is well known for its wildlife.

Hunter's Range Area (Map 37/A4) 🚶 🎿 🥾 🎿

North of Ashton Creek off the Watershed Road or the Brash Creek Road, this is a popular snowmobile area following an old sub-alpine road network. With over 240 km (146 miles) of trails, there is a lot to see and do up there. During the summer, this high elevation area is accessible by vehicle and provides hiking on undeveloped trails with spectacular displays of wildflowers.

Joss Mountain Trail (Map 46/C7) 🚶 👤 🥾

This trail can be reached by a 4wd road from the North Shuswap Forest Service Road, the roads south of Three Valley Gap or the Derry Creek Road. The trail leads to fabulous views and the old Dominion Lookout on Joss Mountain at 2,385 m (7,751 feet). From there, it is possible to traverse the scenic ridge south to the Tsuius Mountain trail system. Beware of Grizzly Bears in the area.

Kingfisher Interpretive Centre (Map 37/E4) 🚶 🥾

One of the most biodiverse areas in the province, the 30 km (18.3 mile) stretch along the Shuswap River east of Enderby is a transition area between the dry area of the North Okanagan and the wet belt of the Shuswap. Over the past 15 years, the Kingfisher Environmental Interpretive Centre has evolved from a community-run hatchery to a year-round interpretive centre with an easy 1.5 km (0.9 mile) hiking trail near the hatchery.

Larch Hills Trail Network (Map 36/F1)

🚶 🐴 🚴 🎿 🥾 🎿

Located on the Larch Hills FSR southeast of Salmon Arm, Larch Hills has 150 km (91.5 miles) of clearly marked cross-country ski trails. In the spring, the trail network becomes popular with hikers, horseback riders

and mountain bikers. Detailed maps of the area are available from the Forest Service.

Little Mountain Park (Map 36/C1)
In the heart of Salmon Arm, this popular area offers 8 km (4.9 miles) of easy hiking trails that are set in a figure 8 leading to the top of Little Mountain. The trail network is also used by joggers, mountain bikers and cross-country skiers and offers an excellent view of Salmon Arm. The trails are accessed from the east end of Okanagan Avenue or from 10th Avenue S.E.

Margaret Falls Trail (Map 44/E7)
From Herald Provincial Park, this easy 1 km (.6 mile) (15 minute) walk takes you through a creek draw (Reinecker Gorge) with old growth cedar and moss covered canyon walls to a beautiful cascading waterfall. The trail is very popular and well-maintained (wheelchair access). If you want to get away from the crowds, try exploring the easy walking trails that meander along the creek to the Shuswap Lake and along the beach through Herald Park.

Mount Copeland–Eagle Pass Mountain Trail (Map 46/D1-A2)
This is a very difficult 25 km/15 mile (3 day) one-way route from Mount Copeland to the Crazy Creek FSR. You will need a compass and topographic maps as well as good route finding skills to follow the ridges and valleys between Hiren Creek and Eagle Pass Mountain. You will also require a vehicle at each end of the trail.

Mount Begbie Trail (Map 46/G5)
From Highway 23 south of Revelstoke, this 12 km/7.3 mile (5+ hour) steep difficult hike brings you from the valley bottom to the foot of a glacier. Experienced mountaineers can continue up to the 2,732 m (8,965 ft) summit or explore the alpine lakes in the area. Mountain bikers and horseback riders can use the lower section of the trail.

Mount Ida Trail (Map 36/D3)
This is a popular hiking area south of Salmon Arm. The main trail starts from the Mount Ida FSR (825 Road) and leads 13 km/7.9 mile (6 hour) return to the two scenic viewpoints. The moderate trail is fairly steep and requires climbing 1,100 m (3,575 feet) in elevation to the top at 1,500 m (4,875 feet). To reduce the hike to 6 km (3.6 miles/2 hours) return, it is possible to drive the 4wd road to a saddle set below the two summits. From the top, you will get an excellent view of the surrounding valley and mountains. Mountain bikers should note that the West Peak Trail is not rideable while the steep demanding East Peak Trail may require some dismounting.

Mount Fowler (Map 44/G1)
Depending on how far you can drive up the roads from the Ross Creek-Ruckle Point FSR, it is about a 10 km/6.1 mile (3 hour) trek to the summit of Mount Fowler. From the Y in the road, an undeveloped trail leads through alpine meadows and beautiful wildflowers to the summit. It is possible to continue down to Crowfoot Mountain trails. In the winter, snowmobilers, who maintain an emergency hut at the summit, use the area.

Mount Mara Lookout (Map 37/C1)
Part of the Owlhead Snowmobile system, in summer a 6 km/3.6 mile (3 hour) moderate hike leads along the deteriorating Mount Mara Road (4wd road) to the alpine and lookout at 2,200 m (7,150 feet). It is possible to short cut along a steep old horse trail near the top. An alternative route is to hike the 16 km/9.9 mile (8 hour) trail south from the end of the Owl Creek FSR. This route requires a very steep climb near the summit, where wildflowers dot the alpine meadows.

Notch Hills Falls Trail (Map 44/A6)
South of Sorrento off Taylor Road, there is a 1.5 km (20 minute) hike from a parking lot of a private residence (1536 Taylor Road) to the falls. Please ask permission from the private landowner to use the trail. The best time to visit the falls is during the spring run-off when McEwan Creek is at its highest.

Prudential Trail (Map 36/E2)
At the end of 10th Ave in Salmon Arm, an enjoyable 14.5 km (8.8 mile) mountain bike loop begins. This moderate trail offers it all; rocks, roots, streams and, of course, mud!

Pukeashun Trail (Map 52/C6)
From the Kwikoit Creek FSR, this 13 km/7.9 mile (4 hour) moderate hike takes you to the open meadows of a seemingly endless alpine. The area is popular with horseback riders, guide outfitters and, in winter, snowmobilers.

Quaaout Lodge Trails (Map 43/D6)
Along the northern shores of Little Shuswap Lake, the Quaaout Lodge maintains 4 km (2.4 miles) of nature trails ideal for a family outing. Mountain bikers as well as cross-country skiers can use the trails.

Queest Mountain Trail (Map 45/C3)
The attraction to this area is the sub-alpine meadows with wildflowers in July, the excellent view and the wilderness camping at the rustic campsite at the top. The area is also a popular handgliding area. For hikers and bikers, the route follows a 4wd road/trail for about 9 km/5.5 miles (2.5 hours) up to the lookout at 2,085 m (6,776 feet). In the winter, the area offers a series of groomed snowmobile trails along old roads leading to the alpine as well as a chalet.

Roderick Haig-Brown Park (Map 43/E5)
Within the provincial park are 26 km (15.9 miles) of well-developed trails, mostly along both sides of Adams River from Adams Lake to the Shuswap Lake. The trails are generally flat and easy to follow. The area is famous for its Sockeye Salmon spawning beginning in October with the peak years being every 4 years (2006, 2010, etc.). In the winter, beginner to intermediate cross-country skiers can ski 14 km (8.5 miles) from the river mouth to the gorge and back. More advanced skiers can travel 18 km (11 miles) return from the river mouth to the south end of Adams Lake.

The **Bear Creek Flume** Trail is an 8.5 km5.2 mile (3 hour) moderate side trail that follows a good trail up Bear Creek and out of the park. The trail is part of an 18 km (4.9 miles) long log flume built in 1912 by the Adam River Logging Company used to transport logs from the Bear Valley to the river below.

Ross Creek Trail (Map 44/E2)
From the wash out on Ross Creek FSR, it is possible to follow the old road network in the area. The roads provide many kilometres of hiking and biking/ATV extending as far east as Mount Fowler or Ruckle Point. For a one-way trip, leave a second vehicle on the Rock Creek-Ruckle Point Road.

Salmon Arm Nature Trails (Map 36/C2)
From the Salmon Arm Wharf, two short boardwalks, totaling 1.5 km (0.9 miles) in length, lead through marshland. The trails are ideal for waterfowl viewing and leads to a viewing platform overlooking Christmas Island on Shuswap Lake. This area is part of a Nature Enhancement Preserve.

Seymour Lookout Trail (Map 53/C3) 🚶 🚴
To reach this former forestry lookout requires a steep, difficult 3.8 km/2.3 mile (2 hour) one-way grunt up a poorly maintained trail through the sub-alpine. The trailhead is found at the 66 km marker on the Ratchford Creek FSR.

Skimilkin Lake Trail (Map 44/A7) 🚶 🚴 🛶 ⛷
There are 15 km (9.2 miles) of unmaintained cross-country skiing trails surrounding Skimilkin Lake and connect with the Fly Hill Snowmobile Trails to the south. During the summer, the trails provide an opportunity for an easy walk through a gently sloping landscape. The Forest Service campsite at the lake provides access to the trails.

Skmana Lake Trail (Map 43/C6) 🚶 🚴 🛶 ⛷
At Skmana Lake off the Loakin-Bear Creek Road, there are 10 km (6.1 miles) of groomed cross-country ski trails. During the off-season, the trails offer a stroll or mountain bike ride around the marshy lake that provides the ideal setting for wildlife viewing.

Spring Falls Trail (Map 36/G3) 🚶 🚴
At the end of Garrett Road is a private homestead that provides access to this is a 6 km/3.6 mile (2 hour) moderate hike. Please ask permission before crossing the private property, which leads to Lambert Creek and a cascading waterfall. Since the springs dry up in the summer, it is best to try the hike during spring run-off.

Swanson-Rose Mountain Trail (Map 36/C7) 🚶 🐎 🚴 ⛷
The trailhead to this well-marked 10 km/6.1 mile (4 hour) hike is found at the end of Camberlaine Road. It is considered an easy climb despite gaining 300 m (975 feet) to the summit of two mountains. The main attraction to the area is the great view of Armstrong from the top.

Tsuius Mountain Trails (Map 38/D2) ⛺ 🚶 ⛷
To access Tsuius Mountain at 2,490 m (8,093 feet), you can take any one of four trails. The most popular trail is the shortest; a 6 km (3.7 miles) one-way trip from a logging spur off the North Shuswap FSR past Mirror Lake gaining 900 metres (2,925 feet). The longest trail is a 16 km (9.8 mile) hike from Tsuius Creek Road along Paintbrush Ridge. This scenic route should take the better part of a day. When you reach the mountaintop, you will be rewarded with spectacular scenery and views of distant snowfields. Many hikers use Mirror Lake as a base camp for wilderness hikes north to Joss Mountain and Joss Pass.

White Lake Lookout Trail (Map 44/D5) 🚶 🚴 🛶 ⛷ 🎣
From Pari Road, a 3 km/1.8 mile (30 minute) easy hike leads up the cliffs at the north end of White Lake. The area has an abundance of wildflowers and wildlife as well as a good view of the Tappen Valley from the cliffs.

White Lake Trails (Map 44/E5) 🚶 🐎 🚴 🛶 🎣
The White Lake Trail begins at the Settle Road turnaround and leads 5 km/3 miles (2 hours) one-way along the southern shore of White Lake. The trail dissects a cedar and hemlock forest as well as an old burn before reaching the 5 km (3 mile) mark on the Bastion-White Lake FSR. The trail can be quite swampy and wet, especially during the spring. There are also a series of ski trails at the east end of the lake to explore.

Wright Lake Trail (Map 53/B7) 🚶 🎣 ⛷
From Anstey Beach on the Anstey Arm of Shuswap Lake, it is possible to hike 6 km/3.6 miles (1.5 hours) to Wright Lake, which is noted for its good fishing. The trail, which follows an old road through an old growth hemlock forest, begins on the south side of Wright Creek. Also in the area is the Hunakwa Lake Trail. Both routes provide access to good fishing lakes as well as plenty of opportunities to see wildlife.

Okanagan Valley Trails

Surrounding the major centres of Kelowna, Penticton and Vernon are a variety of trails ranging from steep difficult climbs to the tops of a mountain to easy strolls next to Okanagan Lake. This is the heart of the Okanagan and it can get hot here in the summer. Trail users should always bring along plenty of water. Please note some of the trailheads are found on city roads too small to mark on our maps. It is advised to pick up a detailed street map of each centre before venturing out.

Apex Mountain Resort (Map 10/G7) 🚶 🚴 ⛷
There's a lot of hiking/biking to be had at this resort. For the ambitious, it is possible to walk up to the top of Apex on the gentle slope of **Grandfather's Run**. This route features breathtaking scenery and meadows of alpine flowers. If you're feeling lazy, take the lift to the top and walk down. There are also a number of trails in the area for biking, ranging from easy (Scout Cabin Trail, Powerline Road) to challenging (Orange Trail, Apex Mountain Trail).

Bear Creek Park (Map 19/G3) 🚶
In Bear Creek Park north of Kelowna, you will find 23 km (14 miles) of well-marked hiking trails. The trails are found on both sides of Lambly (Bear) Creek canyon and along the shores of Okanagan Lake. Bridges, cleared trails and steps help make the trails easier to walk despite the moderate climb required.

Bella Vista Trails (Map 28/B4) 🚶 🚴
The entrance to this area is found along Bella Vista Road west of Vernon. Some of the trails are hikable, but the primary users are bikers who are looking to get onto trails like **The Race Course** and **Matt's Dust**.

Big White Mountain (Map 21/B7) 🚶 🧗 ⛷
After the skiing season, Big White Mountain at 2,315 m (7,524 feet) becomes a fine hiking destination. It is possible to climb 6 km/3.6 miles (3 hours) return from the parking lot to the top or, if you prefer, take the chair lift up. Once you reach the top, you can enjoy the excellent views, rock climbing opportunities and the alpine flowers (in August). The hiking season runs from mid-July to late September.

Black Knight Mountain Trail (Map 20/C4) 🚶 🚴 🏍 ⛷
To reach this forestry lookout at 1,280 m (4,160 feet), you can either hike, mountain bike or drive to the top. It is about a 6 km/3.6 mile (2 hour) return trip from Pyman Road. Like most other lookouts, the view of the surrounding country is fabulous. Mountain bikers often descend along the challenging single track trail found near the top.

Blue Grouse Mountain Trail (Map 19/G2) 🚶 🚴 🏍 ⛷
This is another hike to the top of an Okanagan mountain, which can also be biked or driven by a 4wd vehicle. If you choose to hike, it is 13 km/7.9 miles (4 hours) return from the Grouse Mountain No 1 sign to the top at 1,250 m (4,063 feet). Once you reach the top, there is an excellent view of Okanagan Lake and Kelowna. This area is also a popular motorbike area.

Blue Mountain Trail (Map 11/C5) 🚶 🚴 🏍 ⛷
To the west of Penticton, it is possible to hike or mountain bike about 18 km (11 miles) return along an old access road to the transmitter and summit of Blue Mountain. At 1,400 m (4,550 feet), the view is excellent. The trailhead is located by driving along Bartlett Road to Rifle Range Road. Give yourself a few hours on bike, or the better part of a day on foot.

Bluenose Mountain Trail (Map 28/G5) 🚶 ⛷
This is a 10 km/6.1 mile (2 hour) scramble from the signed trailhead on Aberdeen Lake Road. The trail takes you steadily upward through a timbered slope to one of two peaks gaining 200 m (650 feet) along the way. From the summits at 1,240 m (4,030 feet), there is a good view of the Coldstream Valley. Please note that there are actually three peaks but the middle peak is privately owned.

Boucherie Mountain (Map 19/F5) 🚶 📷

To reach the top of this mountain at 762 m (2,477 feet) in elevation, simply drive along Boucherie Road to the base of the mountain. From the road it is a 5 km (3 miles) return scramble (there is no formal route) to the top where there is an the excellent view of Kelowna.

BX Creek & Falls Trail (Map 28/E3) 🚶 🚵 📷

The BX Creek Canyon is a melt-water channel from the last ice age. It has carved through layers of the earth revealing glimpses into the Okanagan Valley's formation. From Tillicum Road, just off Silver Star Road, the trail leads you to a viewpoint overlooking the spectacular falls. You can also branch off and follow a steep, short trail that takes you to the bottom of the falls. The southern trailhead is located at the bottom of the switchbacks on Star Road. Also in the area is the Grey Canal Trail (see below).

Camel Hump Trail (Map 29/D4) 🚶 📷

From the Creighton Valley Road, take the road marked "R.V. Schmidt Channel" and follow it past Clier Lake to the signed trailhead. From there, the hike leads 6 km/3.6 miles (3 hours) on a well-developed trail up the gently sloping southern side of The Hump. The elevation gain is 300 m (975 feet) to the summit at 1,331 m (4,326 feet) where there is an outstanding view of the Monashee Mountains.

Carrot Mountain (Map 19/D4) 🚶 🚵 📷

Carrot Mountain is reached by hiking along Smith Creek Road from the gate and then picking a place to scramble up the hillside to the top of the mountain. Once you reach the top at 1,525 m (4,956 feet), you will be rewarded with a view of the McDougall Creek and Powers Creek Valleys. An alternative route is to scrabble up the mountain from the road paralleling McDougall Creek.

Cougar Canyon Trail (Map 28/C6) 🚶 🚵 📷

From just north of Oyama, the trail extends 10 km/6 miles (3 hours) along the powerline to a scenic canyon for a spectacular view of Kalamalka Lake. The trail system can also be accessed from the Cosens Bay Trail in Kalamalka Provincial Park. This route is 18 km (11 miles/5 hour) long and climbs 280 m (910 feet). It is best tackled in the spring when the wildflowers are blooming and the heat of the summer has not set in. The powerline is very popular with mountain bikers.

Damer Lake Trail (Map 28/D6) 🚶 📷

From the junction at Oyama Lake Road, this 12 km/7.3 mile (4 hour) easy walk takes you along a deteriorating road to Damer Lake before the trail branches left to the transmitter and lookout. From the lookout, there is an impressive view of the north Okanagan Valley. Overall the elevation gain is 150 m (488 feet).

Deninson Lake Trail (Map 29/F6) ⛺ 🚶 🎣

This easy 8 km/4.9 mile (4 hour) trail begins on the Bonneau FSR before leading up an old road and then a well-marked trail to the lake. The elevation gain is 200 m (650 feet) to the lake at 1,500 m (4,875 feet), where rustic camping and fishing are possible.

Dixon Dam (Map 28/F2) 🚵

Found off the Silver Star and Tillicum Roads, the bike route around Dixon Dam offers a moderate 8 km (4.9 mile) loop. From Dixon Dam Road, you climb along the steep road to above the dam. From here a technical single track trail will eventually lead you back to the gravel road.

Eagle Rock Viewpoint Trail (Map 28/E1) 🚵 📷

This mountain bike trail starts at the Bobslide Park north of Vernon on Highway 97. From the parking lot, follow the 4wd road heading north and then follow the trail marked with flagging tape. This difficult trail climbs over 950 metres (3,088 feet) up to Proctor Lake. From the lake, you then continue down towards Eagle Rock (and the viewpoint). In all, the loop will cover 28 km (17 miles) back to the parking lot. Several well-defined side trails south of Proctor Lake are highly recommended.

Ellis Creek Demo Forest Trails (Map 12/A6) 🚶 🚵 📷

The Ellis Creek Demonstration Forest is a 2,000 hectare patch of woods to the east of Penticton on the north banks of Ellis Creek. There are still telltale signs of the wildfire that burned through most of the area in 1994. **Canyon View Interpretative Trail** is a 1.5 km (0.9 mile) easy loop offering views of Ellis Canyon and Penticton. The **Ellis Ridge Trail** extends 4 km (2.4 miles) one-way on the southern side of Carmi Road between the Canyon View Trail and the Carmi Cross-Country Ski Trail parking lot. If you start from the north parking lot, you will actually lose 165 m in elevation while enjoying the amazing views and the remnants of the forest fire. Mountain bikers should expect a tough technical ride. The Carmi Ski Trails also offer 24 km (14.6 miles) of marked but often wet trails (follow the blue stakes).

Ellison Park Trails (Map 28/A6) 🚶 📷

Ellison Provincial Park is home to several small trails that make up 6 km (3.6 miles) of easy walking trails. The nature loop is a scenic trail that leads up through an open hill dotted with Ponderosa Pine trees to grassy openings overlooking Okanagan Lake. Shorter trails lead down to the beaches and protected bays of the big lake.

Flamingo Flats Trail (Map 20/A6) 🚵

Located near the Lower South Slopes Trails, this trail starts at a power station at the end of Stewart Road East. Climb the gravel road for about 6 km (3.6 miles), staying right at the forks. The road ends at Flamingo Flats where a pink flamingo (at least it used to be pink) is stuck in the ground in a clearing. Climb the single track trail going up and to the right. After a short climb, it's all downhill to the power station with lots of twisty single track and some fast sandy sections. There are many trail options on the way down, about 15 km (9 miles) total.

Gallagher's (Scenic) Canyon Trail (Map 20/B5) 🚶 🚵 📷

Southeast of Kelowna, at the end of Field Road, there are a series of trails along Gallagher's Canyon and the Mission Creek Canyon. The scenic trails range in length from 3 to 13 km (1.8–7.9 miles) and are used by both hikers and bikers.

Giant's Head Mountain Trail (Map 11/D3) 🚶 🧗

To reach the top of this landmark above the city of Summerland, it is a 2 km/1.2 mile (1 hour) one-way hike from the gate at the end of Milne Road. When you reach the summit at 845 metres (2,772 feet), a number of short easy walks are available to enjoy the view of Summerland and Okanagan Lake. Also found at the summit is a time capsule from 1967 and a sundial.

Kettle Valley Railway (Maps 3, 5, 8, 9, 10 11, 12, 16, 18, 19, 20)

The historic Kettle Valley Railway (KVR) was opened in 1915 to link most of southern BC's towns. Due to a variety of factors (avalanches through the Coquihalla pass, as well as new road and rail routes to Vancouver), the railway was ultimately abandoned. By June 1990, all the tracks had been removed (except for a short section that remains active Summerland), and the route was rediscovered by hikers, mountain bikers, cross-country skiers and snowmobilers. After years of lobbying the trail was given official trail status, and shortly thereafter, became the backbone of the Trans Canada Trail Route through BC. For detailed information on the whole route, be sure to pick up a copy of The Trans Canada Trail, The British Columbia Route.

Today, a 550 km (335 mile) route extends from Hope to Midway, but there are few spur routes to Osoyoos, Merritt and Copper Mountain south of Princeton. Most people who do the whole route start in Midway and head west, as the climbs are generally less steep this way. Highlights include the **Myra Canyon**, the **Adra** and **Othello Tunnel** areas as well as the numerous bridges, trestles and tunnels along the route. The gentle grade (maximum 2.2% grade) and wide tracks make most of the route easy to use, especially for cyclists. There are still a few sections that are impassable, due to access issues or washouts, but there have been many major improvements since the last update of this mapbook. The following is a summary of the various sections. People interested in day trips will find additional write-ups throughout this section of the book.

Carmi Subdivision (Maps 5, 11, 12, 19, 20) extends 215 km (131 miles) from Midway to Penticton. If you are cycling, give yourself at least two days, and more likely three or four, to explore this wilderness route. This section of the KVR slowly climbs 600 m (1950 feet) over 125 km (76 miles), taking you from the dry range country of Midway to the forested wilderness surrounding McCulloch. After two days of non-stop climbing, you will be glad when the trail levels out and begins one of it's steepest descents (or ascents, if you're heading east) from the old Carmi Station down into Penticton. In addition to the remote setting, this section takes you past the spectacular Myra Canyon, to the Adra Tunnel where views open out over the Okanagan Valley. This is certainly one of the most picturesque (and popular) sections of the railway. Watch out for loose sand between Chute Lake and Adra.

Osoyoos Subdivision (Maps 3, 11) extends 58 km (35 miles) from Penticton to Osoyoos. This is an almost perfectly flat stretch of the old railway that takes you through the rural orchards and vineyards and along Skaha and Osoyoos Lakes. Some sections of the route are quite difficult to follow so you may need to divert along the busy Highway 97. This section is easily ridden in a day.

Princeton Subdivision (Maps 8, 9, 10, 11, 16, 18) extends 175 km (107 miles) from Penticton to Brookmere. Give yourself three or four days to ride it. This section climbs 700 m (2275 feet) over 60 km (36 miles) from Penticton to Osprey Lake, which, at an average gradient of 1.1%, is the steepest climb you will face. Near Penticton, you will pass through the Penticton Indian Reserve, which is private land, before crossing the impressive Trout Creek Bridge. This is the highest bridge on the Kettle Valley Railway and it leads to Summerland where a 16 km (9.8 mile) section of track that remains in place. You can hike-a-bike along the track (not fun), catch a ride on the historic steam train that runs this section, or detour through Summerland (not a bad option, as you will pass Summerland Sweets on the way). From Osprey Lake, the route begins its descent into Princeton. This is another highlight of the trip, as the railway loops back and forth through the open grasslands above Princeton. The last 65 km (39.7 miles) to Brookmere climbs gently (400 m/1300 feet in total). This section is more remote, following the Tulameen River Canyon for part of the distance, and offers a more wilderness type setting.

Copper Mountain Subdivision (Map 9) extends 21 km (12.8 miles) south from Princeton. This trail climbs 300 m (975 feet) to the mine but it is mostly impassable due to private residences, and the deterioration of the trestles, tunnels and railbed. The section from Princeton to Smelter Lakes is mostly passable.

Merritt Subdivision (Maps 16, 24) extends 47 km (28.7 miles) from Brookmere to Merritt. The gentle decline combined with the scenic route through the Coldwater River Valley and Canyon makes this a pleasant route. Recent improvements to this section of the trail should encourage more KVR trail users to extend their adventure from Brookmere into Merritt.

Coquihalla Subdivision (Maps 7, 8, 16) extends 87 km (53 miles) from Brookmere to Hope. After a gentle climb to the Coquihalla Summit (100 m/325 feet over 30 km/18 miles), the route begins its most dramatic descent, losing 1000 m (3250 feet) over 50 km (30.5 miles) as it shaves off all the elevation it has gained as it drops down into Hope. Because this section is mostly downhill it can easily be done in a day, or split over two. Unfortunately, the old railbed is deteriorating rapidly or was destroyed or divided with the construction of the Coquihalla Highway, meaning much of this section has had to be re-routed. From the Coquihalla Summit to the old Jessica Station, the official route is to follow the Trans Mountain Pipeline Road (open to cyclists and hikers only). Past Jessica, the route is being developed by Trails BC, although there are still a few sections where you are still forced to travel on the Coquihalla Highway. With the tremendous improvements being undertaken, it will not be long before an entirely off-road route will link Hope with Brookmere. This is certainly one of the most impressive sections of the KVR, with its wild, mountainous setting and the spectacular Othello Tunnels. Visit www.backroadmapbooks.com for up to date information on this section.

Glenmore Trails (Map 20/A3) 🚴

Found north of Knox Mountain off of Clifton Road, a difficult series of mountain bike trails extends north to McKinley Landing. The trails actually start at the end of a small road (Grainger). Due to the number of options, it is easy to get confused. Expect a combination of old roads with technical single track trails and fabulous views.

Graystokes Protected Area (Map 21/C2) ⛺ 🚶 🐎 🚴 🛶 ⚓ 🎣 ⛷

Characterized by gently rolling hills, the Graystokes Plateau is dotted with a number of large and small lakes interwoven with an extensive complex of swamps, meandering streams and meadows. The plateau plays a vital role in providing mid and late summer range for wildlife once vegetation in the Okanagan Valley bottom has dried up. The area is a maze of old ATV trails. This area is now closed to motorized vehicles (except snowmobiles in winter), but the trails remain open to hikers, horseback riders and bikers looking to explore the area.

Grey Canal Historic Trail (Map 28/E3)

The Grey Canal Historic Trail is a 3.5 km (2.1 mile) trail that follows an old irrigation ditch and provides magnificent views over the entire North Okanagan Valley. The trailhead parking lot is on the west side of Silver Star Road, just below the Silver Star Foothills subdivision. It is also possible to link up with the BX Creek Trail (see above).

Greyback Mountain Trail (Map 12/B2)

The trailhead is located on the Greyback Road (R202 Road) and leads 3 km/1.8 miles (90 minutes) one-way to the top of Greyback Mountain at 2,134 m (6,936 feet). The trail is undeveloped and hard to follow as it dissects the timber and reaches the treeless alpine region where great views of the surrounding area are provided.

Hayman Lake Trail (Map 19/F3)

This is a 12 km/7.3 mile (4 hour) return hike up the McDougall Creek Valley following a well-marked trail then an old road network to the lake at 1,220 m (3,965 feet). The trail begins at the cattle guard on the Bartley Road. Once you are there, you can enjoy the fine view of Kelowna or try your luck fishing. If need be, you can drive up the deactivated McDougall Creek FSR to reduce the hiking distance.

Headwater Lakes Cross-Country Ski Area (Map 18/F6)

At the Headwaters Fishing Camp, which is easily accessed off the Peachland FSR, three easy cross-country ski trails dissect the Lodgepole pine forest around the lakes. **Headwaters Lake Trail** is a 4 km (2.4 miles) loop circling the main lake. **Camp Trail** is a 1 km (.6 miles) loop near the fish camp. **June Lake Trail** is a 6 km (3.6 mile) loop, which leads along the Headwaters Lake Trail but extends onto a smaller lake. Across the road several more challenging trails exist.

James Creek Falls Trail (Map 12/A2)

At about the 12 km mark on the Greyback Road, a signed trail leads 500 metres to a ridge overlooking the cascading falls. It is possible to scramble down the banks to the base of the falls if you so choose.

Kalamalka Lake Park (Map 28/D5)

This park offers several multi-use trails. The main trail, from the gate on Cosens Bay Road, leads 6 km/3.6 miles (1.5 hours) along the road to the beautiful sandy beach. Alternatively, you can try the 8 km/4.9 mile (2.5 hour) easy walk up the gently sloping road to Deep Lake, which will take you through Bear Valley and outside the park. Also, there is an extensive network of trails through the dry grassland of the park. Bring water, stay on the trails and watch for rattlesnakes. Mountain bikers usually explore the single track trails found east of the Coldstream Trail. These trails are quite physically demanding and fairly technical and not recommended for the beginner. **Rattlesnake Hill Trail** is considered the trail to ride with its tough climb and fast technical descent. Allow 1 hour to bike the 9.5 km (5.8 mile) loop, which starts at the Cosens Bay Gate.

Kalamoir Regional Park Trail (Map 19/D3)

Also known as Casa Loma, an easy 4.5 km round trip follows the western shores of Okanagan Lake. The trail begins just before Casa Loma Resort (hence the alternate name).

Kelowna Crags Trail (Map 19/D4)

You can hike or bike to the bottom of these 100 m high (325 feet) basalt cliffs, which are made up of several fascinating columns. A trail also leads up to the cliff top at the north end. Depending on where you left your car, it is about a 6.5 km (4 mile) walk. The view from the top, at about 760 metres (2500 feet), is beautiful.

Kettle Valley Railway: Adra and Little Tunnel (Map 11/F2)

If you want to explore the history of the Kettle Valley Railway, this 20.3 km (12.4 mile) section of abandoned track is a good choice. Many hikers/bikers begin where Smethurst Road meets the railgrade and work their way up to the two tunnels and some old rock ovens. Despite the gentle grade, you actually climb almost 900 metres (2,925 feet) with excellent views of Okanagan Lake along the way. The 484 metre (1,573 foot) long Adra Tunnel is sealed off because it is partly collapsed and full of water. Cyclists often continue past Chute Lake to the trestle bridges of the spectacular Myra Canyon.

Knox Mountain Trails (Map 19/G3)

Cyclists, hikers and joggers looking for a scenic but challenging trail close to downtown Kelowna use these trails. From the end of Ellis Street, the paved access road climbs 300 metres (975 feet) to the top. Enjoy the view before following any number of routes down. The options include going down the steep face, circling around the backside to **Paul's Tomb** or venturing down to Clifton Road where you can follow the roads back to the start.

Lacoma Lake Trail (Map 19/A3)

This moderate trail runs 11 km/6.7 miles (2 hours) from a parking lot at Clover Creek to the south. The first half of the trail follows an old road, and is bikeable. The second half of the trail was not designed for bikes, and has some steep sections as it climbs 200 metres (650 feet) to the lake.

McCulloch Ski Trails (Map 20/E7)

Located on the McCulloch Road (good 2wd access), there is a series of 45 km (27.5 miles) trails towards the north end of McCulloch Lake. The trails are well-marked by the local ski club and can be used by hikers and bikers in the summer.

McDougall Rim Trails (Map 19/E3)

The McDougall Rim Trail begins off the McDougall Creek Road and is an 18 km/11 mile (8 hour) circuit accessing Hayman Lake, Mount Swite and Carrot Mountain. For mountain bikers, the area offers a more strenuous and challenging 20 km/12 mile (3 hour) loop that ends on one of the best single track trails in the area. Follow Bartley Road out of Westbank to the McDougall Rim Trail sign. From there a grueling climb takes you up (over 600 m/1,950 feet) to Hayman Lake along a 4wd road. Soon you will come upon a smooth single track and the glide back down.

Mission Creek Regional Park Trails (Map 20/A5)

Located on Springfield Road east of the Orchard Park Mall in Kelowna is a series of easy, well developed trails. A map at the entrance distinguishes which trails are open to mountain biking.

Mount Brent Trail (Map 10/G5)

Although red diamonds mark the Mount Brent Trail, it can still be difficult to follow, as a number of cross trails (mostly cattle and game trails) intersect the main route. The trail leads approximately 4 km (2.4 miles) along the Shatford Creek Road (which can be driven with a 4wd vehicle), and the same distance again along a rustic trail to an old forestry lookout at 2,203 m (7,160 feet). The gently rolling alpine of the summit offers spectacular 360 degree views over the Okanagan Valley and the distant Coast and Monashee Mountains. The trailhead is difficult to find along a maze of backroads. Off Apex Road, turn right on the Shatford logging road (just past the 4 km marker). Watch for the old 8 km marker and turn left. Stay left at the next fork; the trailhead is in an old log landing 4.6 km (2.8 miles) past the 8 km marker.

Mount Campbell Trails (Map 11/F5) 🚵
One of the easiest mountain bike trail systems to access from Penticton, these trails are mostly moderate to difficult. There's a lot of uphill climbs and steep, fast descents on smooth trails.

Mount Dilworth Trail (Map 20/A4) 🥾 🎒
Just northeast of downtown Kelowna on the Longhill Road, a series of trails are found along Mount Dilworth. The trails lead across, up and over the mountain, which offers a fine view from the summit at 635 m (2,064 feet). Depending on your route, the hike can range from 3 to 10 km (1.8–6.1 miles) in length.

Mount Drought Trail (Map 19/D6) 🥾 🎒
The trailhead to this hike is found 2.5 km (1.5 miles) south of the Gorman Sawmill on Highway 97. The trail is 6 km/3.6 miles (2 hours) long, and starts out along an old road before leading right along the powerline and the scramble up hill to the summit. From the top, an excellent view of the Peachland area is offered.

Mount Nkwala Trail (Map 11/D4) 🥾 🎒
In Westbench northwest of Penticton, follow Sage Mesa Drive to the trailhead that is south of the Pine Hill Golf Club and near the sign saying "A West Bench Irrigation District". The steep trail to the top of the mountain at 1,020 m (3,315 feet) is 13 km (7.9 miles) long and is well-marked (blue stakes). From the summit, there is a panoramic view of the Okanagan Valley.

Myra-Bellevue Provincial Park Trails (Map 20/A6-C6)
🥾 🐎 🚵 🚣 🎒 🎿
This new provincial park was developed to protect some of Kelowna's most popular recreational areas, including the famed Myra Canyon. The canyon is one of the most popular and most spectacular sections of the Kettle Valley Railway (KVR). Trails include:

Angel Springs Trail leads 9 km/5.5 miles (3 hours) one-way to a steel trestle on the KVR that extends over Pooley Creek. The trail passes by an old cabin at 1 km and then reaches Angel Springs, which are not for soaking at 3 km (1.8 miles). To the springs, the trail is not well-marked. Past the springs, the trail is very faint and difficult to follow. A new interpretive trail to the springs is being built from Little White FSR (Fall 2003, most likely). Along the trail you will see a shallow cave at 4 km (2.4 miles) and eventually walk along Pooley Creek to the trestle. It is recommended that you have two vehicles unless you want to backtrack along the KVR and the Little White Road to the trailhead.

Lower South Slopes Trails were formerly known as the Crawford Trails. This is Kelowna's most popular and largest mountain bike trail network (with over 80km/49 miles of trails) offering a wide variety of terrain that can be enjoyed by all cyclists. The area is found south of Kelowna, at the end of Stewart Road East (follow the signs to the parking lot). The variety and difficulty varies from old roads to technical single tracks (for cyclists at least) and from gradual slopes to steep hills. Pick any old road to ride up and then enjoy the single track trails that take you back down. The powerlines make an excellent landmark.

Kettle Valley Railway: Myra Canyon is an easy 13km/7.9 mile hike or bike that takes you over 18 trestles and through two tunnels, with stunning views of both Myra Canyon (the railway snakes along both sides of the canyon) and the city of Kelowna. This section is accessed either by the Myra FSR or by the Little White FSR. It is easy to extend your hike/bike in either direction.

Nickel Plate Nordic Centre (Map 10/G7)
🏕 🥾 🚵 🚣 🐟 🎒 🎿
The Nordic Centre is home to 50 km (30.5 miles) of ski trails that provide excellent hiking/biking trails anytime after April. In particular, the **Okanagan Vista Trail** offers a nice 8 km (4.9 miles) loop whereas the **Burn Perimeter Trail** is a 12 km (7.2 mile) loop. Both trails are best hiked in the late summer, as they are boggy in the earlier part of the season. The **Twenty Mile Creek Trail** (see below) also begins here.

Okanagan Brigade Trail (Maps 18, 27) 🥾 🎒
Most of this historic trail has now disappeared but a few sections do exist for exploration. The best sections to explore lie on the west side of the Okanagan Lake and are marked by white rectangular pieces of metal and the occasional "HBC Trail" sign along Westside Road. Great views of Okanagan Lake and pictographs are found en route.

Okanagan Highlands Trail (Maps 20/E5, 12/C1, 11/G1)
🏕 🥾 🐟 🎒
This wilderness trail is made up of a series of trails from the Okanagan High Rim trailhead near Mission Creek to Chute Lake. It will eventually be connected with Okanagan Mountain Park. For now, the trail follows logging roads and existing trails south to McCulloch Lake, where it ventures southwest by Canyon Lake and over the Little White Mountain Ridge into Myra-Bellevue Provincial Park. The rugged route continues to Big Meadow Lake before connecting with Chute Lake. Although it is marked, it is not advisable to hike it unless you are with someone who knows the trail well. This trail is best left to experienced backcountry hikers since sections are very rough, and remote.

Okanagan High Rim Trail (Maps 20, 28) 🏕 🥾 🎒
This is a moderate backpacking trip (there is little elevation gain, but it is 50 km/30.5 miles long) on a well-marked trail from Highway 33 north to Cosens Bay along the east side of Okanagan Lake. The trail follows the mountain ridge above the lake and has many viewpoints of the valley. To hike the whole route will take two or three days. To reduce the length of the hike, you can find the trail at several access points. The most popular access points are Kalamalka Lake Park in the north or Philpot Road on Highway 33 in the south. No mountain bikes or horses are allowed on the trail system.

Okanagan Mountain Park (Maps 11, 19)
🏕 🥾 🚵 🐎 🐟 🎒
This wilderness park is accessed by the Lakeshore Road from the north, Chute Lake Road from the south or by boat to the west. Within the park, there are miles of interconnecting trails with the highlights including canyons, four mountain lakes, sandy beaches, six marine camping areas and wilderness lakes. Mountain biking is allowed on all trails, but horseback riding is restricted to the Divide Lake Trail North. Be sure to bring along plenty of water and your bug repellant.

Baker Lake Trail is a 2 km (1.2 mile) offshoot of the Frederickson Creek Trail. There is tenting and fishing at the lake.

Boulder Loop Trail is a 5 km (3 mile) trail that starts from the North Parking lot along Dead Horse Creek.

Divide Lake Trail is a 20 km (12.2 mile) hike following the old microwave road past Divide Lake. This trail is the only trail open to horseback riders and is the main route into the heart of the park from the north. It is very scenic in late May– early June because of the wildflowers along the trail as you approach the lake. From the lake, several trails lead south and west.

Fredrickson Creek Trail is a 4 km/2.4 miles (2 hour) trail linking Divide Lake Trail and the Mountain Goat Trail.

Gemmill Lake Trail is a 2 km/1.2 mile (1 hour) hike from Chute Lake Road to Gemmill Lake (just outside the park boundary). There is tenting at the trailhead.

Goode's Basin Trail is a 2.5 km (1.5 mile) one-way trail branching south off the Boulder Trail to the Pinnacles.

Mountain Goat Trail is a 10 km/6.1 mile (5 hour) trail starting from the south parking lot and climbing steadily to Divide Lake. The trail is not maintained and the footing in places requires the sure footedness of a mountain goat.

Rim Trail is a 1 km/0.6 mile (45 minute) offshoot from the Wildhorse Canyon Trail to a lookout over Okanagan Lake.

Wildhorse Canyon Trail begins from the North Parking Lot and extends 22 km (13.3 miles) into a spectacular canyon. The trail initially dips into the creek draw before climbing the hillside dotted with beautiful Ponderosa Pine trees and granite rock bluffs offering impressive vantage points of Okanagan Lake. The trail eventually leads into the canyon and past a few offshoot trails leading down to the lakeside camping areas. This trail makes an excellent overnight destination.

Postill-Swalwell Lake Trails (Map 20/E1) 🥾 🚵 🛷 🐟

A 65 km (39.7 mile) network of trails extends around Postill Lake and Swalwell Lake with one trail (Postill Lake Trail) connecting the two trail networks. The trails range in length from 5 km (3 miles) to 11 km (6.6 miles) and are accessed by the Postill Lake Road or the Beaver-Dee Lake Road. Due to the wet and fragile nature of the area in summer, no mountain bikes or ATV's are allowed.

Riddle Road Trails (Map 11/F3) 🚵 🏕

A series of mountain bike trails are found at the end of the steep Riddle Road, which in turn is found north of Penticton on the Naramata Road. From the gate at the end of the road, a great single track trail is yours to explore. It is possible to pick your way north to Naramata while you enjoy the terrific views of Okanagan Lake.

Rose Valley Reservoir (Map 19/F4) 🥾 🚵 🐟

The popular Rose Valley Reservoir can be reached by hiking west from the Westside Estate area to the ridge east of the reservoir then by walking down to the reservoir. An alternative route is to hike from the cattle guard on Bartley Road along a Forest Service trail to the south end of the reservoir and then along the western shores. Yet another route is to drive past the cement plant in the Westside Industrial Park and access the north end of the reservoir.

Shatford Creek/Sheep Rock Trail (Map 10/G6) 🥾 🚵 🛷 🏕 🎿

This well-marked, easy to follow trail climbs 720 m (2,340 feet) up into the alpine of Sheep Rock along a 10 km (6.1 mile) trail. Sheep Rock is made up of rolling sub-alpine and alpine meadows and affords panoramic views to the Coast and Monashee Mountains as well as the Okanagan Valley. Give yourself 7–8 hours for a round trip. It is possible to hook up with the Brent Mountain Trail or follow the old road to the abandoned Gold Zone Mine. The trailhead is just past the Shatford Creek Bridge about 2.3 km (1.4 miles) along the Shatford logging road.

Shorts Creek Canyon Trail (Map 27/F6) 🥾 🏕

From the parking lot on a spur road of the Whiteman Creek Road, a 12 km/7.3 mile (5 hour) moderate hike follows a well developed trail along the edge of the Short Creek Canyon. After viewing the canyon, you can continue down the creek to the Westside Road near Fintry for an additional 8 km/4.9 miles (2 hours) one-way.

Silver Star Provincial Recreation Area (Maps 28/G1, 29/A1) 🥾 🐎 🚵 🛷 🏕 🎿

Silver Star Mountain provides excellent hiking opportunities in July through September from the top of the ski lift (which can be ridden in the summer months for a small fee). The trails, which are found along the ski runs and access roads, provide a chance to walk through beautiful wildflowers in the sub-alpine. The area also offers world-class mountain biking opportunities along designated and well-marked trails. These alpine trails range from 5 km to 10 km (3 miles to 6.1 miles) and take around an hour for the intermediate rider to complete. Short paved trails around the village will keep the family riders happy. The bike trails around the ski resort include:

The **Cross-Country Loop** starts from the village and heads south. This moderate trail does have some uphill sections.

The **Repeater Road-Gold Mountain Trail** starts with a ride up the Summit Chair (for a small fee). From here you soar down the Repeater Road for 5 km (3 miles).

The **Gold Mountain Trail** (also 5km/3 miles) is more of a roller coaster ride.

Putnam Creek Trail also starts from the summit, at 1,890 m (6,143 ft), but requires one long uphill section before the 5 km (3 miles) downhill coast to the base.

Inside the park boundaries trail users will also find an incredible variety of backcountry trails to explore. The **Sovereign Lake Ski Area** has 42 km (25.6 miles) of trails, while the **Trinity-Ricardo Trails** offer 60 km of trails connecting Silver Star area with the Trinity Valley (see below). The **Ganzeveld Trail** links these two trail systems. Also in the area is the **Tuktakamin Mountain Trail**. This steep difficult trail extends 12 km/7.3 mile (4 hours) from Silver Star Mountain to the Trinity-Ricardo Trail system. To reduce the elevation gain of 400 m (1,300 feet), you can drive the maintenance road to the top of the mountain at 1,770 m (5,753 feet). The trail is generally well-marked although there is some scrambling up the open ridges. These trails are best hiked later in the summer after they have dried and the mosquitoes are less abundant.

Spionkopje Mountain Trail (Map 28/A7) 🥾 🚵

Also known as Spine-cop, riders will find this trail fast, steep and insane. This is a great place to ride, with a couple of named trails and a maze of forest service roads to explore. Hikers also frequent the area, so be careful.

Sugar Loaf Mountain (Map 27/G5) 🥾 🏕

To reach the summit of Sugar Loaf Mountain requires a 400 metre (1,300 foot) climb from the Whiteman Creek Road. The 3 km/1.8 mile (one hour) one-way trail follows an old skid road and well-marked trail to a deteriorating lookout platform overlooking Okanagan Lake.

Summerland Trails (Map 11/B2) 🥾 🚵 🏍

The main trail area here has actually been developed by motorcyclists. This means the trails are generally on loose sandy surfaces and often lead to dead ends. To get to the area follow the Princeton-Summerland Road and turn right about 2 km (1.2 miles) past the landfill sign. From the trailhead, follow the road and explore the options. The **Race Course Loop** heads left at about 3 km (1.8 miles). This is a moderate 6 km (3.7 mile) trail that makes it way back to the Summerland Road.

Terrace Mountain Trail (Map 27/E7) 🥾 🚵 🏍 🏕

To reach the highest mountain in the Vernon area at 1,950 m (6,338 feet), you can hike (or drive) up the deteriorating road. From the summit, you get a great view of Okanagan Lake.

Trinity-Ricardo Trails (Maps 28, 36, 37)

For adventurous hikers and bikers, a fantastic 40 km (24.4 mile) one-way adventure will take you from Silver Star Park north to Ashton Creek. From the Sovereign Lake Cross-Country Area you must climb 10 km (6 miles) to the park boundary (follow Repeater Road and Ganzeveld Trail). From the boundary, continue along the main (Ganzeveld) trail as it descends toward Ashton Creek. Along the way, you will pass the snowmobile chalet at 18 km (11 miles) and several side trails. The high alpine terrain, the long distance and difficult climb makes this an area for experienced trail users prepared for wilderness travel.

Twenty Mile Creek Trail (Map 10/E7)

The 20 mile Creek Trail leads 22 km (13.4 miles) one-way from Apex Mountain to Hedley, with an overall loss of elevation of 1,400 m (4,550 feet) as you pass by remnants of old gold mines to the valley below. The rugged route follows old roads and crosses several unbridged creeks making it is necessary to bring ropes (for the creek crossings), a topographic map and a compass. The trail begins from the Nickel Plate Cross-Country Ski Area.

Vernon Hill Interpretation Forest (Map 28/F4)

To the east of Vernon along the 2wd Becker Lake Road, the Interpretation Forest showcases 1,850 hectares of good forest practices in the Okanagan. Within the forest are a number of short trails, which allow you to explore different forest ecosystems, enjoy the wildlife of the area and visit a small pond with waterfowl. The **Easthill Trail** is the only trail with a steep climb, but you will be rewarded with a good view of the pond and the Coldstream Valley when you reach the top.

Vernon Hill Trail (Map 28/E4)

East of Vernon, a 12 km/7.3 mile (4 hour) moderate hike gains 600 metres (1,950 feet) to the summit of Vernon Hill (at 1,385 m/4,501 feet). From Cypress Drive, the hike involves a scramble through an open range to an old road that leads to the summit. Mountain bikers and motorcyclists also frequent the numerous trails in the area. The trails are best left to the moderate and expert riders as you can expect a lot of climbing and technical challenges as you weave your way through the network of single track trails, old roads and powerline routes. These trails can also be accessed from Hartnell Drive in the north, Cypress/Ravine Road in the south or Coldstream Creek Road/Becker Lake Road in the southwest.

Whiterock Mountain (Map 19/B1)

From the Whiterock Main, scramble up the slopes through a recent cut block to the mountain top at 1,865 m (6,061 feet). The reward is a fine view from the top.

Woodhaven Nature Conservancy (Map 20/A5)

In the heart of downtown Kelowna on Raymer Road, this 1.5 km (0.9 mile) easy walk takes you around the conservancy. The trail leads through a variety of different ecosystems including a forest of giant cedars and a dry hillside.

Wrinkly Face Cliffs (Map 20/C1)

From the Beaver/Dee Lake Road, follow the old road northeast to the base of the mountain. From there, you must scramble up some fairly steep sections before reaching the top at 1,220 m (3,965 feet) for a superb view.

South Okanagan/Boundary Trails

Stretching from Princeton to Grand Forks, the Crowsnest Highway (Hwy 3) provides good access to the southern reaches of the Okanagan and Boundary Country. This area is characterized by dry, rolling hills intermixed with pine and fir forests. Many of these trails in the area access small fishing lakes and offer backcountry camping opportunities. Trail users should always bring along plenty of water. While in Grand Forks be sure to pick up a copy of the Boundary Trails Guide.

Border Lake Trail (Map 1/E7)

Border Lake Trail is one of a series of rugged mountain trails between Manning Provincial Park and Cathedral Park. This particular trail leads 10 km (6.1 miles) from Trapper Lake to Border Lake. Hikers and equestrians use the trail primarily to access the fairly good fishing lake.

Cathedral Provincial Park Trails (Maps 1-2)

This is truly one of the best backcountry wilderness opportunities in the province. The spectacular rock formations, great views, good fishing, plentiful wildlife and unbelievable rock climbing opportunities are just some of the attractions. To reach the northern boundary of the park, take the Ashnola River Road (good 2wd access) west of Keremeos. Upon reaching the park, there is a private road (gated) to the Core Area (at 2,330 m/7,573 feet) but you will have to hike into the sub-alpine unless you pay a significant fee (currently $55/person). If you choose to reach the Core Area by foot, you have a choice of three routes:

- **The Lakeview Trail** is the shortest of the three at 16 km (9.8 miles). It will take about seven hours climbing 1,300 m (4,225 feet) in elevation.

- **The Wall Creek Trail** is a 20 km/12.2 miles (7-8 hour) trip gaining 1,100 m (3,575 feet).

- **The Ewart Creek Trail** is a daunting 28 km (17.1 miles) hike gaining 1,740 m (5,655 feet). Allow at least ten hours to complete the hike in.

These distances are for one-way trips. Once you reach the Core Area, there are plenty of areas to camp as well as a lodge to stay at. From your base camp, you can then choose any of a number of trails to explore. Distances for the trips listed below are for a round trip:

- **Diamond Trail** is an 8 km (5 miles) hike around Scott Mountain via Scott Lake gaining 225 m (731 feet). Allow four hours as the trail winds up through clusters of flowers over rock bluffs and past a small rock glacier where the rocks are slowly moving and pushing into the soil. The Diamond Trail offers great views of the Ashnola Corridor.

- **Glacier Lake Trail** is the quickest way into the alpine but it is fairly steep, gaining 200 metres (650 feet) in 3 km (1.8 miles). It is one of the main access routes to the Rim Trail.

- **Goat Lakes Trail** is an ideal trail when the weather is poor since it stays in the valley bottom (gaining a mere 150 m/488 feet). Allow four or five hours to hike the 10 km (6.1 mile) trail that follows the outlet creek through wetlands and riparian vegetation.

- **Ladyslipper Lake Trail** covers 7 km (4.2 mile) while climbing 150 m (488 feet) to the lake. For most people, it will take about three hours to wind through the larch and spruce to Ladyslipper Lake, which has great views of Grimface, the Matriarch and Macabre Tower. Ladyslipper is the best spot in the park for fishing.

- **Lake of the Woods** is a short 3 km/1.8 miles (1 hour) hike with minimal elevation gain.

- **Lakeview Mountain Trail** climbs to the highest point in the park and offers panoramic views of surrounding landscape. The trail is 12 km (7.3 miles) return, and will take the better part of the day (10 hours) to hike, gaining 600 m (1,950 metres) to the peak.

Pyramid Loop Trail is a short 2 km (1.2 mile) loop that passes Lake of the Woods and Pyramid Lake. There are bridges and boardwalks to help you cross the creeks and wet areas.

Pyramid Mountain Trail takes you past Glacier Lake over steep terrain to the mountain gaining 475 m (1544 feet). It is a 7 km/4.3 mile (3.5 hour) hike.

Quiniscoe Lake is the hub of the park from which trails and routes radiate to most of the surrounding lakes and peaks. An easy 2 km (1.2 mile) trail loops around the lake and passes a small waterfall.

Quiniscoe Mountain towers above Glacier Lake and is reached by a fairly easy, well-marked route. The plaque atop the mountain is a positional marker that once aided in mapping the area. This is an 8 km (5 mile) hike past Glacier Lake over steep terrain to the mountain gaining 500 m (1,625 feet) along the way.

Red Mountain is reached by a 10 km (6.1 mile) trail that should take most hikers 6 hours. You only climb 250 m (813 feet) but the trail provides some of the best views in the park. Since you are required to scramble through the open mossy alpine, the trail is not recommended for inexperienced hikers. The trail is reached off the Glacier Lake Trail.

Scout Lake requires a 3 km/1.8 mile (1 hour) hike gaining 125 m (406 feet). The lake is found along the Diamond Trail.

Stone City is certainly one of the highlights of the park. The quartz monzonite formation has been eroded by the action of wind over the millennia, while the Giant Cleft was formed when softer basalt rocks eroded, leaving a split in the granite. The 12 km (7.3 mile) hike takes you past Glacier Lake gaining 500 m (1,625 feet). Allow 7–8 hours for this hike.

Centennial Trail (Maps 1-2) 🛆 🛉 🛉 🐎 🖼 🛉 🐟 🛉

This trail extends 420 km (256 miles) from The Plaza of Nations in Vancouver to Joe Lake near Keremeos. In the Okanagan region, the trail extends from Manning Park to Keremeos offering a fantastic wilderness trek for experienced mountaineers or horseback riders. The trail leads past alpine lakes, rugged peaks and panoramic viewpoints. The best part of the trail is the 26 km (15.7 km) section that connects Manning Park and Cathedral Provincial Park through the backcountry. From the Monument 83 Trail in Manning Park, the Pasayten River Trail heads east. This trail requires a dangerous river crossing over the Pasayten River. After the river, the trail leads along a series of logging roads and eventually into the pristine wilderness near Trapper Lake. From the lake, the trail follows along Easygoing Creek, through Cathedral Provincial Park, and on to Joe Lake. From Joe Lake a trail leads to Susap Creek FSR, which will take you down to Highway 3 south of Keremeos.

China Ridge Cross-Country Ski Trails (Map9/B5) 🛉 🛉 🐎 🎿 🛉 🛉

Located just west of Princeton at the Snowpatch Ski Hill, there is a 35 km (21.4 mile) network of ski trails that follow old roads and skid trails through open timber, some cut blocks and across natural grassy slopes. In summer, hikers, bikers and horseback riders use the trails. The trails are at around 1,200 m (3,900 feet) in elevation and offer the occasional view of the Tulameen River Valley.

Clark-Maloney Lake Trail (Map 13/B3) 🛆 🛉 🐟

This is a 9 km (5.5 mile) one-way circuit that leads past three wilderness lakes, with rustic Forest Service campsites at two of them. The trailhead is found 7.9 km (4.8 miles) along the Lassie Lake Road. The lakes provide some fairly good fishing in the spring and fall.

Collier Lakes Trail (Map 13/C4) 🛆 🛉 🐟

This trail takes you 5 km (3 miles) return to two wilderness lakes through rolling hills and a park-like setting. The trailhead is at the Sago Creek Forest Service Site, which is 18 km (11 miles) along the Beaverdell–State Creek FSR. The Collier Lakes are popular fishing lakes with rustic backcountry camping areas.

Copper Kettle Lake Trail (Map 13/E1) 🛆 🛉 🐟

The Copper Kettle Lake Trail begins near the 66 km (40 mile) marker on the Christian Valley Road and leads 3 km (1.8 miles) one-way over fairly steep terrain to Copper Kettle Lake. The lake offers reasonably good fishing and a wilderness campsite.

Crater Mountain Trails (Map 2/D4) 🛆 🛉 🐎 🛉

This trail follows the old road to the top of Crater Mountain at 2,290 m (7,443 feet) where you will have a great view of the surrounding countryside. When you reach the top, you can explore the open alpine, which includes several tarns as well as tiny Crater Lake. The length of the hike will depend on how far you can drive along the Crater Mountain FSR with the distance from the Ashnola River Road to the top being 11 km (6.7 miles) one-way and an elevation gain of 1,140 m (3,705 feet). The deactivated road has a gate at the bottom, which is usually open and the road is ditched several kilometres up. It may be possible to drive beyond that ditch with a 4wd.

Crystal Lake Trail (Map 13/A6) 🛆 🛉 🐟

Crystal Lake is a small fishing lake, accessed by a 2 km (1.2 mile) one-way hike from a rough 4wd road off the Boyer Creek FSR to the south. Add another 4 km (2.4 miles) if you can't make it to the end of the road. The lake can also be reached by bushwhacking along an old trail from the north. Crystal Lake makes a good overnight fishing destination.

Eagle Creek Trail (Map 22/D3) 🛉 🐎 🛉

The trailhead is found on the Burrell Creek FSR southwest of Edgewood (see the Kootenay Backroad Mapbook). The moderate pack trail extends 40 km/24.4 miles (2–3 days) along an old trail north of Eagle Creek into the foothills of Gunwad Mountain and beyond. Guide outfitters accessing the rich hunting grounds below Mount Young, Gunwad Mountain and Mount Scaia primarily use the trail. Be careful, this is Grizzly Bear country.

Garrison Lakes Trail (Map1/A3) 🛆 🛉 🐟

The Sunday Summit FSR (4wd recommended) leads to the trailhead of this 4 km (2.4 miles) one-way hike. The trail leads to two mountain lakes and to a Forest Service campsite on the larger Garrison Lake. Anglers are the primary users of this trail.

Gladstone Provincial Park (Map 6) 🛉 🐎 🚲 🐟 🛉

This park encompasses most of Christina Lake and the pristine forests to the north of the lake. There are a number of well-developed trails in the park that will allow you to explore the park. Choose from one of the following:

Deer Point Trail is a moderate 20 km (12 mile) return trail leading along the eastern shores of Christina Lake through a semi-open forest from the Texas Point Campsite. Give yourself about six hours to hike the trail, which follows an old roadbed—partly completed in the early 1900s—to the north end of Christina Lake. It provides a good opportunity to hike or mountain bike on the slopes above Christina Lake. It is also possible to access the Sandner Creek Trail at the north end of the lake but you will have to obtain permission in order to cross private property. Cyclists should be warned that this single track travels over undulating and rooty terrain.

Mount Faith Trail begins from the end of Lynch Creek FSR (4wd required) and is a very well maintained horse trail leading 36 km (22 miles) to the top of Mount Faith within Gladstone Provincial Park. Hikers will need two days, while horseback riders can do the trail in a day. Guide outfitters looking to access the rich Mule Deer hunting grounds below the mountain use this trail extensively. Hikers will find the trail moderately steep and fairly difficult to hike.

Sandner Creek Trail requires the better part of a day (or two) to explore the old homestead and unique geological formations that are accessed by this trail. It begins at the north end of Christina Lake and extends some 18 km (11 miles) return along Sander Creek. Please respect private property at the north end of the lake.

Xenia - Christina Lake Trail begins at the end of the Miller Creek FSR (2wd access) and extends 6 km (3.7 miles) one-way over the summit from the Granby River Valley to Christina Lake. The trail is steep and difficult so it is not a good choice for a family outing. The hike should take less than three hours.

Goat Lookout (Map13/A7)

It is possible to drive to within 1 km of the flat-topped rock known as Goat Mountain but the road is water barred. Without a 4wd vehicle the hike will be longer and more challenging. The trail is well-marked and offers an excellent panorama view once you reach the lookout, at 1,740 metres (5,655 feet).

Golden Mile Trail (Map 3/D3)

A new concept in hiking. This 10 km (6 mile) easy trail connects a trio of wineries, and a historic stamp mill west of Oliver. Stop in at each winery for a tour and some sampling; how long it takes you to complete this trail depends on how long you want to spend at each winery. The trailhead is at the Tinhorn Creek Winery.

Granby River Trail (Map 14/B4)

The trailhead is found off the Bluejoint Mountain FSR. From here it is a short jaunt to the Traverse Creek Forest Service Site along an old road. This is an easy overnight trip, covering 25 km (15.2 mile) of relatively level trail along the Granby River and entering the south end of the Granby Provincial Park. The trail provides access to fishing pools, old-growth cedar trees, sandy beaches and views of the canyon. Although the first part of the trail is open to bikers, beyond the park boundary only horseback riders and hikers are allowed. Please remember that the park protects important Grizzly Bear habitat so an unfriendly encounter is possible.

The Harpolds (Map 6/E7)

It's Baby Harpold and Papa Harpold. Yes ladies and gentlemen, it's the Harpolds! These two hills are home to some of the best mountain biking in Grand Forks, and there is a maze of difficult mountain bike trails around and over the pair. Expect to take at least an hour to ride any of these routes, or just spend the day exploring.

Inkaneep Cross-Country Ski Trails (Map 4/B6)

North of where the Camp McKinney Road crosses Inkaneep Creek, a parking lot marks the beginning of a 10 km (6 mile) cross-country ski trail system. The **Prospector Trail** is the main trail that extends south of the road, and there are a number of shorter trails near the road. The area is rich in history of gold mines from the early 1900's and is an interesting place, so explore during the summer months.

Jewel Lake Trails (Map 6/A4)

From the Jewel Lake Lodge at the south end of the lake, three short loop trails (up to 5.8 km/4.9 miles long) lead through the forest and to an old mine site (at the end of the Roderick Dhu Trail). These trails are well-marked and groomed in winter for skiing. In summer, they provide an enjoyable outing for hikers and bikers.

Joan-Cleo Lake Trail (Map 13/B2)

The trail to this pair of wilderness fishing lakes involves a 5 km (3 mile) return hike that will take under two hours if you were just to walk there and back. However, most people will spend a few hours fishing or even spend the night at one of the Forest Service campsites. The trail is fairly flat and not too strenuous. The trailhead is found at 6.5 km (4 miles) on the Lassie Lake Road.

Joe Lake Trail (Map 2/G5)

Although this is the terminus of the historic Centennial Trail, the access from the west will require extensive route finding skills. But a good trail has been cut from the end of the Susap Creek FSR to the lake where well-kept cabins and good fishing can be found. The sheep trails make exploring the surrounding area a delight.

Jubilee Mountain Trail (Map 5/D3)

Behind a tall red building on Togo Street in Greenwood is the trailhead for this trail that switchbacks past an old mine shaft on its way up the west ridge above Greenwood. The climb is fairly easy to the top of Jubilee. The trail splits at the 1.5 km mark (0.9 miles). Keep left.

Keremeos Columns Provincial Park (Map 3/A2)

This popular 4 km/2.4 mile (2 hour) hike begins at the second gate on Liddicoat Road north of Keremeos. The hike gains 210 m (683 feet) in elevation through an open sage brush range along an old road eventually leading to a series of basalt pillars that tower 100 m (325 feet) tall. To reach the columns, it is necessary to obtain permission to cross private property. Watch for rattlesnakes and bring water.

Kettle Valley Railway: Oliver Area (Map 3/C)

A relatively flat section of the old railway passes through the orchards around the town of Oliver. But it is the hard packed dykes that parallel the old railbed that are recommended for smoother cycling. Access is from Road 22 south of Oliver or where Highway 97 crosses the river north of Oliver.

Lincoln Trail (Map 6/C4)

This is an easy walk along the Granby River, past the slag piles and beach. While the easiest access should be from the end of Riverside Drive, there is private property and access is not allowed. Instead, turn left on 85 Ave, and follow the trail up to the fence, then skirt the fence down to the river (about 1 km). From here, you can follow the riverside trail all the way to the Old Dam, or head left at the power line pylon up Observation Mountain (see below).

Little Nipple (Map 12/C2)

If you want to reach the Little Nipple (and who wouldn't?), you will have to bushwhack from the Wilkinson Creek FSR to the top, at 1,764 m (5,733 feet), where you will be rewarded with a spectacular view of the Kettle River Valley. This is a difficult route.

Lower Granby (Wolf) Trail (Map 14/C4)

This easy 5 km/3 mile (1.5 hour) one-way trail begins approximately 1 km past the 28 Mile Bridge on the Granby FSR. The signed trail follows an old trappers trail next to the Granby River to the Gable Creek Rec Site. It provides access to fishing holes and is a pleasant walk.

Marshall Lake Trails (Map 6/A5)

Easily accessed on a good 2wd road (Phoenix Mountain Road) off Highway 3A, there are 17.5 km (10.7 miles) of cross-country skiing trails that can be used in summer by horseback riders, mountain bikers and hikers. The area surrounding the ski trails is rich with a history of old gold mines and the remains of an old gold rush town. Be careful when exploring these old mine works and please stay out of private property in the area.

McIntyre Canyon Trail (Map 3/G2)

From the bridge on Highway 97 over Vaseux Creek, this 3 km/1.8 mile (1 hour) hike takes you to a spectacular 4 km (2.4 mile) long canyon. The best time to hike into the canyon is during low water (July-October)

Boundary Pathway (Maps 5 & 6)

Like the Kettle Valley Railway, the Boundary Pathway is part of the Trans Canada Trail and is built upon the remains of an old railbed. This particular section of trail follows the old Columbia and Western Railway between Midway and Robson (a community west of Castlegar) and open to all trail users, including ATVs. This 162 km (99 mile) trail has seen a lot of work in the past few years, especially the portion that helps form the Trans Canada Trail. The Boundary Trail passes through some spectacular scenery, clinging to the sides of mountains, and passing through some major tunnels (bring a flashlight). As an added bonus, the old railway breaks away from the highway north of Christina Lake into a wonderfully remote area. This section is notorious for it's long dark tunnels and spectacular trestle views over Arrow Lake. But, the most popular section of the pathway carries you from the old Eholt Station down to Grand Forks. The gentle (downhill) grade adds to the enjoyment as you skirt the hills west of Grand Forks. For more detailed information, pick up The Trans Canada Trail, The British Columbia Route.

because you will need to wade into the creek on your way to the canyon. An alternate route is to walk along the gated road near Vaseux Lake Provincial Park to the rim of the canyon. Look for bighorn sheep and pictographs in the area.

Midway Village (Map 5/E7)
From 1 km (0.6 miles) on the Myers Creek Road, this 9 km (5.5 mile) trail is used by mountain bikers and hikers to reach a scenic viewpoint on the international border southeast of Midway.

Morrissey Lookout (Map 6/C4)
This is a difficult mountain bike route that is well rewarded with a great view from the top. You climb about 1,200 m (3,900 feet) in elevation along logging roads (starting from Morrissey Road) before a rip-roaring descent along the Gilpin Creek FSR.

Mount Baldy Area (Map 4/D4)
If you want a great view along with splendid wildflowers in season (July-August), then hike up the ski lift at Mount Baldy. From the top, at 2304 metres (7,487 feet) you get a true feel for the vast wilderness in the south Okanagan.

Mount Kobau Trails (Map 3/D5)
At the top of the Richter Pass on Highway 3, the Mount Kobau FSR takes off to the northwest and eventually leads to the top of the mountain at 1,870 m (6,078 feet). Approximately 1.5 km below the summit is a parking lot with toilet facilities, picnic tables and two marked trails. From here, you can either hike the deteriorating 4wd road 1.5km/0.9 miles (one-way) to the top for a great view of the Osoyoos area, or you can hike to the southwest through the timbered slopes below Mount Kobau for a 5km/3 mile (2 hour) loop. This loop is called the **Testalinden Trail**.

Mount Moore Trail (Map 21/D4)
A 12 km/7.3 mile hike follows an old pack trail to the top of Mount Moore at 2,166m (7,106 ft). Expect to take about four hours. From the top is an excellent view of the Kettle River Valley. The trail is well developed and is used by mountain bikers, horseback riders and hikers in summer and snowmobilers in winter.

Observation Mountain (Map 6/D7)
There is a maze of unmarked trails in the Copper Ridge/Observation Mountain area. The most popular route to the top of the latter is along a route just southeast of Copper Ridge Estates. A shorter, but steeper route starts at the turnaround at the bottom of the gravel road that goes to the Wildlife Hall on Second Street. Many of these trails are on private property, so use with respect.

Phoenix Interpretive Forest Trails (Map 6/A5)
This series of trails and old roads dissect the Phoenix Interpretive Forest between Greenwood and Grand Forks. The longest trail—the Outside Loop—is about 31 km (18.9 miles) long. These trails hook up with the Thimble Mountain Trails (below) or the Boundary Trail/TCT.

Phoenix Wagon Road (Map 6/A3)
Look for the trailhead to this old wagon road at the sharp bend near the first bridge over Twin Creek on the Greenwood side of the Phoenix Road. At the time of this writing, only 1.5 km (0.9 miles) of this historic route had been cleared, although there is an alternate trail that climbs steeply to the right where a fence currently blocks the route. Heading left to parallel the creek will bring you to an old forestry road, which in turn will bring you back to Phoenix Road.

Snowy Mountain Trail (Map 3/A4)
This 12 km/7.3 mile (6 hour) hike begins along a well-maintained trail, but ends with a scramble to the top of the mountain through alpine meadows. From the top at 2,595 m (8,434 feet), you will be rewarded with an excellent view of pristine wilderness between the mountain and the US border. Given the high elevation, the hike is limited to the summer months only.

State Lake Trail (Map 13/B2)
It will take less than two hours of easy walking to cover the 4 km (2.4 miles) to State Lake and back again. The trail leads through some low-lying areas, which can be particularly wet during the spring, so bring some boots. There is a Forest Service campsite at the lake, which is primarily used by fishermen. The trailhead is easily accessed at the 9 km mark on the Barth Creek Road.

Thimble Mountain Trail (Map 6/B3)
The trail system begins at about the 3 km (1.8 mile) mark on the Knob Hill Forest Service Road, which is found to the southeast of Wilgress Lake on Highway 3. The trail extends 4.6 km (2.8 miles) one-way to the base of Thimble Mountain and is used by both mountain bikers for single track riding and by hikers. From the base of the mountain, there is a further 2 km (1.2 miles) hike to a viewpoint overlooking the Granby River Valley. The moderate trail system is fairly steep (climbing 300 m/985 ft) but is well maintained.

Tramway Viewpoint (Map 5/D4)
Head left from the end of Berta Street to the Greenwood Phoenix Tramway Bore. It is about an hours hike uphill to the viewpoint. The Bore is very dangerous, so please do not enter.

Trapper Lake Trail (Map 1/B3)
This difficult 20 km/12 mile (day+) trail extends from a branch road of the Pasayten River FSR into some remote wilderness area to the west of Cathedral Provincial Park. The historic pack trail once lead from Similkameen Falls, but logging activity has made it easier to drive further up the valley. At Trapper Lake, the trail connects with the Centennial and Border Lake Trails (see above), while further south Flat Top Mountain and Placer Lake are accessible. Many hikers use Trapper Lake as a base camp for further excursions around the area.

Westlake Trail (Map 1/B3)
From the 6.5 km mark on the Stewart Creek FSR, this difficult 34 km (20 mile) bike route follows an old road towards Christina Lake. There are several viewpoints and berry bushes to help you enjoy the descent down to a residential area that leads to West Lake Drive along Christina Lake.

Vancouver, Victoria and Eastern Railway (V V & E)
(Maps 2, 3, 4, 5)
This old railway used to run 220 km (134 miles) from Midway to Princeton. Unfortunately, most of the old railbed has disappeared. The best section is from Bridesville to Myncaster, although some sections are overgrown. This 34 km (20.7 mile) section descends 250 metres (813 feet) through the dry ranch country.

Wilgress Lake Trail (Map 6/B5)
Branching from the TCT/Boundary Pathway, just east of Eholt, is a 1 km side trail to Wilgress Lake. The lake makes a fine fishing destination complete with a rest area (picnic tables & washrooms).

Thompson/Nicola Area Trails

This region covers the western portion of this book, extending north from Hope, past Merritt and into the hills around Kamloops. This is a diverse area, ranging from the steep dry hillsides of the Fraser Canyon to the high elevation plateau of the Bonaparte Plateau. In between, trail users will find trails leading up the dramatic mountain peaks of the Coquihalla, through mixed forests and ranch country and even into remote fishing lakes.

Antler Lake Trail (Map 24/E1) 🚶 🚵 🐟

Antler Lake can be reached by a 4 km/2.4 mile (1 hour) hike on a 4wd road and deteriorating trail. There is a Forest Service Site at the lake, which is popular with anglers.

Blackwell Lake Trail (Maps 34/E7-26/E1) 🚶 🐟

From the Pratt Lake Forest Service Site on the Monte Creek-George FSR, this trail extends 3 km (1.8 miles) one-way to Blackwell Lake. The trail also passes by two smaller lakes and is popular with anglers.

Bonaparte Provincial Park (Maps 41, 49) ⛺ 🚶 ⛵ 🐟 🏕

Bonaparte Provincial Park is a remote backcountry park dotted with endless lakes, Lodgepole pine and sub-alpine meadows. The high elevation of the Bonaparte Plateau makes this a fine area to visit when other areas of Southern BC are too hot to hike or fish. Due to the relatively flat terrain, the trails are not too difficult but they are in various states of repair (or disrepair). Fishing is the primary attraction to the trail systems.

Deadman Trail (41/E1) is a 12 km/7.3 mile (4 hour) moderate hike along a fairly level, well-marked trail from Shelley Lake to Hiahkwah Lake. The trail leads past several small swampy lakes and through beautiful meadows. The trailhead is at 7 km (4.3 miles) on the Shelly Lake Road or 8 km (4.9 miles) on the Deadman Creek Road. The trail can be shortened, in fact, many anglers only travel the 4 km/2.4 miles (1.5 hour) trail into Shelley Lake.

Heller Lake Circuit (49/C7) leads past several lakes following an old road and some hard to follow trails. The distance of the trail really depends on how many lakes you want to visit as it can take several days to explore the entire route, which joins up with the Masters Subalpine Trek (see below). It is highly recommended that you bring a compass and topographic map, as it is easy to get lost. The trail is best accessed off the Deadman Creek Road.

Skoatl Point Trail (49/F7) begins from 8.5 km (5.2 miles) on the Windy Lake Road. It is a 12 km/7.3 mile (4 hour) moderate hike that follows a well-marked and popular trail to the base of a dramatic volcanic cone. Once you reach the base, it is possible to climb the eastern side of the cone for a great panoramic view of the surrounding lakes and forests. You can also examine the basaltic columns on the cone or fish the many lakes en route.

Bush Lake Interpretive Forest (Map 33/E5) 🚶 🚵 📖

Found on Goose Lake Road, hikers will enjoy the short, easy loop trails that display interpretive forest practices. Also in the area is a network of rewarding mountain bike trails. For the advanced rider, **Quickdraw** heads east (left) from the parking lot and eventually loops back after a grueling 11.5 km (7 miles). This single track trail offers several hills, technical sections and mud. **Trappers Line** is an easier and shorter 5.5 km (3.4 mile) loop starting at the back of the parking lot. This trail combines single track and old roads.

Cabin Lake Trails (Map15/F2) 🚶 🚵 🐟 🏕

To reach Cabin Lake, you can use a 4wd vehicle/ATV or walk along the rough, Cabin Lake Road (7km/4.3 miles) gaining 215 m (700 feet) to the lake. Hiking time is about four hours. Given the elevation (1,860 m/6,045 feet), the best time to sample the area is in June through September. From the lake, it is possible to access the alpine of Stoyoma Mountain by hiking 7 km (4.3 miles) gaining 420 m (1,375 feet).

This hike is considered moderate in difficulty and involves hiking through sub-alpine timber to the open alpine ridge below the summit (at 2,282 m/7415 feet). Another alternative is to access Heather Basin to the west via a 15 km (9.2 mile) hike along an alpine ridge. This difficult route leads past an old aircraft wreck. Another option is to hike to Lightning Lake, which involves a steep 5 km (3 mile) excursion along an old road.

Chewels Mountain Trails (Map 33/C5) 🚵 🏍 🚵 🏕

There are 46.5 km (28.3 miles) of motorcycle trails in the Chewels Mountain area. These trails are also popular with mountain bikers and in winter, snowmobilers. The road leads up to a microwave tower at 1,896 m (6,220 ft) for a fine view of the surrounding area.

Clapperton Falls Trail (Map 25/B5) 🚶 🏕

This trail extends 6 km/3.6 miles (2 hours) along an old road and undeveloped trail from Mill Creek Road to the falls gaining 100 m (325 feet) along the way. It is an easy hike and is best visited in March through October.

Coquihalla Summit Recreation Area (Maps 7/G3-8/A2) 🚶 📷 🏕

At the summit near the toll booth is a series of dramatic peaks and sub-alpine avalanche shoots. There are several strenuous hikes that allow the experienced mountaineer to reach the peaks for a fantastic view of the Coquihalla River Valley. These high elevation routes are best traveled from July to October.

The Falls Lake Trail begins off the short road leading from Exit 221 of the Coquihalla Highway. From the parking lot, it is a nice 1.5 km (0.9 mile) return walk to the small mountain lake. The lake provides good fishing for small rainbow trout. East of the main trail is Bridalveil Falls, but accessing the falls requires bushwhacking along the creek. (An easier approach is along the old KVR railgrade.)

Needle Peak Trail begins off an old road opposite to the highway yard on the Coquihalla Highway. Simply cross the creek behind the sheds and follow the old road to the trailhead. From there, it is a very strenuous hike that gains 855 m (2,779 feet) as you climb up the back side of the Needle. From the top, at 2,105 m (6,841 feet), the reward for this difficult 13 km/7.9 mile (6 hour) trip is the great view. This hike should only be attempted by experienced hikers.

Vicuna & Guanaco Peaks Trail are found at the end of the Upper Coldwater FSR. The trails lead straight up to excellent vantage points.

Thar Peak Route begins from the Boston Bar Rest Area and follows the gas pipeline before heading upwards along a faint trail to the peak. The trail leads up the back of the mountain and provides a phenomenal view when you reach the summit. Although you only travel 5 km (3 miles), you should allow five hours return as you climb 700 metres (2,275 feet) to the peak, at 1,920 metres (6,240 feet).

Zoa Peak Route begins along the powerline off of the Falls Lake Trail or from the Upper Coldwater FSR. A faint trail leads 635 metres (2,064 feet) to the 1,875 metre (6,094 foot) summit. The 11 km (6.7 mile) round trip should take about 6 hours. This is the easiest of the climbs to the alpine.

Zopikos Ridge Trail is a difficult daylong route that is accessed from the Zoa Peak Route. The dramatic rock face of Zopikos Ridge is seen on the Coquihalla Highway just south of the toll booth. The view from the top is breathtaking.

Dunn Peak Trail (Maps 51/A1-50/G1) 🚶 🏕

Rumour has it that there is a way to access Dunn Peak from the west. But this route has fallen out of use and is all but impossible to find. Instead, most hikers will follow the forestry trail off the Harper Creek FSR in the east. This difficult hike will lead you up Dunn Peak.

Knight (Echo) Lake Trail (Map 24/C1) 🚶🐟
Knight Lake is a sheltered treed lake with good fishing potential if you can bring in a boat to work past the muddy shoreline surrounded by lily pads. From the western shore of Roscoe Lake, a 2 km/1.2 mile (45 minute) easy walk follows a flat well-marked trail.

Elkhart Lake Trail (Map 17/G3) 🚶📷
This 6 km/3.6 mile (2 hour) hike leads from the Bob's Lake Forest Service Site to the Elkhart Lake Forest Service Site. Both lakes offer wilderness camping and good fishing opportunities.

Embleton Mountain Trail (Map 42/E6) 🚶📷
The trailhead to this challenging 9.5 km (5.8 mile) hike begins at the Heffley Lake Forest Service Site on the Sun Peaks Road. Expect to take about four hours as you climb steeply upward to the summit.

Gate Mountain Trail (Map 15/C7) 🚶🐎📷
Also known as the First Brigade Trail, this steep, difficult trail climbs 1.2 km (3,900 feet) along a 16 km/9.8 mile (7 hours) old pack trail. The trailhead is found just south of the Coopers Corner Rest Area (watch for a pullout on the west side of the road). The hike follows a mixture of logging roads, old pack trails as well as a newer trail and is best hiked in June-October. Eventually, you will pass through a meadow with wildflowers before reaching the Notch and then finally the summit of Gate Mountain. Both the Notch and the summit both provide excellent views over the Fraser Canyon.

Godey Creek Trails (Map 24/G7) 🚶📋📷
Located right behind the Merritt Travel Info Centre, there is a network of short interpretive trails highlighting forestry practices. The trails are about 1km (0.6 miles) in length and lead the forest to a clearing overlooking the valley.

Greenstone Park Trails (Map 33/B3) 🚶🐎🚴🏍📷
Found west of Kamloops, this provincial park is found off the Greenstone Mountain Road. A forest fire in 1999 and recent logging have played havoc with the series of mountain bike trails found near the radio tower. There are still a series of ATV and hiking trails in the park.

Gypsum Mountain Trail (Map 24/F2) 🚶📷
Gypsum Lake is found off the Aberdeen Road south of Dot Lake. It is a 4 km/2.4 mile (1.5 hour) easy hike leading to the summit of Gypsum Mountain at 1,546 metres (5,024 feet).

Hamilton Mountain Trail (Map 25/G6) 🚶🚴🏍📷
From the Douglas Lake Road, a 11 km/6.7 mile (3.5 hour) moderate hike leads along an old driveable forest service lookout road. You will gain 600 m (1,950 feet) to the top at 1,508 m (4,901 feet) where there is an excellent view of the dry Douglas Lake range country.

Harper Mountain Trails (Map 34/C1) 🚶🚴🎿📷⛷
Found east of Kamloops off the Paul Lake Road, is a 14 km (8.5 mile) cross-country trail system. These trails are found on the north side of Mount Harper, around the downhill area. Hikers and bikers can follow these trails in summer. For advanced cyclists, the downhill ski trails feature some seriously technical riding.

Hope Brigade Trail (Maps 8/E6-7/E7) ⛺🚶🐎📷
This trail leads from Lodestone Lake southwest of Tulameen to Mount Davis (see Southwestern BC Mapbook) covering over 25 km (15.3 miles). From Mount Davis, the route veers northwest branching from Sowaqua Creek to the western trailhead off Peers Creek FSR. This trail is designated as a National Heritage Trail and is used by both hikers and equestrians. The trail leads through rugged pristine wilderness north of Manning Park. Although the portion south of Lodestone Lake is much easier to follow, this trail should only be attempted by well equipped and experienced wilderness travellers. A compass and topographic maps are essential.

Hope Lookout Trail (Map 7/B7) 🚶📷
The trailhead is located at the junction of Highway 1 and the Old Hope Princeton Highway across from the Rainbow Inn. You have a choice of a short 2 km (1.2 miles) loop around the base of Hope Mountain or a 5 km/3 mile (2 hour) hike to the lookout. The latter hike involves a 500 m (1,625 feet) climb as you switchback up the talus slopes to the lookout.

Hope Mountain Trail (Map 7/B7) 🚶📷
The rough 4wd road leading to this trailhead is found opposite the Nicolum Campground. From the trailhead, the difficult 14 km/8.5 mile (8 hour) hike leads sharply upwards with some dangerous talus slopes and open rock faces to cross. The trail gains 800 metres (2,600 feet) to the summit at 1,836 metres (6,023 feet). Needless to say, there are some excellent views of the Fraser Valley and Hope from the top.

Hope-Nicola Valley Trail (Map 7/C7) 🚶🐎📷
From the parking lot for the Othello Tunnels (Coquihalla Canyon), follow the easy rail trail through the tunnels, and watch for the kiosk for the Nicola Trail on your right. This 8 km (4.8 mile) trail heads north over the hill and back to the parking lot.

Hyas-Shaw Trails (Map 42/G7) 🚶🎿⛷
Located off the Hyas Lake Road, there are 6 km (3.6 miles) of cross-country ski trails that extend northward from the road. The trails are currently in a state of disrepair (the bridges are washed-out) but hikers still use the trail system in the summer.

Inks Lake Area (Map 33/E3) 🏍🏍
Found off the Coquihalla Highway, Inks Lake Road accesses a large network of motorcycle trails that can be enjoyed by the experienced mountain biker. Following the first road left will give access to some single track trails. Several options are available including making your way south to Timber Lake Road. This difficult trail climbs 650 m (2,112 feet) over 21.5 km (13 miles) return. **Reggie's Roost** is another popular route that is found 7.5 km (4.6 miles) down the first road left. It is a moderate single track trail that links back with the Inks Lake Road.

Iron Mountain Powerline Trail (Map 16/G1) 🚵 🏇

From the top of Iron Mountain Road, a steep, technical mountain bike trail leads down to the Fox Farm Road, which can be accessed south of Merritt on the Coldwater Road. It is best to leave a car here and cycle up to the top, then ride back down.

Isobel Lake Interpretative Trail (Map 41/F6)
🚶 🚵 ⛷ 🗑 🎣 ⛷

It's an easy 3 km (1.8 mile) walk around Isobel Lake with interpretative signs describing the ecology of region. If you wish a longer hike/bike, you can continue on the 10 km (6 miles) of cross-country ski trails in the area. Another alternative is to bike down the roads next to Dairy Creek from Isobel Lake to Westsyde Road. Along the way, you will cross several trails and roads (stay right at all intersections). This moderate ride is 14.5 km (8.8 miles) long.

Jamieson Creek Falls (Map 42/A3) 🚶 🏇

This is a short, easy walk (30 minute) down a steep bank to a wooden bridge across Jamieson Creek then along the creek to the base of the cascading waterfall. The trailhead is before the 13 km mark on the Jamieson Creek FSR (2wd access). The falls are best visited in May or June during spring run-off.

Kane Valley Ski Trails (Map 17/A2) 🚶 🏇 🚵 ⛷ 🎣 🏇 ⛷

In addition to the 43 km (26.2 miles) of ski trails cum hiking/biking trails in the summer, there is an additional 2.5 km (1.5 mile) stroll through the demonstration forest near Harmon Lake. The trails follow old roads and skid trails through open timber and across sloping meadows. In the spring, the area becomes very popular with fishermen.

Kentucky Lake Trail (Map 17/C3) 🚶 🎣 🏇

There is a 4 km/2.4 mile (2 hour) easy walk that follows a well-marked trail around Kentucky Lake. The trail leads through old growth timber and is ideal for wildlife viewing and for access to the lake for fishing.

Kettle Valley Railway: Ladner Creek (Map 7/E5)
🚶 🚵 🏇

This hiking/biking trail leads along a section of the historic Kettle Valley Railway through tunnels and over an abandoned trestle. The 3 km (1.8 mile) hike will take about an hour, and makes an excellent side trail from the newly established Trans Canada Trail, which leads south of Highway 5. Alternatively, many visitors simply scramble up the talus slope from the east side of the creek off of the highway. Please be careful as this trail is not maintained and the trestle is in a state of disrepair.

Kettle Valley Railway: Othello Tunnels (Map 7/C7)
🚶 🏇 🚵 🏇

From the parking lot off Kawkawa Lake Road, this popular trail is part of the Kettle Valley Railway Trail, which is in turn a part of the Trans Canada Trail. Most people only hike though the canyon itself, an easy walk that's less than a kilometre return. The trail cuts south through the dramatic Coquihalla River Canyon to the equally impressive Othello/Quintette Tunnels. It is possible to stretch this into a 12 km/7.3 mile trek west along the north side of the river, all the way to the Hope Cemetery. East, the route follows the old Kettle Valley Railway across half the province, and then along the Trans Canada Trail to Alberta and eventually St Johns Newfoundland on the East Coast.

Lac Du Bois Provincial Park (Maps 33 & 41/D1)
🚶 🚵 ⛷ 🎣 🏇 ⛷

Found north of Kamloops, this area offers an incredible variety of trails and old roads through the sprawling grasslands. Most of the area is closed to vehicle traffic making it an ideal place for hikers, bikers, cross-country skiers and even snowshoers to explore. Although there are few maintained trails, the biking community has created a few fine routes to follow. Due to the distances involved, hikers will find these routes challenging.

The **Lac Du Bois Trail** (41/G7-33/F1) climbs from Westsyde Road up and over Long Lake Road and the Lac Du Bois Road to the lake after which the trail and park are named. The route follows the gated road south and back to the Lac Du Bois Road, which eventually brings you back to Westsyde Road just south of the starting point.

Mara Hill Trail (33/E1) is a difficult mountain bike route that climbs over 550 metres (1,625 feet) to the top of the hill (mostly along old roads). From the summit you can enjoy the breathtaking views over Kamloops and Kamloops Lake before following the single track trail that will eventually bring you back to Tranquille Road and the start. The complete loop covers 22.5 km (13.7 miles), combining roads and trails.

Lac Le Jeune Ski Trails (Map 33/E7) 🚶 🏇 🚵 ⛷ 🏇 ⛷

This network of trails and old roads circle the lake and are well used throughout the year. The entire network is about 73 km (44.5 miles) long with many of the trails being moderate in difficulty because they have steep long climbs and are not maintained. It is also possible to link up with the Home Ranch and Stake Lake Trails in the area.

Landstrom Ridge Trail (Map 7/A7) 🚶 🏇

From the west end of the weigh scales on Highway 7, cross the railroad tracks and look for the trailhead on the left. From here, it is a 3 km (1.8 mile) hike gaining 150 m (488 feet) to the scenic viewpoint.

Little Douglas Lake Trail (Map 8/A2) ⛺ 🚶 🎣

The trailhead is located at the Zum Peak Forest Service Site on the Upper Coldwater FSR. It is a short 1.5 km (0.9 mile) one-way hike to the small mountain lake where you will find another Forest Service Site. Fishing is the primary attraction to the lake. Be careful! This high elevation area is prone to Grizzly Bears.

Master's Subalpine Trek (Maps 41, 49) ⛺ 🚶 🎣 🎣 🏇

This difficult 4–5 day trek extends through the sub-alpine terrain and past numerous wilderness lakes and meadows of the Bonaparte Plateau. The access points are from the Tranquille Lake Resort to the south or from around the 63 km (38.4 miles) mark on the Jamieson Creek Road to the north. It is also possible to access the trail at several other locations if you wish to shorten the hike. Along the route are several cabins, which you can overnight in, as well as many remote fishing lakes. The trail is very isolated and wanders through vast stretches of unspoiled wilderness. Hikers should come prepared with topographic maps and compass as well as being bear aware.

Monck Park Trails (Map 25/C5) 🚶 🗑 🏇

Within Monck Provincial Park is a well developed 5 km (3 mile) interpretive loop trail with three trailheads. The trail explores the shores of Nicola Lake and leads up to an ancient volcanic outcropping and Indian pictographs on the slopes above the lake.

Moonscape Trail (Map 34/A2) 🚶 🚵 🏇

Moonscape is located on the Kamloops Indian Reserve amidst the dramatic looking hoodoo formations and sagebrush north of the Thompson River. The trailhead is on Shuswap Road, just east of Highway 5. Hikers prefer to follow the trail up to Peter and Paul Peaks (see below), while cyclists seem to frequent this easy route. Instead of continuing up the peaks, you cut east along a sandy old road and single track. The complete loop takes you 12 km/7.3 miles (4 hours). A permit (acquired from the Indian Band) is required before setting out.

Mount Dufferin Trails (Map 33/G2) 🚶 🚵 🏇

Mount Dufferin is a popular and easily accessible hiking/biking area in Kamloops. From the Kenna Cartwright Park trailhead on Hillside Drive, follow the road up to the tower (about 2 km/1.2 miles). At the top, a couple of moderate trails will give you a wide variety of options. It is possible to poke your way north to Mission Flats Road or to loop back on the Old Race Course Loop, which starts from the second switchback. This moderate 9 km (5.5 mile) loop returns you to the tower road.

Mount Lincoln Trail (Map 7/B3) 🚶🥾

Found 100 m (325 feet) north of the "Historic Yale" sign on Highway 1, you will find the trailhead to this strenuous 5 km/3 mile (3 hour) hike. The beginning of the trail is quite intimidating, as you must use secured ropes to assist you up a steep incline over a bare rock face. However, after you have climbed the 580 metres (1,885 feet) to the summit (at 655 m/2,129 feet), the view is fantastic.

Mount Peter & Paul Trails (Map 34/A2) 🚶🚲🥾

In the heart of Kamloops country along the Shuswap Road, it is possible to hike to the top of the two peaks just north of Kamloops. The hike is 2–3 hours long and involves passing through an Indian Reserve and desert like topography before reaching the tree line and eventually the top. From the summit at 1,095 m (3,559 feet), you will be rewarded with a great view of Kamloops. Since this is very dry country, bring some water. A permit (acquired from the Indian Band) is required before setting out.

Nicklemine Riding Area (Map 7/A5) 🏍

After the closing of the Homestake Mine, the area was opened up to motorcycle riders. The tailing ponds are a great place to test your skills, while more difficult roads/trails radiate north to Emory Creek.

Nicola, Kamloops & Similkameen Coal & Railway Company (N K & S) (Maps 23, 24, 25, 31) 🚶🐎🚲🐟🥾

Extends 75 km from Nicola to Spences Bridge and if followed east to west it's all downhill. From the ginseng farm west of Nicola this beautiful route descends along the scenic Nicola Valley. While the railbed is still fairly unbroken (even the eight bridges over the Nicola are still in good condition), there are three Indian reserves on the route that must be routed around, or permission gained to cycle through.

Paul Lake Area (Map 34/D1) 🚶🚲🥾

From the west end of Pinatan Lake, a well-marked mountain bike trail climbs (about 20 minutes) to the top of the hill for a good view. From here, you can make your way down to Paul Lake where you can loop around the lake and return to the start.

Rea Lake Circuit (Map 41/F2) ⛺🚶🐟

This 12 km/7.3 mile (5 hour) moderate wilderness circuit leading past several remote wilderness lakes. The trail is generally well-marked but can be tough to follow in places. The circuit also links up with the Tsintsunko Lake Trails (see below). The trailhead is found at the end of Bob Lake Road or the Rea Lake Road.

Round Lake Trail (Map 41/C1) ⛺🚶🐟

From the 8 km (4.9 miles) mark on the Deadman Creek Road, this 3 km/1.8 mile (1 hour) one-way hike leads through a second growth Lodgepole pine stand with little elevation gain. While it is not a long trail, it is seldom used and can be quite difficult to follow the old blaze marks. A compass and topographic map are definitely in order.

Roscoe Bluff (Map 24/B1) 🚶

The bluff is accessed along a 2.5 km (1.5mile (1 hour) well-marked (with yellow triangles) trail around the south end of Roscoe Lake through a second growth forest.

Roscoe Lake Trail (Map 24/D1) 🚶🐟

The trail around Roscoe Lake is well-marked (with yellow triangles), has little elevation gain and is well maintained. It is a 4 km/2.4 mile (1.5 hour) easy walk through an immature pine stand on the western shores of the lake. The lake is a popular fishing destination reached via the Chataway Lake Road.

Spirit Caves Trail (Map 7/B3) 🚶🥾

The trailhead is located off Highway 1, across from the Pioneer Cemetery at the south end of Yale. This 5km/3 mile (3 hour) trail gains 500 metres (1,625 feet) to the caves, as well as some great views of the Fraser River and Yale.

Sun Peaks Trails (Map 42/D3) 🚲

A series of lift accessed downhill trails accessed off the Sunburst Express at Sun Peaks. Some people think the lift is cheating, but most riders can bomb down the trails, and back up a couple of times before the die-hards have finished grunting their way to the top.

Swakum Mountain Trail (Maps 24/G2-25/A3) 🚶🚲🏍🐟🥾⛷

The slopes below Swakum Mountain are home to 78 km (48 miles) of interconnecting trails and logging roads for the snowmobilers in the winter. In the summer, Helmer Road is closed to vehicle travel but the area does offer a hike in Forest Service Site and opportunities to fish and explore. Helmer Road is accessed from Exit 315 on the Coquihalla Connector.

Thacker Mountain Trail (Map 7/A4) 🚶🚲🥾

In the heart of Hope, this trail leads 5 km/3 miles (1.5 hours) along an old road to the summit of Thacker Mountain. You gain 160 metres (520 feet) up to the summit, which provides a good view of the Fraser Valley and Hope.

Thynne Mountain/Mount Henning Trails (Maps 8/C1-16/D7) 🚶🚲🏔🥾⛷

This area is easily accessed from Coquihalla Lakes. An 8 km/4.9 mile (3.5 hour) hike/bike leads along an old road to a viewpoint and then along a faint trail through some alpine meadows to the base of Mount Henning. Overall, the elevation gain is 550 m (1,805 ft) to the summit at 1,818 m (5,965 ft). Most hikers return to the parking lot by way of another faint trail passing by an old mining camp and then leading along the old road. Another option is to hike the 7.5 km trail that leads through the sub-alpine between Thynne Mountain and Mount Henning. In the winter, the area becomes an extensive series of snowmobile trails including 55 km of trails around Thynne Mountain and 50 km of trails around Mount Henning. The trail between Mount Henning and Thynne Mountain links the two trail systems.

Tsintsunko Lake Trails (Map 41/E2) 🚶📷🐟

From the 14 km mark on the Shelley Lake/Beaverhut Road, this 4 km/2.4 mile (1 hour) easy walk follows a well-marked trail through second growth timber to the Tsintsunko Lake. The trail is wide and flat enough to pack a small boat to the main lake. At the north end of the lake, it is possible to join up with a few other trails in the area. Anglers may wish to follow the 3 km/1.8 mile (1 hour) one-way route to Caribou Lake. This trail is not maintained and is becoming overgrown.

Valleyview–Barnhartvale Area (Map 34/A2) 🚶🚲🥾

From the Valleyview Arena on Todd Road to the east of Kamloops, an easy 4.5/2.7 mile (2 hour) one-way hike leads along an old road through the hills. The main route accesses a plateau above Valleyview for a view of Kamloops and the Thompson River. Mountain bikers often explore a number of additional trails that are found in the area.

Whatcom Trail (Map 8/C5-D7) ⛺🚶🐎🐟🥾

Most travellers start this trail from the Cascade Recreation Area parking lot off of Highway 3 (see Southwestern BC Mapbook). The northeast trailhead is found southwest of Tulameen at Lodestone Lake. The trail begins on the Hope Brigade Trail (see above) before branching south to the Paradise Valley and Wells Lake. The lake makes a fine camping and fishing destination in late summer or early fall. The trail continues to climb through second growth forest to the sub-alpine meadows of Whatcom Pass and the Punch Bowl. From here you will drop 650 metres (2,113 feet) to Highway 3, covering a total distance of 17 km (10.4 miles) one-way. You will probably want to arrange for a shuttle.

Wilderness Camping
(Forest Recreation Sites)

The Ministry of Forests, in cooperation with the forest industry, have developed an extensive network of forest service recreation sites. These sites provide rustic but free camping sites throughout the southern interior. The sites are user maintained and are often found next to a lake, river or scenic vista.

Unfortunately, these sites, as well as access issues to these sites, have been thrown into a state of confusion by the recent government cutbacks. While the Forest Service and local interest groups strive to keep as many sites open as they can, remember that these sites can, and will, close with little prior notice. The public can help keep the system in place by doing their part to help maintain the sites. Remember to pack out all your garbage, and leave the site in better condition than when you found it. If users work together to keep these sites clean and safe, they will stay open. If not…

Below we have included brief descriptions on over 300 recreation sites and organized the sites by district. We have also done our best to add the symbols of the activities in the immediate area. Visitors will find that some of the recreation sites offer picnic tables, outhouses and fire rings, but many of the sites are simply a designated place to stay in the outdoors.

100 Mile House Forest District Sites
The northern reaches of this mapbook border with the Cariboo Forest Region. As a result, several of the recreation sites around Green Lake and Bonaparte Lake fall under the 100 Mile House Forest District.

Beaver Dam Lake Rec Site (Map 47/A4)
Located on the Meadow Lake Road, this small recreation site is ideal for fishermen wanting to try their luck at Beaver Dam Lake and the surrounding lakes. With good road access and plenty of room for RVs, this site is often busy throughout the fishing and hunting seasons.

Bonaparte Lake Rec Site (Map 49/B5)
Although there are several resorts around this popular lake, many visitors prefer to use the recreation site on the northwest end of the big lake. Most visitors take advantage of the boat launch to try their luck fishing or spend an afternoon exploring the shoreline in a canoe.

Bonaparte River Rec Site (Map 47/G5)
On the Clinton-Loon Lake Forest Service Road (3400 Rd), this recreation site is located right next to Bonaparte River. River anglers and hunters use it.

Hammer Lake Rec Site (Map 49/A5)
This site is found off the Egan-Bonaparte FSR and contains a boat launch as well as several camping spots. The recreation site is found at the north end of Hammer Lake, which is a popular fishing hole.

Little Scot Lake Rec Site (Map 48/G5)
The small recreation site is located on the north end of a small mountain lake next to the Egan-Bonaparte FSR (3700 Rd). Access to the site is good, and small RVs often fill the five spaces available.

Moose Lake Rec Site (Map 48/E4)
This small recreation site (space for about three vehicles) is located on the Egan- Bonaparte FSR (3700 Rd) at the west end of the lake. It has a boat launch as well as some camping facilities.

Pressy Lake Rec Site (Map 48/C2)
This is a small campsite, with space for three vehicles, located on the northeast end of this long narrow lake. The access is good enough for small RVs and there is a boat launch on the lake.

Scot Lake Rec Site (Map 48/G5)
Scot Lake is easily accessed off the Egan-Bonaparte FSR and provides not only a boat launch but also several camping spots at the north end of the lake. There is also a small, sandy beach on the lake.

Sharpe Lake Rec Site (Map 48/G4)
Sharpe Lake is found on the Egan Lake FSR and offers space for six vehicles. A cartop boat launch provides access to the lake.

Arrow Forest District Sites
Located in the dry southeastern portion of this book, the Boundary District is focused around two main valleys. The Christian Valley follows the Kettle River north of Rock Creek and is home to numerous backcountry lakes. The next valley to the east is the much quieter Granby River Valley. Both valleys offer good fishing and hunting retreats.

Arlington Lakes Site (Map 12/G2)
Arlington Lakes are a trio of lakes that are very popular during the summer and fall for fishing, hiking and biking opportunities. There are a total of 12 campsites on both sides of the southernmost lake. Most of the sites can be accessed by larger RVs since they are only 3 km (1.8 miles) from Highway 33. People exploring the Kettle Valley Railway will find the northwest site a little more suited for tents.

Bluejoint Creek Rec Site (Map 14/E6)
Located about 4 km (2.4 miles) along the West Burrell Creek FSR (good 2wd access), this site is found in a grassy, semi-open area next to Bluejoint Creek. Although rarely busy, this site would allow room for several units but only offers a couple picnic tables.

Buck Lake Rec Site (Map 13/A4)
This small site has three camping units set in the forest that surrounds Buck Lake. The lake and the site are accessed along a rough 4wd road and set below China Butte in the hills dividing the Kettle River and the West Kettle River. Toilet and table facilities as well as a cartop boat launch are offered.

Burns Lake Rec Site (Map 14/C5)
This is a small rustic lakeside campsite that is accessed by foot. Depending on how far you can drive on the rough Burns Lake Road, it is about a 1.5 km (0.9 mile) hike into the lake.

Canyon Creek Rec Site (Map 13/D7)
Canyon Creek is a popular destination for anglers and swimmers. There are three campsites set in the forest, and a nice swimming hole with a sandy beach on the Kettle River. The recreation site is 32 km (19.5 miles) along the paved Christian Valley Road and can be accessed by smaller RVs and trailers.

Canyon Flats Rec Site (Map 13/D6)
This is a small but well used site on the banks of the Kettle River. While fishing and hunting are popular pursuits, so is swimming in the hot summer. There is a sandy beach that is found after a short walk downstream. The recreation site has space for three vehicles/small RVs and is found at the 31 km (18.9 mile) mark on the paved Christian Valley Road.

Clark Lake Rec Site (Map 13/B3)
It is a 3.5 km (2 mile) hike from Cup Lake along the Clark-Malone Lake Trail to this small site on the shores of Clark Lake. Anglers looking for a nice backcountry retreat mostly use the trail and campsite.

Cleo Creek Rec Site (Map 13/B3) ▲ 🚶 🐟

Another hike-in campsite found in the hills above the Christian Valley. The Cleo Creek site is a small, open campsite that requires following a 2.5 km (1.5 mile) trail past Joan Lake from the 6.5 km (4 mile) mark on the Lassie Lake Road.

Collier Lake Rec Sites (Map 13/C4) ▲ 🚶 🐟

Collier Lakes are two small mountain lakes that are accessed from the Sago Creek Recreation Site at the 18 km (11 mile) mark on the Beaverdell-Stake Creek FSR or from the end of Dear Creek Road (4wd access). The Lower Collier Lake Rec Site is a small, walk-in campsite found along a rough 1 km (0.6 mile) trail beginning from Sago Creek. Upper Collier Lake offers two separate sites. The first is found off the Dear Creek Road, while the second is a walk-in site at the north end of the lake. It is about a 1 km hike from the end of the road. A rustic trail links the two lakes.

Copperkettle Lake Rec Site (Map 13/E1) ▲ 🚶 🐟

This small campsite is located at the end of a 3 km (1.8 miles) trail leading from around the 66 km (40 miles) mark on the Kettle River Main. This mountain lake provides good fishing as well as a rustic tenting area at the south end.

Cup Lake Rec Site (Map 13/C3) ▲ 🐟 🏕

Cup Lake is found off the Lassie Lake Road (2wd access) and has two camping spots located in a clearing next to the lake.

Damfino Creek Rec Sites (Map 13/E1) 🏕 🐟 🏕

This pair of recreation sites are found 68 km (41.5 miles) along the Kettle River Main (good 2wd access). Located on both sides of Damfino Creek, these two sites are large enough for group camping and RVs.

Eight Mile Flats Rec Site (Map 14/B6) ▲ 🚣 ⛵ 🐟 🏕

Eight Mile Flats is located at an old bridge site and provides good access to the Granby River. The small site is located on a rough 2wd road off the Boulder-Traverse Creek FSR and on the opposite side of the river from the Granby FSR. There is room for three units but there are no picnic tables or facilities.

Five O'Clock Lake Rec Site (Map 13/C3) ▲ 🚶 🐟

Backcountry anglers will find this small site (big enough for one group of tenters), after a short 1 km (.6 mile) hike. The trailhead is found on the 12.5 km (7.6 mile) mark on the Lassie Lake Road.

Gable Creek Rec Site (Map 14/B7) 🏕 🚶 🚣 ⛵ 🐟 🏕

Found at the bottom of a steep hill on the Gable Creek FSR, this site is located in a scenic gorge created by Gable Creek and the Granby River. Anglers and hunters primarily use the Forest Service Site, which has a table, pit toilets and plenty of room for RVs or bigger units.

Granby-Burrell Site (Map 14/C7) 🏕 🚶 🚣 ⛵ 🐟 🏕

This semi-open campsite is used mainly by river fishermen in the summer and hunters in the fall. There are three official sites but there is plenty of room to accommodate more campers then that. The site is located right at the 28 Mile Bridge and is the most popular recreation site in the Granby River Valley.

Hoodoo Lake Rec Site (Map 13/B7) ▲ ⛵ 🚣 🐟

There are three small camping spots located in an opening next to the lake. Hoodoo Lake is accessed by the rough Waddell Creek FSR and there is a cartop boat launch for fishermen and paddlers.

Howe Creek Rec Site (Map 14/B5) 🏕 🐟 🏕

Accessed from approximately 1 km (.6 miles) down the Traverse Creek Road, this is a large, open campsite on the west side of the Granby River. Small RVs and tent trailers can access the site.

Joan Lake Rec Site (Map 13/B2) ▲ 🚶 🐟

This is a small, walk-in site next to Joan Lake. To reach the lake, it is a short 1 km (0.6 mile) walk from the 6.5 km (4 mile) mark on the Lassie Lake Road.

Jolly Creek Rec Site (Map 4/G6) 🏕 ⛺ 🚶 🚴 🛝 🏕

An open, grassy site is found a short distance from Highway 3 near Bridesville. The rec site is easily accessed by cars and RVs and sees a lot of day-use in the summer. An old road in the area leads past old prospector cabins and mining artifacts.

Kettle Bench Rec Site (Map 13/D5) 🏕 🛶 ⛵ 🐟 🏕

This is a large, grassy site that provides an opportunity for fishing on the Kettle River as well as swimming in a large pool next to a sandy beach. The beach is found a short distance downstream from the camping area. The recreation site is 39 km (23.8 miles) down the Christian Valley Road.

Kettle Canyon Rec Site (Map 13/E5) ▲ ⛵ 🐟 🛝 🏕

There are four camping spots in the thick forest next to the Kettle River. There is a good swimming hole on the river, and it is only a short walk to a waterfall. The larger pools in the area also make fine holding areas for trout. The site is located at the 41 km (25 mile) mark along the Christian Valley Road.

Kettle River Crossing Rec Site (Map 21/F6) ▲ 🐟 🏕

A small, open grassy site next to the Kettle River, this site is found at the 80 km (49 mile) mark on the Kettle River Main. Despite the long bumpy road, small RVs and trailers can access the site.

Lassie Lake Rec Site (Map 13/C3) ▲ ⛵ 🐟 🏕

There are seven camping spots in the thick forest next to the shores of Lassie Lake. The site receives heavy use during the summer and fall and is located on the Lassie Lake Road.

Maloney Lake Rec Site (Map 13/C3) ▲ 🚶 🐟

A small lakeshore site that is reached by hiking the Clark-Maloney Lake Trail. The trailhead can be reached from the 7.9 km (4.8 miles) mark on the Lassie Lake Road.

Marshall Lake (Providence) Rec Site (Map 6/A6) ▲ 🚶 🚴 🐟 🛝 🎿

On the Phoenix Road, this popular recreation site is an excellent staging ground for year round recreation adventures. In the summer, you can try fishing the lake, exploring the abandoned mines, mountain biking the old rail grades or logging roads or hiking one of the several trails. In the winter, Phoenix Hill provides downhill skiing and the Marshall Lake Trails offer great cross-country skiing, snowshoeing and even snowmobiling.

Moore Lake Rec Site (Map 13/B7) ▲ 🐟

Moore Lake is a small, shallow lake with spotty fishing. There is only one camping spot on the opening next to the lake, which is found 11 km (6.7 miles) along the Waddell Creek FSR.

Nevertouch Lake Rec Site (Map 21/E6) 🏕 ⛵ 🚣 🐟 🏕

This small, treed site at the north end of a very popular lake has space for about ten vehicles. The access to Nevertouch Lake is fairly good (along a 2wd road) and facilities include a boat launch an outhouse and picnic tables.

Pete Lake Rec Site (Map 5/B1) 🏕 🐟 🏕

This site is found at about the 9 km (5.5 miles) mark on the Waddell Creek FSR. There are three campsites within the timber next to the south shores of this small lake. Small RVs can make their way into the area.

Sago Creek Rec Site (Map 13/B4) 🔺 🏕 🚶 ⊶ 🎣
This is a small, pretty site with space for three groups, located next to Sago Creek at the 18 km (11 mile) mark of the Beaverdell-State Creek Road. It is used primarily as a staging ground for hikers to the Collier Lakes.

Sandrift Lake Forest Service Sites (Map 13/D2) 🔺 ⊶ 🎣
The Sandrift Lakes are a trio of small lakes in the Christian Valley. The southern two of the three lakes sport Forest Service Sites. The lakes are found just off the road and the campsites are small (the site at the third lake only has space for two units)

Sandy Bend Rec Site (Map 21/F6) 🔺 🔺 🚣 🐟
This site is only half a kilometre south of the Kettle River Crossing Site and is a small, semi-open site next to the Kettle River, which offers a sandy beach and a good swimming hole.

Saunier Lake Rec Site (Map 12/F7) 🔺 🚣 🎣 🐟
The recreation site at Saunier Lake has two small camping sites set in the dense forest on the shores of the lake. There is also a cartop boat launch. The site is found at about the 8 km (4.9 miles) mark on the Tuzo-Eugene Creek Road (good 2wd access).

St. Anne's Meadow Rec Site (Map 14/E5) 🔺 ⊶
 St. Anne's Meadow is a large, grassy field overlooking Burrell Creek that offers a secluded summer camping area. Although there are only two picnic tables, there is room for several groups in the area. The rec site is found 7.5 km (4.6 miles) up the West Burrell FSR (rough 2wd access).

State Creek Rec Site (Map 13/E4) 🏕 🚣 ⊶ 🎣
A large site located in a grassy, semi-open area next to State Creek. It is located at the 46 km (28 mile) mark on the Christian Valley Road and is ideal for a stopover for larger RVs or for picnicking.

State Lake Rec Site (Map 13/D3) 🔺 🚶 🐟
State Lake is a popular fishing lake that is located 2 km (1.2 mile) along a trail, which begins at the State Lake Road Forest Service Site. There is a small camping area at the north end of the lake.

State Lake Road Rec Site (Map 13/D2) 🔺 🚶
This site is found along the Sandrift Road and marks the beginning of the trail to State Lake. It is a large semi-open site that is mostly used by anglers heading for State Lake.

Taurus Lake Rec Site (Map 5/B1) 🔺 🚣 🎣 ⊶
Taurus Lake is found at the 10 km (6.1 miles) mark on the Ouellette Creek Road east of Highway 33. There are ten camping sites located on both the east and west sides of the lake as well as a cartop boat launch.

Thone Lake Rec Site (Map 13/E5) 🔺 🚣 ⊶ 🎣
There are nine small camping spots, which are extremely popular especially during the summer with fishermen and in the fall with hunters. The recreation site is accessed by a good 2wd road (Thone Road), which leads from the Christian Valley Road at around the 27 km (16.5 mile) mark.

Traverse Creek Rec Site (Map 14/B5) 🔺 🚶 🏕 🚵 ⊶
A small campsite on the east side of the Granby River that is used as a staging ground for travellers on the Granby Wilderness Trail. Access to this site is by foot from the footbridge crossing Howe Creek.

Williamson Lake Rec Site (Map 5/E1) 🔺 ⊶
This site is accessed by either the Sebastian Creek Road (rough 2wd access) to within 300 metres (975 feet) of the recreation site or via the Windfall Creek Road (rough 4wd access) to the south. This small site provides a tenting site and fishing opportunities at Williamson Lake.

Kamloops Forest District Sites

The Kamloops Forest District is a popular recreational area that is dominated by dry rolling hills and thick Lodgepole pine forests. It is a large area that stretches east from the Deadman River Valley, past the Bonaparte Plateau and Barriere Lakes to Adams Lake. Home to a variety of big and small lakes, this area is notorious for its fast growing and feisty Kamloops Rainbow Trout.

Allan Lake Rec Site (Map 49/G5) 🔺 🚣 ⊶ 🚻
Allan Lake Recreation Site has 15 campsites along with a cartop boat launch. The lake is a popular place for anglers throughout the ice free season, so space here can be limited, especially on weekends.

Badger Lake Rec Site (Map 42/C2) 🔺 🚤 🚣 ⊶
Located in a forest next to Badger Lake, this site has 15 open camping spots. There is a cartop boat launch at the site, which is used primarily by fishermen.

Barnes Lake Rec Site (Map 31/F1) 🏕 🚤 🚣 🚵 ⊶
To the southeast of Ashcroft, this site is set in an open range next to the lake and receives heavy use throughout both the winter and summer. There is a cartop boat launch at the 60 unit site, which is RV accessible. In winter, this is a popular ice fishing lake.

Bose Lake Rec Site (Map 32/D6) 🔺 🚤 🚣 ⊶
This small recreation site is comprised of eight camping units together with a cartop boat launch at the north end of Bose Lake. A 4wd vehicle is required to access the campsite, which is used primarily by fishermen. An interesting side trip is to visit the Bethlehem Copper Mine to the south.

Campbell Lake Site (Map 34/C3) 🏕 🏕 🚤 🚣 ⊶
This relatively new recreation site is located on the southwest side of Campbell Lake. Managed as an enhanced site (there is a fee), there are 30 campsites and a nice day-use area on a small bay on the lake. The access into the lake is good as long as the road is dry.

Community Lake Rec Site (Map 42/E4) 🔺 🚤 🚣 🐟
Community Lake has a boat launch together with a wharf. Fishing is the primary attraction to the site, which also offers room for ten camping units.

Dairy Lake Rec Site (Map 33/A3) 🔺 🚤 🚣 ⊶ 🚻
Located on the Duffy Lake Road, this site is set below Greenstone Mountain. The site is split between two locations, containing a total of 13 camping units. The northern site is 4wd accessible and there is a cartop boat launch at each site.

Deadman Lake Rec Site (Map 48/F7) 🏕 🏕 🚤 🚣 🐟 🚻
Deadman Lake is found in the eerily named valley north of Kamloops Lake. The Forest Service site is found next to the Vidette Road and has ten treed camping sites together with facilities such as tables and a cartop boat launch.

Dennis Lake Rec Site (Map 43/B7) 🔺 🚤 🐎 🚣 🐟
Found on a rough side road of the McGillivray Lake FSR, this small site has five vehicle units and a cartop boat launch.

Duffy Lake Rec Site (Map 33/A2) 🔺 🚤 🚣 ⊶
Located on the Duffy Lake Road, this site is set below Greenstone Mountain. There are 30 camping units together with a boat launch for anglers to test their luck.

Dunn Lake Site (Map 50/D1) 🏕 🚤 🚣 ⊶ 🚻
At the north end of Dunn Lake (south of the resort), this semi-open, grassy site has room for ten vehicles. Despite the steep climb from the valley (& ferry) below, the access is fair from Little Fort.

Dunsapie Lake Rec Site (Map 49/G7) ⬛ ⬛ ⬛ ⬛ ⬛
This site is located on the Jamieson Creek FSR and receives heavy use throughout the summer months. It has five camping units as well as a cartop boat launch.

East Barriere Lake Site (Map 51/A5) ⬛ ⬛ ⬛ ⬛ ⬛ ⬛ ⬛
This is a large, 20 unit site which is set in a forested area on the northwestern shores of the lake. The enhanced site is easily accessed on the East Barriere Road and offers full facilities including an improved boat launch and picnic tables.

Face Lake Rec Site (Map 33/B5) ⬛ ⬛ ⬛ ⬛
Located on a 4wd road leading past the resort, there is a small ten unit camping site set in a forested area at the north end of Face Lake. There is a cartop boat launch for anglers and canoeists.

Gannett Lake Rec Site (Map 52/B1) ⬛ ⬛ ⬛ ⬛
This medium sized, open site is located at the southwest end of Gannett Lake, well hidden from the main road. The recreation site is used by fishermen and hunters accessing the high elevation area.

Gordon Bay Rec Site (Map 52/A2) ⬛ ⬛ ⬛ ⬛ ⬛
This small site is the northernmost site on the Adams Lake and accessible by road or water. There is a nice beach and a rustic boat launch onto the lake.

Gorman Lake Rec Site (Map 50/A6) ⬛ ⬛ ⬛ ⬛
The edge of Gorman Lake is quite swampy, making it difficult, but not impossible to launch a cartop boat here. There are five camping units in a grassy area next to the lake.

Heffley Lake Rec Site (Map 42/E7) ⬛ ⬛ ⬛ ⬛ ⬛ ⬛ ⬛
This lake is found on the paved Sun Peaks Road and the recreation site is often full of RVs and other large units throughout the summer months. If you can find a campsite, canoeing, swimming and fishing are the main pastimes in the spring through fall. Ice fishing is also popular as the lake can be accessed year round. There is a cartop boat launch and picnic tables at the Forest Service site.

Hihium Lake Rec Site (Map 40/B2) ⬛ ⬛ ⬛ ⬛ ⬛
Easily accessed off the Clinton-Loon Lake FSR (3400 Rd), this recreation site is found at the southeast end of Hihium Lake. Fishing is the main attraction to the area.

Honeymoon Bay Rec Site (Map 51/G5) ⬛ ⬛ ⬛ ⬛ ⬛
Honeymoon Bay offers 15 campsites on the western shores of Adams Lake. The sites are set in the forest and there is a nice sandy beach on the lake. We have yet to see any newlyweds vacation here.

Hyas Lake Rec Site (Map 42/G7) ⬛ ⬛ ⬛ ⬛ ⬛
Hyas is a day-use only site with a cartop boat launch as well as picnic tables. In the winter, this is a popular starting point for ski touring.

Isobel Lake Site (Map 41/F6)
⬛ ⬛ ⬛ ⬛ ⬛ ⬛ ⬛ ⬛ ⬛
Part of the Isobel Lake Interpretive Forest, this Recreation Site is a wheelchair accessible site with four campsites. There is also a group camping area that can be reserved as well as a cartop boat launch and a well developed cross-country ski trail system in the area.

Johnson Lake Rec Site (Map 51/C7) ⬛ ⬛ ⬛ ⬛ ⬛
This is a seven unit site located at the eastern end of the lake (on the opposite side of the lake from the resort). It has a cartop boat launch and is used primarily by anglers.

Little McGillivray Lake Site (Map 43/A6) ⬛ ⬛ ⬛ ⬛ ⬛ ⬛
Little McGillivray is accessible via a 4wd road. This rec site contains five camping units and a cartop boat launch. The small lake is particularly swampy around the edges and a boat is necessary if you want to fish it. Also, insects are a real problem at the lake.

Lodgepole Lake Site (Map 33/D6) ⬛ ⬛ ⬛ ⬛ ⬛ ⬛
On the Chewhels Mountain Road, this small (ten unit) recreation site is used primarily by fishermen or visitors to the Chewhels Mountain Motorcycle Trails. This is a very good fishing lake.

McGillivray Lake Site (Map 43/A6) ⬛ ⬛ ⬛ ⬛ ⬛ ⬛
With good road access and plenty of recreational activities in the area, this site can be busy. Unfortunately, the swampy nature of the lake also attracts many voracious mosquitoes during wet season. The rec site offers five campsites and a cartop boat launch.

Mayson Lake Rec Site (Map 49/F6) ⬛ ⬛ ⬛ ⬛ ⬛
Mayson Lake is a large, scenic lake just south of Bonaparte Lake. Access to the rec site with five camping units as well as a cartop boat launch is off the Jamieson Creek Road (rough 2wd).

Morrissey Lake Sites (Map 43/A6) ⬛ ⬛ ⬛ ⬛ ⬛ ⬛ ⬛
There are two different sites on Morrissey Lake, east and west. The western site is a small, timbered site with nice camping spots and a cartop boat launch. The eastern site has eight camping units and a cartop boat launch. Both sites are frequented by snowmobilers in the winter and fishermen through the spring and fall.

Paska Lake Rec Site (Map 33/B5) ⬛ ⬛ ⬛ ⬛
The Paska Lake Recreation Site has 50 campsites that are extremely popular in the summer. The site is set in a semi-open area and can be accessed by a small RV. There is also a cartop boat launch available at the site.

Pass Lake Rec Site (Map 41/E6) ⬛ ⬛ ⬛ ⬛ ⬛
A medium sized (15 vehicle units) site set in a forest on the shores of Pass Lake. The scenic lake is found off Lac Du Bois Road and is a fine angling destination.

Pemberton Lake Site (Map 42/G7) 🏕️ ➰ 🚶 🛶 ➰ 🐟

Pemberton Lake is the small lake found just south of Hyas Lake. There is a small four unit campsite complete with a cartop boat launch on Pemberton. In addition to angling and paddling, visitors can explore the nearby Hyas Shaw Trail System.

Rocky Point Rec Site (Map 52/A2) 🥾 ➰ ➰ ➰ 🐟

Rocky Point is named for its exposed rocky beach, located on the northwestern shores of the Adams Lake. A cartop boat launch is also available at the site.

Ross-Moore Lake Site (Map 33/F7) 🏕️ ➰ 🚶 🚴 🛶 ➰ 🐟

To the east of Lac le Jeune Provincial Park, there is a small undeveloped site, which is used primarily by fishermen. Access to the lake is by rough 2wd road from the Long Lake Road to the east. There is also a cartop boat launch at the site, which is usually not very busy.

Sandy Point Rec Site (Map 51/C4) 🥾 ➰ ➰ ➰ ➰ 🐟

This site is located on the western shores of Adams Lake south of Brennon Creek. It is a larger site (room for about 30 units) and the sandy beach is a favourite with the families. The boat launch provides good access to the lake.

Saskum Lake Rec Site (Map 51/D2) 🥾 ➰ ➰ ➰ ➰ 🐟

This 25 unit site at the north end of Saskum Lake is easily accessed along the Saskum Lake Forest Service Road. The rec site provides a sandy beach but also a cartop boat launch.

Saul Lake Rec Site (Map 41/B5) 🏕️ ➰ ➰ ➰ 🐟

Saul Lake is a popular year round destination. Anglers test their luck during the open water season and through the ice, while snowmobilers can explore the trails leading to nearby Truda Lake. On the western shores of Saul Lake there is a four unit campsite with a cartop boat launch.

Scott Lake Rec Site (Map 50/A6) 🏕️ ➰ ➰ ➰ 🚻

This small recreation site has five camping units together with a cartop boat launch. The site is located on the east end of the lake in a forested area.

Skmana Lake Rec Site (Map 43/C6) 🏕️ ➰ 🚶 ➰ ➰ 🛷

There is a small open site with five campsites set on the shores of Skmana Lake. There is a wharf, cartop boat launch and a series of trails in the area.

Skwaam Bay Site (Map 43/B1) 🏕️ ➰ ➰ ➰ ➰ ⚓ ➰

On the western shores of Adams Lake, Skwaam Bay is a popular, medium sized (ten unit) site with full facilities. Access is by a steep road with a limited turn-around so it is not recommended for RVs. There is a cartop boat launch, beach and picnic tables at the Forest Service site.

Skookum Lake Rec Site (Map 40/F1) 🏕️ ➰ ➰ 🐟

An open, grassy site with 15 campsites. While the Deadman Vidette Road is a good road, access into the site from the main road is poor.

Snohoosh Lake Rec Site (Map 40/F1) 🏕️ 🍴 ➰ ➰ ➰

Found in the forest at the north end of the narrow Snohoosh Lake is a five unit campsite. This recreation site also offers a cartop boat launch and fuel facilities and is easily accessed on the Deadman Vidette Road.

South Barriere Lake Rec Site (Map 51/B6) 🏕️ ➰ ➰ 🐟

Located on the South Barriere Lake FSR, this medium-sized, 15 unit site is found at the west end of the lake. There is a cartop boat launch together with picnic tables and toilet facilities at the Forest Service site.

Sullivan Lake Rec Site (Map 42/C3) 🥾 ➰ ➰ 🐟

Better known as Knouff Lake, the Sullivan Lake Recreation Site is a busy place in the summer as both campers and small RVs flock to the area for the good fishing. The site is located at the northeast end of the lake and is easily accessed from the Knouff Lake West Road. There is also a resort on the lake, which can be fished both through the ice in winter and from spring through fall.

Tsikwustum Creek Sites (Map 52/A2) 🥾 🍴 ➰ ➰ 🐟 🛶

This popular day-use area is broken up across two locations on the eastern shores of Adams Lake where Tsikwustum Creek drains into the lake. On the north side of the creek is a medium sized site located in an opening next to Adams Lake. It has a good boat launch together with picnic tables and toilet facilities. On the south side of the creek is a small, treed site. Both sites can be used by RVs.

Three Sisters Creek Rec Site (Map 31/B2) 🏕️ 🚻

Located on the Hat Creek Road just north of Oregon Jack Provincial Park, there is a small campsite next to the creek. The campsite, which has five units set in an opening, is used by visitors to the nearby parks. Alternatively, there are pictographs to explore by following the faint trail at the bend in the road. There is limited (4wd) access to the site when the area is wet.

Tranquille Crossing Rec Site (Map 41/C7) 🏕️ 🍴 ➰ 🚻

Not as popular as the nearby Tranquille Meadow Site, Tranquille Crossing is not nearly as big either. There is only space for two vehicles here.

Tranquille Meadow Rec Site (Map 41/C7) 🥾 🍴 ➰ 🚻

A 50 unit, motorhome accessible site on the banks of the Tranquille River. Visitors can test their luck fishing or spend a few quite moments looking for the wildlife that frequents the area.

Vermelin Creek Rec Site (Map 51/B3) 🥾 ➰ ➰ ➰ ➰ 🐟

Located on the northern shores of North Barriere Lake, there are five open camping spots at the lake. The sandy beach and cartop boat launch allow visitors to enjoy swimming, fishing and other water sports.

Vidette Lake Rec Site (Map 48/E7) 🏕️ ➰ ➰ 🐟

Just north of Deadman Lake, Vidette Lake is a narrow lake offering anglers a chance to test their luck. The small rec site on the lake has two campsites and a cartop boat launch. Access into the area is quite good (via Deadman Vidette Road).

Whitewood Lake Rec Site (Map 41/G1) 🥾 ➰ ➰ 🐟

Accessed by the Jamieson Creek Forest Service Road north of Kamloops, it is possible to haul in a small RV to this site. In addition to a cartop boat launch, visitors have a choice of either camping in the open or under the trees. There is room for about 15 camping units at this recreation site.

Willard Lake Rec Site (Map 31/F2) 🏕️ ➰ 🚶 🚴 ➰ 🐟

To the southeast of Ashcroft, this site is located on the Barnes Lake Road. The site is located in an open range next to the lake and receives heavy use throughout the year. It has two camping spots and a cartop boat launch. Activities in the area include fishing (ice fishing and open water fishing) as well as hiking and biking.

Windfall Lake Rec Site (Map 49/G6) 🏕️ ➰ ➰ ➰ 🚻

This small lake is found along the Jamieson Creek Road (rough 2wd access) not far from Bonaparte Lake. The high elevation, forested recreation site offers five camping sites as well as a cartop boat launch for anglers and paddlers.

Windy Lake Rec Site (Map 41/F1) 🏕️ ➰ ➰ 🐟

Found on the Bonaparte Plateau, Windy Lake can live up to its name. Luckily, the five unit campsite is set in a dense forest.

Cascades Forest District Sites

The southwest portion of this book is found around the city of Merritt. Once again, fishing is the primary focus of recreation in the area but there are plenty of other things to do when out and about.

Abbott Lake Rec Site (Map 24/C3)

Abbott Lake is found off the Tyner FSR and has four camping units in a semi-open area. There is a cartop boat launch and picnic tables for day-trippers.

Andy's Lake Rec Site (Map 16/D7)

Andy's Lake Recreation Site is set in an opening next to the lake. It is best accessed by Thynne Mountain Road and the two units are used mostly by fishermen in the spring through fall and by snowmobilers in the winter. There is a short walk to reach the lake.

Antler Lake Rec Site (Map 24/E1)

Antler Lake is located northeast of Chataway Lake on a 4wd spur road. There are three tenting sites set in the forest on the east side of the lake.

Big OK (Island) Lake Site (Map 32/A6)

Located to the west of Highland Valley and off the Pimainus Lake Road, this recreation site has six camping units and is set in the trees next to a small lake. Despite its size, the lake is one of the better fishing holes in the southern interior. There is a cartop boat launch as well as tables at the Forest Service site.

Billy Lake Rec Site (Map 32/E7)

Billy Lake is found north of Chataway Lake and has three camping units in a semi-open area next to the lake. There is also a cartop boat launch at the lake, which is accessed by 4wd vehicle.

Bluey Lake Rec Site (Map 17/C4)

There are seven camping units set in a Douglas-fir forest next to the lake. A 4wd road south of Bates Road and the popular Kentucky-Alleyne Recreation Area reaches the recreation site.

Bob Lake Rec Site (Map 25/C2)

Bob Lake has three vehicle units located on a difficult to find 4wd access road. Please keep in mind that access is not off the Coquihalla during May through October because of road closures. Rather, access must be gained from Monck Park Road and the extensive logging road network that leads to the north.

Bob's Lake Rec Site (Map 17/G3)

Bob's Lake is located on the Elkhart Road just north of the Coquihalla Connector (Hwy 97C). There are two semi-open campsites next to the lake as well as picnic tables and access to the lake.

Boot Lake Rec Site (Map 17/G3)

Boot Lake is found on a 4wd road off the Elkhart Road. There are a total of four forested campsites and a cartop boat launch.

Boss Lake Rec Site (Map 16/G4)

Boss Lake is one of three very popular lakes in the Voght Valley. The good road access allows RVs and cars into the area. As a result, the 13 campsites in the semi-open area are often full. There is a cartop boat launch at the Forest Service site.

Botanie Lake Rec Site (Map 23/A1)

This small, semi-open recreation site is located next to Botanie Lake off the Botanie Valley Road. The access to the lake is good enough so allow small RVs to reach the site. Please note that the lake is on an Indian Reserve and so access may be restricted.

Brook Lake Rec Site (Map 16/B4)

Brook Lake offers a day-use only site at the end of a deteriorating road. This is a popular place for anglers to go chasing small rainbows.

Buck Lake Rec Site (Map 17/E5)

Buck Lake is located on the Siwash Creek FSR south of the Loon Lake Exit on the Coquihalla Connector (Hwy 97C). There are eight campsites as well as a boat launch for visitors to enjoy.

Cabin Lake Rec Site (Map 15/F2)

This is a small (two unit) site located by rough 4wd/ATV road. Hikers accessing the Heather Basin Trail frequent the area.

Calling Lake Rec Site (Map 32/A7)

Found south of Big Ok Lake, Calling Lake is often a little quieter place to visit. There are three campsites, which are easily accessed off the Pimainus Lake Road.

Chain Lake Rec Site (Map 10/A1)

Chain Lake is a popular destination next to the Princeton-Summerland Road. The large site offers room for 25 units in a semi-open location next to the lake. Due to the good road access, this is a favourite site with RVs and larger trailers. There is an opportunity to launch a small boat onto the lake or explore the Kettle Valley Railway trail.

Clifford Lake Rec Site (Map 16/D4)

The first of a series of small fishing lakes found in the Otter Valley, Clifford Lake offers three campsites. Access into the area is by Youngsberg Road.

Copper Creek Rec Site (Map 1/C4)

This small site is located 1 km from Highway 3 on the Placer Mountain FSR. There are a total of four units in a semi-open location next to the creek. RVs can access the site so it makes a good stopover for travelers on the Hope-Princeton Highway.

Davis Lake Rec Site (Map 16/G4)

Davis Lake is perhaps the most popular lake in the Voght Valley. Despite the size of the rec site (57 campsites) it is often difficult to find a site. The semi-open forest and good road access make this site ideal for RVs. A boat launch provides access to the lake.

Deadman Lake South Site (Map 17/B7)

Deadman Lake is located on a 4wd road off the Ketchan Lake FSR. There are a total of three semi-open camping units next to the lake.

Dewdney Rec Site (Map 9/E5)

Dewdney is the closest site to Princeton on the Old Hedley Road. The good road access and open setting under Ponderosa pine trees allows room for about three RVs or campers. Visitors can test the waters with a fishing line or on a canoe or explore the surrounding area for Indian pictographs.

Dot Lake Rec Site (Map 24/E1)

Dot Lake is found just southeast of Chataway Lake on a 2wd spur road off the Aberdeen Road. There are two camping units on a forested shore of the lake.

Eastmere Lake Rec Site (Map 18/A4)

Just north of Osprey Lake, Eastmere Lake is a difficult to access lake. Visitors will find two campsites next to the lake.

Elkhart Lake Rec Site (Map 17/G4)

Although the road leads by Elkhart Lake, a short hike accesses the rec site. There is room for two tenting parties in the forest next to the lake. It is possible to haul a canoe or small boat to the lake.

Garrison Lake Rec Site (Map 1/A3)

With new road activity in the area, it is rumoured that Garrison Lake is no longer a hike-in lake. But visitors looking to access this lake will need our Southwestern BC mapbook. For the rest of you, a trailhead is found on a 4wd access road off of the Sunday Summit FSR. Given the difficult access, the recreation site is not particularly busy.

Gillis Lake Rec Sites (Map 16/C3)

The Murray Lake Road to the west of Kingsvale accesses Gillis Lake East and West Recreation Sites. There are six treed camping sites at the west site, while the east site is day-use only. There is also a boat launch at the west site for anglers testing their luck.

Glimpse Lake Rec Site (Map 26/A4)

This recreation site is made up of two separate campgrounds, one at the north end and one at the south end of the lake. The northernmost site has 14 camping units and is located in a Douglas fir forest. The southernmost site has nine camping units and is in the Douglas fir/spruce forest next to the lake.

Goose Lake Forest Service Sites (Map 16/G7)

There are 11 camping units divided between two sites on Goose Lake. The south has nine camping units set in the forest, while the north only has two rather open sites. If they are busy, there are several other lakes in the vicinity that offer camping areas.

Gordon Lake Rec Site (Map 24/C3)

Gordon Lake is found on a 4wd road off the Tyner FSR. There are four camping units set in the trees next to the lake. A cartop boat launch is also at the site.

Granite Creek Site (Map 9/A5)

Granite Creek Recreation Site is found just south of Coalmont on the Lodestone Lake FSR. Its proximity to the main road (Tulameen Road.), the scenic Tulameen River and the Kettle Valley Railway makes it a very popular Forest Service site. There are 12 campsites together with a picnic facility and a cartop boat launch.

Gwen Lake Rec Site (Map 16/G1)

Although found close to the Coquihalla Highway, access into Gwen Lake is rather rough and not recommended for RVs. The recreation site is situated in the trees next to the west side of the lake and offers a total of three campsites.

Gypsum Lake Rec Site (Map 24/E1)

Gypsum Lake is found on a 2wd spur road off of the Aberdeen Road. There are two camping units set in the trees next to the lake. There is also a cartop boat launch in the area.

Harman Lake Rec Sites (Map 17/A2)

The Kane Valley is extremely popular with fishermen and finding a camping area anywhere is often difficult. This is particularly true at Harman Lake since it is big enough to allow RVs. There are two different locations totaling 25 camping units, 16 in the east, nine in the west. The easternmost site is located in an opening and is often windswept, whereas the westernmost site is more sheltered and found within the trees. In addition to a boat launch at the east site, there is an impressive trail system in the area to explore.

Helmer Lake Site (Map 25/A2)

Despite its proximity to the Coquihalla Highway, vehicle access into this site is rather difficult. The road leading from the Helmer Exit is closed from May to October. People willing to walk the short distance in will often find their choice of the three nice camping sites on the south end of the lake. During the summer, it is possible to access the site by vehicle from the south.

Hook Lake Rec Sites (Map 17/C6)

There are two recreation sites at Hook Lake as well as a cartop boat launch. There is no camping at the south site, while there are five vehicle units at the north. Hook Lake is a small lake west of Missezula Lake that is found off the Ketchan Lake FSR.

Island Lake Rec Site (Map 18/A3)

This lake is known as a trophy fishing lake and visitors will find a small site with five campsites together with a cartop boat launch. Due to the rough access, the site is not suitable for RVs or trailers.

Jacobson Lake Site (Map 8/A7)

Found well down the Tulameen River Forest Service Road, this small three unit site is not accessible to hunters in the fall. It is used primarily by backpackers using the HBC Brigade Trail.

Johnny Lake Rec Site (Map 16/G7)

Yet another small fishing lake found off Youngsberg Road, next to the Otter Valley. There are three campsites on the forested south end of the lake.

Kane Lake Site (Map 17/A1)

The Lower Kane Lake offers a scenic but busy site next to the bulrushes on the south side of the lake. There is room for five camping units as well as a deteriorating wharf and cartop boat launches scattered around both lakes. These lakes are RV accessible and receive heavy use during the summer primarily by fishermen. There is also an excellent trail system in the area.

Kump Lake Rec Site (Map 17/A7)

Found just off Highway 5A, there are two semi-open sites on the east side of the Kump Lake.

LeRoi Lake Rec Site (Map 24/C1)

LeRoi Lake is another one of the lakes in the popular Chataway Lake area. The rec site offers room for one camping party on the shores of the small lake.

Link Lake Rec Site (Map 10/A1)

Link Lake is one of a series of popular lakes found on the Princeton-Summerland Road and next to the Kettle Valley Railway trail. This lake offers ten RV accessible campsites and a cartop boat launch. The site is less than 1 km southwest of Osprey Lake.

Lightning Lake Rec Site (Map 15/D2)
This campsite is found in a heavily forested area next to a small mountain lake. There is room for about two units. A 4wd vehicle is required to access the lake.

Lily Lake Rec Site (Map 16/D1)
Located on the Lily Lake Road (2wd access), this recreation site offers five campsites in a semi-open area next to the lake. There is a cartop boat launch together with a day-use area. Fishing is the primary attraction to this Forest Service site.

Little Box Canyon Rec Site (Map 24/B7)
A day-use site showcasing the scenic Little Box Canyon on Spius Creek. The nearby Spius Creek Hatchery is another interesting sight in the area.

Little Douglas (Map 8/A2)
A hike-in site below Zum Peak, this high elevation lake is a nice summer getaway for anglers or hikers.

Lodestone Creek Rec Site (Map 8/E5)
Lodestone Lake is located on a 4wd road (Lodestone Lake FSR). The Forest Service site, which is located in a semi-open forest, has two camping spots and is used by fishermen and as a stopover for hikers or horseback riders on the Hope Brigade Trail.

Lodwick Lake Forest Service Sites (Map 16/G7)
There are two small sites at either end of this popular fishing lake. In total, there are eight camping units, including five at the more open south end.

Loosemore Lake Rec Site (Map 17/A7)
Loosemore Lake is a small fishing lake sandwiched between the Otter Valley and Highway 5A. There are four camping sites at the north end of the lake.

Lundbom Lake Rec Sites (Map 25/B7)
There are a pair of popular campgrounds on Lundbom Lake. In total there are 55 campsites, 20 sites at the eastern site, and 35 in the western. Both sites have a choice of camping units in the forest or in the open. The better boat launch is found at the east end of the lake.

Marquart Lakes Rec Site (Map 25/A7)
There are 14 vehicle units set in a grassy area next to the east side of the lake. Due to the proximity to Highway 5A, the lake and rec site make a nice picnic destination.

Martin's Lake Rec Site (Map 9/D5)
Martin's Lake is located on the Princeton-Summerland Road just north of Princeton and provides two campsites easily accessed by paved road. There is a boat launch and picnic facilities, but fishing is the main recreation pursuit at the site.

Missezula Lake Rec Site (Map 17/C6)
Located on the eastern shores of the lake, this site has eight camping units. The site is treed and has a cartop boat launch. The scenic lake is found east of Highway 5A on the Missezula FSR.

Murphy Lake Forest Service Sites (Map 8/D3)
There are sites on both the east and west end of the lake but all the camping happens at the west site (there are four spaces). Both sites are popular with fishermen and hikers.

Murray Creek Rec Site (Map 31/A6)
Located on the Murray Creek FSR, this is a small semi-open site, which requires a 4wd to reach. The recreation site is next to Murray Creek and is used primarily by hunters in the fall.

Murray Lake Forest Service Sites (Map 16/B6)
There are two campgrounds found on Murray Lake, which, in turn, is found on the Murray Lake Road north of Exit 240 of the Coquihalla Highway. In total there are 15 campsites on the lake, 12 at the north and three at the south, with the primary users being fishermen.

N'Kwala Rec Site (Map 24/B6)
This nine unit site is found on the Nicola River, and is a popular put-in or take-out for canoeists and kayakers exploring the river.

Old Hedley West and East Sites (Map 10/B4)
On the Similkameen River, these two sites share a total of 16 sites; nine at the east site, the remaining at the west site. They are located in a semi-open Ponderosa pine forest and allow room for RVs. There are several Indian Pictograph sites in the area.

Peterhope Lake Rec Site (Map 25/G3)
There is room for 15 vehicle units at this forest service site, set on the northern shores of Peterhope Lake. The lake is very popular with anglers looking for large rainbow trout.

Pimainus Lake Rec Site (Map 24/A1)
Located on a 2wd road (Pimainus Lake Road) south of Highland Valley, this recreation site has three camping units set in the trees next to the lake. The area is popular throughout the year with fishing, paddling and snowmobiling being the primary recreation pursuits.

Placer Lake Rec Site (Map 1/D6)
In the southwest reaches of this book, Placer Lake is a remote hike-in lake. There are four campsites set in the trees next to the lake.

Plateau Lake Rec Site (Map 26/A2)
Found in the hills west of Stump Lake, Plateau Lake offers six tenting units and access to the lake. The access into the lake requires a 4wd vehicle following the road from Peter Hope Lake.

Prosser Lake Rec Site (Map 17/B7)
Prosser Lake has four vehicle units, and is located on a 4wd access road off the Ketchan Lake FSR. Anglers are the main visitors.

Rampart Lake Rec Site (Map 9/D1)
To the north of Princeton, Rampart Lake is found on logging roads off the Summers Creek Road. There are six campsites at the south end of the lake as well as a cartop boat launch for anglers.

Reservoir Lake Rec Site (Map 18/B3)
Reservoir Lake is accessed by 4wd road off the Bear FSR. There are a total of four sites in a semi-open area next to the lake. The cartop boat launch can be used by anglers and canoeists.

Rickey Lake Rec Site (Map 16/G7)
Part of a series of good fishing lakes next to the Otter Valley, Rickey Lake offers a small rec site with four camping units. There is also a cartop boat launch to aid anglers.

Robertson Lake Rec Site (Map 17/A7)
Robertson Lake is a small fishing lake found west of Highway 5A. There are four semi-open camping sites at the lake.

Roscoe Lake Rec Site (Map 24/D1)
Roscoe Lake is found on a 2wd road to the northwest of Chataway Lake. There are four campsites at the south end of the lake together with a cartop boat launch. A hiking trail leads around Roscoe Lake and over to Knight Lake.

Shea Lake Rec Site (Map 16/D2)
Despite the pothole-laden road leading up the hill from the Voght Valley Road, this site can be busy on weekends throughout the

summer. There are a total of five sites located on the north end of the lake in a semi-open forest. It is possible to hand launch small boats onto the lake.

Silver Lake Rec Site (Map 15/G2)

Located in a spruce/Lodgepole pine stand next to the lake are four camping units and a cartop boat launch. The site is found on a rough 2wd road west of Spius Creek.

Stoney Lake Rec Site (Map 17/A7)

Yet another lake in the cluster of fishing lakes southwest of Aspen Grove. Stoney Lake has two treed sites located on the east side of the lake. In winter, this site is used by snowmobilers.

Stringer Lake Rec Site (Map 9/C1)

To the north of Princeton, the Stringer Lake Recreation Site is located on a 4wd access road from Allison Lake. There are three campsites that are used primarily by fishermen.

Sussex Lake Rec Site (Map 25/B1)

Access into Sussex Lake requires a 4wd vehicle from the road leading past Surrey Lake. Sussex offers room for two camping units.

Sutter Creek Rec Site (Map 8/B6)

This site is found on the Tulameen River FSR in a quaint little area next to the creek. There are two campsites within a semi-open forest. Hiking to Treasure Mountain and hunting are popular pastimes.

Tahla Lake Rec Site (Map 16/G4)

Tahla Lake is the quietest of the three lakes in the Voght Valley but still sees its share of visitors. The small rec site has three campsites in the trees at the south end of the lake. There is a cartop boat launch.

Thalia Lake Rec Sites (Map 16/G7)

There is one camping area at the south end of Thalia Lake and one at the north end. When combined, they offer nine campsites together with a cartop boat launch. The southernmost site is more open than the northernmost site.

Third Lake Rec Site (Map 24/A1)

Found west of the more popular Pimainus Lake, Third Lake often makes for a quieter retreat. There is room for four camping units in the area.

Tupper Lake Rec Site (Map 32/E7)

There are three camping units and a cartop boat launch at this small lake southwest of Logan Lake. The area surrounding Tupper Lake is rich in history of mining activity.

Tyner Lake Rec Site (Map 24/D3)

Tyner Lake is found on the Tyner FSR and has three sites set in the forest next to the lake. There is also a cartop boat launch for anglers and paddlers to explore the lake.

Vinson Lake Rec Site (Map 17/E6)

Found 200 metres from the nearest road, Vinson Lake is a day-use only site.

Vuich Falls Rec Site (Map 8/B6)

This small two unit recreation site is located on the Tulameen River FSR near Sutter Creek. The scenic site is used primarily by hunters.

Wells Lake Rec Site (Map 8/E7)

Although it is possible to access Wells Lake by a 4wd road off the Tulameen River Forest Service Road, most visitors into the area come via trail. There are a total of four rustic tenting pads located next to the small fishing lake. Fishermen or travellers on the Whatcom Trail are the primary users of this site.

Okanagan Shuswap Forest District-Penticton Area

The following sites are found around the city of Penticton in the southern portion of the hot Okanagan Valley. Although this area is famous for its beautiful sandy beaches and warm lakes, it is the small mountain lakes that host the majority of the recreation sites in the region.

Allendale Lake Rec Site (Map 12/C7)

Allendale Lake is located on a rough 2wd spur road off the Okanagan Falls FSR. It is a small, forested site complete with toilet and table facilities. The recreation site is used as an alternative to the nearby commercial fishing camp.

Brenda Lake Rec Site (Map 18/E4)

There are five vehicle units in this small site on the shores of Brenda Lake, which is a popular fishing hole. Although the lake is easily accessed, snow can linger into June at this high elevation area.

Browne Lake Rec Site (Map 20/E6)

Browne Lake is to the north of McCulloch Lake on a 2wd road. There is a small (five unit), semi-open site next to the lake complete with toilet and table facilities. The main attraction to the area is the fishing at the three small lakes in the area.

Burnell (Sawmill) Lake Site (Map 3/E3)

This is an open site with space for about ten camping units next to the lake. The site is used mainly by fishermen and provides a cartop boat launch as well as toilet and table facilities. There is also a trail around the lake as well as a day-use area for picnicking.

Cameo (Cameron) Lake Site (Map 19/A2)

Cameo Lake is located on the Bear Creek Main and is a small open site with four campsites as well as a cartop boat launch. The recreation site is used as a stop-over for fishermen trying their luck in a number of nearby lakes or by hunters in the fall.

Chute Lake Rec Site (Map 11/G1)

Found at the south end of the lake near the Chute Lake Resort, this is a popular place for fishermen and bikers and hikers traveling along the Kettle Valley Railway. This small, treed site has space for four campsites and is user-maintained.

Crescent Lake Rec Site (Map 18/D5)

Crescent Lake is located a few kilometres to the east of the Headwater Lakes on the Peachland FSR (good 2wd access). It is a small site with four campsites set on the dam in an open, exposed area. It is not particularly beautiful but it does provide good access to the lake for fishermen.

Hatheume Lake Rec Site (Map 18/E2)

Found near the Hatheume Lake Resort, there are 12 forested campsites at this rec site. The lake is popular with anglers interested in a good catch and release fishery.

Headwater Lakes Rec Site (Map 18/E5)

This small (seven unit), forested site is located in the centre of the Headwater Lakes. It provides a quiet, scenic camping spot for individuals wishing to try their luck fishing at one of the four Headwater lakes. Access to this recreation site is a little rough so RVs should not try to reach this site. There is also a resort and cross-country ski trails in the area.

Horseshoe Canyon Rec Site (Map 2/E5)

Horseshoe Canyon is located 11 km (6.7 miles) along the Ashnola River Road and offers room for two units. The site is primarily used as a stopover for visitors heading into Cathedral Provincial Park or for fisherman, hikers and hunters in the Ashnola River area.

Hydraulic Lake Rec Site (Map 20/E7)

The lakes in this area are collectively known as the Hydraulic Lakes. This enhanced site is located on the north end of McCulloch Lake (the biggest lake of the bunch) and offers 14 forested campsites and a cartop boat launch. Also in the area is a commercial resort, a 3 km (1.8 km) hiking trail, a series of cross-country trails and the famed Kettle Valley Railway.

Idleback Lake Rec Site (Map 12/C5)

This medium-sized (15 unit), forested site is located on the shores of Idleback Lake. There is a trail around the lake, which is restricted to electric motors only and fly fishing.

Isintok Lake Rec Site (Map 10/F4)

Located on a good 2wd, this medium-sized (five vehicle units), forested site has toilet and table facilities as well as a cartop boat launch. The recreation site is set beneath Isintok Mountain and next to the lake providing a beautiful setting. It is used primarily by fishermen and hunters.

Jackpine Lake Rec Site (Map 19/A3)

Jackpine Lake is found off the Jackpine FSR (2wd access) and offers six open campsites next to the lake. The site is used by fishermen as well as prospectors interested in exploring the surrounding area including the gold mine nearby. A commercial fishing camp is also located on Jackpine Lake.

James Lake Rec Site (Map 20/D3)

This is a small, semi-open site located on a rough 2wd road. The recreation site is mainly used by fishermen and offers a cartop boat launch.

Lambly (Bear) Lake Rec Site (Map 19/B3)

This medium-sized (14 unit), open recreation site is located next to Lambly Lake and provides a more rustic alternative to staying at the resort on the lake. The recreation site is mainly used by fishermen and offers a cartop boat launch.

MacDonald Lake Rec Site (Map 18/E4)

MacDonald Lake is found next to Brenda Lake. Although the lake is smaller, the rec site is slightly larger offering room for six units and a boat launch.

McCulloch (Minnow Lake) Rec Site (Map 20/E7)
$

This is a medium-sized, treed site located towards the south end of the popular McCulloch Lake. The site marks the beginning of McCulloch Canoe Route, which is a pleasant route joining the Hydraulic Lake. In addition to a place to launch a boat, there are toilet and table facilities as well as a hiking trail leading to the Hydraulic Lake Rec Site. There is also a series of cross-country ski trails and the Kettle Valley Railway trail in the area.

Madden Lake Rec Site (Map 3/E3)

Found northwest of Oliver, Madden Lake is found just south of Ripley Lake. The rec site on Madden is located in an open area and has room for eight vehicle units next to the lake. In addition to a cartop boat launch, there is a trail around the lake.

Mount Kobau Trails Rec Site (Map 3/B3)

Mount Kobau provides a scenic vantage point over both the Similameen and Okanagan Valleys. Although there is space for three vehicle units to overnight, most visitors simply picnic at the lookout or enjoy exploring the trails in the area.

Nickle Plate Lake (Map 10/E1)

On the boundary of Nickle Plate Provincial Park, there is a three vehicle unit campsite for visitors to enjoy. The lake is a popular fishing destination and there are a series of good trails to explore in the area. The small rec site is set in an opening next to the lake and sports a cartop boat launch.

Peachland Lake Site (Map 18/F5)

Peachland Lake is a pretty lake with a little island in the middle. RV's and other campers will find good access from the Brenda Mine Road and room for about eight units in an open area on the eastern shores of the lake.

Pinnacle Lake Rec Site (Map 18/E2)

This small, five campsite rec site is set in a forested area next to a small lake. Visitors to the area either fish here or venture to one of the many surrounding lakes.

Red Bridge Rec Site (Map 2/E4)

Named after the easily identified landmark signaling the start of the Ashnola River Road, this site is found 8.6 km (5.2 miles) down the road. It is a medium-sized (nine vehicle units) site next to the river with room for RV's. The site is primarily used as a stopover for visitors heading into Cathedral Provincial Park or for anglers, hikers and hunters in the Ashnola River area.

Ripley Lake Rec Site (Map 3/E3)

Ripley Lake is located to the north of Madden Lake on a rough secondary road. The recreation site provides a nice, quiet spot to try some fishing. Each camping unit (there are seven) has a table.

Silver Lake Rec Site (Map 19/A5)

This six-unit site is located on the north end of Silver Lake near the BC Forestry Camp. The site is set in the sylvan shoreline and has toilet and table facilities.

Solco Lake Rec Site (Map 12/D7)

There are six vehicle units at this site, found on the Solco Lake Branch Road (rough 2wd access). The site is user-maintained and is used mostly by anglers.

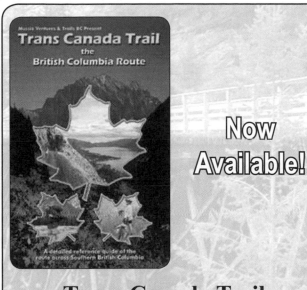
Thirsk Lake Rec Site (Map 18/C7)

The biggest of the series of lakes found on the Princeton-Summerland Road, Thirsk Lake is actually a reservoir. Plans are to flood the area. In the meantime, there is room for six units in the opening on the northern shores of Thirsk Lake. In addition to fishing, visitors can explore the famed Kettle Valley Railway in the area.

Trout Creek Crossing Site (Map 10/G1)

Found next to Trout Creek, the Princeton-Summerland Road and the Kettle Valley Railway is a small (five unit) campsite. Despite the nice forested setting and good road access, this site is not as busy as others in the area.

Whitehead Lake Rec Site (Map 18/B6)

Whitehead Lake is located in the hills above Chain Lake along a deteriorating 2wd road. The recreation site is located in the trees next to the lake and has toilet and table facilities as well as six campsites. Whitehead Lake offers reasonable fishing but it is a domestic reservoir for Summerland, so it is subject to draw down.

Windy Lake Rec Site (Map 18/G2)

Windy Lake is found just west of Cameo Lake along the Bear Creek Main. The small (two unit), forested site offers a quaint camping experience on a high elevation lake.

Okanagan Shuswap Forest District-Salmon Arm

Shuswap Lake is the focus point of recreation in this area but this lake is managed by BC Parks as well as numerous commercial facilities. The forest service focuses its facilities on the more remote lakes and interesting backcountry features in the area.

Bryden Lake Rec Site (Map 35/G1)

Bryden Lake offers a small, user-maintained site, which is accessed by trail from a branch road of the Charcoal Creek FSR.

Cooke Creek Rec Site (Map 37/D4)

This site is located along the Enderby-Mabel Lake Road (good 2wd access) on the banks of the Shuswap River. The area is particularly popular during the fall when the sockeye salmon are running. There is a fish hatchery and hiking trails in the area.

Cummings Lake Rec Site (Map 45/F6)

This is a small, forested site that is reached by trail off the Cummings Branch Road. The trail is used by fishermen in the summer and by snowmobilers/cross-country skiers in the winter.

Dale Lake Rec Site (Map 37/D3)

This site is easily accessed off the Cooke Grassy FSR and is found next to a small, marshy lake. The recreation site has several camping pads in the forest next to the lake. Fishing is the primary attraction.

Elbow Lake Rec Site (Map 37/D3)

Located on a rough spur road from Cooke Grassy FSR, this site has several treed lakeshore sites with picnic tables. The small, shallow lake is best fished from the water but there are no boat launching facilities.

Frog Falls Rec Site (Map 46/C5)

A small site located in a dense forest near Frog Falls on Wap Creek. A short hike leads to the scenic falls.

Grassy Lake Rec Site (Map 37/E3)

Grassy Lake is a small lake, northeast of Elbow Lake along a rough 4wd spur road off the Cooke Grassy FSR. The lake has a marshy shoreline, which limits shore fishing and boat launching.

Harper Lake Rec Site (Map 35/C1)

On a 2wd road south of Chase, this small site is found on the shores of a scenic mountain lake. The fishing at the lake remains fairly good throughout the spring and fall. The site has toilet and table facilities for the overnight camper.

Herman Lake Rec Site (Map 44/F5)

This is a small timbered site near Herman Lake that has a boardwalk built along the marshy shoreline of the lake. The area has hiking trails that circle the lake that allow you to see plenty of waterfowl. The recreation site is easily accessed on the Bastion-White Lake FSR from the west or the Bastion-Ivy FSR from the north.

Holiday Lake Rec Site (Map 37/F2) ▲ ♨ ◅ ⬜

This site is located on the shores of a marshy lake, which offers reasonable fishing during the spring and fall. It is found off a 2wd spur road off the Beattie Road. There are several camping pads set in the trees next to the lake complete with picnic tables. Fishing is the primary attraction to the recreation site.

Humamilt Lake Sites (Maps 52/E4, 53/A4) ⬜ ♨ ⬛ ◅ ⓘ ⬜

Humamilt Lake is a long narrow lake in the hills between Adams and Shuswap Lakes. There are two separate campgrounds, one at the west end of the lake and one at the east end of the lake. The western site is a medium sized site with easy access from Humamilt Lake Road. The eastern recreation site is a smaller site with a cartop boat launch.

Kernagan Lake Rec Site (Map 36/A3) ▲ ◅

The rough 4wd access limits visitors to this small lake west of the Salmon River Valley. It is possible to hand launch small boats at the lake.

Kidney Lake Rec Site (Map 37/G1) ▲ ⬛ ⬜ ◅ ⓘ

Despite the rough access, the scenic, mountain lake receives heavy use by fishermen during the spring and summer months. A reasonable boat launch is available at the site as are a number of picnic tables.

Kwikoit Creek Rec Site (Map 44/A2) ⬜ ◅ ⓘ ⬜

This small, timbered site is easily accessed on the Scotch Creek Forest Service Road and provides camping for tents and small RVs. Most visitors try their luck fishing the creek or hunting in the fall. Plans are to close this site in the near future.

Nellie Lake Rec Site (Map 53/A6) ⬜ ♨ ⬛ ◅

Nellie Lake is a small lake just north of Albas Provincial Park. The rec site contains picnic tables and toilet facilities and can be accessed by small RVs.

Noisy Creek Site (Map 37/G2) ⬜ ♨ ⬛ ⬜ ⬜ ⬜ ⬜ ◅ $

Most of the activities at this small sheltered site on the western shores of Mabel Lake are focused around the lake and at the nice sandy beach. There is also a boat launch at the rec site.

Noreen Lake Rec Site (Map 37/F2) ▲ ⬜ ⬜ ◅

This site is located next to the tiny lake off a 4wd spur road from the Beattie Road north of Kingfisher. There are several forested, lakeside campsites as well as a rough cartop boat launch.

Pement Lake Rec Site (Map 35/G1) ▲ ⬜ ◅

This small, user-maintained site is found on the same trail as Bryden Lake. Both sites have picnic tables and tenting facilities and are primarily used by fishermen.

Queest Mountain South Site (Map 45/C3) ▲ ♨ ⬜ ⓘ

This small recreation site is located on the top of Queest Mountain at the forestry lookout. It is possible to drive to the top but most visitors prefer to hike up or bring their snowmobile in the winter.

Rosemond Lake Rec Site (Map 36/G1) ▲ ♨ ◅

Rosemond Lake is really an extension of Mara Lake. On the western shores of the lake is a small recreation site, which provides tenting facilities as well as picnic tables. Access into the area is restricted by private property; therefore, it is necessary to take the longer route that switchbacks east from the Rosemond Branch Road down to Rosemond Lake.

Seymour River Falls Rec Site (Map 53/C4) ⬜ ⓘ

This is a small day-use area, which marks the beginning of the short trail to the scenic waterfalls.

Skimikin Lake Site (Map 44/A7) ▲ ♨ ⬜ ⬜ ⬜ ◅ ⬜

This semi-open, medium-sized site is easily accessed on the Skimikin Lake Road west of Tappen Valley. The lake is a popular fishing hole and is home to a series of cross-country trails in the winter. Snowmobiling as well as biking and hiking in the summer are other popular activities here.

Spruce Lake Rec Site (Map 37/D3) ▲ ♨ ◅

Spruce Lake is just north of Dale Lake, not far off the Cooke Grassy FSR. The recreation site is used primarily by fishermen trying their luck at this small, marshy lake and has several lakeshore tent pads and some picnic tables.

Stoney Lake Rec Site (Map 37/F1) ▲ ♨ ◅

There are several camping pads located on the forested shoreline of Stoney Lake, which is located just northeast of Holiday Lake on a 4wd spur road. The recreation site is a good choice for a secluded weekend get-away as the poor access limits the number of visitors.

Wallensteen Lake Rec Site (Map 36/A3) ▲ ⬛ ⬜ ⬜ ◅

This small lakeshore site, which has a cartop boat launch, is used mostly by hunters and fishermen. The area also comes alive in winter as snowmobilers follow the endless road system around Fly Hill.

Wap Lake Rec Site (Map 46/A6) ⬜ ♨ ⬛ ⬜ ⬜ ◅ ⓘ

Wap Lake is a scenic lake with good road access. Although the forested site is small, there is room for smaller RVs and campers. A cartop boat launch provides access for anglers and canoeists to explore the lake.

Okanagan Shuswap Forest District-Vernon Area

At the north end of the hot Okanagan Valley, the Vernon Forest District offers an excellent array of mountain lakes to visit. Access into these areas is not always easy as the myriad of roads can make backroad travel a little confusing. With the right vehicle and a little patience, visitors will find this region a joy to explore.

Aileen Lake Rec Site (Map 28/F7) ⛺ 🚤 🎣 🐟
This small (3 unit) site is accessed by a very rough 4wd road from the Dee Lake Road. There is a good cartop boat launch at the recreation site.

Arthur Lake Rec Site (Map 36/A5) ⛺ 🏕 🚤 🎣 🐟 📷
This forested site is to the south of Spa Lake and has eight camping spots. It is accessed off the 2wd Bolean Lake Road and has a rough cartop boat launch.

Baird Lake Rec Site (Map 37/E5) ⛺ 🏕 🚤 🎣 🐟 📷
Despite the size of this small mountain lake, there are two separate campgrounds on the lake. The seven campsites are used primarily by fishermen. The lake is easily accessed off the Hidden Lake Road, just east of Hidden Lake, and has a good cartop boat launch.

Bardolph Lake Site (Map 28/G3) ⛺ 🚤 🎣 🏍 🐟 📷
Located in the Vernon Hills Interpretive Forest, this site provides a few tenting pads and a rough cartop boat launch on the north end of the lake. The access into the lake is quite rough.

Bear Lake Rec Site (Map 28/E6) ⛺ 🚤 🎣 🐟
There are three camping units together with a rough cartop boat launch at this site on Bear Lake. It is accessed by a reasonably good 2wd road east of King Edward Lake.

Becker Lake Rec Sites (Map 28/F3) ⛺ 🚶 🚲 🏍 🐟
The Becker Lake Recreation Site has ten camping units in two different areas on the north side of the lake. Becker Lake is part of the Vernon Hill Interpretative Forest and there are several trails in the area to explore if you are not into fishing.

Bisson Lake Rec Site (Map 22/A1) ⛺ 🚤 🎣 🐟 📷
Located on a rough 4wd spur road off of the Kettle Valley FSR near Highway 6, this small lakeshore recreation site has a cartop boat launch and five camping units. It is used mainly by fishermen.

Blackwell Lake Rec Site (Map 26/E1) ⛺ 🚶 🐟
Blackwell Lake is accessed by a 3 km (1.8 mile) trail from Pratt Lake to the north. Blackwell makes a fine overnight camping destination for anglers.

Bolean Lake Rec Site (Map 35/G5) 🏕 🏕 🚤 🎣 🐟
Bolean Lake is a popular fishery that is easily accessed by the Bolean Lake Road north of Falkland. The rec site is located just past the fishing lodge. There are eight campsites next to the lake together with a good cartop boat launch.

Bouleau Lakes Sites (Map 27/D3) 🏕 ⛺ 🚤 🎣 🐟 📷
Accessed by the Bouleau Main to the west of Okanagan Lake, there are two sites for visitors to the Bouleau Lakes. On the east side of the bigger lake is the **Bouleau Lake Recreation Site**, which has ten campsites together with a good cartop boat launch. At the west end of the lake system and next to the smaller lake is the **Little Bouleau Lake Recreation Site**. This site is often less busy as it only offers three campsites and a rough cartop boat launch. Both sites are situated in a forested setting and are used mainly by fishermen and hunters.

Bruer Creek Rec Site (Map 21/G2) 🏕 🐟 📷
Found at the junction of Bruer Creek and the Kettle River, this roadside site can be a little noisy when the logging trucks are running. There are four campsites that are used by fishermen and hunters.

Brunette Lake Rec Site (Map 28/F7) ⛺ 🚤 🎣 🐟
Brunette Lake is accessed by rough 2wd road from the Flyfish Lake No. 1 Forest Service Site. There is a rough cartop boat launch at the site as well as a few tenting pads.

Cascade South Sites (Map 37/F6) ⛺ 🏕 🏖 🚤 🐟 🚻
This site is located about 15 km (9.1 miles) along the Mabel Lake FSR on the eastern shores of Mabel Lake. There is no vehicle access to the camping area and beautiful beaches but there is a short trail to a scenic waterfall near the lake.

Charcoal Creek Rec Site (Map 35/E3) 🏕 🏕 🐟 📷
The Charcoal Creek site is located on a large, grassy bench above the creek and is ideal for larger RVs or for group camping. It is easily accessed by the Chase-Falkland Road. Charcoal Creek is a good fly fishing creek.

Chase Creek Rec Site (Map 35/E4) 🏕 🏕 🐟
Located a few kilometres to the north of Pillar Lake on the Chase-Falkland Road, this site is set in a forest alongside Chase Creek. There is good road access to the five campsites with picnic tables.

Cherryville Lake Site (Map 30/A3) 🏕 🏕 🏖 🚤 🐟 📷
A large, open site on the banks of the Shuswap River, this rec site provides a beach for sunbathing as well as picnic tables. This site is easily accessed along the Sugar Lake Road and is often used as a stop-over for visitors to Sugar Lake or the Monashee Mountains.

Cottonwood Bay Site (Map 37/G3) 🏕 🏕 🏖 🎣 🚤 🐟
This popular 20 vehicle unit recreation site is located on the eastern shores of Mabel Lake. The site has a good cartop boat launch as well as a sandy beach.

Damer Lake Site (Map 28/D6) ⛺ 🚤 🚶 🎣 🐟 🚻 📷
There are 11 vehicle units at this site, which is accessed by the Oyama Lake Road (4wd access). It has a rough cartop boat launch and is also used as a staging ground for hikers to the Kalamalka Lookout as well as the High Rim Trail.

Denison Lake Rec Site (Map 29/E6) ⛺ 🚶 🐟
This small lake is ideal for fishermen who want to access a rustic wilderness camping experience. The recreation site is found at the end of a 2 km (1.2 mile) trail off the Bonneau FSR south of Creighton Valley.

Doreen Lake Rec Site (Map 28/F7) 🏕 🚤 🎣 🐟 📷
This site is found at the south end of Doreen Lake and offers room for 20 units as well as a good boat launch. The good roadside access makes this recreation site very popular with campers and fishermen.

Edwin Lakes Rec Site (Map 29/A6) ⛺ 🚤 🎣 🐟
Edwin Lakes are located on a fairly good road off the Haddo Main. There are three lakeshore camping pads together with a cartop boat launch.

Flyfish Lakes Rec Sites (Map 28/F7) ⛺ ⛺ 🚤 🚶 🐟
There are two different water bodies that make up the Flyfish Lakes. Flyfish No. 1 is accessed by a short hike off a rough 2wd road that leads near the lake. It is possible to pack a small boat or canoe to the lake. On the other hand Flyfish No. 2 is accessed by a 4wd road leading to the eastern shores of the lake. There are six campsites, a good cartop boat launch and a trail leading south to tiny Ruth Lake.

Goat Mountain Lake Site (Map 29/B7) ⛺ 🚤 🎣 🐟 📷
Easily accessed by the Buck Hill Road, there are four campsites and a good cartop boat launch at this forest service site.

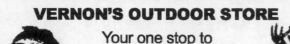

Greenbush Lake Site (Map 46/E7)

This remote lake is located near the headwaters of the Shuswap River in Grizzly Bear country. The scenic backcountry vista has five camping units and is used as a staging ground for travelers to the Joss Mountain Trail or by anglers.

Haddo Lake Rec Site (Map 28/G7)

Haddo Lake is one of many lakes in this area that offers good fishing throughout the spring and fall. On the north end of the lake, there are ten campsites as well as a good boat launch. Access to Haddo is via a rough road. Please note that the small site on the west end of the lake is now closed.

Haggkuist Lake Rec Site (Map 29/G1)

This small mountain lake offers three quaint campsites. Access into the area is via a rough 2wd road.

Hidden Lake Sites (Map 37/D5)

This site is comprised of three separate campgrounds that surround this popular getaway lake. There are a total of 46 camping units, reasonable boat launches and several old roads in the area to explore in the summer and winter. The lake is easily accessed by the Hidden Lake Road.

High Lake Rec Site (Map 28/D6)

High Lake is accessed by either the Oyama Lake Road (4wd access) or the King Edward Lake Road (2wd access). Whichever way you choose, you will have to park beside the cattle guard and walk a short distance along a rough trail to the lake. There is room for a few tents at this small lake.

Holmes Lake RecSite (Map 30/F7)

Located to the east of Keefer Lake, Holmes Lake offers five campsites together with a rough boat launch. The recreation site can be accessed by either the Keefer Lake or the Fife Creek Roads.

Holstein Lake Rec Site (Map 29/G2)

Holstein Lake is accessed by a rough 4wd spur road, directly east of Kathy Lake. The recreation site has a few treed campsites as well as a rough cartop boat launch.

Ideal Lake Rec Site (Map 20/G1)

Ideal Lake is a popular fishing hole located on a good 2wd road off the Philpot Road. The rec site offers room for about 30 camping units and is set in a forest at the south end of the lake. There is a boat launch as well as table and toilet facilities.

Island Lake RecSite (Map 28/E7)

Virtually an extension of Crooked and Deer lakes, Island Lake is easily accessed by the Dee Lake Road. It has 15 sites as well as a good boat launch. This high elevation lake is exposed to the wind but still makes a fine paddling and fishing destination.

Jimmy Lake Rec Site (Map 27/A2)

The access into Jimmy Lake is good but you will have to come in from the south (off the Sucker Lake Forest Service Road) as the access from the Douglas Lake Road is gated. Jimmy Lake has 15 camping units with a good cartop boat launch.

Joyce (Green) Lake Site (Map 35/E5)

This site has eight campsites and a good cartop boat launch on the shores of Joyce Lake. The site is easily accessed by the Chase-Falkland Road (good 2wd road).

Kaiser Bill Lake Rec Site (Map 28/E6)

Kaiser Bill Lake is located on a 4wd road off the King Edward Lake Road. The recreation site has three campsites together with a rough cartop boat launch.

Kate Lake Rec Site (Map 38/D7)

Kate Lake is reached by a 2 km side trail off the Sugar Mountain Trail. (You'll cover 9 km/5.5 miles by the time you get to the lake, as the side trail starts at the 7 km mark of the Sugar Mountain Trail). It is a rustic tenting site used primarily by fishermen to the sub-alpine lake. Beware of Grizzly bears in the area.

Kathy Lake Rec Site (Map 29/F2)

Kathy Lake is easily accessed by the Silver Hills Road and offers three treed sites next to the lake. There is a cartop boat launch for anglers and paddlers to use.

King Edward Lake Site (Map 28/E6)

One of many good fishing lakes in the area, King Edward Lake has a good cartop boat launch for anglers to use. Campers will find room for five vehicle units on the western shores of the popular lake.

Little Pinaus Lake Rec Site (Map 35/D4)

Little Pinaus Recreation Site is a small, user-maintained site with a good cartop boat launch and three campsites. It is the last of four sites along the Pinaus Lake Road

Loon Lake Rec Site (Map 28/F7)

This small site has three camping units and is accessed by a very rough 4wd road from the Dee Lake Road. There is a rough cartop boat launch.

Monashee Kettle River Rec Site (Map 30/B4)

There is a small, open campsite next to the Kettle River, which is used primarily by river fishermen or as a stop-over for visitors to the Keefer Lake area. The recreation site is easily accessed off the Keefer Lake Road and has room for five units.

Mohr Creek Rec Site (Map 21/G6)

This is a three unit site right next to the Kettle River and the busy logging road.

Moore (Bulman) Lake Site (Map 20/E1)

This small six unit rec site is located on the western shores of Moore Lake and is accessed by a rough 2wd road from Postill Lake. There is a rustic boat launch at the lake.

Nicklen Lake Forest Service Sites (Map 29/A6)

Nicklen Lake is the water source for local residents and is found on the Buck Hills Road east of Aberdeen Lake. There is a total of 30 camping units split evenly between the two sites (east and west). Each site also sports good boat launches.

Nugget Lake Rec Site (Map 27/A2)

To the south of Jimmy Lake, Nugget Lake is found on a rough 4wd road that is better left to hikers or ATV riders. There are five camping units at the lake together with a place to launch small boats or canoes.

Okanagan Lake Rec Site (Map 28/A5)

Perhaps the most popular recreation site in the district, Okanagan Lake offers 30 enhanced, lakeshore campsites. The site has a nice beach. There is a rough boat launch as well as some hiking trails and pictographs in the area.

Oyama Lake Rec Site (Map 28/C7)

This scenic lake is home to a resort as well as a 15 campsite recreation site with a good cartop boat launch. Access into the rec site is by a very rough spur road off the Oyama Lake Road.

Pillar Lake Rec Site (Map 35/E4)

Pillar Lake is found off the Chase-Falkland Road and offers four lakeshore campsites and a good cartop boat launch. While in the area, it is recommended that you hike the short distance to the basalt pillars above the road.

Pinaus Lake Rec Site (Map 35/E7)

When you reach Pinaus Lake, you will find a 25 unit rec site with a good boat launch set in a forest on the north shore of the lake. This lake is very popular during the summer and the access is good enough to allow RVs into the area when the roads are dry.

Postill Lake Rec Site (Map 20/E1)

The recreation site is located at the east end of Postill Lake, not far from the resort. It is a popular site with 12 camping units as well as a cartop boat launch for fishermen. Near the recreation site is a series of ski trails, which provide excellent hiking in the summer. Due to the sensitive nature of the area, no bikes or ATVs are allowed on the trails.

Pratt Lake Rec Site (Map 34/E7)

Pratt Lake is accessed by a good 2wd road from the Monte Creek FSR. The recreation site has ten campsites together with a boat launch.

Rottacker Lake Rec Site (Map 30/F1)

This site is located on the north end of the small mountain lake. It is reached by a rough trail leading from near the 20 km (12.2 mile) mark on the Kate-Sitkum FSR. The lake makes a good backcountry camping and fishing destination but beware, this is Grizzly Bear country.

Ruth Lake Rec Site (Map 28/F7)

A walk-in site accessed by a 1 km (.6 mile) trail leading south from the Flyfish Lakes No. 2 Lake. There is room for a couple of tents on the north end of the lake.

Salmon River Rec Site (Map 27/A1)

This is a large, grassy site on a bench above the Salmon River, which use to be the home of the Dominion Ranger Station. This site is ideal for group camping and is used by fishermen trying their luck at Salmon River or by hunters in the fall. The recreation site is easily accessed on the Douglas Lake Road.

Sigalet Lake Rec Site (Map 29/D1)

Anglers often seek out Sigalet Lake since it has a reputation of being a good fly fishing lake. In addition to three campsites, there is also a cartop boat launch at the forest service site. The access road into the lake is narrow and best left to 4wd vehicles.

Spa Lake Rec Site (Map 36/A5)

There are five vehicle units at this site on the shores of Spa Lake, which is accessed by a spur road off the Bolean Lake Road. There is also a rustic cartop boat launch.

Spanish Lake Site (Map 35/G6)

This site is located on the Silvernails Road (2wd access) and is set below Mount Connaught. It has four camping units together with a good cartop boat launch. Skiing in the winter and mountain biking/hiking or fishing in the summer are the attractions to the area.

Specs Lakes Rec Site (Map 28/G7)

Specs Lakes are found on a spur road at about the 24 km (14.6 mile) mark on the Aberdeen Road. There are six campsites ideal for fishermen or paddlers who want to explore a chain of small lakes to the east of Grizzly Lake. The cartop boat launch at the site is very rough.

Square Lake Rec Site (Map 35/F7)

Just past Pinaus Lake on the Pinaus Lake Road, Square Lake Recreation Site has seven camping spots. There is a rough cartop boat launch at the site together with toilets and tables.

Streak Lake (Map 28/D7)

The last of the series of fishing lakes with recreation sites in the hills southeast of Vernon, Streak Lake offers a seven unit campsite. The road into the site itself is rough but there is a cartop boat launch.

Sugar Creek Site (Map 30/C1)

The Sugar Creek Site is located on the eastern shores of Sugar Lake at 600 metres (1,950 feet) in elevation. The enhanced site has room for 12 vehicle units together with a nice beach with a cartop boat launch. The site is found at the 14 km mark of the Kate Creek FSR.

Sugar Lake Sites (Map 30/B1)

There are four separate sites on the western shores of Sugar Lake with a combined total of 48 campsites. Some sites have boat launches and beaches and as a result are very popular in the summer with fishermen and people looking for a nice place to relax. Access into the area is quite good at the North Shuswap FSR and is considered a good 2wd road. The enhanced **Two Mile Rec Site** is the largest of the four areas, with room for 40 vehicle units.

Swalwell (Beaver) Lake Rec Site (Map 20/D1)

Located on the western shores of Swalwell Lake, this medium-sized site offers a series hiking and cross-country ski trails in the area. The lake is known locally as Beaver Lake and also makes a fine paddling and fishing destination. There are 20 campsites and a good boat launch at the recreation site as well as a resort on the lake.

Weyman Creek Falls Rec Site (Map 26/G1)

This is a small picnic site next to the Douglas Lake Road with a short but steep trail leading to a spectacular waterfall.

Winnifred Creek Falls Rec Site (Map 21/G3)

There are eight campsites set in a forest next to Winnifred Creek, near a small falls. There is little to do here, other than look at the falls, and enjoy the still, quiet site.

Woods Lake Rec Site (Map 27/B1)

Woods Lake is accessed by a spur road leading from the Ingram Creek Forest Service Road to the south. The 30 unit rec site is often busy during weekends with anglers testing their luck. There is a cartop boat launch is at the Forest Service site.

Wildlife Viewing

Super Natural British Columbia has an international reputation as being an excellent place to see wildlife. Despite the development and hot, dry climate, the southern interior offers an abundance of species to view. In addition to birds and animals common to the rest of BC, this region is one of the best areas of the province to see mountain goats and California Bighorn Sheep.

What follows isn't a complete list of where you can see animals and birds, but it is a fairly good start. Some of the sites below cater mostly to birders, while other sites feature large mammals like deer and bighorn sheep. Still other sites focus on fish. All of them are worth checking out. For more information on wildlife watching, contact an area club, like the Kamloops Naturalist Club or the South Okanagan Naturalist Club.

Allan Brooks Nature Centre (Map 28/C5)
Inside the Allan Brooks Nature Centre you can take a virtual tour of the North Okanagan Valley in the Habitat Room. Visitors can also stroll on the Grassland Trail, wander through the Naturescape Gardens or take in a scheduled interpretive program outside the Nature Centre. The centre is located at the end of Allan Brooks Way above Vernon in the old Environment Canada weather station. Visit www.abnc.ca for more details.

Antlers Beach Regional Park (Map 19/B7)
Found along Highway 97, on the shores of Okanagan Lake, the park provides good access to Hardy Creek. A trail alongside leads to Hardy Falls, where kokanee can be seen spawning from mid September to mid October. American Dippers also frequent the area year round.

Bear Creek Provincial Park (Map 19/G3)
Bear Creek Provincial Park is situated in the Central Okanagan Basin on the west side of Okanagan Lake. The park features 5 km (3 miles) of hiking trails and a picturesque canyon that has been carved into the bedrock. Kokanee spawn in the creek from mid September to mid October, while White-throated Swifts are seen frequently from mid May to mid October.

Bertram Creek Regional Park (Map 19/F6)
On the shores of Okanagan Lake, this is a good birding site in spring and fall. Watch for kinglet, vireos, warblers and sparrows.

Boothman Oxbows (Map 6/E7)
This site just east of Grand Forks contains a large wetland, which was an old oxbow of the Kettle River. Bird lovers will find a variety of species ranging from songbird to woodpeckers and waterfowl. April to September is the best time to visit, as Bobolink, Yellow-headed Blackbird, Mourning Dove, Western Meadowlark, Marsh Wren, Common Yellowthroat, Virginia Rail, Sora and Long-billed Curlew are often seen in the area.

Cathedral Provincial Park (Maps 1, 2)
This huge park is home to mountain goats and California Bighorn Sheep. Although they are seen throughout the year, the best time to see these mammals is in summer when they come further down the rock bluffs to feed. Also watch for birds and raptors like the Prairie Falcon, Boreal Owl, Rock Wren and American Pipit.

Chopaka Border Area (Map 3/D7)
This area stretches along Nighthawk Road from Highway 3 to the border crossing west of Osoyoos. This dry desert habitat is a popular location with birders and is especially good during spring migration. The land on both sides of the road is private but there is ample room to stop off the road and observe. Common birds from May to July include Long-billed Curlew, Mountain Bluebird and Western Meadowlark.

Coalmont (Map 9/A5)
The Tulameen Road from Princeton to Coalmont is a picturesque drive and is a good place to watch for Elk from December to February, and for Mule Deer from December to May. The best viewing begins about 5.7 km from Princeton.

Ellison Provincial Park (Map 28/A6)
Ellison Provincial Park includes 200 hectares of forested bench lands above a rocky shoreline of scenic headlands and sheltered coves. Songbirds are most visible from late April to early June and in September. Look and listen for Olive-sided Flycatcher, Western Wood-Pewee, Hammond's Flycatcher, Western Kingbird, Eastern Kingbird, warblers, Western Tanager and Evening Grosbeak.

Fintry-Nahun (Map 27/G7)
Westside Road provides a longer but more scenic route along Okanagan Lake between Vernon and Kelowna. During winter, in the hills above the stretch of road between Nahun and Fintry you can see California Bighorn Sheep.

Gardom Lake Park (Map 36/E4)
This small park offers a few trails that provide access along the lakeshore and a floating bridge to Main Island. In May and June this is a good place to view waterfowl such as Red-necked Grebes and American Coots on their floating nests. There is also good songbird viewing in spring and summer, while Western Painted Turtles are best viewed in May, June and September.

Ginty's Pond (Map 3/A3)
Found just east of Keremeos, this small wetland pond is home to a variety of wetland birds in the spring through fall. In addition to wetland birds, you'll find blackbirds, orioles, kingbirds and wrens. To find the pond, head east on Highway 3 from its junction with 3A to Couthard Avenue. Turn right, then left on V.L.A. Road.

Granby River Valley (Map 6/C6–4)
The Granby River Valley is a great place to watch for both Mule and White-tailed Deer. The fleet-footed deer are most often seen about 12 km (7.3 miles) north of Grand Forks for on both sides of the river. But it is the herd of California Bighorn Sheep that are often seen on the Brown Creek Road that will amaze even the most casual viewer.

Haynes Point Provincial Park (Map 4/A7)
Haynes Point sits on a pencil of land jutting into Osoyoos Lake. Families of California Quail are common in summer, and from April through September watch for Marsh Wrens, Eastern Kingbirds, Gray Catbirds, Cedar Waxwings, Yellow-headed Blackbirds and orioles. The best viewing times are when there are fewer visitors in the park.

Hedley-Keremeos Cliffs (Map 2/G3)
More than 150 goats call the south-facing cliffs along Highway 3 between Hedley and Keremeos home. Viewing is best done with binoculars from the highway since the goats are usually high up on the hillside. While present year round, the goats are best seen from April to October.

Hell's Gate Fishways (Map 15/B6)
More than 31 million sockeye were harvested from the 1913 run on the Fraser River. When the remaining fish reached Hell's Gate, they ran into an almost impenetrable obstacle caused by the construction of what is now the Canadian National Railway. All but the hardiest fish were blocked by a rockslide that shrank the already narrow channel and created a five metre high waterfall. By 1915, the removal of 45,000 cubic metres of rock from the channel had eased the problem, but the 33 metre wide Hell's Gate gorge still remains one of the toughest obstacles on the river. The migrating salmon have since been aided in their passage through Hell's Gate by specially designed fishways,

the first of which was built in 1946 at a cost of $1 million. The design and construction of the fishway was complicated by the fact that Hell's Gate carries the water from 220,000 square kilometres of British Columbia-about one quarter of the province-and the river levels can fluctuate as much as five metres in a day. The first fishway proved successful and more were added in 1947, 1951, 1965 and 1966.

Inkaneep Provincial Park (Map 3/F3)
The park protects a few hectares of habitat along the Okanagan River and is a good bird watching area. California Quail are best viewed from April to June, while Eastern Kingbirds, orioles and Gray Catbirds can be seen in May and June. Woodpeckers are also common visitors to the park, which is 6 km (3.6 miles) north of Oliver on Highway 97.

Jim Grant Island (Map 28/A7)
Formerly known as Whisky Island, this island was purchased with the assistance of the North Okanagan Naturalists Club and renamed after one of its members. The small island is home to a sizable nesting colony of Ring-billed Gulls, as well as other gulls. The island is found on Okanagan Lake between Vernon and Kelowna at Carrs Landing.

Kalamalka Lake Provincial Park (Map 28/D5)
Surrounded by grassland, dotted with ponderosa pine and groves of Douglas fir, this largely undeveloped park has an all season appeal. The spring wildflower show is truly spectacular, while a variety of animals, bird-life and reptiles can be seen throughout the year. Amazingly, nature lovers will also find 432 varieties of vascular plants that have been identified in the park.

Kalamoir Regional Park (Map 19/G5)
This is another bird watching site that is found on the western shore of Okanagan Lake. Watch for Western and Eastern Kingbirds, Cedar Waxwing, Western Wood-Pewee, orioles, Nashville Warbler and many more.

Kettle River Provincial Park (Map 5/A5)
An open bunchgrass prairie and large stands of ponderosa pine make this great habitat for White-tailed and Mule Deer. Coyote are also common in the area.

Kingfisher Hatchery (Map 37/D4)
This is one of many fish hatcheries around British Columbia that is open to the public. This hatchery rears Chinook Salmon, Coho Salmon and Rainbow Trout. It is located along Cooke Creek about 21 km (12.8 miles) northeast of Enderby, just north of Enderby-Mabel Lake Road.

Knox Mountain Nature Park (Map 19/G3)
This local park offers many recreational opportunities, including a number of trails that provide access throughout the park and its habitats. You will find songbirds and small mammals here.

Lac du Bois Grasslands Protected Area (Maps 33 & 41)
Rising above the hot, dry Thompson Valleys, this area helps protect three grassland communities surrounded by forested hills. Nowhere else in western North America will you find these grassland communities in such close proximity to each other. California Bighorn Sheep, Mule Deer, moose and waterfowl are common residents and visitors to the park, while the Western Rattlesnake, Sharp-tailed Grouse and Flammulated Owl live more secretive lives within its boundaries.

Loon Creek Hatchery (Map 39/C2)
The Loon Creek Hatchery is one of five such hatcheries run by the province. This one produces kokanee and Rainbow Trout. Combined, these hatcheries populate about 1,200 lakes with between 10 and 12 million fish each year. The hatchery is located 20 km (12.2 miles) north of Cache Creek on the paved Loon Lake Road.

Mission Creek Linear Park (Maps 19/G5-20/A5)
The dyke trails along both sides of Mission Creek provide good bird watching for shore birds and songbirds. The park is located along the

lower reaches of Mission Creek between Lakeshore Drive and K.L.O. Road. There is limited parking at major road crossings.

Monashee Provincial Park (Map 38/G6)
Summer is the best time to see wildlife in Monashee Provincial Park. Species such as the Mountain Caribou, Mule Deer, Columbian Ground Squirrels and American Pikas are often spotted at this time. The park has 24 km (14.6 miles) of well maintained, yet rugged trails as well as a developed camping area at Spectrum Lake.

Mount Kobau (Map 3/D5)
Originally destined for an observatory that was never built, this is a good site to star watch. The mountain is also a place for nature lovers. Mule Deer are present year round, while from May to August, Hermit Thrush, Brewer's Sparrow and Vesper Sparrow are some of the birds common to the area.

Okanagan Falls Provincial Park (Map 3/F1)
Just above the Okanagan River, a stand of deciduous trees provides a contrast to the parched hills in the area. This oasis is famous among naturalists for its bird watching, wildlife viewing, nature study, and bats. In fact, this is one of the best sites in the Okanagan to watch for bats. A variety of species have been recorded here and several interpretive signs provide information. The best bat viewing is in the evening just before sunset from the middle of May through July. In autumn, the fall colours make this area particularly appealing.

Okanagan Mountain Provincial Park (Map 19/C4)
Above Okanagan Lake, this large park covers over 10,000 hectares of rugged landscape with mountain lakes, grasslands as well as spruce and fir forests. The park is only accessible by boat, on foot, horseback or bicycle and is a good bird watching area. A variety of large and small mammals can also be seen on occasion.

Old Hedley Road (Map 9/D5-10/C7)
This interesting backroad is located along the north side of the Similkameen River east of Princeton. Watch for Mule Deer in April and May. The road is also host to a large number of pictographs as well as a pair of Forest Service Sites.

Osoyoos Desert Centre (Map 3/G7)
The Desert Centre is an interpretive education and research facility offering insight into the flora and fauna of this unique area. The area is the only pocket desert in Canada and an elevated boardwalk trail provides access into this special place. The area is of international importance and home to over 100 rare plants and over 300 rare invertebrates, many of which are species at risk.

Osoyoos Oxbows Wildlife Reserve (Map 3/F6)
The Okanagan River north of Osoyoos is a great spot for birders, and an amazing list of species may be observed here. The list includes Burrowing Owls, Long-billed Curlew, Bobolink, California Quail, Black Swift, Yellow-headed Blackbird, Gray Catbird, Canyon Wren, Common Yellowthroat and Lazuli Bunting and hundreds more. There is dyke and road access along the river as well as many trails for visitors to get close to the various habitats.

Paul Lake Provincial Park (Map 34/C1)

Nestled in a mixed forest of Douglas-fir, pine and aspen, this park is within a half-hour drive of Kamloops. As a result, the park can be extremely busy during the summer and birdwatchers will find it more difficult to see the Bald Eagles, falcons, osprey, swallows, and White-throated Swifts common to the area. The park also protects habitat for coyote and Mule Deer.

Paul Peak (Map 34/A2)

Paul Peak is located outside of Kamloops, on the Kamloops Indian Reserve. Access is by permission only but this doesn't seem to deter the bighorn sheep prevalent on this rocky peak.

Roderick Haig-Brown Provincial Park (Map 43/E5)

Roderick Haig-Brown Provincial Park captures the section of the Adams River that is world famous for its Sockeye Salmon Run. This amazing display of nature occurs every fall, but it is the dominant runs, where millions of fish jam the stream, that attracts all of the attention. The dominant runs occur every four years—2006, 2010, 2014, etc. At other times of the year, birds and small mammals can be seen along the well developed trail system in the park. Be sure to catch the Annual Salmon Festival every September.

Salmon Arm Nature Park (Map 36/C2)

The Salmon Arm Nature Bay Enhancement Society operates an information centre at Marine Park in the north end of town. With their help, you will get a better understanding of what to see along the 10 km (6 mile) nature trail. In addition to bird blinds, every May there is a Grebe Festival in honor of the Western Grebes that make this area home.

Shannon Lake Regional Park (Map 19/E5)

A good bird watching lake. Watch for waterfowl and shorebirds, including Great Blue Herons, with the best time to visit being May to August. A wide range of birds has been recorded at the park, which is located about 3km (1.8 miles) north of Westbank.

Shuswap River Hatchery (Map 29/E3)

Chinook Salmon are raised at this small hatchery on a scenic section of the Shuswap River. The hatchery is open to the public, and is found about 32 km (19.5 miles) east of Vernon.

Shuswap River (Maps 36 & 37)

The Shuswap River winds back and forth through the flatlands around Enderby. Watch for Osprey and their nests on the hydro towers along the river just east of the small town. Chinook, Coho and Sockeye Salmon as well as kokanee can be seen spawning in the river from mid September to mid October. The best viewing areas are between Enderby and the hatchery at Cooke Creek.

Silver Star Provincial Park (Maps 28 & 29)

Best known for its winter recreation, the best time to view wildlife is when the snow is gone. Watch for birds such as the Gray Jay, Hermit Thrush, Fox Sparrow, Pine Grosbeak, Red Crossbill and White-winged Crossbill.

Skaha Lake (East Side) (Map 11/F7)

The stretch of road running along the east side of Skaha Lake is another interesting backroad to explore. California Bighorn Sheep can be seen in the cliffs from October to March. Also hidden on the rocks above the road are Indian pictographs.

Skihist Provincial Park (Map 23/A3)

This hot, dry area is home to a variety of birds, which frequent the campsite and the nature trail taking you to the scenic bench above the river. There is also a herd of Elk that have been introduced in the area.

Spences Bridge (Map 31/D7)

Large herds of bighorn sheep are visible in and around the community of Spences Bridge throughout the year. Although the site of the sheep excites visitors, they do cause the local residents grief by often eating laundry that is hanging to dry. A patient wildlife observer in the area surrounding Spences Bridge may also see elk, deer, coyote, black bears, cougar, bobcat, lynx, bald eagles, ospreys and many other wildlife species.

Spius Creek Hatchery (Map 24/B7)

Approximately 15km (9.1 miles) west of Merritt on Sunshine Valley Road, this hatchery features self-guided tours, and is open every day except Christmas, Boxing Day, and New Years. The hatchery raises Chinook Salmon, which return in September and Coho Salmon, which return in November. Juveniles can be seen all year.

South Thompson River (Maps 34, 35 & 43)

The shores of the South Thompson are usually a good place to see waterfowl and shore birds, but the big attraction to this stretch of river is winter viewing of trumpeter swans. Although they can be seen anywhere between Kamloops and Chase, the swans are more often found around Pritchard.

Summerland Trout Hatchery (Map 11/D3)

This provincial hatchery is popular with visitors looking to learn more about Rainbow Trout and Brook Trout. Facilities include a fisheries interpretative centre and spawning channels. The hatchery is located 14 km north of Penticton on Highway 97. Turn right on Lakeside Drive and continue for 1 km.

Sutherland Hills Park (Map 20/A5)

Situated along the Mission Creek corridor, this park has many trails to explore and is a good bird watching location. The best time to visit is from April to September. Watch for Calliope Hummingbird, Rufous Hummingbird, Western Wood-Pewee, Dusky Flycatcher, nuthatches, Western Bluebird, vireos, Warblers, Western Tanager, Black-headed Grosbeak and orioles.

Swan Lake (Map 28/D2)

Swan Lake is a birding hotspot in the North Okanagan area. The lake is located just north of Vernon and is host to a variety of species. During the spring and fall migration, Sharp-tailed Sandpiper and Lesser Golden-Plover are spotted on occasion, while American Avocet, Black-necked Stilt and Black-crowned Night-Heron are seen less frequently. Common waterfowl species includes Green-winged, Blue-winged and Cinnamon Teals, Ruddy Duck, Barrow's and Common Goldeneyes, Bufflehead, Canada Geese and American Coot.

Tranquille Marsh (Map 33/C1)

Located 10 km (6 miles) west of North Kamloops on Tranquille Road, the marsh is often completely flooded in late spring. Access is difficult at this time but improves from May to mid-June. Fall is also a good time to visit. Tranquille Marsh is known for migratory waterfowl, especially swans.

Vaseux Lake Wildlife Area (Map 3/G2)

Connected by trail to Vaseux Lake Provincial Park, the best time to visit is in spring and fall, especially during bird migrations. The area is a National Waterfowl Sanctuary and Provincial Wildlife Management Area that is host to a wide variety of bird species, and in winter, watch for California Bighorn Sheep in the hillsides east of the parking area.

Vernon Heronry (Map 28/C4)

Great Blue Herons nest in a stand of tall Cottonwood trees just west of Highway 97 in Vernon, behind the McDonald's. Viewing is best from mid March to mid July.

Ward's Lake (Map 6/D7)

This small lake contains good wildlife habitat, especially for birds and migratory waterfowl. However, in recent years the water level has been a problem. When water levels are up, watch for yellowlegs and sandpipers, while many songbirds, including bluebirds, blackbirds, kingbirds, flycatchers, sparrows and warblers, can be seen from April to September. Also common to the lake are Western Tanager, Lazuli Bunting, Common Yellowthroat and California Quail.

Winter Recreation

(Cross-Country Skiing, Snowshoeing and Snowmobiling)

People living in the Southern Interior have long known that winter is a sacred time. Although the days are shorter, there is a certain beauty and stillness that only winter brings. Even better, many of the trail systems are often abandoned during the week allowing for a more peaceful adventure.

Many of the locations described below are groomed and maintained, often on a volunteer basis. Some of these locations require you to purchase trail passes, while others are free of charge. All of them offer you a chance to get out and enjoy winter in a safe, enjoyable fashion.

Allen Creek Snowmobile Trails (Map 39/A2)

Off Highway 97 south of Clinton, experienced snowmobilers can ride the popular route into a vast alpine area.

Apex Mountain Ski Area (Map 10/G7)

Apex Mountain Resort offers plenty of opportunity to ski tour along ungroomed trails in the winter. The best trail leads from the bunny hill near the lodge around the far side of the ski hill to Mount Riordan. The return distance is 6 km (3.6 miles), gaining 275 metres (894 feet) along the way. On the same trail, there is a detour to Beaconsfield Mountain, which is approximately 10 km (6 miles) return gaining 350 m (1,138 feet) along the way.

The variety in the surrounding area helps make the Apex area one of the best cross-country skiing areas in the province. Also in the area are the Nickel Plate Nordic Centre, the Okanagan Vista Trails and the Southward Ho Backcountry Route. From Apex Mountain, a 6 km (4.7 mile) trail links to the Nickel Plate Lake Ski Trails. You will climb 100 m (328 feet) along the way.

Bear Creek Main Area (Maps 19/E2-27/B7)

Bear Creek Main west of Kelowna provides access to hundreds of unplowed logging roads and clearcuts. The local snowmobile club uses the Esperon FSR to gain access to most of the area and helps maintain a shelter at Esperon Lake. During the week this area is active with logging and it is extremely dangerous (and illegal) to drive a snowmobile on any winter maintained or ploughed roads.

Big White Cross-Country Ski Trails (Map 21/C7)

There are approximately 25 km (15.3 miles) of groomed and well-marked cross-country ski trails at the base of the Big White Ski Resort. These trails dissect the timber in and around the ski village. **Trapping Meadows Trail** is 5 km (3 miles) long and is ideal for beginner skiers. It only has a vertical drop of 75 m (244 feet). Two John **Lake Connection** is 8 km (4.9 miles) long and is better for intermediate skiers, while **Copper Kettle Meadows Trail** is for advanced skiers as it climbs part way up the mountain. It extends some 12.5 km (7.6 miles) gaining 180 m (585 feet) along the way. Snowmobilers will find trails that hook up with the popular Graystokes area to the north.

Boulder Mountain Trails (Map 46/E2)

During the winter, snowmobilers can drive the Boulder Mountain Road as far as it is ploughed. From the end of the road, there is a series of popular snowmobile trails with four routes to choose from. Each trail is named and marked and there are signs showing the way to the chalet at the 2,100 m (6,825 foot) summit.

Carmi Ski Trails (Maps 11/G5-12/A5)

Located in the Ellis Creek Demonstration Forest, there are 17 km (10.4 miles) of well-marked trails. The trails are not groomed in the winter, but are easy to follow, and are usually well broken. The main trail is

quite challenging with steep hills (up to 17 degrees). There is also a popular toboggan hill next to the parking lot.

Chewels Mountain Trails (Map 33/C5)

Set at the base of Chewels Mountain, there are 47 km (28.7 miles) of snowmobile trails, which are also used by motor cross and mountain bikers in the summer. The trail system is accessed off the Chewels Mountain Road from the Coquihalla Highway.

China Ridge Ski Trails (Map 9/B5)

Located west of Princeton at the Snowpatch Ski Hill, there is a 35 km (21.4 mile) network of beginner to intermediate cross-country ski trails. 16 km (9.8 miles) of the trails are groomed. The trails follow old roads and skid trails through open timber, some cut blocks and across natural grassy slopes. The trails are at around 1,200 m (3,900 feet) in elevation with some trails offering a view of the Tulameen River Valley as well as shelters and warm-up huts. A user fee is charged.

Chute Lake Ski Trails (Map 11/G1)

From the Chute Lake Resort, it is possible to follow a ski trail southward to Elinor Lake or on to Big Meadow Lake. With a return distance of up to 16 km (9.7 miles) and a vertical drop of 450 m (1,463 feet) these ungroomed routes are not for beginners. Other skiers use the Kettle Valley Trail and ski to the Adra Tunnel to the south. There is also informal snowmobiling in the area, and along the Kettle Valley Trail.

Crowfoot Mountain Trails (Map 44/C2)

A well established trail network offers about 30 km (18.3 miles) of groomed snowmobile trails and a chalet in the Crowfoot Mountain area north of the North Shore of Shuswap Lake. The trails begin on logging roads before picking up the remains of a road built in the 1800's. This road leads to the endless alpine areas of Crowfoot and Mobley Mountain. Access is found from Onyx Creek and Ross Creek Road near Magna Bay.

Fly Hill Trails (Maps 35/G2-36/A1)

West of Salmon Arm, the Fly Hills have 70 km (43 miles) of snowmobile trails forming three loops along old roads. There is a chalet (at the junction of Wallensteen and Granite Peak Roads) and some warm-up huts available. Access to the area from Salmon Arm is via the Fly Hill Forest Service Road or via the Charcoal Creek FSR to the west.

Graystokes Snowmobile Area (Maps 21/B2, 29/E7)

There are three warming chalets and 350 km (215 miles) of groomed trails found in this huge snowmobile area 41 km (25 miles) east of Kelowna. The vast majority of the trail network centres around the Graystokes Plateau, but there are also connectors to the Big White area and the McCulloch Lakes area in the south or even Lumby in the north.

Harper Mountain Ski Trails (Map 34/C1)

Found east of Kamloops on the Paul Lake Road, a 14 km (8.5 mile) cross-country trail system exists. These beginner to moderate trails are found on the northside of Mount Harper around the downhill area.

Headwater Lakes Cross-Country Ski Area (Map 18/E6)

At the Headwaters Fishing Camp, three easy cross-country trails dissect the Lodgepole pine forest around the lakes. **Headwaters Lake Trail** is a 4 km (2.4 mile) loop circling the main lake. **Camp Trail** is a short 1 km (0.6 mile) loop near the fish camp, while **June Lake Trail** is a 6

km (3.7 mile) loop. The June Lake Trail begins on the Headwaters Lake Trail before branching to the smaller lake. Across the road, several more challenging, unmaintained trails exist.

Snowmobilers can follow unploughed logging roads in the area as far west as they choose. There are many lakes and meadows to explore as well as a scenic view from atop Pennask Mountain. Accommodations may be obtained at Headwaters Fishing Camp.

Hunters Range Trails (Map 37/A4-D2)
A mix of groomed and ungroomed snowmobile routes are found northeast of Enderby. The trails follow old roads up into the semi-alpine of the Hunters Range. It is also possible to hook up with the Owlhead trail system (see below) to the north.

Inkaneep (McKinney) Ski Trails (Map 4/B6)
North of where the McKinney Road crosses Inkaneep Creek, a parking lot marks the beginning of a 12 km (7.3 mile) cross-country trail system. The Prospector Trail is the main route extending south for 10 km (6 miles), and there are a number of shorter trails near the road. Most of the trails are beginner to intermediate trails although the Quick Silver Trail is fairly difficult because of the hill you have to traverse. The area is also rich in history of gold mines from the early 1900s and is an interesting place to explore during the summer months. There are trail fees to ski here.

Isobel Lake Trails (Map 41/F6)
There is a 3 km (1.8 mile) interpretive trail around Isobel Lake that is popular in both summer and winter. There are also 10 km (6.1 miles) of ungroomed ski trails in the area for winter enthusiasts to explore.

Jewel Lake Ski Trails (Map 6/A4)
From the Jewel Lake Lodge at the south end of the lake, three short loop trails (up to 5.8 km/3.5 miles long) lead through the pine forest. These trails are well-marked and groomed and provide an enjoyable outing for all levels of skiers. Also in the area is the more challenging Calypso Trail, which leads up Mount Roderick Dhu. This route is a popular snowmobile destination.

Kane Valley Cross-Country Trails (Map 17/A1)
The beautiful Kane Valley is home to a well-established 43 km (26.2 mile) trail system between Harmon and Corbett Lakes. Designed for beginner to intermediate skiers, the trails follow old roads and skid trails through open timber and across sloping meadows. The ski season runs from December to March and unlike the surrounding areas, offers good snow conditions. The **Menzies Loop** winds 15 km/9 miles (3 hours) through the open country west of the road. **Matthew's Loop** is found 3.7 km (2 miles) down the Kane Valley Road and is best skied in a clockwise direction. The trail leads south for 5 km (3 miles) through open woods and meadows climbing 100 m (328 feet) along the way. **Robinson's Loop** is actually a series of loops along the old logging roads to the south of the road. There is a fair bit of hill on this loop, which eventually hooks up with Matthew's Loop.

Lac Le Jeune Ski Trails (Map 33/E7)
This network of trails and old roads circle the popular recreational lake south of Kamloops. Since the trails are not groomed and have steep long climbs, the 73 km (43.5 mile) long network is considered moderate in difficulty. The variety of terrain ranges from open meadows and hillsides to narrow forested trails.

Larch Hills Trail Network (Map 36/F1)
Located on the Larch Hills FSR southeast of Salmon Arm, Larch Hills has 150 km (91.5 miles) of ski trails to explore. 40 km of the trails are groomed and there are several chalets and shelters to help take the edge off those cool days. The trail system follows a network of old and new logging roads, which criss-cross their way throughout the area. A detailed map is available from the Salmon Arm Forest Service. Snowmobilers are prohibited in the area.

Lichen Mountain Trails (Maps 44/B1-52/C7)
If the Kwikoit Creek FSR is ploughed, you can drive to the base of Little Lichen Mountain and then explore the series of trails leading to Lichen Mountain. The trails are groomed and follow old logging roads and trails to the alpine. There is a small chalet available.

Logan Lake Cross-Country Trails (Map 32/F6)
At Logan Lake, there are 36 km (28.1 miles) of groomed ski trails for all abilities. 2 km (1.2 miles) of the trails are lit at night, and the trails are tracked set for both skating and classic skiing. During the summer, hikers and bikers use the trails.

Marshall Lake Ski Trails (Map 6/A5)
Easily accessed on a good 2wd road (Phoenix Mtn Road) off Highway 3A, Marshall Lake is a fine winter destination. There are 17.5 km (10.7 miles) of trails for skiers of all levels of abilities as well as room for snowshoers and even snowmobilers (please stay off the set ski tracks). The cross-country ski trails are linked to the nearby Phoenix Alpine Ski Area and are found in an area rich in history of old gold mines. There is even the remains of an old gold rush town in the area. Be careful when exploring these old mine works.

McCulloch Ski Trails (Map 20/F6)
This series of cross-country trails in the McCulloch/Hydraulic Lake area offers 50 km (31 miles) of groomed trails, plus 12 km (7.3 miles) of ungroomed trails. There is a heated cabin at the trailhead and trail users are asked to contribute through club membership or day-use donations. To get here, take Highway 33 from Kelowna and look for the turn-off just over 6 km (3.7 miles) past the Big White Road. The trailhead is about 4.5 km (2.7 miles) from the highway. The trails are also available for hikers/bikers to explore in the off-season.

Mount Morrissey Ski Trails (Map 43/A6)
Found just east of the Sun Peaks Ski Area, there are 20 km (12.2 miles) of both track set ski trails and ungroomed trails. A day-use cabin is found at Morrissey Lake.

Nickle Plate Nordic Centre (Map 10/F7)
Nickel Plate Nordic Centre is the home of 50 km (30 miles) of ski trails for all levels of ability. In total, there are 30 km (18.3 miles) of groomed trails that are track set for skating and classic skiing, while the other 20 km (11.7 miles) offer more challenging ski-touring opportunities. In particular, the **Okanagan Vista Trail** offers a nice 8 km (4.9 mile) loop, and the **Burn Perimeter Trail** provides a 12 km (7.3 mile) loop. A large log cabin at the trailhead offers a stop over after a long day of skiing. The ski season lasts from November until April and there is a fee to use the ski trails.

Owlhead Snowmobile Trails (Maps 37/C1-45/D7)
A series of logging roads wind their way up Mara Mountain and into extensive alpine meadows. The local snowmobile club groom the road and maintain a warming chalet on the trail system. The attraction of the area to snowmobilers is the vast alpine area and interconnecting trails.

Postill-Swalwell Lake Ski Trails (Map 20/E1)

A 65 km (38.7 mile) network of trails extends around Postill Lake and Swalwell Lake northeast of Kelowna. The **Postill Lake Trail** connects the two networks, which are considered for beginner to intermediate cross-country skiers. The trails range in length from 5 km (3 miles) to 11 km (6.7 miles) and are flat with a maximum elevation drop of 150 m (488 feet). There are also snowmobile trails in the Swalwell (Beaver) Lake area and the chance to get out and explore on snowshoes.

Queest Mountain Trails (Map 45/C3)

Heading north from Sicamous along logging roads will eventually lead snowmobilers to the alpine area of Queest Mountain. There is a warming chalet at the top and a great view of Shuswap Lake.

Silver Star Mountain Area (Map 28/G1)

During the winter, there are 35 km (21.4 miles) of groomed cross-country trails at the base of the Silver Star Ski Hill east of Vernon. The cross-country trails connect up with the Sovereign Lake Trails to offer over 100 km (60 miles) of trails with at least 70 km (42.7 miles) of these trails being groomed daily. If this is not enough variety, the Trinity-Ricardo Trail network (see below) extends north offering a true backcountry experience. There is a fee to access the ski system.

Skimikin Lake Trails (Map 44/A7)

There are 15 km (9 miles) of mostly easy, unmaintained cross-country trails surrounding Skimikin Lake. Snowmobilers can follow the unploughed roads south into the Fly Hills area.

Skmana Lake Ski Trails (Map 43/C6)

There are 15 km (9.1 miles) of groomed and track set trails for beginners to advanced skiers. One of the easiest and most popular of these is a 4.5 km (2.7 mile) trail around Skmana Lake itself. The rest of the trails wind through the surrounding hills along old logging roads. There is a small warming hut near the lake about 500 meters (1,625 feet) from the parking area.

Southward Ho Backcountry Route (Map 10/F7)

This is a marked trailhead for an unmarked route, or rather, series of routes, for backcountry skiers looking to get out into the Apex Mountain and Mount Beaconsfield areas. This area is for experienced backcountry skiers only. The trailhead is located on a sharp curve on the Hedley-Nickle Plate Road, about 5 km (3 miles) past Apex Village.

Sovereign Lake Ski Area (Map 28/G1)

The Sovereign Lake area offers 50 km (30 miles) of groomed cross-country ski trails together with a day lodge and three warm-up huts. The series of short loop trails (up to 5.5 km/3.3 miles long) dissect the beautiful sub-alpine meadows of the area. It is also possible to link up with the Silver Star and Trinity-Ricardo trail networks. There is a fee to access the ski system.

Spanish Lake Tour (Maps 35/G6-36/B7)

This backcountry ski route starts at the end of Silvernails Road east of Falkland. From the end of the road, an old road network leads past Spanish Lake to Yankee Flats in the Salmon River Valley. The return trip will cover about 13 km (7.9 miles) gaining about 150 m (488 feet) along the way.

Stake Lake Ski Trails (Map 33/E6)

These trails are located to the south of Stake Lake and offer a total of 45 km (27.5 miles) of track set cross-country trails for all abilities. The roller coaster trail network offers a warm-up hut at the Stake Lake parking lot. There is a fee to access the ski system.

Stucci Cross-Country Centre (Map 35/G7)

Located on Cedar Hills Road, there are 60 km (36 miles) of trails, which extend from the rustic lodge all the way to the west end of Pinaus Lake and onto Falkland. The route to **Pinaus Lake** is 8 km (4.9 miles)

one-way with a vertical drop of 360 m (1,170 feet), whereas the trip to **Falkland** is 6.5 km (4 miles) one-way dropping 120 m (390 feet). Shorter and easier trails are found around the lodge.

Swakum Mountain Snowmobile Trails (Maps 24/G4-25/A2)

From the Helmer Exit on the Coquihalla Highway, a series of 78 km (47.6 miles) of snowmobile trails offer fine views along with plenty of variety. The trails lead along a series of logging roads at the base of the mountain.

Telemark Cross-Country Trails (Map 19/C5)

Near the Crystal Mountain Ski Hill on the Glenrosa Road, there are over 45 km (27.5 miles) of cross-country trails, which are groomed for classic and freestyle skiing. The trails range in difficulty from beginners to advanced and are anywhere from 1.5 km to 10 km (6.1 miles) long. Maintained by the Telemark Ski Club, the trails have 2.5 km of lit track for night skiing and can be used for a fee.

Thynne Mountain Trails (Maps 8/C1-16/E6)

In the winter, the area around Thynne Mountain and Mount Henning becomes an extensive series of snowmobile trails. The Merritt Snowmobile Club maintains the 55 km (33.5 miles) of trails around Thynne Mountain, while the Cheam Whiskey Jacks Club of Chilliwack maintains the 50 km (30.5 miles) of trails around Mt Henning. A 7.5 km (4.6 mile) trail links the two systems.

Tod Mountain Trails (Maps 42/G5-43/A5)

A snowmobile trail snakes up the backside of Tod Mountain from the road leading beyond Sun Peaks Village. Access is highly restricted as there is the ski hill and cross-country trails in the area. If you stick to the designated trails and do not go south of the peak (and into the ski area) you will discover a scenic paradise.

Trinity-Ricardo Trails (Maps 28/G1-36/G7, 37/A6)

Backcountry skiers and snowmobilers can explore this popular network of 60 km (36 miles) of groomed snowmobile trails connecting Silver Star with the Trinity Valley to the north. From the south, you can access the network from the Sovereign Cross-Country Ski Area. Follow the **Ganzeveld Trail** as it climbs steeply to the north end of Silver Star Provincial Park before descending into the scenic Trinity Valley. At the summit, several old roads and trails criss-cross and make excellent side trips. Along the way, you will pass the snowmobile chalet.

Trudra Lake Snowmobile Trail (Map 41/B4)

To the west of Tranquille Lake off the Sawmill Lake FSR, there are a series of trails often used by snowmobilers to explore the plateau south of Truda Lake.

Tsintsunko Lake Trail (Map 41/E1)

Originally a hiking trail, this short (2.5 km/1.5 mile) trail is now used in the winter by snowmobilers and on occasion skiers or snowshoers looking to get out onto the ice of Tsintsunko Lake. This is one of the few provincial parks in the area that allows snowmobiles.

Uren Snowmobile Trail (Maps 40/G1-41/A3)

Never mind the name! In winter, the logging road network to the east of the Deadman River Valley becomes a 52 km (32 mile) network of snowmobiling trails. The main route leads south past a series of lakes, crosses Criss Creek and skirts Gisborne Lake before eventually connecting with the Sawmill Lake FSR northeast of Tundra Lake.

White Lake Area Trails (Map 44/E5)

At the east end of White Lake, there is a 30 km (18.3 mile) network of trails for you to explore in the summer or winter. Other possibilities are to head south on the second road east of the 5 km marker on the Bastion-White Lake FSR, which takes you along Reinnecker Creek to the Bastion Mountain Road.

Reference 88

Kamloops/Okanagan Mapkey

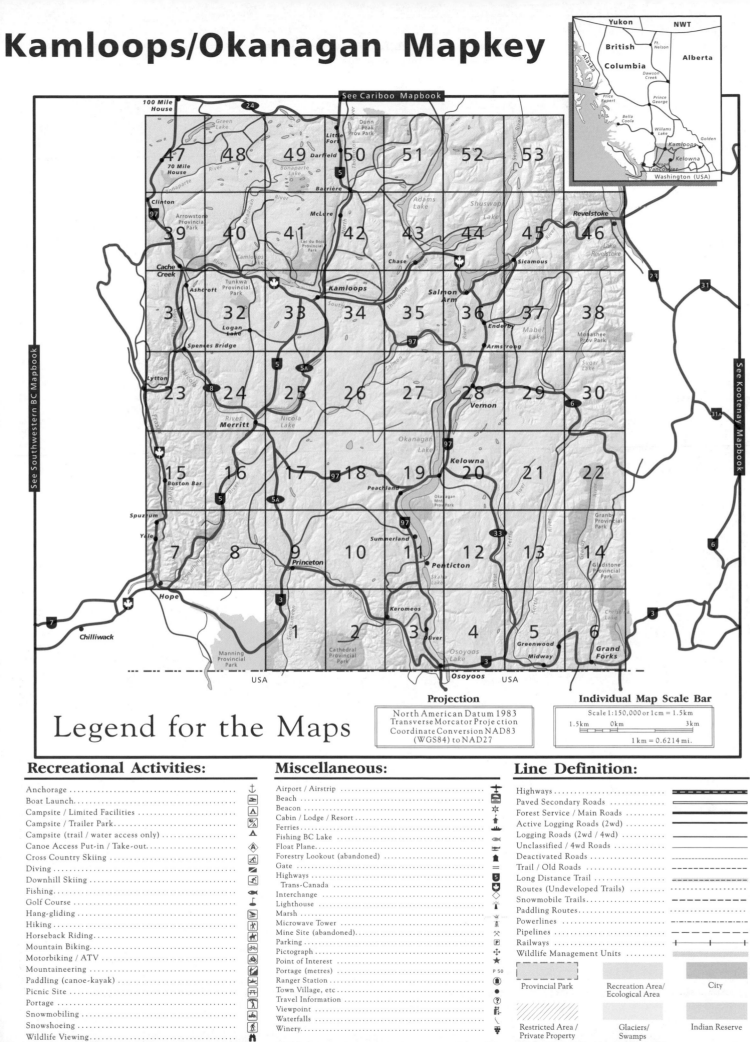

Legend for the Maps

Projection
North American Datum 1983
Transverse Mercator Projection
Coordinate Conversion NAD83
(WGS84) to NAD27

Individual Map Scale Bar
Scale 1:150,000 or 1cm = 1.5km

1.5km   0km   3km

1 km = 0.6214 mi.

Recreational Activities:

Anchorage	⚓
Boat Launch	
Campsite / Limited Facilities	
Campsite / Trailer Park	
Campsite (trail / water access only)	
Canoe Access Put-in / Take-out	
Cross Country Skiing	
Diving	
Downhill Skiing	
Fishing	
Golf Course	
Hang-gliding	
Hiking	
Horseback Riding	
Mountain Biking	
Motorbiking / ATV	
Mountaineering	
Paddling (canoe-kayak)	
Picnic Site	
Portage	
Snowmobiling	
Snowshoeing	
Wildlife Viewing	

Miscellaneous:

Airport / Airstrip	
Beach	
Beacon	
Cabin / Lodge / Resort	
Ferries	
Fishing BC Lake	
Float Plane	
Forestry Lookout (abandoned)	
Gate	
Highways	
Trans-Canada	
Interchange	
Lighthouse	
Marsh	
Microwave Tower	
Mine Site (abandoned)	
Parking	P
Pictograph	
Point of Interest	★
Portage (metres)	P 50
Ranger Station	
Town Village, etc	●
Travel Information	?
Viewpoint	
Waterfalls	
Winery	

Line Definition:

Highways	
Paved Secondary Roads	
Forest Service / Main Roads	
Active Logging Roads (2wd)	
Logging Roads (2wd / 4wd)	
Unclassified / 4wd Roads	
Deactivated Roads	
Trail / Old Roads	
Long Distance Trail	
Routes (Undeveloped Trails)	
Snowmobile Trails	
Paddling Routes	
Powerlines	
Pipelines	
Railways	
Wildlife Management Units	

Provincial Park

Recreation Area/
Ecological Area

City

Restricted Area /
Private Property

Glaciers/
Swamps

Indian Reserve

See Map 2

See SWBC Mapbook

Kam/OK Maps

Placer Mountain

1

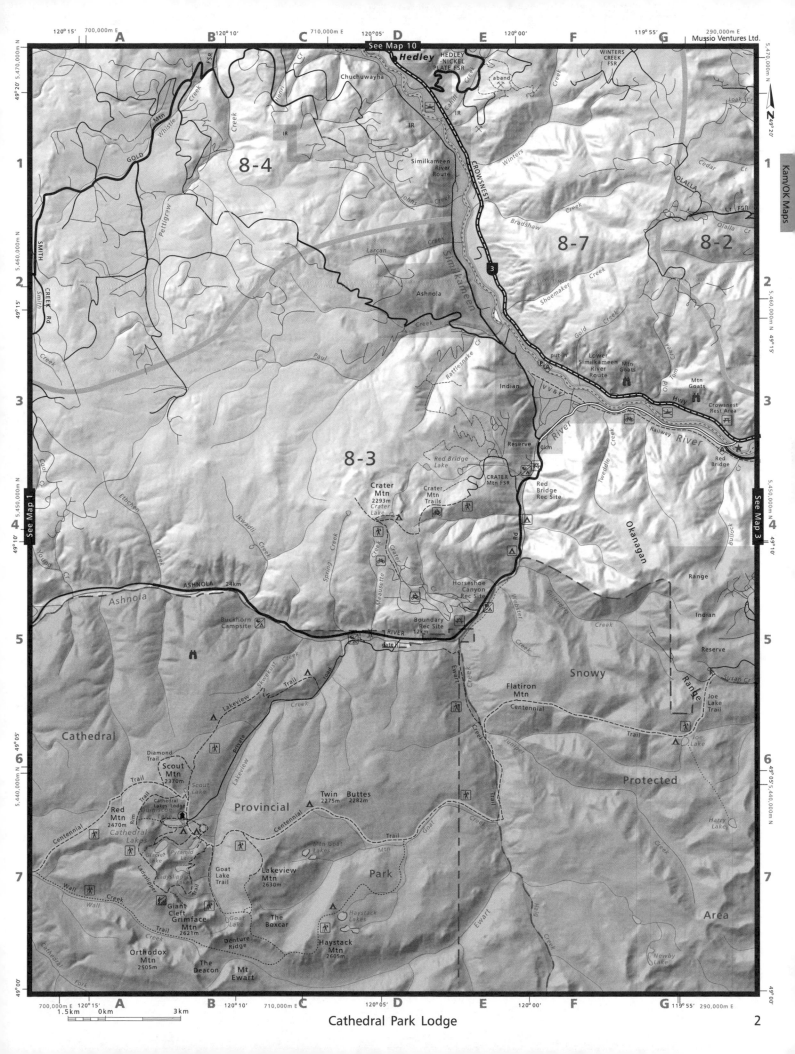

See Map 10

Hedley

HEDLEY
NICKEL
PLATE FSR

WINTERS
CREEK
FSR

Chuchuwayha

aband

8-4

IR

IR

Similkameen
River
Route

Winters

OLALLA

8-7

8-2

CROWSNEST

Bradshaw

Creek

Larcan

Shoemaker

Johns

Ashnola

Creek

Gold

Olalla

Cr

Cr FSR

Loak Cr

Cedar

Cr

Smith

SMITH

CREEK Rd

Weigelia

Pettigrew

GOLD Mtn

Whistle Creek

FSR

Henri

Creek

Creek

Paul

Rattlesnake Cr

Creek

put in

Lower
Similkameen
River
Route

Mtn
Goats

Pio Tom

Mtn
Goats

Smith Creek

Cool Cr

Ethchen Creek

Young Cr

Ikwadili Creek

Spring Creek

8-3

Creek

Meausette

Crater Creek

Crater
Mtn
2293m
Crater
Lake

Crater
Mtn
Trails

Indian

Reserve

9km

Red Bridge
Lake

CRATER
Mtn FSR

Red Bridge
Rec Site

Rd

3

VV&E

Similkameen River

Railway

River

Crowsnest
Rest Area

Red
Bridge
Cr

See Map 3

Horseshoe
Canyon
Rec Site

Boundary
Rec Site
12km

gate

ASHNOLA 24km

Ashnola

Buckhorn
Campsite

RIVER

Webster Creek

Okanagan

Tweddle Creek

Gilandri Creek

Range

Indian

Reserve

See Map 1

Cathedral

Lakeview

Trail

Skyekust Creek

Creek

road

private

Ewart Creek

Flatiron
Mtn

Snowy

Range

Bullock

Susap Cr

Joe
Lake
Trail

Centennial

Trail

Joe
Lake

Diamond
Trail

Scout
Mtn
2370m

Scout
Lake

Lakeview

Cathedral
Lakes Lodge

Red Mtn
2470m

Rim Trail

Cathedral
Lakes

Centennial

Glacier
Lake

Pyramid
Lake

Ladyslipper
Lake

Giant
Cleft
Grimface
Mtn
2621m

Wall Creek

Orthodox
Mtn
2505m

The
Deacon

Mt
Ewart

Denture Ridge

Goat
Lake

Goat
Lake Trail

Provincial

Twin
Buttes
2275m 2282m

Lakeview
Mtn
2630m

The
Boxcar

Mtn Goat
Lakes

Trail

Centennial

Park

Goat Mtn

Trail

Haystack
Lakes

Haystack
Mtn
2605m

Ewart Creek

Juniper Creek

Hail Creek

Protected

Harry
Lake

Area

Newby
Lake

1.5km 0km 3km

3 km

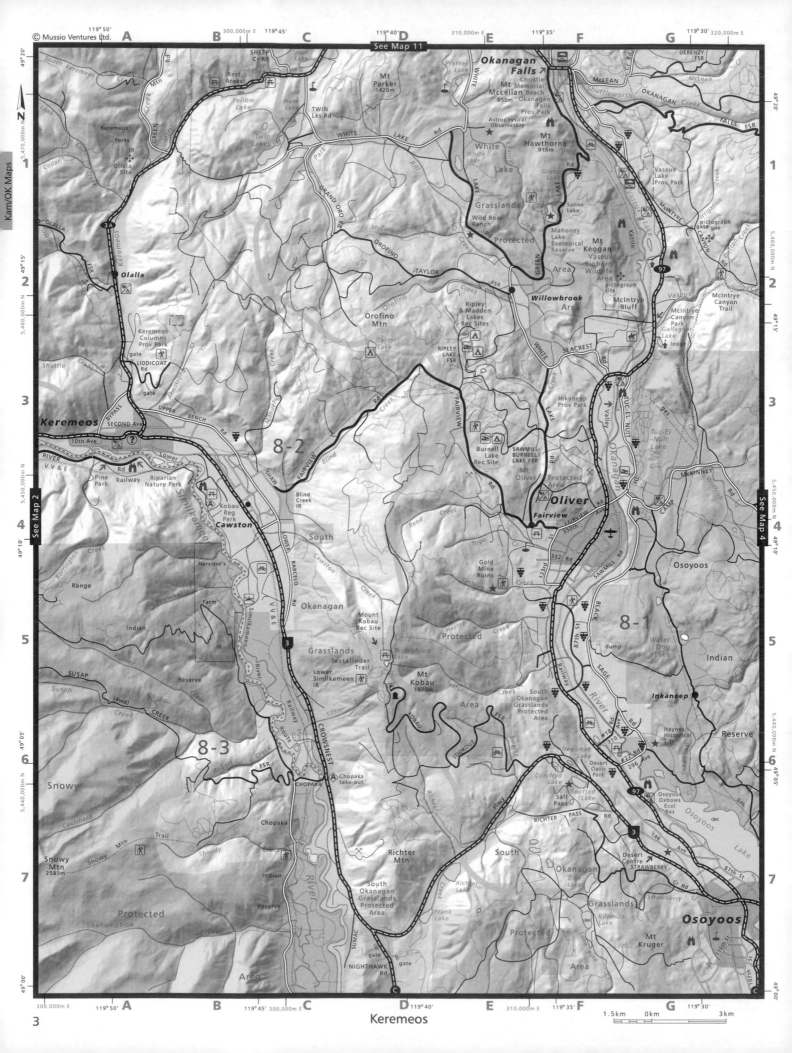

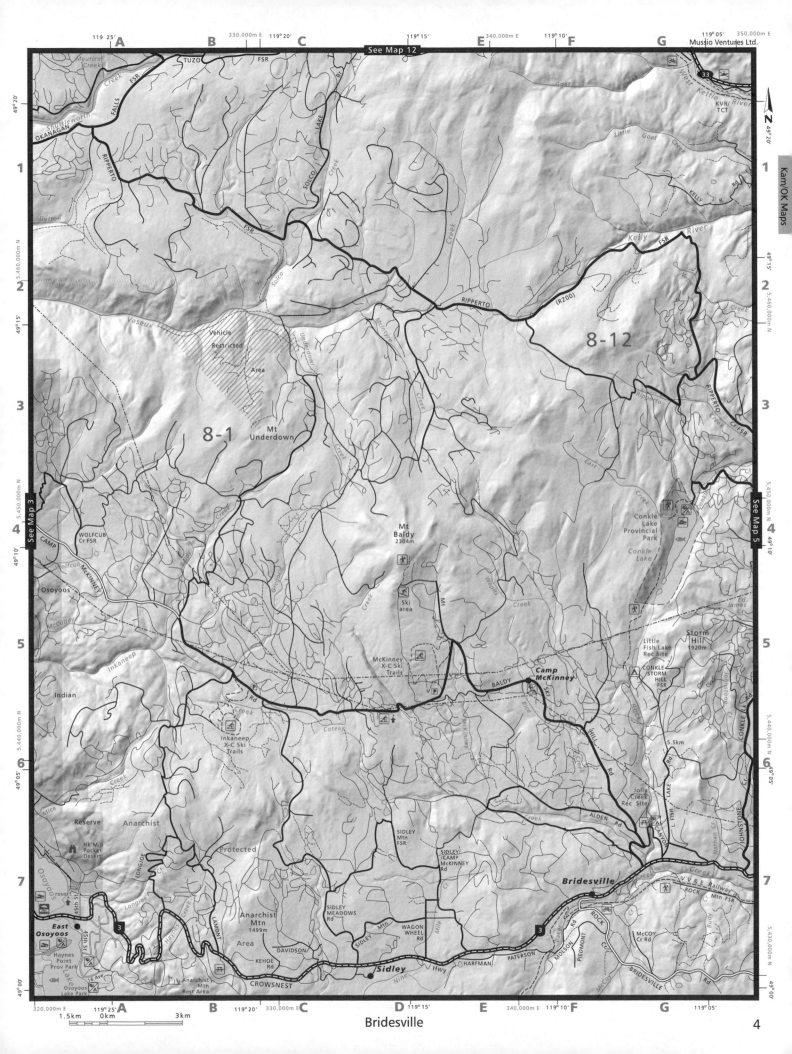

Mussio Ventures Ltd.

See Map 12

8-12

8-1

Bridesville

4

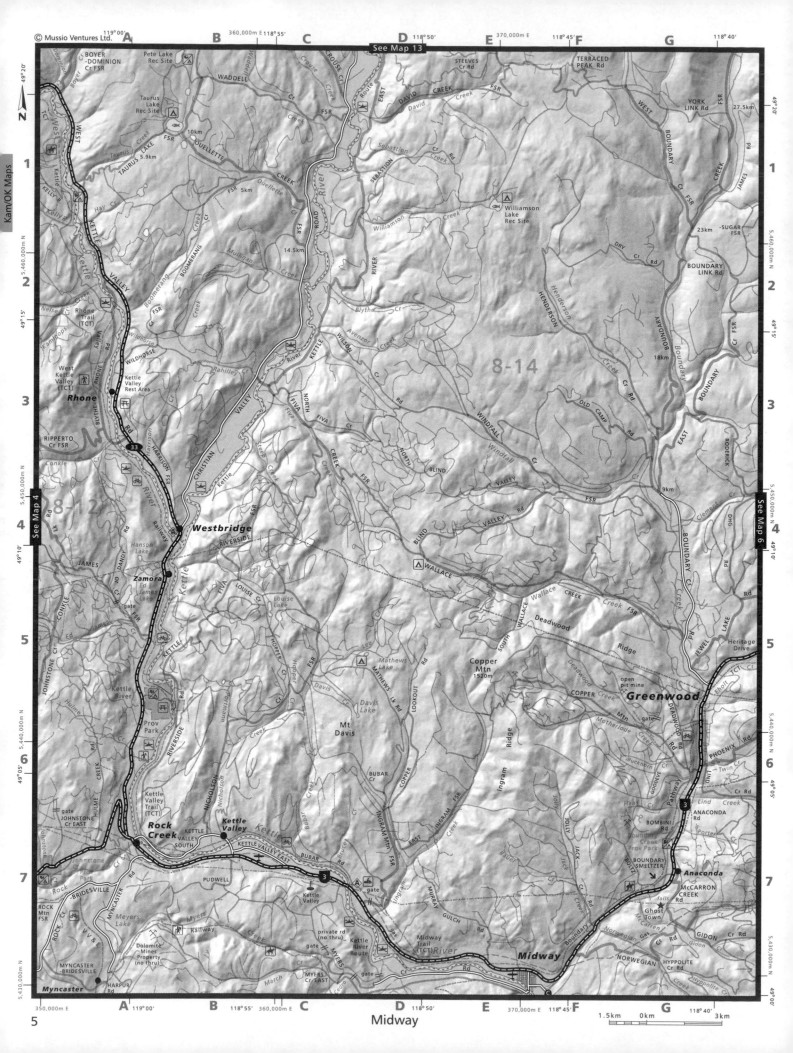

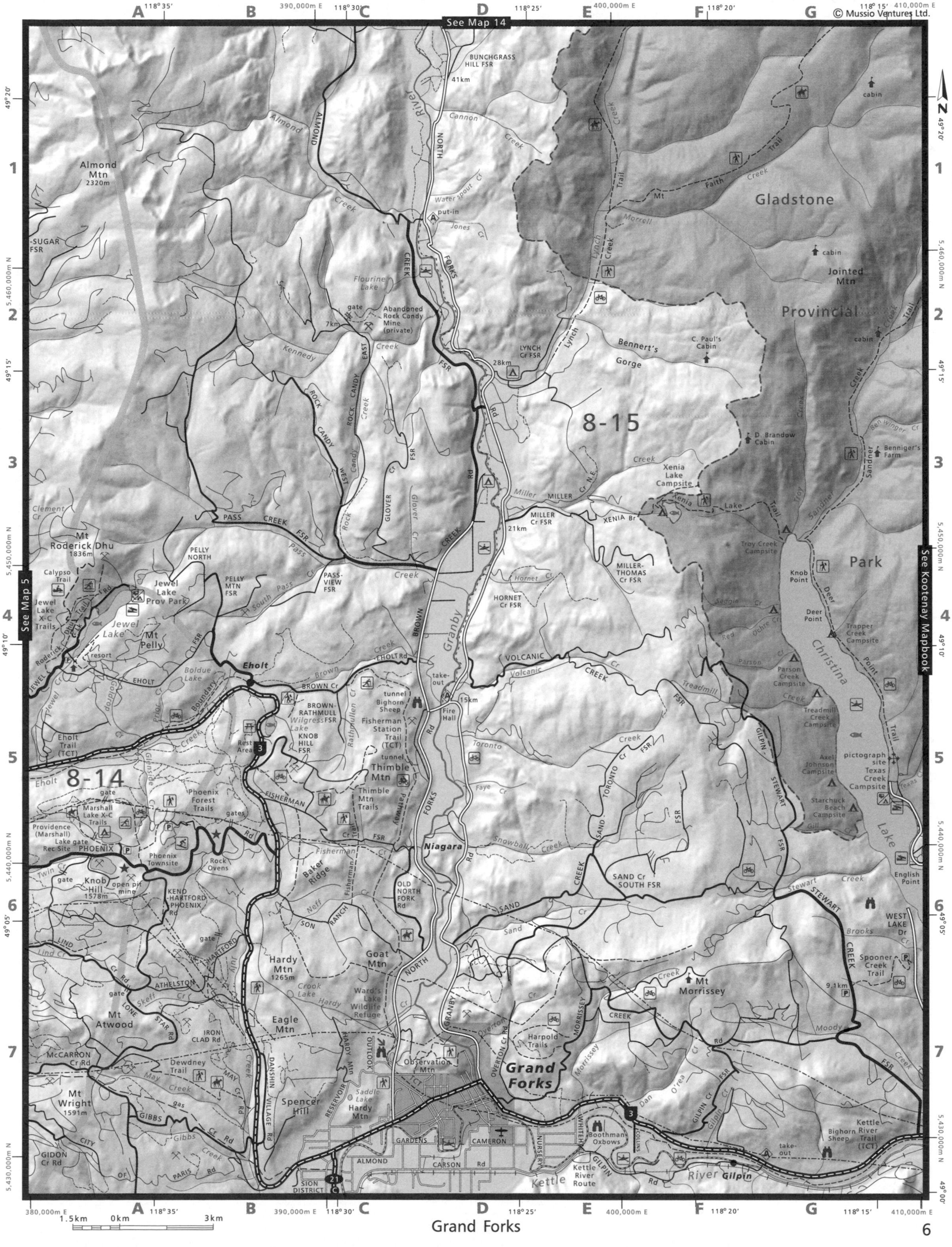
See Map 14
See Map 5
See Kootenay Mapbook
BUNCHGRASS HILL FSR
41km
Almond Mtn
2320m
-SUGAR FSR
ALMOND
Almond
Creek
North Fork River
NORTH FORKS CREEK
Cannon Creek
Waterspout Cr
put-in
Jones Cr
Flourine Lake
gate
7km
Abandoned Rock Candy Mine (private)
Kennedy
EAST ROCK CANDY Creek
ROCK CANDY
CANDY WEST
Rock Candy Cr
GLOVER FSR
Glover Cr
FSR Rd
28km
LYNCH Cr FSR
Lynch
Lynch Creek
Trail
Mt Faith Creek Trail
Morrell
Gladstone
cabin
Jointed Mtn
Provincial
Park
C. Paul's Cabin
Bennert's Gorge
8-15
8-14
D. Brandow Cabin
Benniger's Farm
Ben Winger Cr
Sandner Creek
Troy Creek
Xenia Lake Campsite
Xenia Lake Trail
XENIA Br
Miller
MILLER Cr N.E.
MILLER Cr FSR
21km
Troy Creek Campsite
Knob Point
Deer Point
Deer
Christina Lake
Trapper Creek Campsite
Parson Creek Campsite
Treadmill Creek Campsite
Axel Johnson Campsite
pictograph site
Texas Creek Campsite
Starchuck Beach Campsite
English Point
Clement Cr
Mt Roderick Dhu
1836m
PASS CREEK FSR
Pass
PELLY NORTH
PELLY MTN FSR
PASS-VIEW FSR
South Pass Cr
Creek
Calypso Trail
Jewel Lake X-C Trails
Jewel Lake Prov Park
Jewel Lake
Mt Pelly
Roderick Dhu Trail
resort
JEWEL
Boldue Lake
EHOLT
Eholt
Boundary
Eholt Trail (TCT)
Eholt
MILLER-THOMAS Cr FSR
Hornet Cr
HORNET Cr FSR
BROWN
Granby
EHOLT Rd
BROWN Cr
Brown
take-out
15km
Fire Hall
VOLCANIC CREEK
Volcanic
Treadmill
FSR
tunnel
Bighorn Sheep
BROWN-RATHMULL FSR
Wilgress Lake
KNOB HILL FSR
Rathmullen Cr
Fisherman Station Trail (TCT)
Rest Area
3
Thimble Mtn
Thimble Mtn Trails
FISHERMAN
Pathway
FORKS Rd
Toronto Creek
TORONTO Cr FSR
GILPIN STEWART FSR
Faye Cr
gate
Marshall Lake X-C Trails
Phoenix Forest Trails
gates
Providence (Marshall) Lake gate Rec Site
PHOENIX
Phoenix Townsite
Rock Ovens
Knob Hill
1578m
open pit mine
Twin Cr
Niagara
Snowball Creek
SAND CREEK
SAND Cr SOUTH FSR
Baker Ridge
Fisherman
OLD NORTH FORK Rd
KENO-HARTFORD-PHOENIX
Neff
SON RANCH
SAND
Sand
Stewart Creek
STEWART CREEK
Brooks
WEST LAKE Dr
Spooner Creek Trail
9.1km
LIND
Lind Cr
gate
HARTFORD
ATHELSTON
Hardy Mtn
1265m
Goat Mtn
NORTH
Crook Lake
Hardy
Ward's Lake Wildlife Refuge
Mt Morrissey
MORRISSEY CREEK
Moody
Mt Atwood
LONE STAR Rd
Skeff Cr
IRON CLAD Rd
Eagle Mtn
GRANBY
Overton
OVERTON Cr Rd
Harpold Trails
McCARRON Cr Rd
Dewdney Trail
MAY Cr Rd
May Creek
DANSHIN VILLAGE Rd
HARDY Mtn Rd
OUTLOOK
Observation Mtn
Grand Forks
Morrissey
Mt Wright
1591m
GIBBS Cr Rd
Gibbs Creek
gas
Spencer Hill
RESERVOIR
Saddle Lake
Hardy Mtn
Dan O'rea Cr
GILPIN Cr FSR
Kettle River Trail (TCT)
Bighorn Sheep
GIDON Cr Rd
CITY
PARIS Rd
GARDENS
CAMERON
ALMOND
CARSON Rd
NURSERY
WHITEHEAD
Boothman Oxbows
COLLINS
take-out
Kettle River Route
GILPIN Rd
Kettle River
Gilpin
SION DISTRICT
21
A
B
C
D
E
F
G
1
2
3
4
5
6
7
118° 35'
118° 30'
118° 25'
118° 20'
118° 15'
49° 20'
49° 15'
49° 10'
49° 05'
49° 00'
380,000m E
390,000m E
400,000m E
410,000m E
5,460,000m N
5,450,000m N
5,440,000m N
5,430,000m N
1.5km
0km
3km

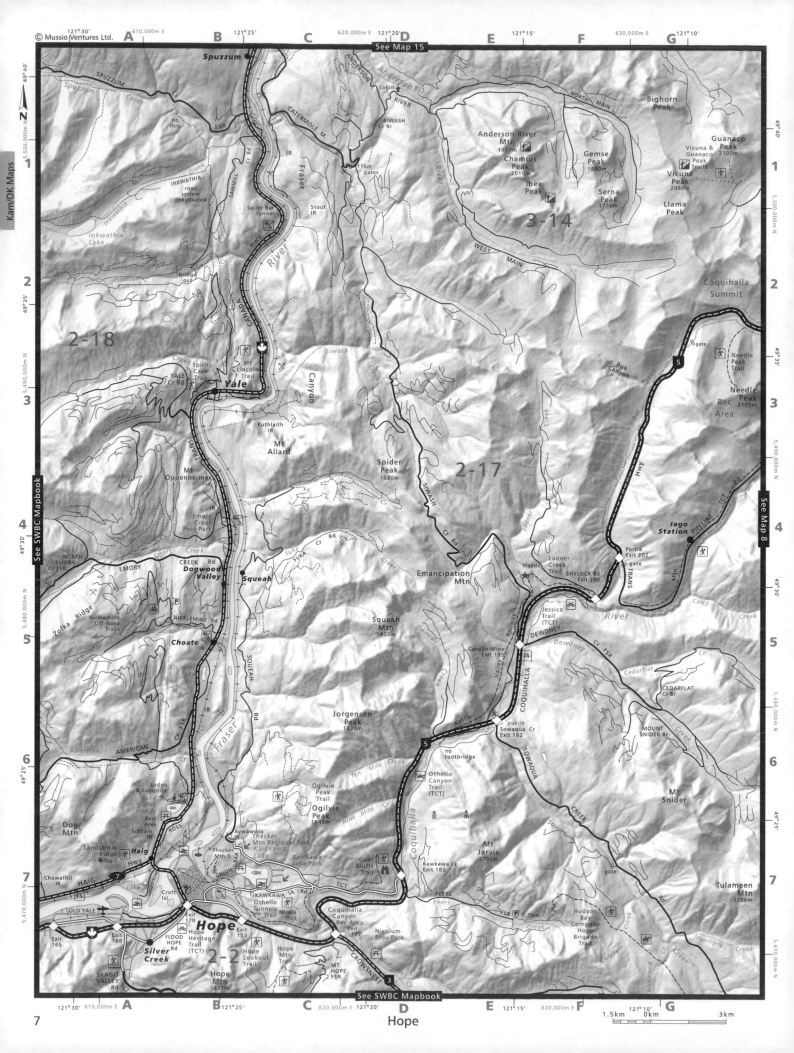

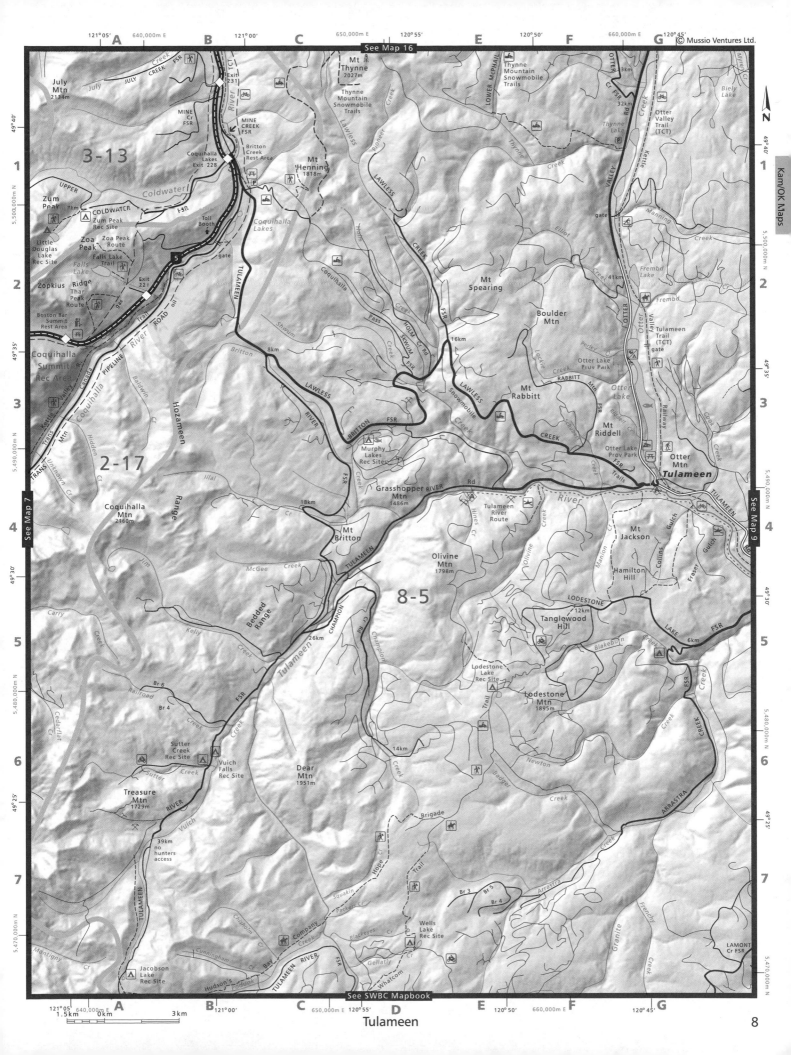

© Mussio Ventures Ltd.

A 640,000m E **B** 121°00' **C** 650,000m E **D** 120°55' **E** 120°50' **F** 660,000m E **G** 120°45'
121°05'

N

July
Mtn
2134m

JULY CREEK FSR

Mt
Thynne
2027m

Thynne
Mountain
Snowmobile
Trails

Thynne Mountain
Snowmobile
Trails

OTTER Cr FSR

3km

Biely Lake

Myrtle Cr

1

3-13

MINE Cr FSR

Exit 231

TCT

Coldwater R

Coquihalla
Lakes
Exit 228

MINE CREEK
FSR

Britton
Creek
Rest Area

Mt
Henning
1818m

Lawless

LOWER McPHAIL

Thynne Lake

VALLEY

Thynne Creek

Otter
Valley
Trail
(TCT)

32km

gate

Upper

Zum
Peak

COLDWATER
FSR

Zum Peak
Rec Site

Toll
Booth

Coquihalla
Lakes

Horn

Coquihalla Creek

LAWLESS

Elliot Creek

Manning Creek

41km

Frembd
Lake

2

Little
Douglas
Lake Rec Site

Zoa
Peak

Zoa Peak
Route

5

gate

TULAMEEN

Shwum

Mt
Spearing

FSR

HOLM Cr Rd

SKWUM

Boulder
Mtn

Lockie Creek

Perley Creek

OTTER

Frembd

Tulameen
Trail
(TCT)

gate

49°35'

Zopkius
Ridge

Thar
Peak
Route

Falls Lake Trail

Falls
Lake

Exit 221

PIPELINE

Britton

8km

Pass

Creek

FSR

LAWLESS

16km

Mt
Rabbitt

RABBITT

Schubert Creek

Otter Lake
Prov Park

Otter
Lake

Railway

3

Boston Bar
Summit
Rest Area

Canada

Coquihalla

Hozameen

Baldwin Cr

ROAD

RIVER

LAWLESS

Snowmobile

CREEK

Mt
Riddell

FSR

Riddell Cr

Otter Lake
Prov Park

Trails

Otter
Mtn

Cook Creek

Coquihalla
Summit
Rec Area

Kettle Valley Trails

Mtn

Hidden Cr

2-17

PIPELINE Trail

Range

Illal Creek

BRITTON

Murphy
Lakes
Rec Sites

FSR

Grasshopper
Mtn
1486m

RIVER

Rd

Tulameen

Tulameen

49°30'

Unknown Cr

TRANS

Coquihalla
Mtn
2160m

18km

Mt
Britton

Creek

Hines Cr

Tulameen
River
Route

Olivine
Creek

Mt
Jackson

Mannon Cr

Gulch

Collins

Fraser Gulch

4

See Map 7

McGee Creek

TULAMEEN

Olivine
Mtn
1798m

Hamilton
Hill

5

Carry Creek

Kelly Creek

Bedded
Range

8-5

CHAMPION

26km

Champion Cr Rd

LODESTONE

Tanglewood
Hill

12km

Blakeburn Creek

LAKE

6km

FSR

Lodestone
Lake
Rec Site

Lodestone
Mtn
1895m

5

Cedarflat Cr

Railroad Creek

Br 6

Br 4

Creek

FSR

Sutter

Trail

14km

Newton Creek

6

Sutter
Creek
Rec Site

Vuich Falls
Rec Site

Dear
Mtn
1951m

Creek

Badger Creek

ARRASTRA

49°25'

Treasure
Mtn
1729m

RIVER

Vuich Cr

Brigade

Arrastra Creek

CREEK

Frenchy Creek

Granite Creek

7

Montigny Cr

TULAMEEN

39km
no
hunters
access

Hope Cr

Trail

Br 3

Br 5

Br 4

LAMONT
Cr FSR

Chisholm Cr

Squakin Cr

Packer Cr

Wells Lake
Rec Site

Jacobson
Lake Rec Site

Hudson's
Bay

Cunningham Cr

Company
Creek

TULAMEEN RIVER

Podunk Cr

Blackeyes Cr

Gellatly Cr

Whatcom Cr

FSR

A 640,000m E **B** 121°00' **C** 650,000m E **D** 120°50' **E** **F** 660,000m E **G** 120°45'
121°05'
1.5km 0km 3km

See Map 9

Tulameen

8

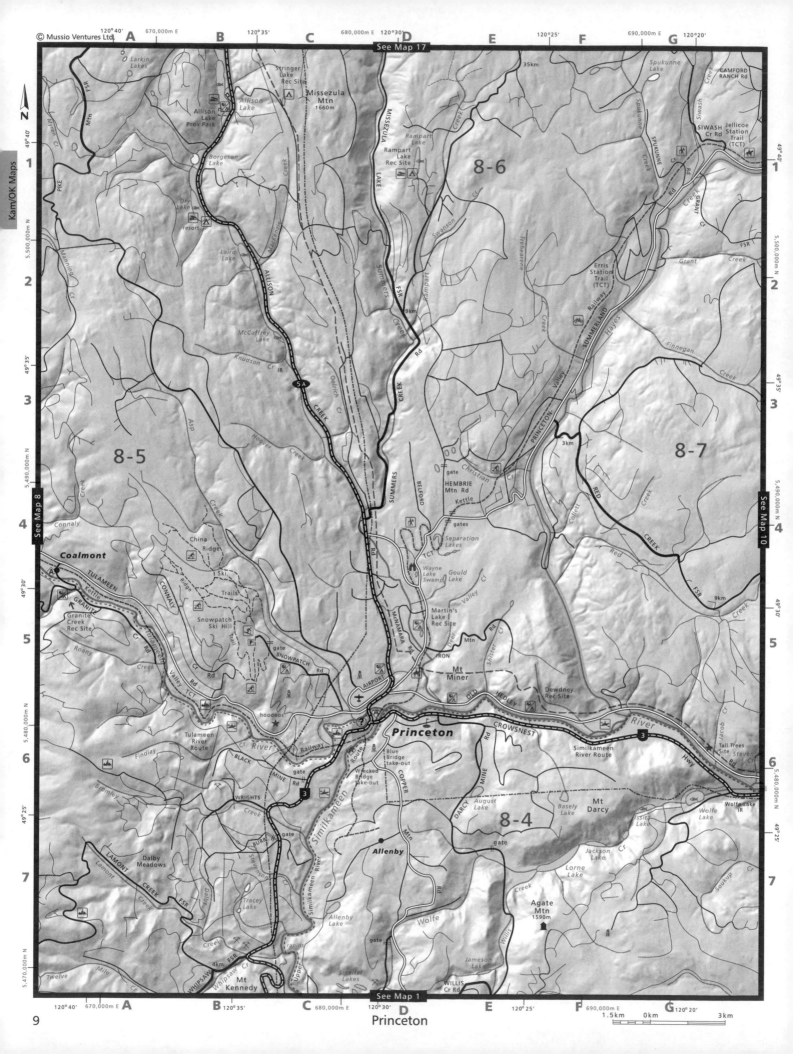

See Map 17

See Map 8

See Map 10

See Map 1

8-6

8-5

8-7

8-4

Coalmont

Princeton

Allenby

Mt
Miner

Mt
Darcy

Mt
Kennedy

Larkin
Lakes

Allison
Lake

Allison Lake
Prov Park

Stringer
Lake Rec Site

Missezula
Mtn
1660m

Borgeson
Lake

Dry
Lake
resort

Laird Lake

McCaffrey
Lake

Knudson Cr

5 A

Rampart
Lake

Rampart
Lake
Rec Site

Swanson

Treharne

Erris
Station
Trail
(TCT)

Spukunne
Lake

SIWASH
Cr Rd

Jellicoe
Station
Trail
(TCT)

CAMFORD
RANCH Rd

GRANT
Creek

FSR

Grant
Creek

Hayes

Finnegan
Creek

Christian

HEMBRIE
Mtn Rd

Kettle

gate

gates

Separation
Lakes

TCT

Wayne
Lake
Swamp

Gould
Lake

Martin's
Lake
Rec Site

IRON

Dewdney
Rec Site

Collett

Red

Siwash

China
Ridge

Connaly

Ridge

Ski
Trails

Snowpatch
Ski Hill

P

gate

SNOWPATCH

Rd

AIRPORT

hoodoos

Tulameen
River
Route

Railway

Route

gate

Blue
Bridge
take-out

Wrecked
Bridge
take-out

Similkameen
River Route

Tall Trees
Site

Steven

Wolfe Lake
IR

Wolfe
Lake

Issita
Lake

Jackson
Lake

Basely
Lake

August
Lake

Lorne
Lake

Agate
Mtn
1590m

Jameson
Lake

Soukup

WILLIS
Cr Rd

Tracey
Lake

Dalby
Meadows

WRIGHTS

Smelter
Lakes

Allenby
Lake

rapids

gate

Findlay

Bromley

Roany

Connaly

Granite
Creek
Rec Site

TULAMEEN

PIKE

Myeth Cr

Manning Cr

Asp

Hoover
Creek

Oehrich Cr

ALLISON
CREEK

SUMMERS
CREEK

MISSEZULA
LAKE

Summers
Creek

Rampart

FSR
9km

Rd

BELFORD

MCNAMARA
Rd

Rd

TCT

Valley

Tulameen

LAMONT
CREEK
FSR

Lamont
Creek

Dalby
Creek

Stevenson
Cr

BURR

BLACK
MINE
Rd

COPPER

Similkameen
River

Upper

Whipsaw Cr

4km FSR

WHIPSAW

Twelve
Mile

DARCY
MINE
Rd

Wolfe
Creek

Willis
Cr

Jacob
Cr

RED
CREEK
FSR
9km

PRINCETON-
SUMMERLAND
Railway

3km

35km

3

3

3

Mt

Stevenson Cr

9

Princeton

1.5km   0km   3km

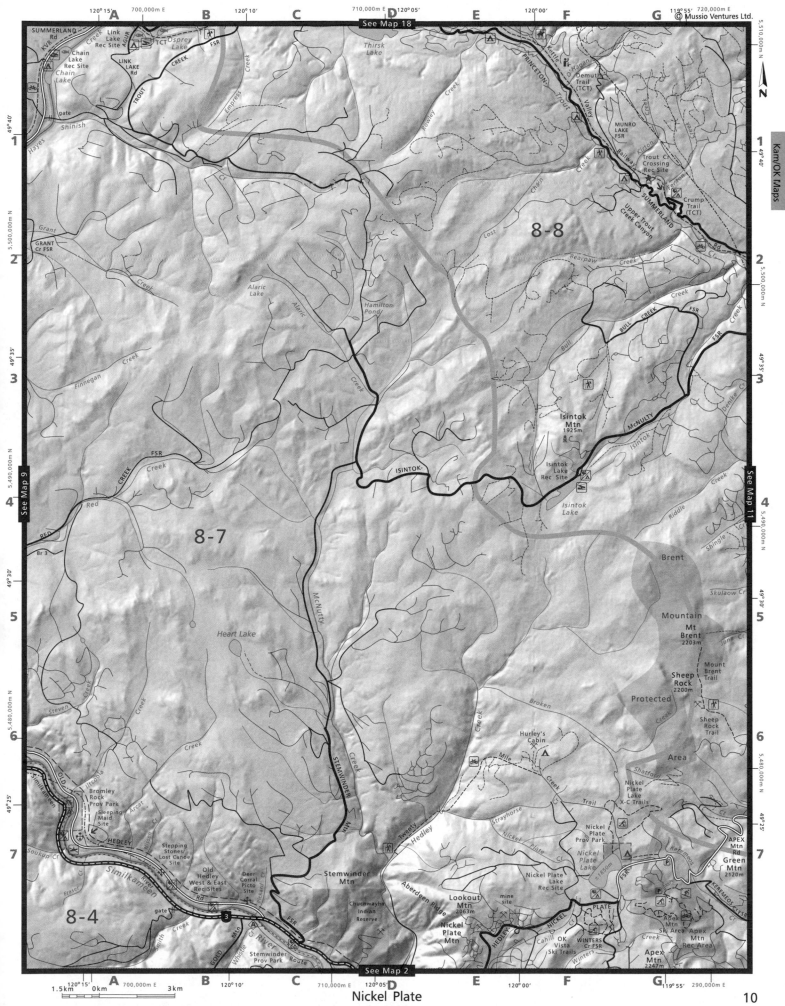

© Mussio Ventures Ltd.

See Map 18

See Map 9

See Map 11

8-8

8-7

8-4

Nickel Plate

See Map 2

10

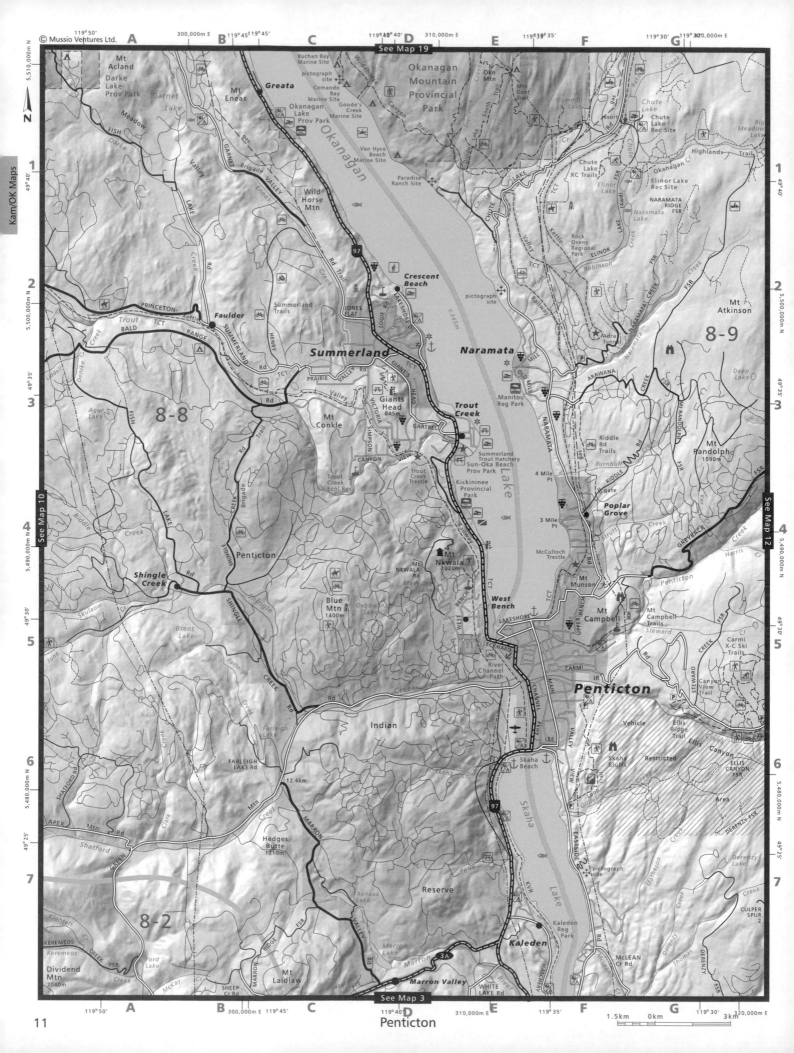

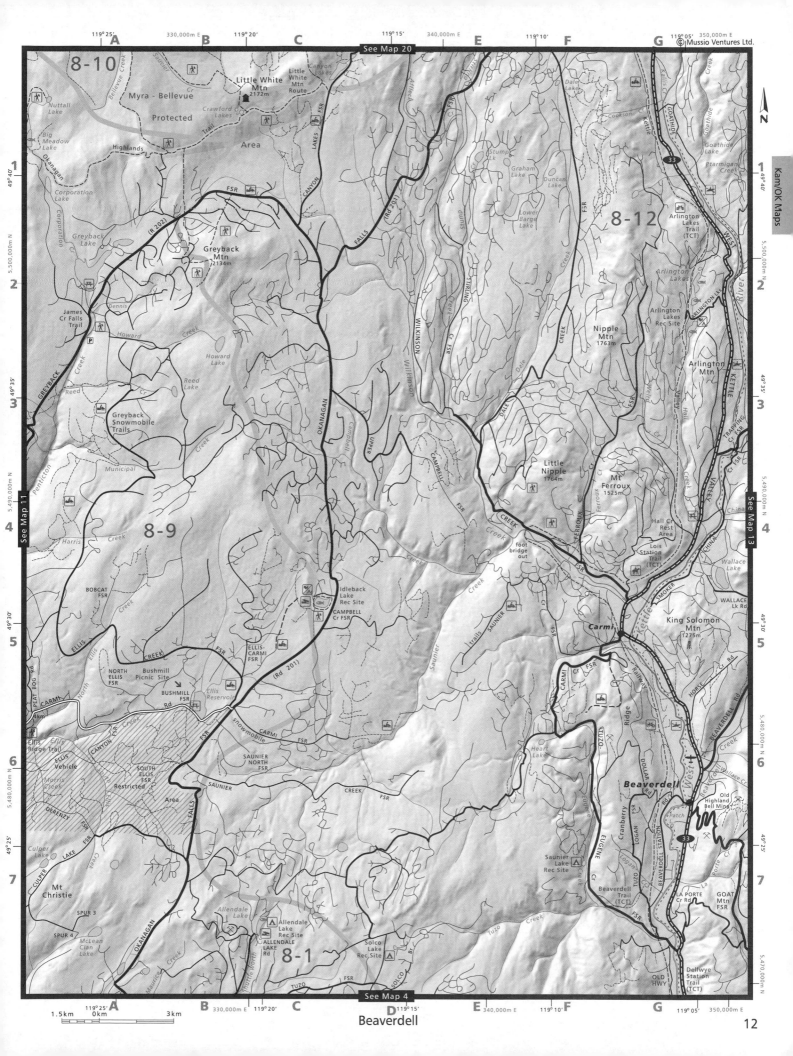

8-10

Myra - Bellevue
Protected
Area

Nuttall
Lake

Big
Meadow
Lake

Highlands

Okanagan

Corporation
Lake

Corporation

Greyback
Lake

Bellevue Creek

Little White
Mtn
2172m

Crawford
Cr
Lakes

Little
White
Mtn
Route

Canyon
Lakes

See Map 20

8-12

Arlington Lakes
Trail (TCT)

Goathide
Lake

Ptarmigan
Creek

33

FSR

Stump
Lk

Graham
Lake

Duncan
Lake

Lower
Barge
Lake

Arlington
Lakes

Arlington Lakes
Rec Site

Greyback
Mtn
2134m

FSR

CANYON

FALLS

WILKINSON

Willkinson

STIRLING

Nipple
Mtn
1763m

Arlington
Mtn

KETTLE

WEST

River

Dennis

James Cr Falls
Trail

Howard

Creek

Howard
Lake

Reed
Lake

OKANAGAN

Campbell

UPPER

CAMPBELL

Creek

DALE

Dale

Little
Nipple
1764m

Mt
Ferroux
1525m

FERROUX

Ferroux

Hall Cr
Rest
Area

Lois
Station
Trail (TCT)

China

Wallace
Lake

WALLACE
Lk Rd

VALLEY

Penticton

Reed

Cr

8-9

Harris

Creek

Municipal

FSR

CREEK

foot
bridge
out

CREEK

Cr

SMOKER

Greyback
Snowmobile
Trails

BOBCAT FSR

Creek

ELLIS

NORTH
ELLIS
FSR

Bushmill
Picnic Site

BUSHMILL FSR

Ellis-Carmi
FSR

FSR

Idleback
Lake Rec Site

CAMPBELL
Cr FSR

(Rd 201)

SAUNIER

Creek

trails

FSR

Carmi

King Solomon
Mtn
1275m

Kettle

CARMI

Ridge

HORSE

BEAVERDELL

Rd

PEAT BOG Rd

CARMI

4km

Ellis

Creek

Ellis Reservoir

Rd

CARMI

snowmobile

FSR

Heart
Lake

TUZO

Beaverdell

West

Creek

Old Highland
Bell Mine

Ellis
Ridge Trail

Ellis
Vehicle

Motris
Creek

SOUTH
ELLIS
FSR

Restricted

Area

CANYON

FALLS

SAUNIER
NORTH FSR

SAUNIER

CREEK

FSR

Eugene

Cr

DOLLAR

EUGENE

Cr

Cranberry

LOGAN

Logan

BEAVERDELL STATION

33

DERENZY
FSR

Culper
Lake

CULPER

LAKE

Creek

Mt
Christie

SPUR 3

SPUR 4

McLean
Clan
Lake

OKANAGAN

Maurice

Creek

Shuttleworth

Creek

Allendale
Lake

Allendale
Lake Rec Site

ALLENDALE
LAKE Rd

8-1

Saunier
Lake
Rec Site

Solco
Lake
Rec Site

Solco
Br

Tuzo

TUZO

Creek

FSR

SOLCO

Beaverdell
Trail
(TCT)

LA PORTE
Cr Rd

La
Porte

GOAT
Mtn
FSR

OLD
HWY

Dellwye
Station
Trail (TCT)

See Map 4

1.5 km   0 km   3 km

© Mussio Ventures Ltd.

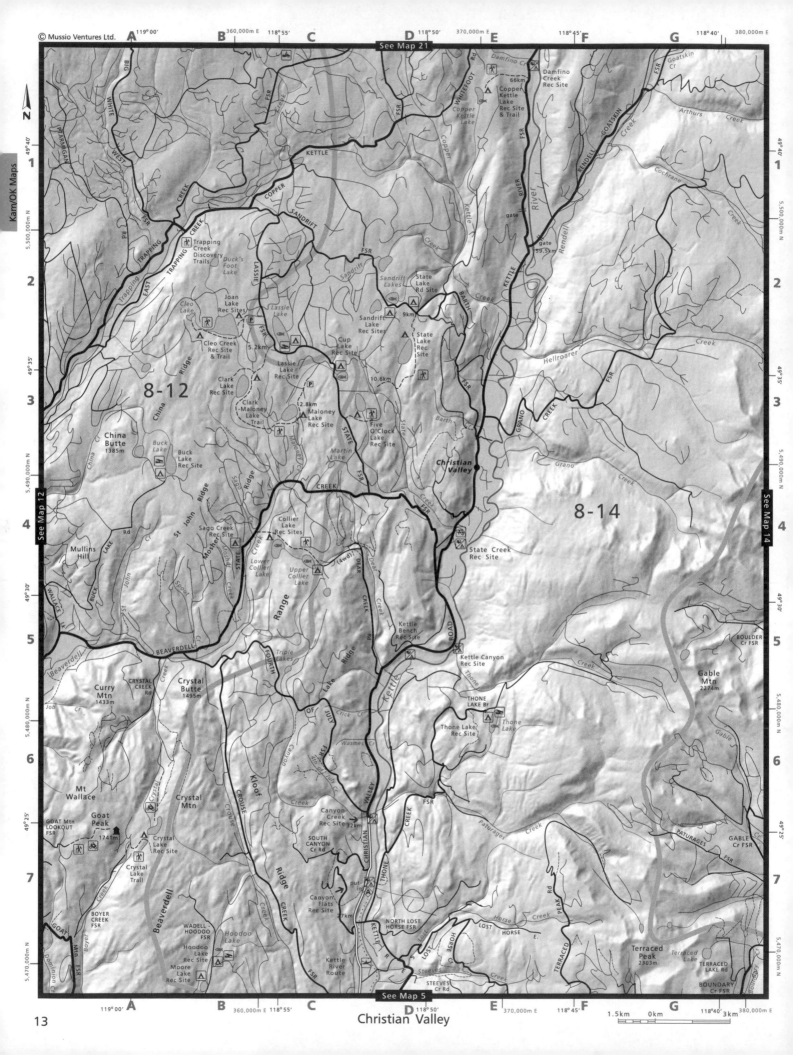

See Map 21

See Map 12

See Map 14

8-12

8-14

See Map 5

Christian Valley

13

1.5km 0km 3km

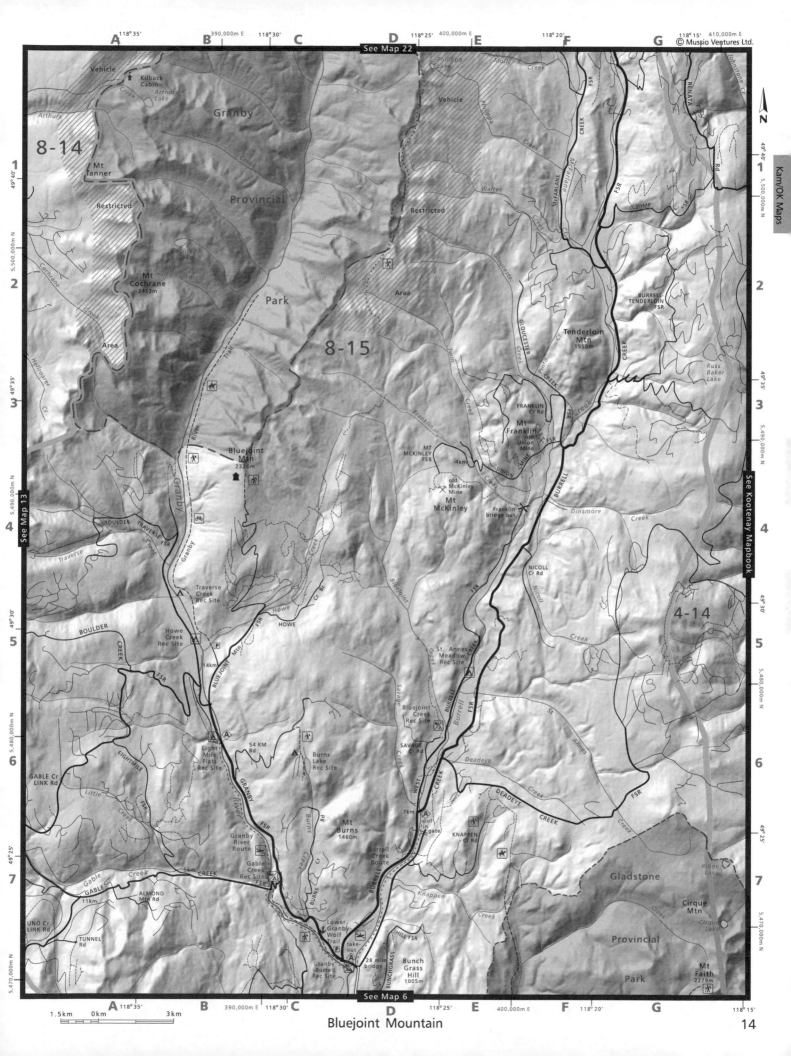

8-14

Granby

Mt Tanner

Restricted

Area

Mt Cochrane 2412m

Provincial

Park

8-15

Kilback Cabin
Arthurs Lake

Vehicle

Cochrane Lake

Cochrane Creek

Helluoaner Cr

Traverse

BOULDER TRAVERSE FSR

Granby River

Bluejoint Mtn 2326m

Traverse Creek Rec Site

Howe Creek Rec Site

14km

BLUEJOINT Mtn FSR

HOWE

Howe Cr Br

BOULDER CREEK FSR

EIGHTMILE

GABLE Cr LINK Rd

Little Gable Creek

Eight Mile Flats Rec Site

54 KM Rd

GRANBY River

FSR

Burns Cr

Burns Creek

Mt Burns 1460m

Granby River Route

Gable Creek Rec Site

GABLE CREEK

5km

ALMOND Mtn Rd

11km

UNO Cr LINK Rd

TUNNEL Rd

Lower Granby Wolf Trail

take-out

Granby Burrell Rec Site

28 mile bridge

BUNCHGRASS

Bunch Grass Hill 1005m

Philippa Lake

Molly Creek

Vehicle

Restricted

Area

Walter Creek

Franklin Creek

Twin Creek

Gloucester Creek

MT McKINLEY FSR

4km

old McKinley Mine

Mt McKinley

FRANKLIN Cr Rd

Mt Franklin

old Union Mine

UNION MINE

Franklin bridge out

BURRELL

Dinsmore Creek

NICOLL Cr Rd

St. Annes Meadow Rec Site

Bluejoint Creek Rec Site

Savage Creek

SAVAGE Cr Rd

BURRELL FSR

WEST CREEK

Deadeye

7km

put in gate

KNAPPEN Cr Rd

Burrell Creek Route

BURRELL

Knappen Creek

HILL FSR

Renata Rd

McFarlane Creek

FSR

JUMP

BURRELL-TENDERLOIN FSR

Tenderloin Mtn 1555m

BURRELL CREEK

851 Creek

Russ Baker Lake

Nicoll Creek

St Ames Creek

DEADEYE CREEK

FSR

4-14

Gladstone

Ridge Lake

Provincial

Park

Cirque Mtn

Cirque Lake

Mt Faith 2279m

See Map 22

See Map 13

See Kootenay Mapbook

See Map 6

1.5km 0km 3km

Bluejoint Mountain

14

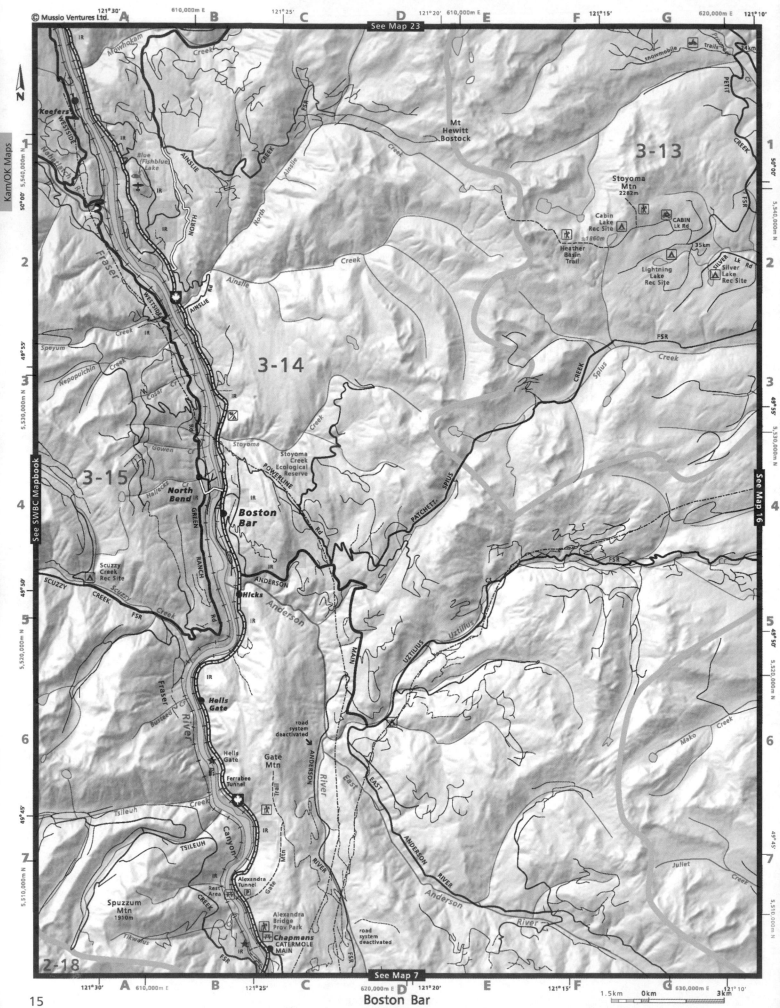

Kam/OK Maps

See SWBC Mapbook

See Map 23

See Map 16

See Map 7

3-13

3-14

3-15

2-18

Keefers

Mt Hewitt Bostock

Stoyoma Mtn 2282m

Cabin Lake Rec Site ±1860m

Heather Basin Trail

CABIN Lk Rd

35km

Lightning Lake Rec Site

Silver Lk Rd

Silver Lake Rec Site

snowmobile trails

4km

Blue (Fishblue) Lake

North Bend

Boston Bar

Scuzzy Creek Rec Site

Hicks

Hells Gate

Ferrabee Tunnel

Gate Mtn

Alexandra Tunnel

Rest Area

Alexandra Bridge Prov Park

Chapmans CATERMOLE MAIN

Spuzzum Mtn 1910m

Stoyama Creek Ecological Reserve

POWERLINE

road system deactivated

road system deactivated

Fraser River

Anderson River

East Anderson River

Uztlius Creek

Mako Creek

Juliet Creek

Spius Creek

15

Boston Bar

1.5km   0km   3km

630,000m E

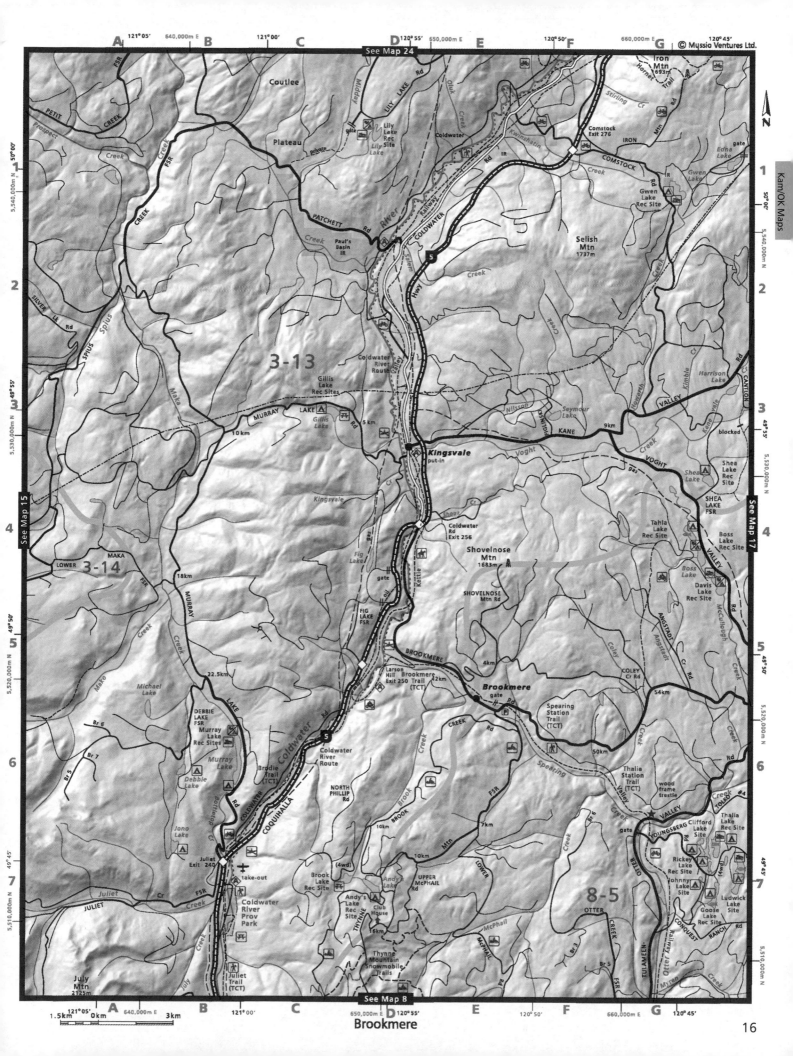

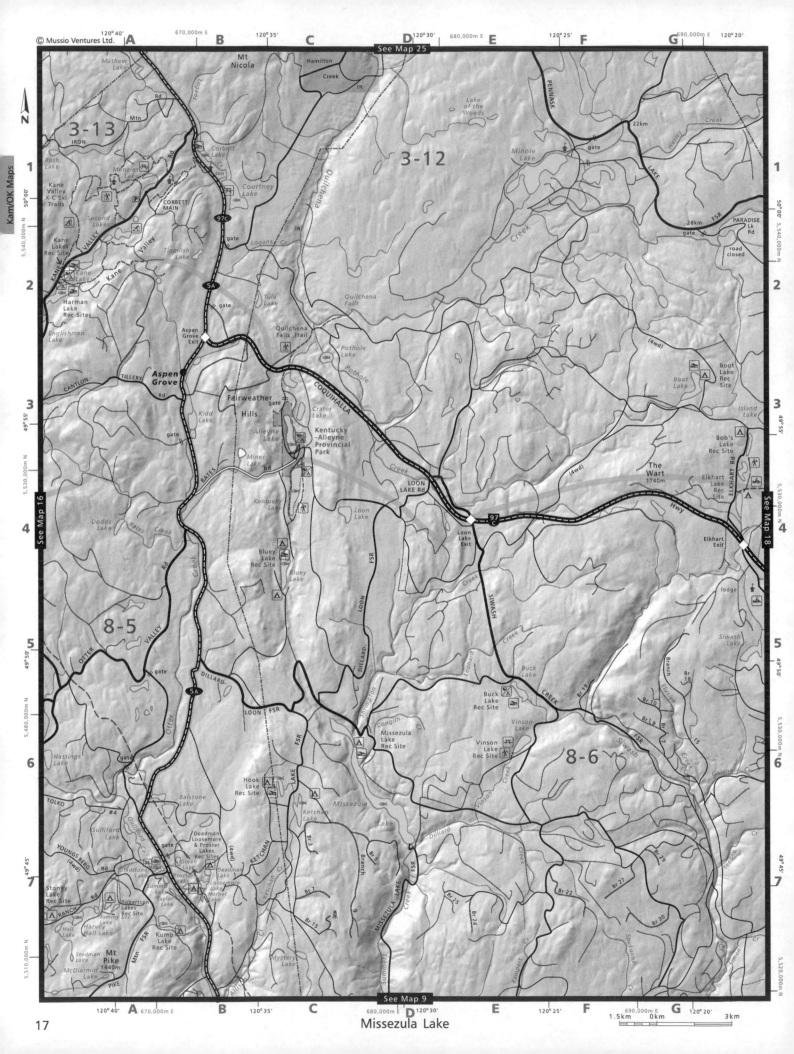

See Map 25

See Map 16

See Map 18

3-13

3-12

8-5

8-6

Missezula Lake

See Map 9

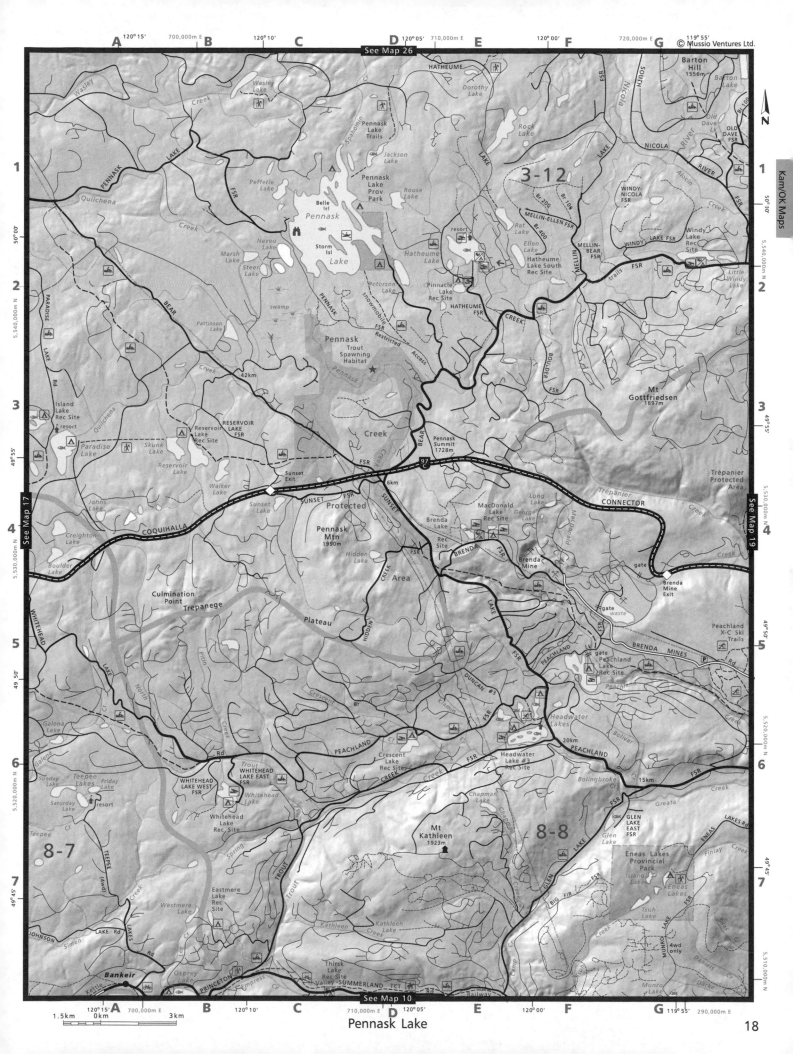

© Mussio Ventures Ltd.

Kam/OK Maps

3-12

Barton Hill 1556m

8-7

8-8

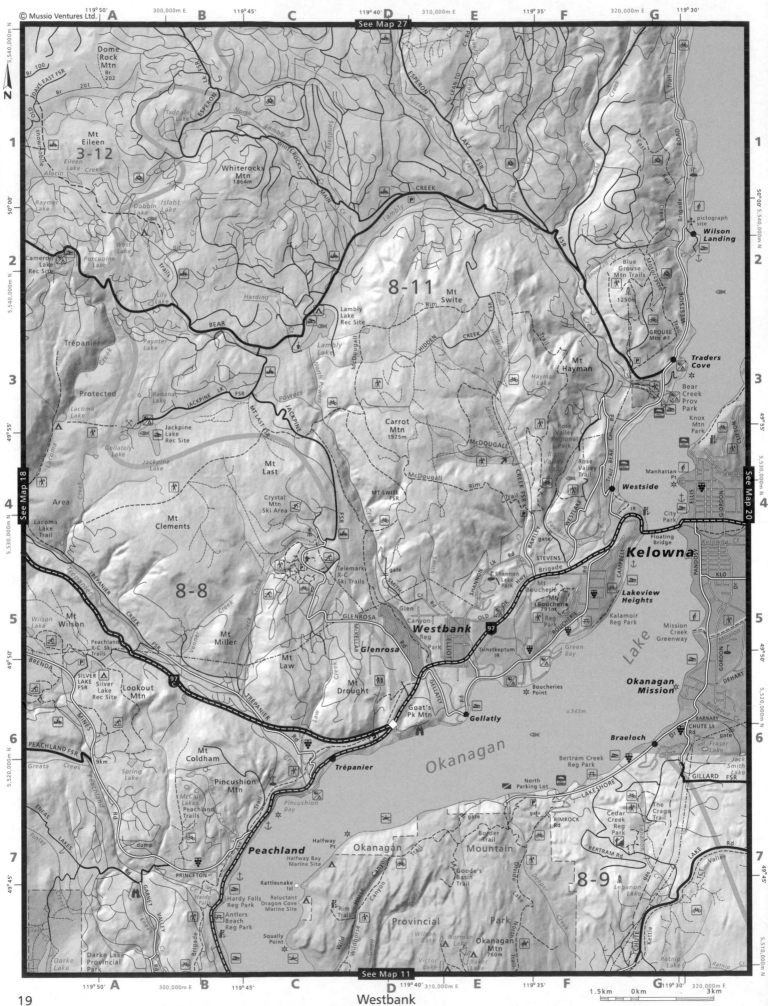

© Mussio Ventures Ltd.

Kam/OK Maps

See Map 18

See Map 20

8-12
Mt Eileen

Dome Rock Mtn

Whiterocks Mtn 1864m

Cameron Lake Rec Site

Trépanier

8-11

Mt Swite

Lambly Lake Rec Site

Mt Hayman

Traders Cove

Bear Creek Prov Park

Protected

Jackpine Lake Rec Site

Carrot Mtn 1525m

McDougall

Knox Mtn Park

Lacoma Lake Trail

Mt Last

MT SWITE FSR

Rose Valley Regional Park

Rose Valley Trail

Manhattan Pt

Westside

Mt Clements

Crystal Mtn Ski Area

8-8

Telemark X-C Ski Trails

Mt Boucherie

Kelowna

Lakeview Heights

Floating Bridge

City Park

Wilson Lake

Mt Wilson

Peachland X-C Trails

Mt Miller

Glenrosa

Mt Law

Westbank

97

Kalamoir Reg Park

Mission Creek Greenway

BRENDA

Silver Lake Rec Site

Lookout Mtn

Mt Drought

Goat's Pk Mtn

Gellatly

Boucheries Point

Green Bay

Okanagan Mission

Peachland FSR

Mt Coldham

Pincushion Mtn

Trépanier

Braeloch

Bertram Creek Reg Park

Cedar Creek Reg Park

The Crags Trail

Jack Smith Lake

Peachland

Peachland Trails

Pincushion Bay

Okanagan

Lake

North Parking Lot

RIMROCK Rd

8-9

Lebanon Lake

Hardy Falls Reg Park

Antlers Beach Reg Park

Halfway Bay Marine Site

Rattlesnake Isl

Reluctant Dragon Cove Marine Site

Okanagan

Provincial

Park

Okanagan Mtn 760m

Darke Lake Provincial Park

Squally Point

Rim Trail

Wilson Lake

Victor Lake

Baker Lake

19

Westbank

1.5km   0km   3km

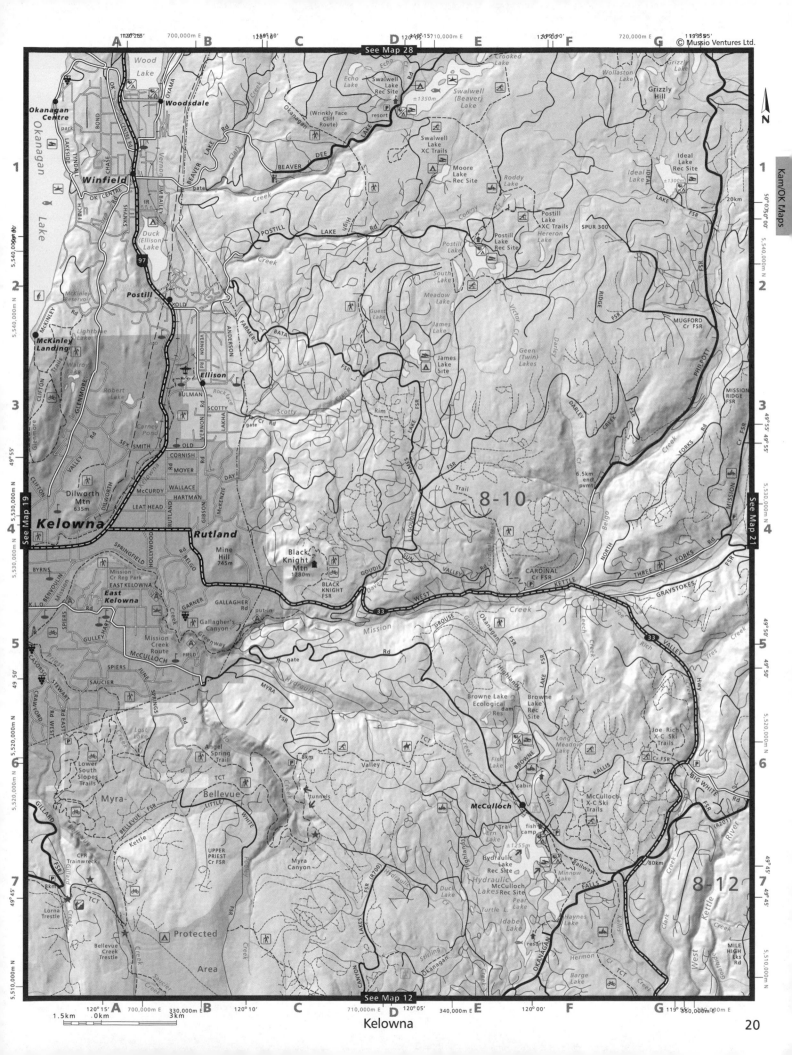

Kam/OK Maps

© Mussio Ventures Ltd.

Wood Lake

Okanagan Centre
park
Okanagan Lake
Woodsdale

Winfield

McKinley Reservoir

Postill

McKinley Landing

Lightblue Lake

Ellison

Robert Lake

Carney Pond

Dilworth Mtn 635m

Kelowna

Rutland

Mission Cr Reg Park

East Kelowna

Mine Hill 745m

Black Knight Mtn 1280m
BLACK KNIGHT FSR

8-10

Gallagher's Canyon
Greenway
Mission Creek Route
McCULLOCH

Myra-
Bellevue

Browne Lake Ecological Res

Browne Lake Rec Site

Joe Rich X-C Ski Trails

Long Meadow Lake

Fish Lake

McCulloch X-C Ski Trails

Lower South Slopes Trails

Angel Spring Trail
TCT

McCulloch

Myra Canyon

UPPER PRIEST Cr FSR

CPR Trainwreck

Hydraulic Lake Rec Site

Fern Lake
±1255m

Hydraulic Lakes
McCulloch Rec Site

Minnow Lake

Duck Lake

Pear Lake

Turtle L.

Idabel Lake

8-12

Lorna Trestle

Bellevue Creek Trestle

Protected
Area

Barge Lake

Swalwell Lake Rec Site
Echo Lake
±1350m
Swalwell (Beaver) Lake
resort
(Wrinkly Face Cliff Route)

Crooked Lake

Wollaston Lake

Grizzly Lake

Grizzly Hill

Ideal Lake Rec Site
±1300m
Ideal Lake

Swalwell Lake XC Trails

Moore Lake Rec Site

Roddy Lake

Postill Lake XC Trails

SPUR 300

Hereron Lake

Postill Lake Rec Site

Postill Lake

South Lake

Meadow Lake

Guest Lake

James Lake

James Lake Site

Geen (Twin) Lakes

MUGFORD Cr FSR

MISSION RIDGE FSR

6.5km end pvmt

CARDINAL Cr FSR

GRAYSTOKES

Mission Creek

Okanagan
Highlands

GROUSE

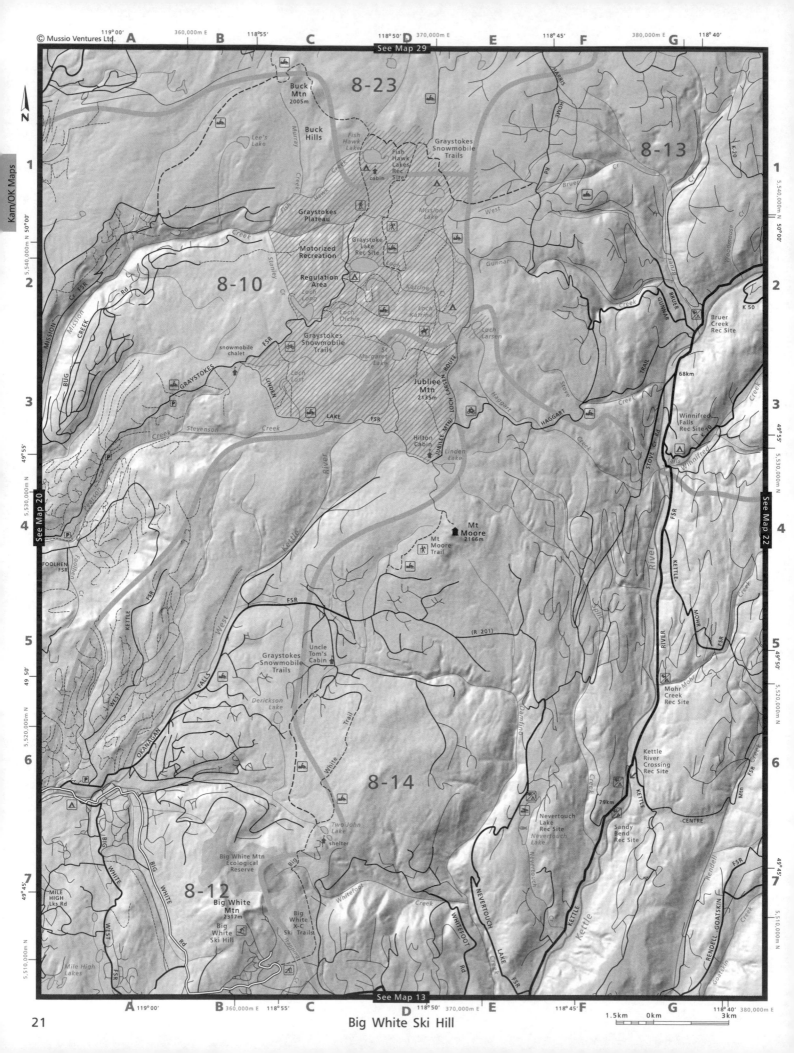

Kam/OK Maps

8-23

8-13

Buck Mtn
2005m

Buck
Hills

Lee's
Lake

Fish Hawk Lake

Fish
Hawk Lakes
Rec Site

cabin

Graystokes
Snowmobile
Trails

Graystokes
Plateau

Mission
Lake

West

8-10

Motorized
Recreation

Graystoke
Lake
Rec Site

Regulation
Area

Gunnar

Loch
Long

Loch
Katrine

Loch Olchia

snowmobile
chalet

GRAYSTOKES

Graystokes
Snowmobile
Trails

Loch
Lost

St
Margaret
Lake

Loch
Larsen

Haggart

Stove

HAGGART

LAKE FSR

Jubliee
Mtn
2135m

Winnifred
Falls
Rec Site

Stevenson   Creek

Hilton
Cabin

Linden
Lake

Kettle

River

Mt
Moore
2166m

Mt
Moore
Trail

8-13

Bruer
Creek
Rec Site

K 50

68km

Winnifred

Stove Grd Rd

KETTLE

MOHR

FOOLHEM
FSR

West

FSR

(R 201)

Split

Damfino

River

Mohr

Mohr
Creek
Rec Site

8-14

Graystokes
Snowmobile
Trails

Uncle
Tom's
Cabin

Derickson
Lake

White

Trail

Kettle
River
Crossing
Rec Site

79km

Nevertouch
Lake
Rec Site
Nevertouch
Lake

Sandy
Bend
Rec Site

-CENTRE

Two John
Lake

shelter

Big

Nevertouch

P

Big White Mtn
Ecological
Reserve

8-12

MILE
HIGH
Lks Rd

Big White
Mtn
2317m

Big
White
Ski Hill

Big
White X-C
Ski Trails

Whitefoot   Creek

WHITEFOOT

NEVERTOUCH

LAKE FSR

KETTLE

Kettle

RENDELL GOATSKIN

Rendell

FSR

Goatskin Creek

Mile High
Lakes

WEST

BIG WHITE Rd

21

Big White Ski Hill

1.5km   0km   3km

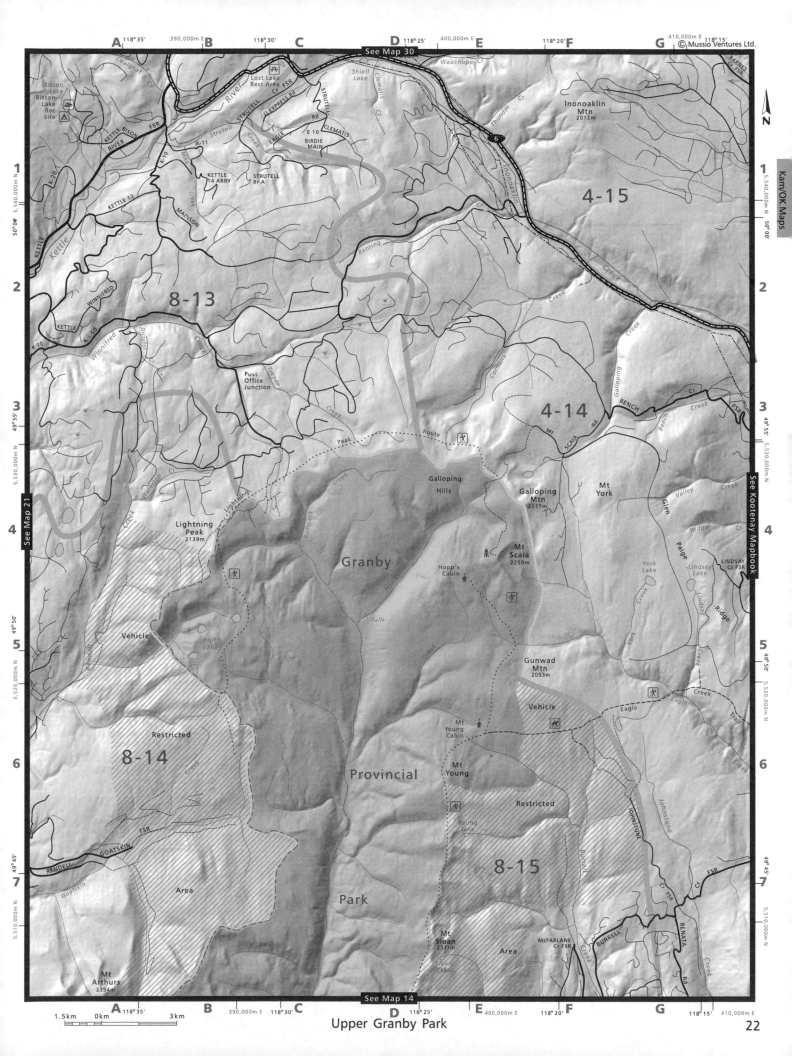

© Mussio Ventures Ltd.

See Map 21

See Kootenay Mapbook

4-15

8-13

4-14

Granby

River

Provincial

Park

8-14

Restricted

Area

8-15

Restricted

Area

Lightning
Peak
2139m

Galloping
Hills

Galloping
Mtn
2217m

Mt
York

Mt Scaia
2259m

Gunwad
Mtn
2053m

Mt Young
Cabin

Mt Young

Mt
Sloan
2331m

Mt
Arthurs
2354m

Inonoaklin
Mtn
2012m

Hopp's
Cabin

Vehicle

Vehicle

York Lake

Lindsay
Lake

Lindsay
Ridge

LINDSAY
Cr FSR

Young
Lake

Sloan
Lake

Bisson
Lake

Bisson
Lake Rec
Site

Lost Lake
Rest Area

Post
Office
Junction

Reith
Lakes

KETTLE
14 ABBY

STRUTELL
Br A

BIRDIE
MAIN

E 10

Shiell
Lake

Wauchope

McFARLANE
Cr FSR

RENATA
Rd

BURRELL
Cr FSR

GOATSKIN
FSR

RENDELL

BARNES
CT FSR

BENCH

SCAIA Rd

JOHNSTONE

Route

Peak

falls

1.5km   0km   3km

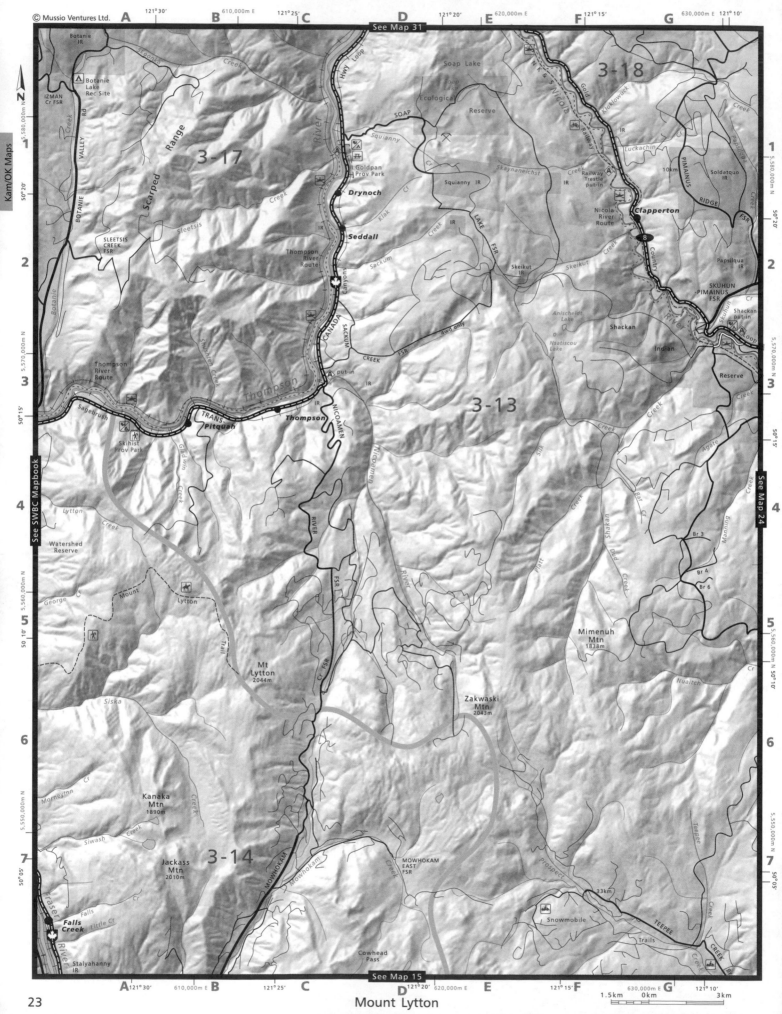

Kam/OK Maps

See SWBC Mapbook

See Map 31

See Map 24

See Map 15

3-17

3-18

3-13

3-14

Scarped Range

Botanie Lake Rec Site

Botanie IR

IZMAN Cr FSR

BOTANIE VALLEY Rd

SLEETSIS CREEK FSR

Sleetsis Creek

Goldpan Prov Park

Drynoch

Seddall

Thompson River Route

Soap Lake

Soap Lake

Ecological Reserve

Squianny

Squianny IR

Skaynaneichst

NK&S Nicola Railway

Gold Railway Rd

Kloklowuck

Luckachin

Pimainus Creek

10km

Soldatquo IR

PIMAINUS RIDGE

Nicola River Route

Railway Trestle put-in

Clapperton

8

Papsilqua IR

SKUHUN -PIMAINUS FSR

Shackan put-in

Shackan

Skeikut IR

Skeikut Creek

Anischeldt Lake

Nsatiscou Lake

Indian Reserve

Hwy Loop

Thompson River

Klak Cr

Sackum Creek

Thompson River Route

Sagebrush

TRANS CANADA

Pitquah

Thompson

Shushen Creek

Gladwin Creek

Watershed Reserve

Lytton Creek

Mount George

Lytton

Mt Lytton Trail

Siska Cr

Kanaka Mtn 1890m

Jackass Mtn 2010m

Siwash Creek

Mornsylnn Cr

NICOAMEN RIVER

IR

IR

put-in

Mt Lytton 2044m

MOWHOKAM Cr FSR

Mowhokam

Mowhokam Creek

Cowhead Pass

Zakwaski Mtn 2043m

MOWHOKAM EAST FSR

Platt Creek

Slok Creek

Shakan Creek

Bat Cr

Gald Creek

Agate Creek

Br 3

Br 4

Br 6

Mimenuh Mtn 1838m

Nuaitch Cr

Prospect Creek

33km

Snowmobile Trails

TEEPEE CREEK

Teepee Creek

Falls Creek

Fraser River

Little Cr

Stalyahanny IR

Skihist Prov Park

N

23

Mount Lytton

1.5km 0km 3km

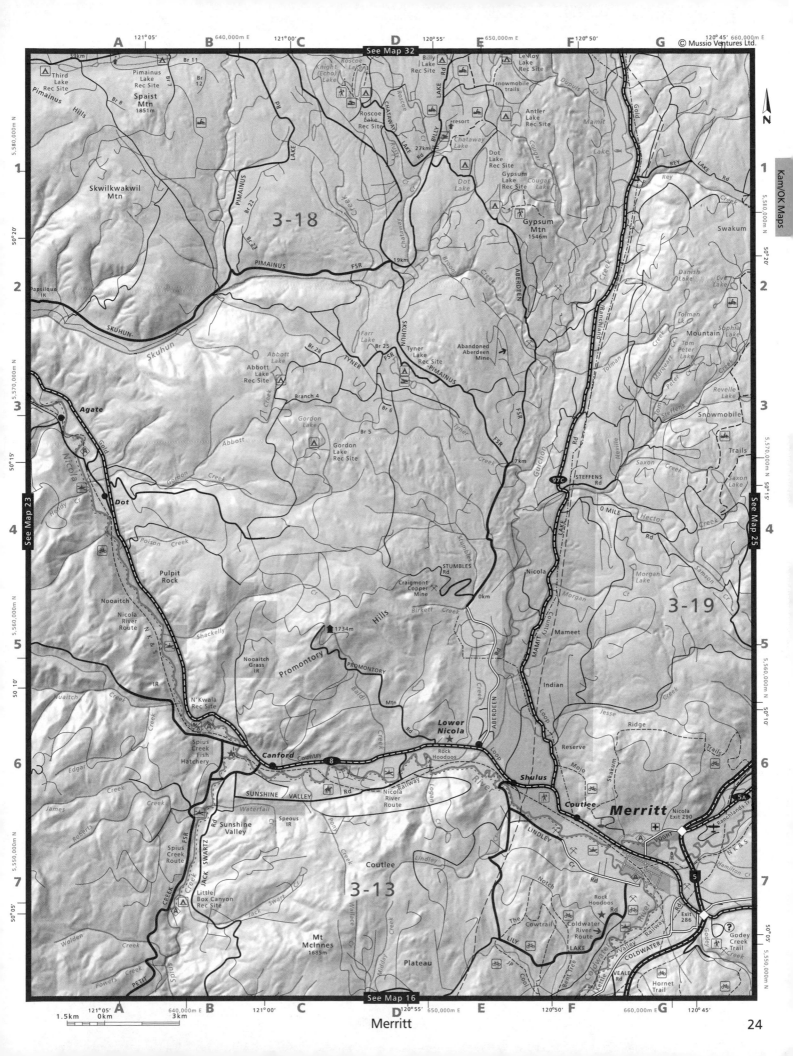

See Map 23

See Map 25

3-18

3-19

3-13

Third Lake Rec Site
Pimainus Hills
Skwilkwakwil Mtn
Pimainus Lake Rec Site
Spaist Mtn 1851m
Br 11
Br 12
Br 7
Br 8

Knight (Echo) Lake
Roscoe Lake
Roscoe Lake Rec Site
Billy Lake Rec Site
Le Roy Lake Rec Site
snowmobile trails
Antler Lake Rec Site
resort
Chataway Lake
27km
Dot Lake Rec Site
Dot Lake
Gypsum Lake Rec Site
Cougar Lake
Gypsum Mtn 1546m
Danish Lake
Eve Lake
Tolman Lk
Sophia Lake
Mountain
Tom Peter Lake
Revelle Lake
Snowmobile
Trails
Saxon Lake
Swakum

PIMAINUS LAKE Rd
Br 22
Br 23
PIMAINUS FSR
19km

Papsilquo IR
SKUHUN
Skuhun

Agate
Nicola
Dot
Handy Cr
Gold

Abbott Lake
Abbott Lake Rec Site
Abbott Creek
Branch 4
Gordon Lake
Gordon Lake Rec Site
Gordon Creek
Br 28
Br 25
Br 6
Br 5
Farr Lake
TYNER
Tyner Lake Rec Site
SKUHUN FSR
PIMAINUS
Tyner Creek FSR
7km
Abandoned Aberdeen Mine
Broom Creek
ABERDEEN

97 C
STEFFENS Rd
Gutchon
Tolman Cr
Neville Cr
Saxon Creek
RANCHLAND Rd
REY LAKE Rd
Rey Creek
Marquart Cr
Tony Cr
Steffens Cr
Samson Cr

Poison Creek
Pulpit Rock
Nooaitch
Nicola River Route
N K & S
IR
Shackelly
Nooaitch Grass IR
Promontory Hills
1734m
PROMONTORY
Baldy Mtn
Craigmont Copper Mine
STUMBLES Rd
0km
Birkett Creek
Stumbles Creek
Nicola
Mameet
Indian Cr
Jesse Cr
Reserve
Mojo
Skakum Cr
0 MILE Rd
Hector Cr
Morgan Lake
Morgan Cr
MAMIT LAKE
Loop
Ridge
Trails

Quaitch Creek
Edgar Creek
James Creek
Roberts Cr
Wolden Creek
Powers Cr
PETIT

Spius Creek Fish Hatchery
Canford
Sunshine Valley
Waterfall
Speous IR
Sunshine Valley
Spius Creek Route
Little Box Canyon Rec Site
Jack Swartz Creek
SPIUS CREEK FSR
JACK SWARTZ Rd

N'Kwala Rec Site
Country 8
SUNSHINE VALLEY Rd
Nicola River Route
Nicola Railway
Rock Hoodoos
Lower Nicola
ABERDEEN Rd
Shulus
Coutlee
Merritt
Coldwater River
Uebo Cr
Wallace Creek
Midday Creek
Mt McInnes 1685m
Plateau
Coutlee
Lindley Cr
LINDLEY
Notch
The Lily
Cowtrail
Rock Hoodoos
Coldwater River Route
Bent Tree
VEALE Rd
Kettle Valley Railway
COLDWATER
Godey Creek
Godey Creek Trail
Hornet Trail
LILY LAKE
Nicola Exit 290
VOGHT
N K & S
Exit 286
Exit 286
5A
5
Ranchlands Tr
Hamilton Cr

1.5km 0km 3km

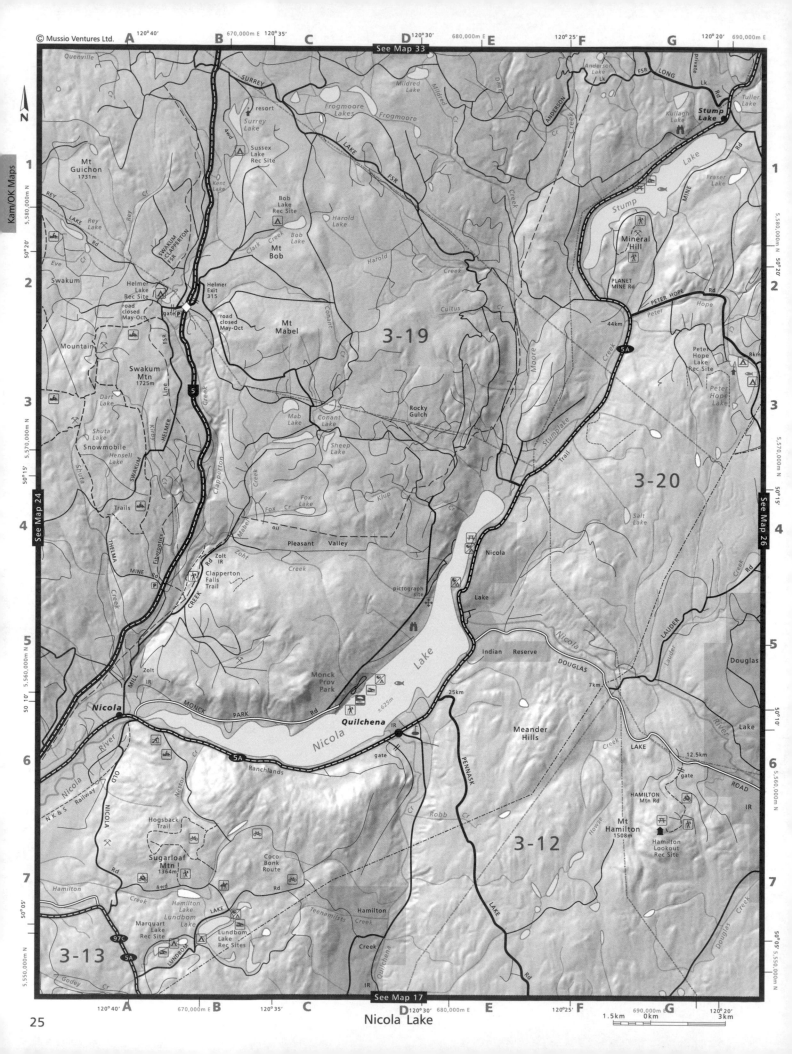

Kam/OK Maps

N

120° 40'   120° 35'   120° 30'   120° 25'   120° 20'

A   670,000m E   B   C   D   680,000m E   E   F   G   690,000m E

Quenville
Cr

Mt Guichon
1731m

REY
LAKE

Rey Lake Rd

Eve Cr

Swakum

Mountain

Shuta Lake

Snowmobile

Hensell Lake

Dart Lake

Shuta Creek

Trails

Swakum Mtn
1725m

SWAKUM   HELMER   Kault   Line   FSR

THELMA

MINE   Fletcherton

CREEK

Zolt
IR

Clapperton Falls Trail

Zolt
Rd

Zolt IR

SURREY
resort
Surrey Lake

Kent Lake

Sussex Lake Rec Site

Clark Creek

Bob Lake Rec Site

Mt Bob

Bob Lake

Harold Lake

Harold

SWAKUM
CLAPPERTON
FSR

Helmer Lake Rec Site

road closed May-Oct   gate   P

Helmer Exit 315

road closed May-Oct

Mt Mabel

Conant Cr

Mab Lake

Conant Lake

Clapperton Creek

Mabel Cr

Zoht

oil

Pleasant   Valley

Fox Cr   Fox Lake

Sheep Lake

Klup   Cr

3-19

Frogmoore Lakes

Mildred Lake

Mildred

Frogmoore

LAKE   FSR

Cultus

Cr

Rocky Gulch

Creek

Moore   Creek

Stumplake Trail

pictograph site

ANDERSON   Creek

Deer   Creek

Anderson Lake   Lk

FSR

LONG   Lk Rd

private   Lk

Kullagh Lake

Stump Lake

Tuller Lake

Stump   Lake

Fraser Lake

MINE

Mineral Hill

PLANET MINE Rd

PETER HOPE Rd

44km   Peter   Hope   Rd

5A

Peter   Creek

Peter Hope Lake Rec Site

Peter Hope Lake

8km

3-20

Salt Lake

Douglas

LAUDER   Creek   Rd

See Map 24   See Map 26

50° 20'

50° 15'

50° 10'

5,580,000m N

5,570,000m N

5,560,000m N

1   2   3   4   5   6   7

Nicola   Lake

Indian   Reserve

DOUGLAS

Nicola

Nicola   Lake

≈625m

Monck Prov Park

MONCK   PARK   Rd

Quilchena   IR

gate

Nicola

Nicola   River

OLD   NICOLA   Rd

NK&S Railway

5A   Ranchlands

Neston   Cr

Hogsback Trail

Sugarloaf Mtn
1364m

4wd

Coco Bonk Route

Rd

Marquart Lake Rec Site

Hamilton Lundbom Lake

LUNDBOM   LAKE

Lundbom Lake Rec Sites

97C   5A

Godey Cr

Hamilton   Creek

Teenamtists   Creek

Hamilton   Creek

PENNASK

Robb   Cr

Meander Hills

7km

12.5km   ROAD

gate

HAMILTON Mtn Rd

Mt Hamilton
1508m

Hamilton Lookout Rec Site

IR

Douglas   Lake

Howse   Creek

Douglas   Creek

LAKE   Rd

Quilchena   Cr

Quilchena   IR

3-12

3-13

50° 05'

5,550,000m N

120° 40'   120° 35'   120° 30'   120° 25'   120° 20'

A   670,000m E   B   C   D   680,000m E   E   F   G   690,000m E

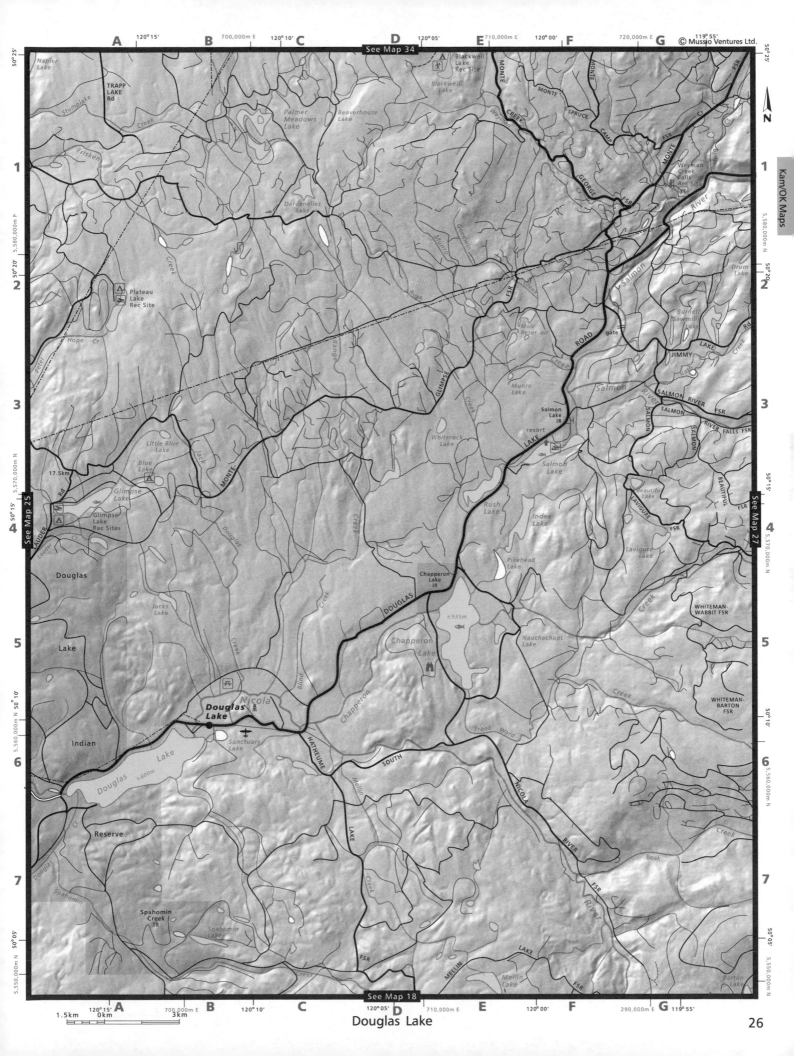

N

A   120° 15'   B   700,000m E   120° 10'   C   D   120° 05'   E   710,000m E   120° 00'   F   720,000m E   G   119° 55'

50°25'

Napier
Lake

TRAPP
LAKE
Rd

Stumplake
Creek

Frisken

1

Blackwell
Lake Rec Site

Blackwell
Lake

MONTE

MONTE

SPRUCE

MONTE

CAMP

Weyman
Creek
Falls
Rec Site

1

Palmer
Meadows
Lake

Beaverhouse
Lake

Dardenelles
Lake

Creek

WEYMAN CREEK

GEORGE

FSR

FSR

River

50°20'

2

5,580,000m N

Plateau
Lake
Rec Site

Hope Cr

Peter

Rush

Creek

Munro

Goodwin

Creek

FSR

ROAD

gate

Salmon

Burnell
(Sawmill)
Lake

Drum
Lake

Rd

2

Moir
Reser oir

Munro
Lake

JIMMY

Nash

LAKE

Creek

Salmon

SALMON RIVER

3

50°15'

Little Blue
Lake

Blue
Lake

17.5km

Glimpse
Lake

Glimpse
Lake Rec Sites

LAUDER

Rd

Lauder Cr

Jack

MONTE

Creek

GLIMPSE

Creek

Whiterock
Lake

Salmon
Lake IR

resort

LAKE

Salmon
Lake

SALMON

SALMON

RIVER FALLS FSR

SALMON

Beautiful
Lake

LAVIGURE

FSR

BEAUTIFUL

See Map 27

50°15'

4

5,570,000m N

Douglas

Lake

Indian

Jacks
Lake

Douglas

Creek

Creek

Chapperon
Lake IR

±935m

Chapperon
Lake

Rush
Lake

Index
Lake

Pikehead
Lake

DOUGLAS

Nauchachapt
Lake

Lavigure
Lake

WHITEMAN-
WABBIT FSR

WHITEMAN-
BARTON
FSR

Creek

4

5

Nicola

Douglas Lake

Blind

Creek

Chapperon

Frank   Ward

5

50°10'

6

5,560,000m N

Douglas

±800m

Sanctuary
Lake

HATHEUME

Mellin

SOUTH

LAKE

Creek

NICOLA

RIVER

Beak

Creek

FSR

6

50°10'

Reserve

Spahomin
Creek
IR

Spahomin
Lake

7

Douglas
Cr

MELLIN

LAKE

Creek

River

Mellin
Lake

FSR

Barton
Lake

7

5,550,000m N

A   120° 15'   B   700,000m E   120° 10'   C   D   120° 05'   E   710,000m E   120° 00'   F   290,000m E   G   119° 55'

1.5km   0km   3km

Douglas Lake

See Map 25

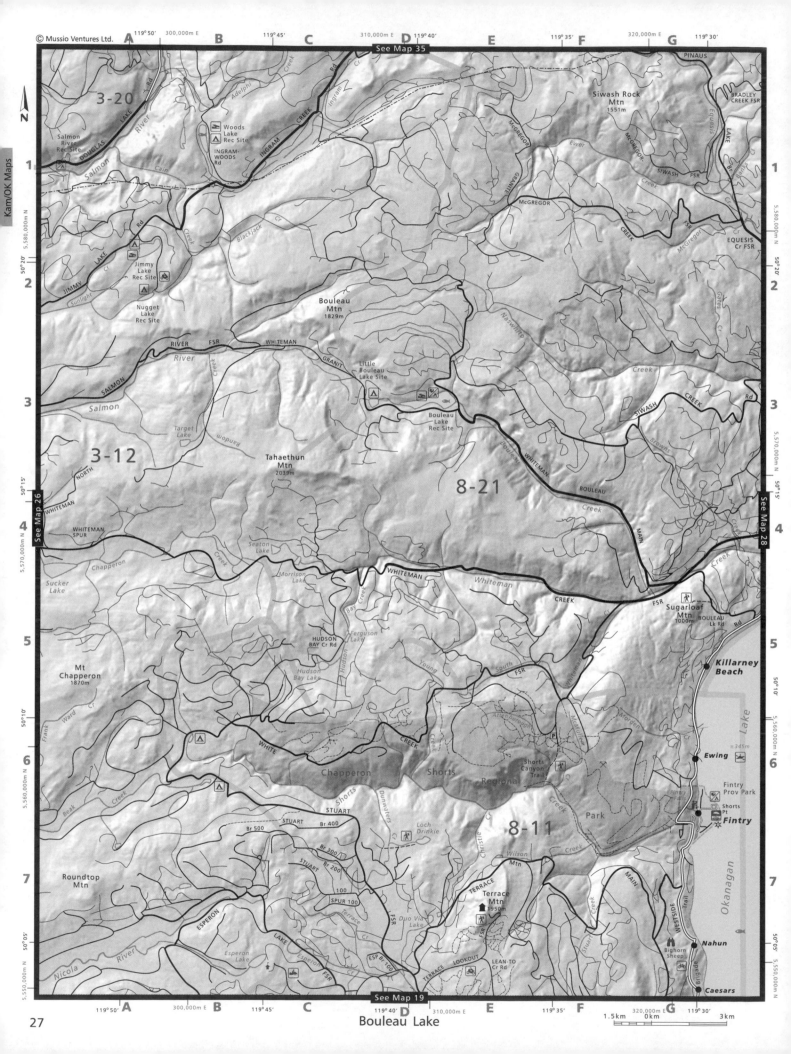

Kam/OK Maps

3-20

Salmon River Rec Site

Woods Lake Rec Site

INGRAM-WOODS Rd

Jimmy Lake Rec Site

Nugget Lake Rec Site

Bouleau Mtn 1829m

WHITEMAN

RIVER FSR

Little Bouleau Lake Site

Bouleau Lake Rec Site

3-12

Tahaethun Mtn 2039m

8-21

Target Lake

See Map 26

WHITEMAN SPUR

WHITEMAN

Chapperon

Seaton Lake

Morrison Lake

WHITEMAN

Whiteman

CREEK

Sucker Lake

Mt Chapperon 1870m

HUDSON BAY Cr Rd

Ferguson Lake

Hudson Bay Lake

Sugarloaf Mtn 1000m

BOULEAU Lk Rd

Killarney Beach

WHITE

Chapperon

Shorts

Regional

Shorts Canyon Trail

Ewing

Fintry Prov Park

8-11

STUART

Br 400

Br 500

Br 300

Br 200

Loch Drinkie

Park

Shorts Pt

Fintry

Roundtop Mtn

STUART

100

SPUR 100

Duo Via Lake

TERRACE

Terrace Mtn 1950m

Wilson Mtn

Christie

Bighorn Sheep

Nahun

ESPERON

Nicola River

Esperon Lake

ESP Br 100

TERRACE

LOOKOUT

LEAN-TO Cr Rd

WESTSIDE

MAIN

Caesars

Siwash Rock Mtn 1551m

PINAUS

BRADLEY CREEK FSR

McGREGOR

SIWASH FSR

McGregor

EQUESIS Cr FSR

SIWASH CREEK

Browns

BOULEAU

MAIN

Okanagan Lake

±345m

See Map 28

Bouleau Lake

1.5km 0km 3km

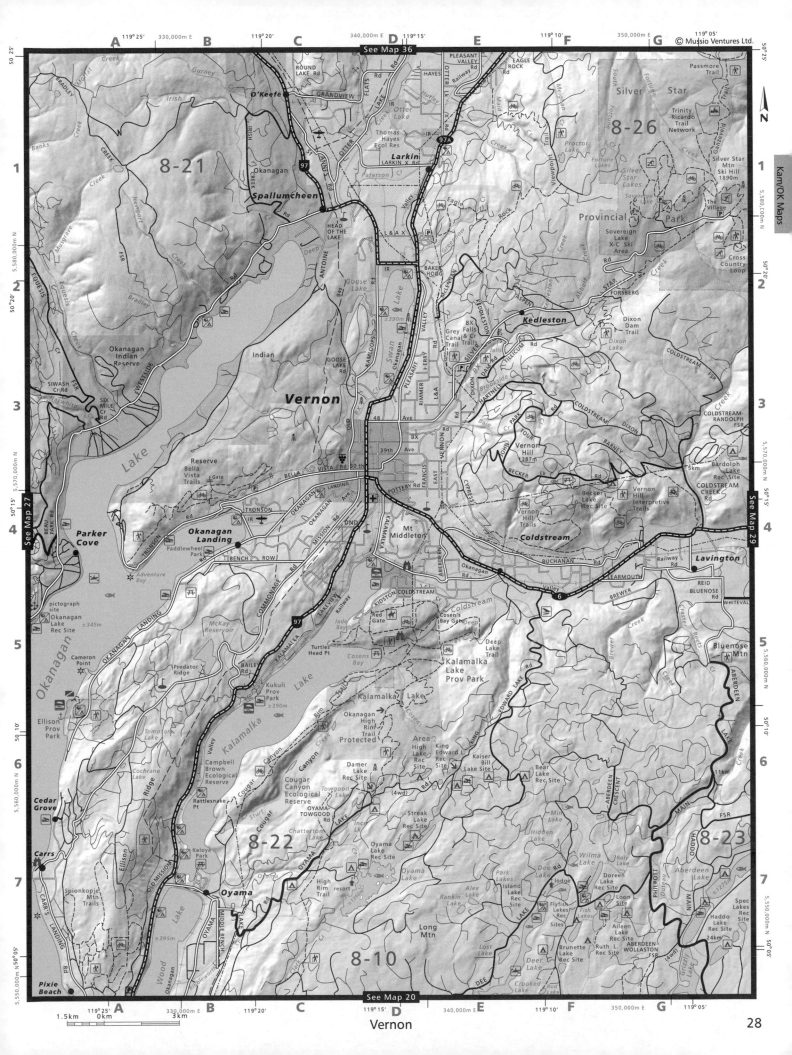

© Mussio Ventures Ltd.

Kam/OK Maps

8-26

Silver Star

8-21

Provincial Park

O'Keefe

Spallumcheen

Larkin

Kedleston

Vernon

Coldstream

Lavington

Parker Cove

Okanagan Landing

Coldstream

Bluenose Mtn

Kalamalka Lake Prov Park

8-22

8-23

Cedar Grove

Carrs

Oyama

8-10

Pixie Beach

See Map 27

See Map 29

1.5km 0km 3km

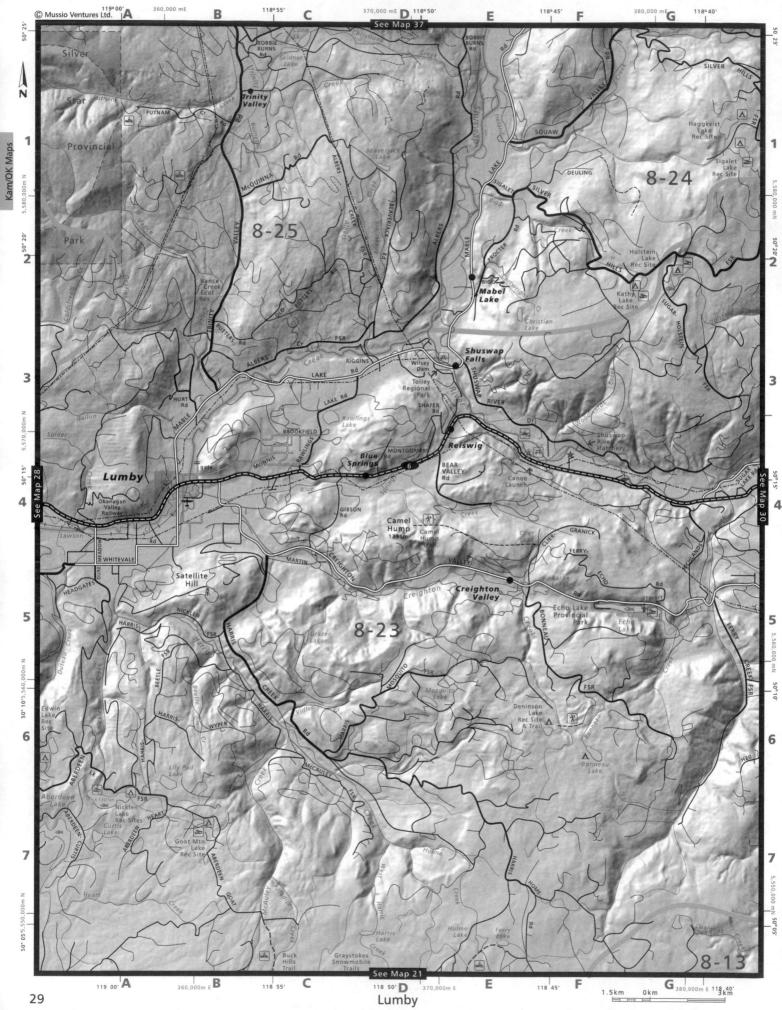

© Mussio Ventures Ltd.

Kam/OK Maps

8-24

8-25

8-23

8-13

See Map 28

See Map 30

Silver Star Provincial Park

Lumby

Trinity Valley

Mabel Lake

Shuswap Falls

Blue Springs

Reiswig

Creighton Valley

Camel Hump 1391m

Echo Lake Provincial Park

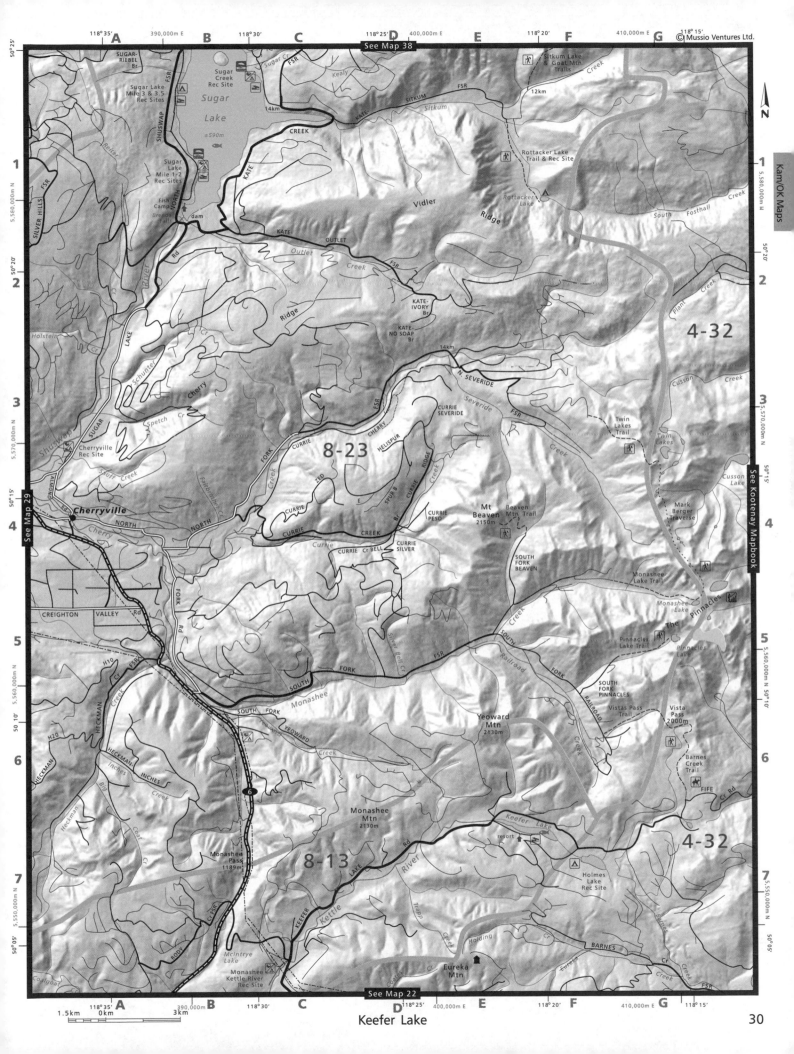

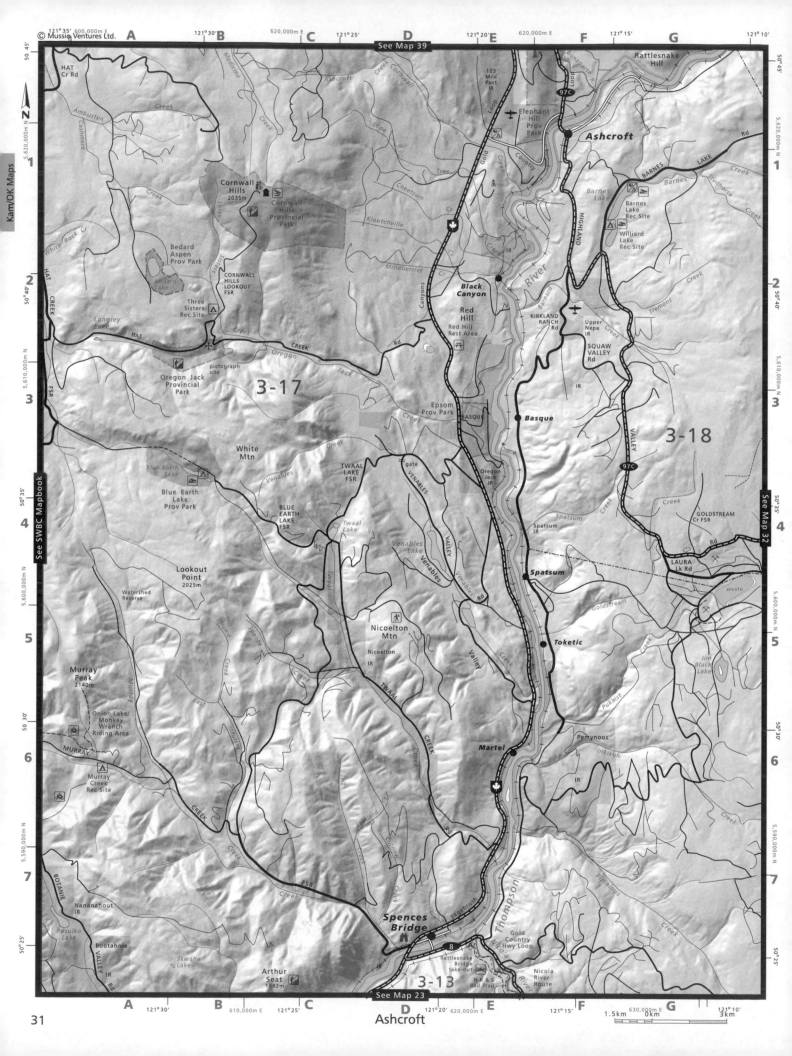

© Mussio Ventures Ltd.
121°35' 600,000m E
50°45'
A
121°30'
B
620,000m E
C
121°25'
See Map 39
D
121°20'
E
620,000m E
F
121°15'
G
121°10'

Kam/OK Maps

HAT
Cr Rd

Ambusten
Creek
Medicine
Creek
Cashmere
White Rock Cr
Creek

1

Cornwall
Hills
2035m

Cornwall
Hills
Provincial
Park

Ashcroft
Creek
Cornwall
Creek

Lone
Creek
Tree
Creek

Cheetsum
Cr

105
Mile
Post
IR

Elephant
Hill
Prov
Park

97C

Rattlesnake
Hill

Ashcroft

BARNES LAKE
Creek
Rd

1

Bedard
Aspen
Prov Park

Bedard
Lake

CORNWALL
HILLS
LOOKOUT
FSR

Three
Sisters

Langley
Lake

HAT
CREEK
FSR

Klootchville

Mindberriet
Creek

Black
Canyon

Red
Hill

Red Hill
Rest Area

Cr
Cr
Creek
River

KIRKLAND
RANCH
Rd

Barnard
Creek

Upper
Nepa
IR

HIGHLAND

Barnes
Lake

Barnes
Lake
Rec Site

Williard
Lake
Rec Site

Barnes
Creek
Studhorse
Creek

Tremont
Creek

2

50°40'

HAT CREEK

Three Sisters
Rec Site

Oregon Jack
Provincial
Park

pictograph
site

OREGON CREEK

Jack
Creek

Epsom
Prov Park

BASQUE

SQUAW
VALLEY
Rd

IR

3

3-17

White
Mtn

Venables
Creek

TWAAL
LAKE
FSR

gate
VENABLES

Oregon
Jack IR

Basque

3-18

97C

VALLEY

3

Blue Earth
Lake

Blue Earth
Lake
Prov Park

BLUE
EARTH
LAKE
FSR

Twaal
Lake

Twaal
Creek

Venables
Lake
Venables
Creek

VALLEY
Venables

Venables
Rd

Spatsum
IR

Spatsum

Goldstream
Creek

GOLDSTREAM
Cr FSR

LAURA
Lk Rd

waste

4

50°35'

See SWBC Mapbook

Lookout
Point
2025m

Watershed
Reserve

Spence
Creek

Huina
Creek

Nicoelton
Mtn

Nicoelton
IR

TWAAL

Venables
Valley

Creek

Toketic

Pukaist
Creek

Jim
Black
Lake

5

Murray
Peak
2140m

Onion Lake/
Monkey
Wrench
Riding Area

MURRAY

Murray
Creek

Murray
Creek
Rec Site

East
Murray
Creek

Thai
Creek

Shetland
Creek

Cupow
Creek

Sagebrush
Creek

CREEK

Martel

Thompson

Pemynoos

Inkikuh

IR

6

50°30'

BOTANIE

Nananahout
IR

Pasulko
Lake

Skwaha
Lake

Arthur
Seat
1662m

CREEK
FSR
Creek

**Spences
Bridge**

8

Rattlesnake
Bridge
take-out

Gold
Country
Hwy Loop

N K & S
Rail Trail

Nicola
River
Route

Nicola
River

Pimainus
Creek

Creek

7

50°25'

BOTANIE
VALLEY
IR
Rd

Bootahnie
IR

IR

3-13

31
A
121°30'
B
610,000m E
121°25'
C
See Map 23
D
121°20'
620,000m E
E
F
121°15'
630,000m E
G
121°10'
Ashcroft
1.5km   0km   3km

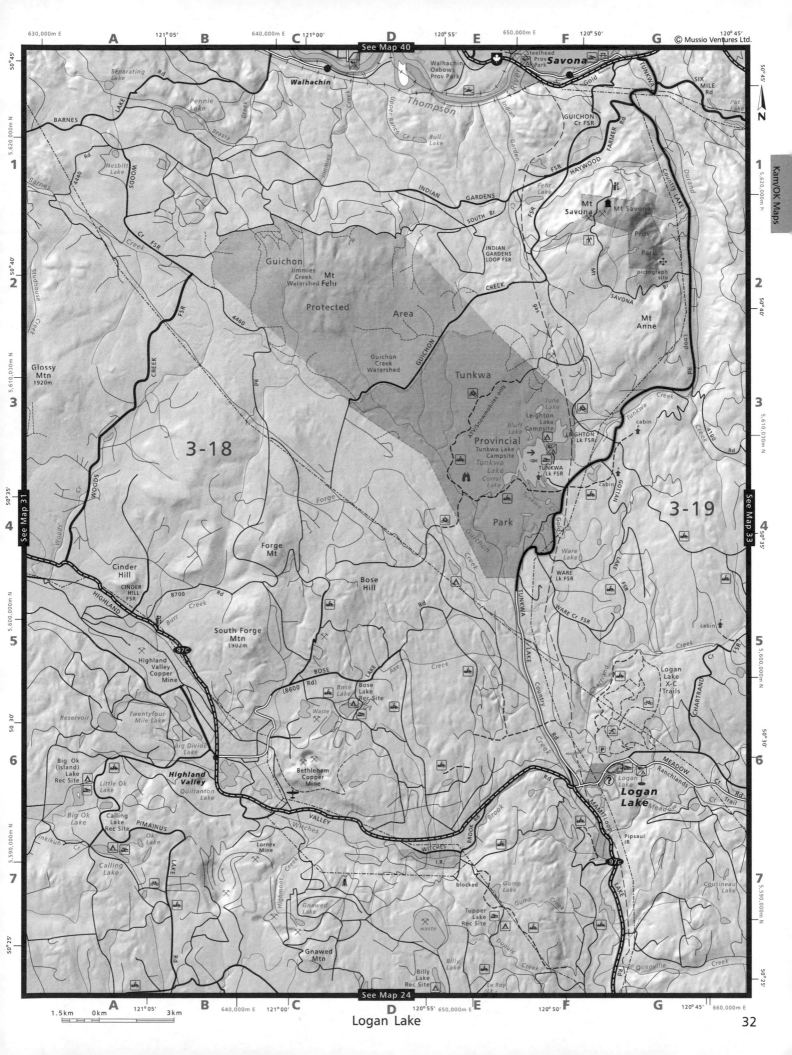

© Mussio Ventures Ltd.

See Map 40

See Map 31

See Map 33

See Map 24

3-18

3-19

Logan Lake

32

1.5km 0km 3km

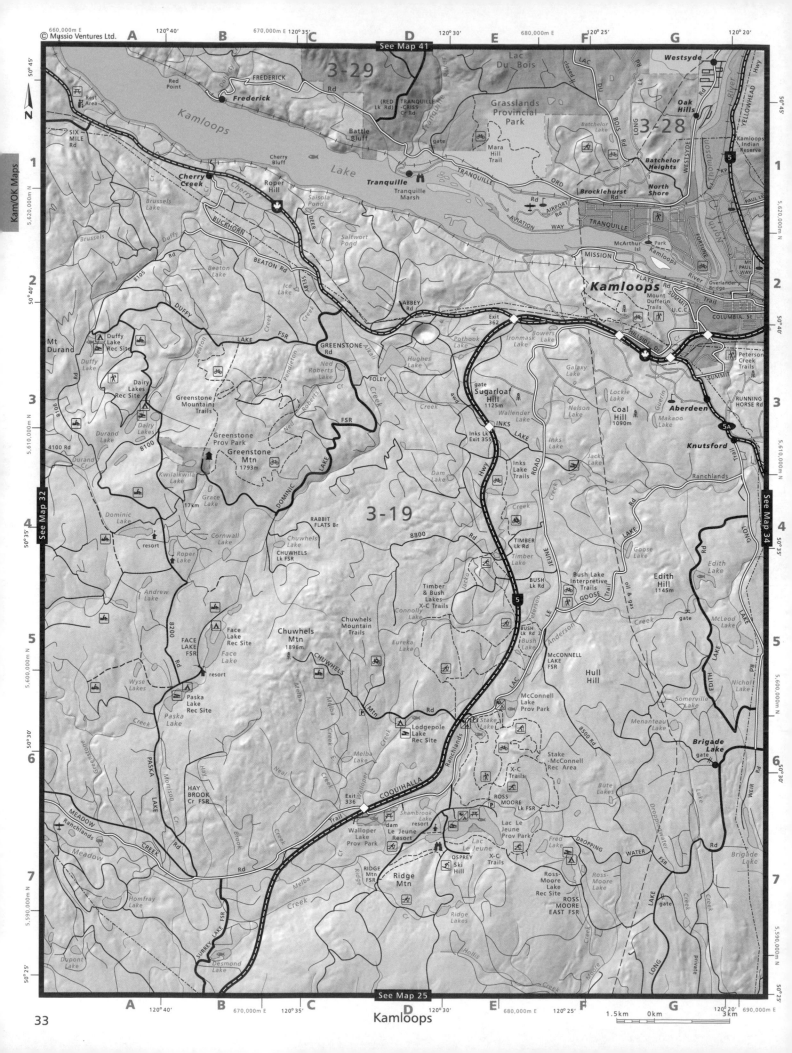

See Map 41
3-29
See Map 32
3-28
3-19
See Map 34
See Map 25

1.5km   0km   3km

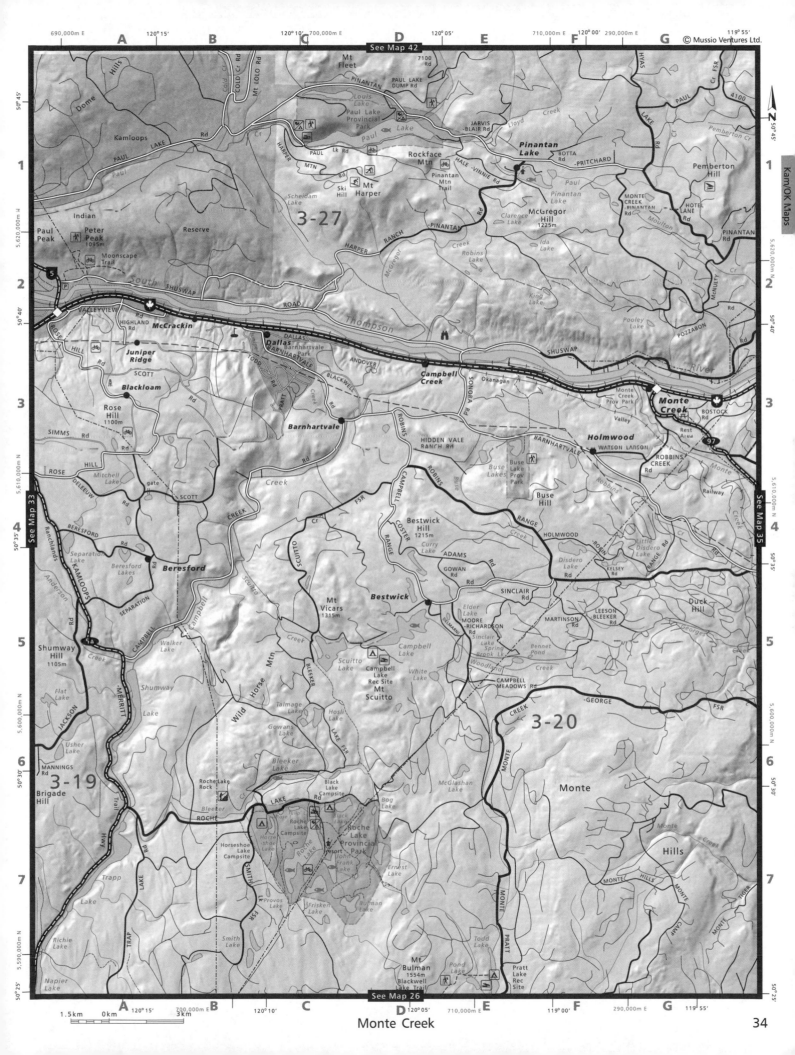

© Mussio Ventures Ltd.

3-27

3-19

3-20

See Map 33

See Map 35

See Map 26

Monte Creek

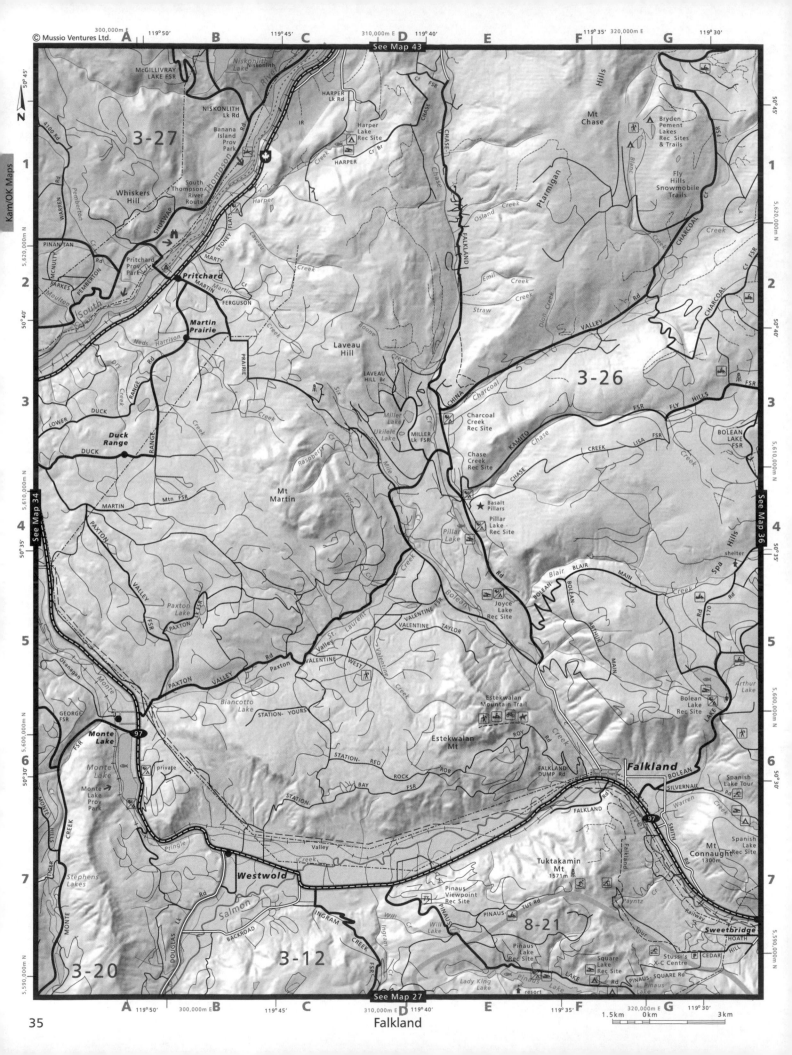

Kam/OK Maps

See Map 34

See Map 36

3-27

3-26

3-12

3-20

8-21

35

Falkland

1.5km   0km   3km

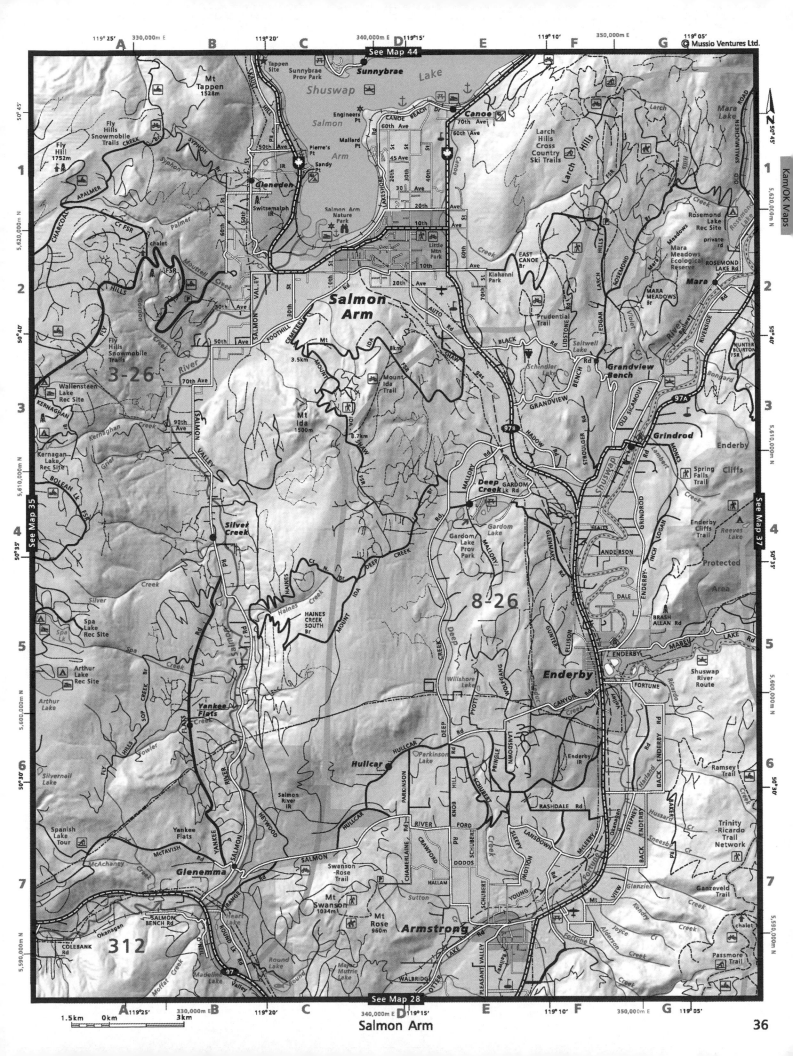

Mussio Ventures Ltd.

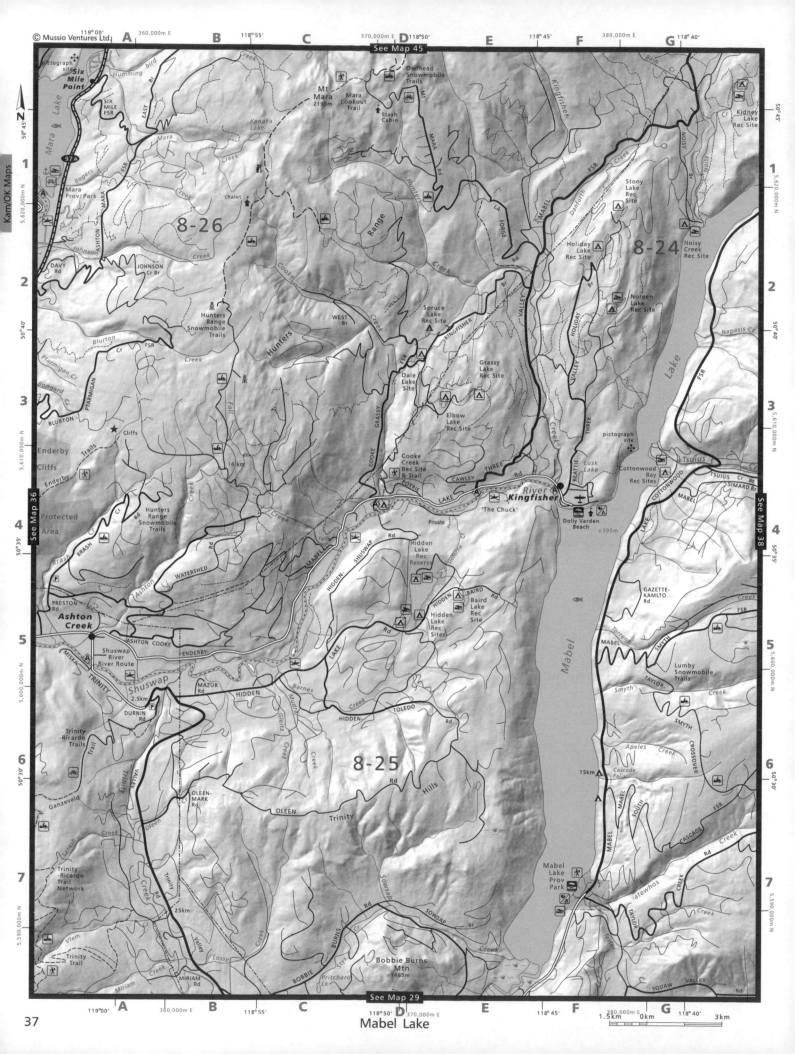

Kam/OK Maps

See Map 45

8-26

8-24

8-25

See Map 36

See Map 38

See Map 29

Mabel Lake

1.5km   0km   3km

Kam/OK Maps

See Map 37

See Kootenay Mapbook

DERRY

Derry Cr Rd

Covanaugh Cr

Wap Cr

Mabel Lake

MABEL LAKE FSR

Iron Cr

Mabel

Iron Dale Creek

Range

Maua Creek

8-24

Mt Mabel 2136m

Napasis Cr

CREEK Br

Hound Creek

WHIP

MABEL

Tsuius Whip

TSUIUS

SIMARD Br

Mimulus Lake

Arnica Lake

Tsuius Creek

Mountain

Tsuius Mtn 2469m

Paintbrush Ridge

Sawtooth

Range

Curven Creek

Curwen Creek

SUGAR- CURWEN

Valerian Creek

Mirror Lake

Mimulus Lake

Tourmaline Trails

SUGAR- FALLS

SUGAR SAWTOOTH

Gates

8-23

Monashee

SUGAR Creek

WESTSIDE TSUIUS

SUGAR- GAGNEY

SUGAR River

Protected Area

BLANKET Creek

Greenbrush Lake Protected Area

Blanket Mtn

Icefield

Armstrong Peak

Lindmark Creek

Vanwyk Creek

Cranberry Mtn 2885m

Icefield

Creek

Torrent Cr

SMYTH FSR

Finlayson Lakes

Doolittle Trail

Smyth Cr

204 Road

Latewhos Cr

Range

Dorky Loop

Lumby Snowmobile Trails

Park Mtn 2057m

Park

SILVER PARK

Sprockton

Squaw Mtn Rd

Great Cr

SUGAR- NELSON Rd

SUGAR- Rd

Straw Cr

Crews Cr

EASTSIDE

SHUSWAP

Shuswap

Range

Rd

SUGAR

Rainbow Falls

Rainbow Spectrum Cr

SUGAR-

Spectrum

SPECTRUM Rd

NORTH

Kate Cr

Sugar Lake

±590m

KATE Cr FSR

Kate Lake Trail

Sugar Mtn Trail

Sugar Cr

Kate Lake

Sugar Mtn

Polly Lake

Pete Lake

Falls

Jarad Cr

Parmigan Cr

Bill Fraser Cr

Vigue Creek

Protected Area

Mt Gunnarson

Monashee

Slate Mtn

Cariboo Mtn

Peters Lake

Mikes Lake

Peters Lake

Cirque Lake

Provincial

Mt Fosthall 2680m

Park

Pillar Pass

Trail

Spectrum Lake

South Cariboo Pass

Twin Peaks

Bill Fraser Lake

Goat Mt

Sitkum Lake & Goat Mtn Trails

Sitkum Cr

Sitkum Lake

Sitkum Plateau

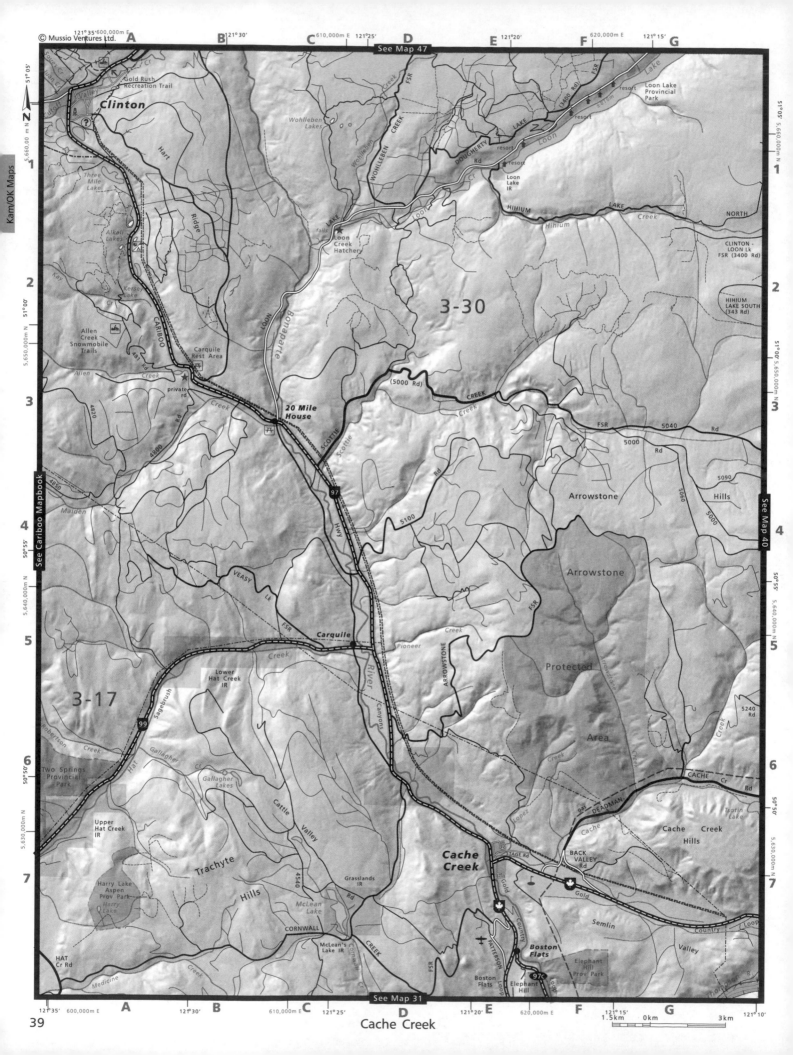

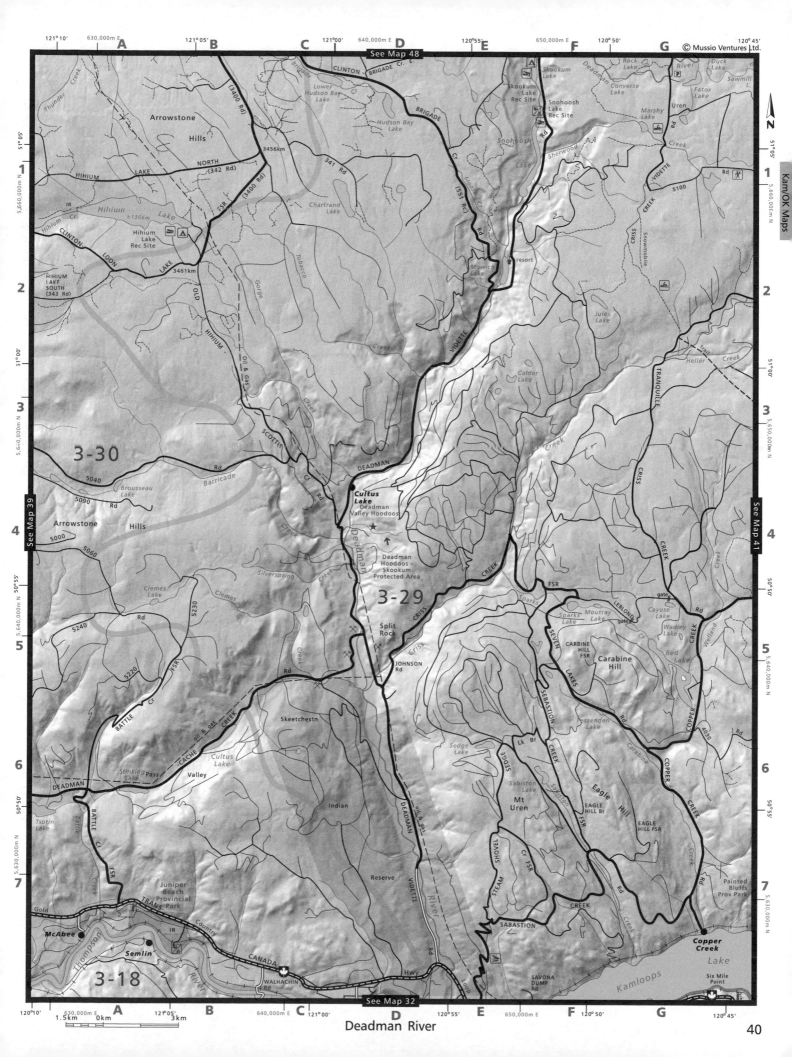

Kam/OK Maps

See Map 39

See Map 41

3-30

3-29

3-18

Deadman River

40

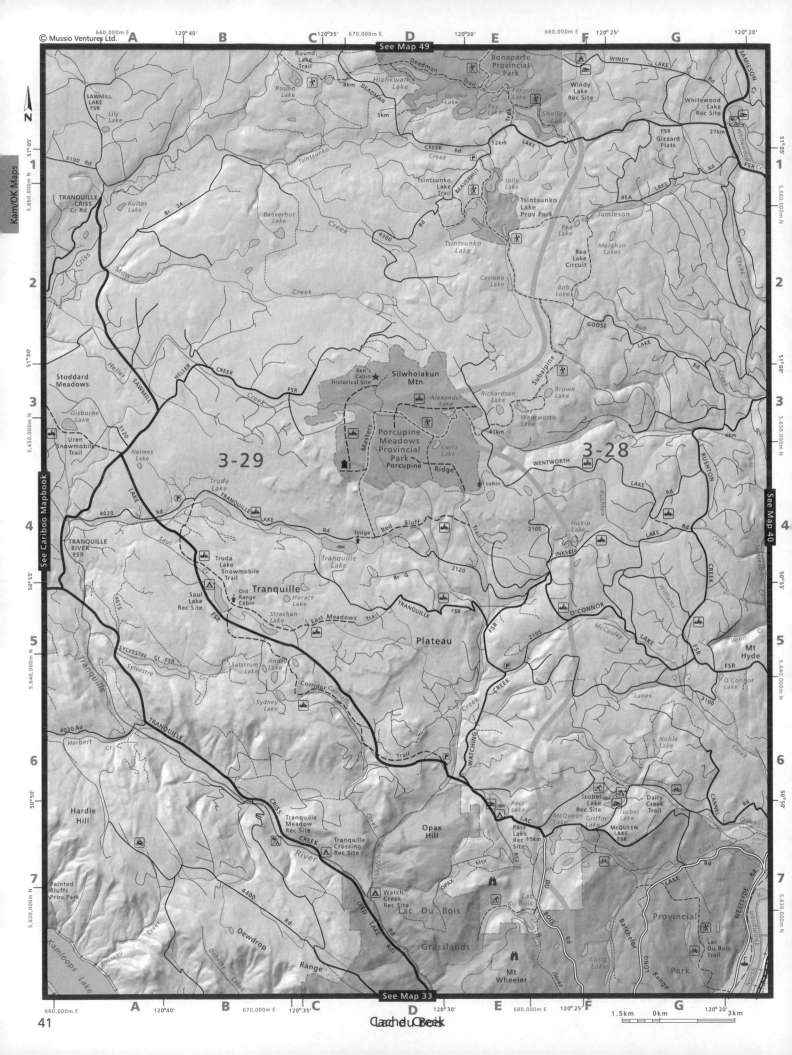

See Map 49

See Cariboo Mapbook

See Map 40

See Map 33

3-29

3-28

Silwhoiakun Mtn

Porcupine Meadows Provincial Park
Porcupine Ridge

Ben's Cabin Historical Site

Bonaparte Provincial Park

Tsintsunko Lake Prov Park

Tranquille

Plateau

Opax Hill

Lac Du Bois Grasslands

Mt Wheeler

Provincial Park

Mt Hyde

SAWMILL LAKE FSR

TRANQUILLE-CRISS Cr Rd

Stoddard Meadows

TRANQUILLE RIVER FSR

Hardie Hill

Painted Bluffs Prov Park

Windy Lake Rec Site

Whitewood Lake Rec Site

Gizzard Flats

1.5km 0km 3km

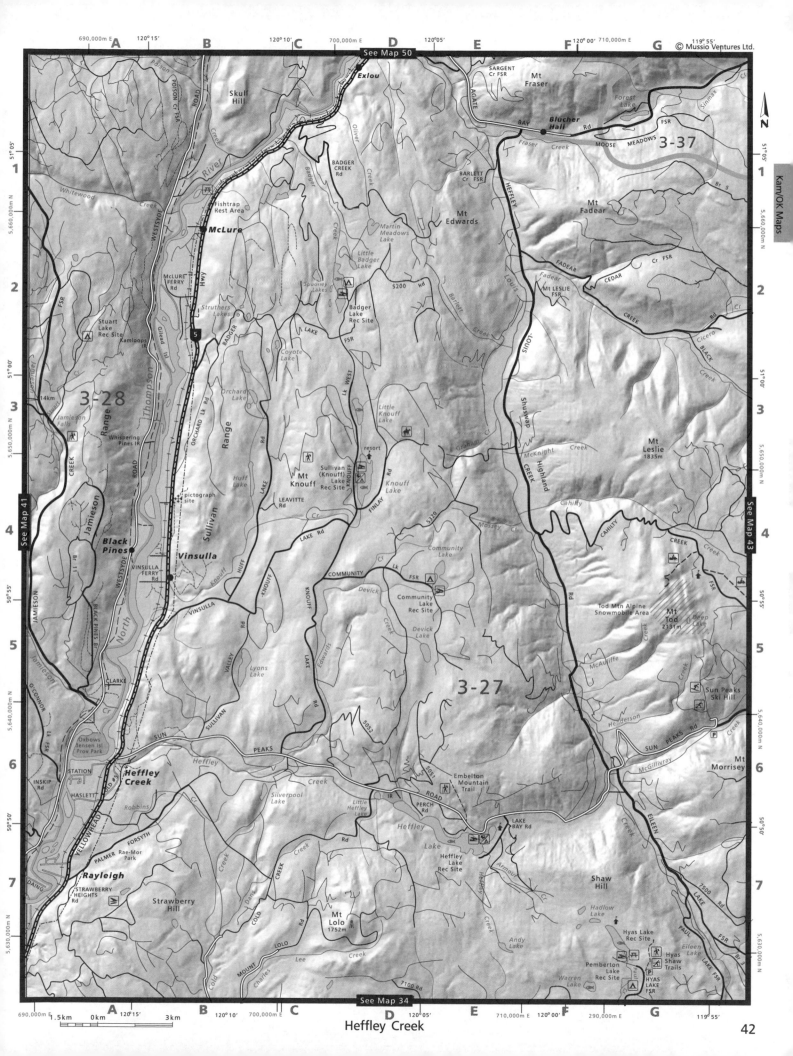

Kam/OK Maps

See Map 41

See Map 43

Heffley Creek

42

Row 1: A 120°15' B 120°10' C 120°05' D E F 120°00' G 119°55'

690,000m E   700,000m E   710,000m E   290,000m E

Exlou

Skull Hill

SARGENT Cr FSR

Mt Fraser

Forest Lake

Blucher Hall

MOOSE MEADOWS

3-37

BADGER CREEK Rd

Mt Edwards

BARLETT Cr FSR

Mt Fadear

Fishtrap Rest Area

McLure

Martin Meadows Lake

Little Badger Lake

Spooney Lakes

5200

Mt LESLIE FSR

CEDAR

McLURE FERRY Rd

Struthers Lakes

Badger Lake Rec Site

Stuart Lake Rec Site

Kamloops IR

Coyote Lake

Orchard Lake

Little Knouff Lake

Mt Leslie 1835m

3-28

Jamieson Falls

Whispering Pines IR

resort

Sullivan (Knouff) Lake Rec Site

Knouff Lake

Mt Knouff

Huff Lake

LEAVITTE Rd

Community Lake

Tod Mtn Alpine Snowmobile Area

Mt Tod 2131m

Deep Lake

Black Pines

Vinsulla

VINSULLA FERRY Rd

Devick Lake

Community Lake Rec Site

Sun Peaks Ski Hill

pictograph site

Lyons Lake

3-27

Mt Morrisey

CLARKE

Heffley Creek

Oxbows Jensen Isl Prov Park

Silverpool Lake

Little Heffley Lake

Embelton Mountain Trail

PERCH Rd

Heffley Lake

Shaw Hill

STATION

INSKIP Rd

HASLETT

Heffley Lake Rec Site

Lake Bay Rd

Rayleigh

STRAWBERRY HEIGHTS Rd

Strawberry Hill

Mt Lolo 1752m

Hadlow Lake

Hyas Lake Rec Site

Hyas Shaw Trails

Rae-Mor Park

Andy Lake

Warren Lake

Pemberton Lake Rec Site

HYAS LAKE FSR

1.5km 0km 3km

690,000m E   700,000m E   710,000m E   290,000m E

120°15' 120°10' 120°05' 120°00' 119°55'

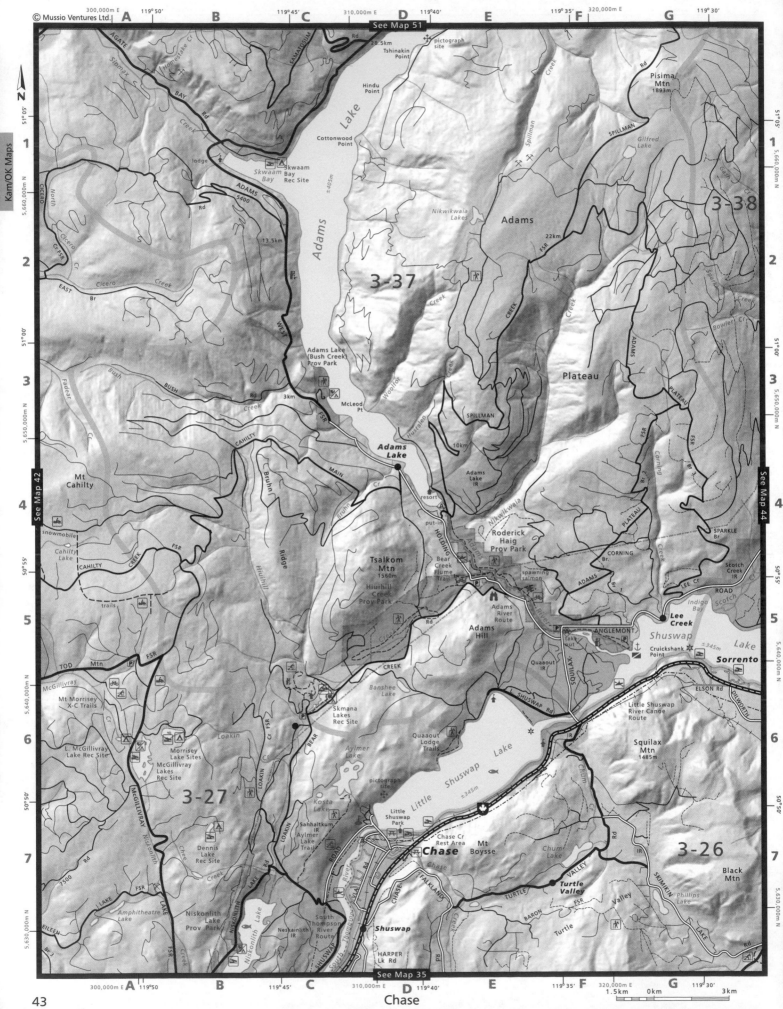

See Map 51

See Map 42

See Map 44

Adams Lake
(Bush Creek)
Prov Park

3-37

Adams Plateau

Adams Lake

Mt Cahilty

Tsalkom Mtn 1560m

Hiuihill Creek Prov Park

Roderick Haig Prov Park

Bear Creek Flume Trail

Adams Hill

Nikwikwaia

Adams Lake IR

Lee Creek

Sorrento

Shuswap Lake

TOD Mtn

Mt Morrisey X-C Trails

L. McGillivray Lake Rec Site

Morrisey Lake Sites

McGillivray Lakes Rec Site

3-27

Skmana Lakes Rec Site

Banshee Lake

Aylmer Lake

Quaaout Lodge Trails

Little Shuswap Lake

Squilax Mtn 1485m

Little Shuswap River Canoe Route

3-26

Dennis Lake Rec Site

Kosta Lake

Sahhaltkum IR
Aylmer Lake Trail

Little Shuswap Park

Chase

Mt Boysse

Chum Lake

Black Mtn

Turtle Valley

Phillips Lake

Amphitheatre Lake

Niskonlith Lake Prov Park

Neskainlith IR

South Thompson River Route

Shuswap

HARPER Lk Rd

See Map 35

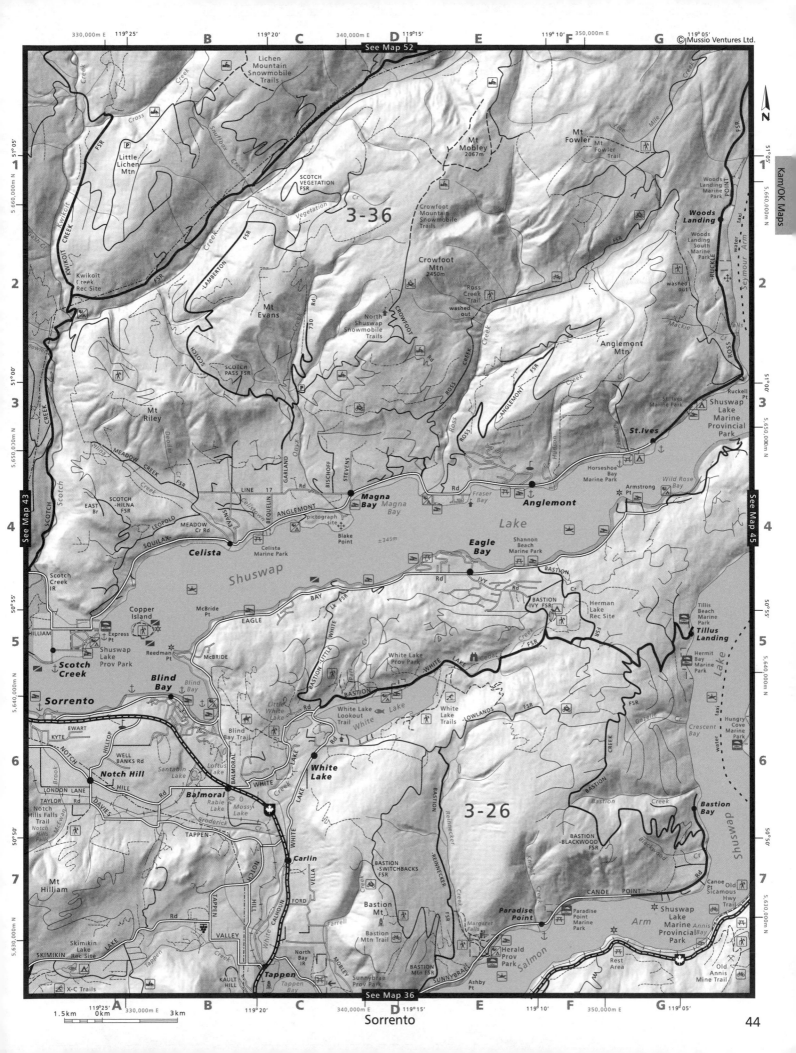

© Mussio Ventures Ltd.

See Map 43

See Map 45

See Map 36

Sorrento

44

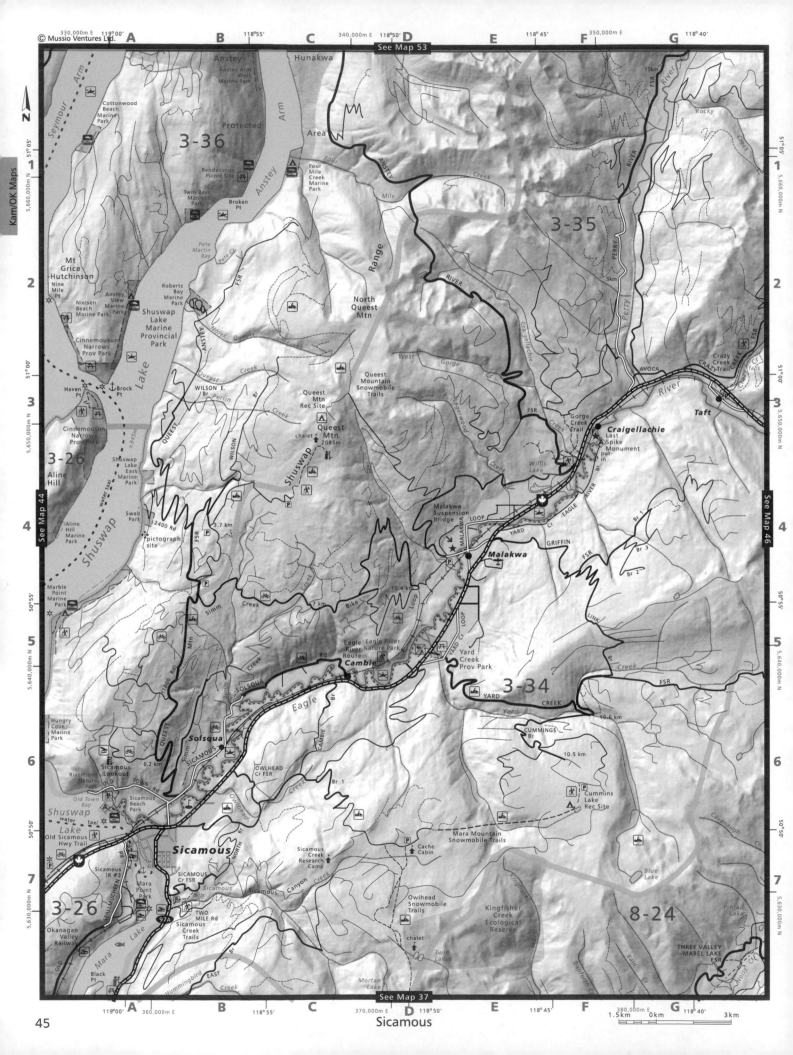

Kam/OK Maps

A   119°00'   330,000m E   **B**   118°55'   **C**   340,000m E   118°50'   **D**   **E**   118°45'   **F**   350,000m E   **G**   118°40'

See Map 53

Seymour Arm

Hunakwa

3-36

Anstey Arm West Marine Park

Cottonwood Beach Marine Park

Protected

Anstey Arm

Rendezvous Picnic Site

Four Mile Creek Marine Park

3-35

Rocky

Twin Bays Marine Park

Broken Pt

Pete Martin Bay

Anstey

Range

Mile

Creek

15km FSR River

51°05'

5,660,000m N

Mt Grice Hutchinson

Nine Mile Pt

Nielsen Beach Marine Park

Anstey View Marine Park

Roberts Bay Marine Park

FSR

North Queest

North Queest Mtn

West Gorge

Craigellachie

Perry

5km

51°00'

5,650,000m N

Cinnemousun Narrows Prov Park

Shuswap Lake Marine Provincial Park

Creek

WILSON E. Br Perrin

Queest

Queest Mtn Rec Site

Queest Mountain Snowmobile Trails

FSR

RIVER

Gorge Creek Trail

Avoca

Taft

CRAZY Creek Trail

Crazy Creek Falls

Cr falls

Haven Pt

Brock Pt

Queest

WILSON

chalet

Queest Mtn 2085m

Creek

Leigerwood

Willis Lake

Craigellachie Last Spike Monument put-in

3-26

Cinnemousun Narrows Prov Park

Shuswap Lake East Marine Park

Creek

Shuswap

Malakwa Suspension Bridge

Br

RIVER

EAGLE

Br 1

50°55'

5,640,000m N

Aline Hill

Aline Hill Marine Park

Shuswap

Swall Park

2400 Rd

3.7 km

FSR

pictograph site

Cr

MALAKWA LOOP

YARD

Malakwa

GRIFFIN

FSR

LINK

Br 2

Br 3

Marble Point Marine Park

Simm

Creek

10.4 km

Bike

Loop

Eagle River Route

Eagle River Nature Park

Yard Creek Prov Park

Creek

Br

50°55'

Hungry Cove Marine Park

Mtn

11800 Rd

Rd

Cambie

YARD CREEK

Yard

3-34

FSR

10.6 km

5

Solsqua

Eagle

Br

CAMBIE

CUMMINGS Br

10.5 km

QUEEST

SICAMOUS

Simm Creek

OWLHEAD Cr FSR

Br 1

Cummins Lake Rec Site

50°50'

5,630,000m N

Riverfront Nature Park

Sicamous Lookout

OLD TOWN Rd

6.2 km

Owlhead

Creek

Cache Cabin

Mara Mountain Snowmobile Trails

Shuswap Lake

Old Town Bay

Sicamous Beach Park

NORTH

Sicamous Creek Research Camp

Owlhead Snowmobile Trails

Blue Lake

Water taxi

Sicamous

Old Sicamous Hwy Trail

SICAMOUS Cr FSR

Sicamous Trails

Sicamous Canyon

Kingfisher Creek Ecological Reserve

8-24

Pintail Lake

50°50'

3-26

Sicamous IR #3

Mara Point Park

97A

TWO MILE Rd

Sicamous Creek Trails

chalet

THREE VALLEY -MABEL LAKE FSR

Okanagan Valley Railway

Black Pt

Mara Lake

Hummingbird Creek

EAST

Twin Lakes

Mortan Lake

Noisy Cr

See Map 37

119°00'   **A**   360,000m E   **B**   118°55'   **C**   370,000m E   **D**   118°50'   **E**   118°45'   **F**   380,000m E   **G**   118°40'

1.5km   0km   3km

Sicamous

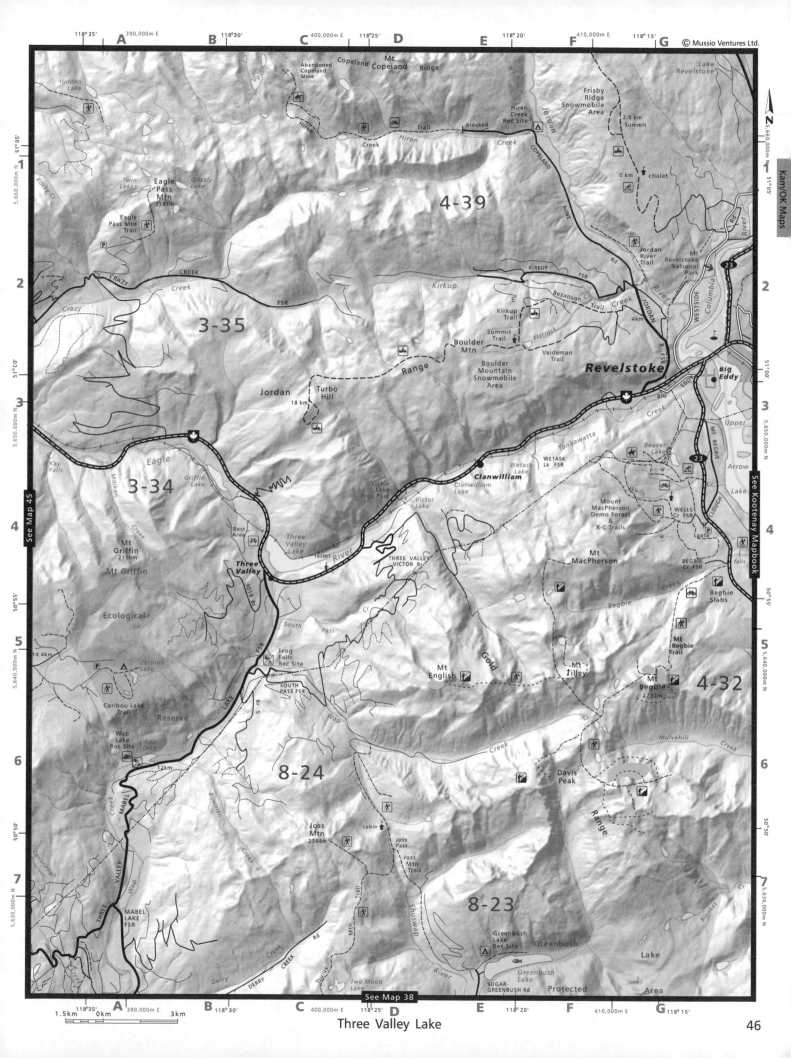

Kamy/OK Maps

Hidden Lake

Rocky Cr

Twin Lakes

Eagle Pass Mtn 2351m

Grizzly Lake

Eagle Pass Mtn Trail

P

Crazy

CRAZY CREEK

Creek

FSR

3-35

Abandoned Copeland Mine

Copeland

Mt Copeland

Ridge

Hiren

Creek

Hiren

Trail

blocked

Hiren Creek Rec Site

4-39

Copeland

Jordan

MINE

Frisby Ridge Snowmobile Area

2.5 km Summit

0 km

chalet

Lake Revelstoke

Rd

River

Jordan River Trail

Mt Revelstoke National Park

23

WESTSIDE

Columbia

River

Kirkup

Creek

KIRKUP

Bezanson Cr

Trail

4km

JORDAN

R. FSR

FSR

Revelstoke

Big Eddy

Kay Falls

Eagle

Griffin Lake

Mitikan

Creek

3-34

Boulder Mtn

Range

Jordan

Turbo Hill

18 km

Boulder Mountain Snowmobile Area

Kirkup Trail

Summit Trail

Flatrock

Veideman Trail

Tonkawatta

BIG

Creek

EDDY

MT BEGBIE

Upper

Arrow

Wetask Lake

WETASK Lk FSR

Clanwilliam Lake

Clanwilliam

Beaver Lake

Wells

23

Lake

Mt Griffin 2156m

Mt Griffin

Griffin Lake

Rest Area

Victor Lake Prov Park

Victor Lake

Three Valley Lake

River

90.9 Br

Three Valley

THREE VALLEY - VICTOR Br.

Cr

Mount MacPherson Demo Forest & X-C Trails

Mt MacPherson

WELLS Cr FSR

gate

P

Begbie

Creek

BEGBIE Cr FSR

falls

Begbie Slabs

Ecological

Three Valley Lake

South

Pass

Gold

Mt English

Mt Tilley

Mt Begbie Trail

Mt Begbie 2732m

4-32

14.4km

P

Caribou Lake

FSR

Frog Falls Rec Site

SOUTH PASS FSR

Wap

Creek

Davis Peak

Mulvehill

Creek

Caribou Lake Trail

Reserve

Br 5

Wap Lake Rec Site

Wap Lake

12km

8-24

Range

Creek

MABEL

Bowman

Joss Mtn 2384m

cabin

Joss Pass

Joss Mtn Trail

Shuswap

8-23

Blanket

Cr

LAKE

THREE VALLEY

MABEL LAKE FSR

Wap

Cavanaugh

Creek

Derry

DERRY CREEK

Rd

Tsuius

Two Moon Lake

Mtn

Trail

River

Greenbush Lake Rec Site

Greenbush Lake

SUGAR-GREENBUSH Rd

Greenbush

Lake

Protected

Area

See Map 45

See Kootenay Mapbook

1.5 km   0km   3km   **A**   390,000m E   **B**   118°30'   **C**   400,000m E   **D**   See Map 38   **E**   118° 20'   **F**   410,000m E   **G**   118°15'

Three Valley Lake

46

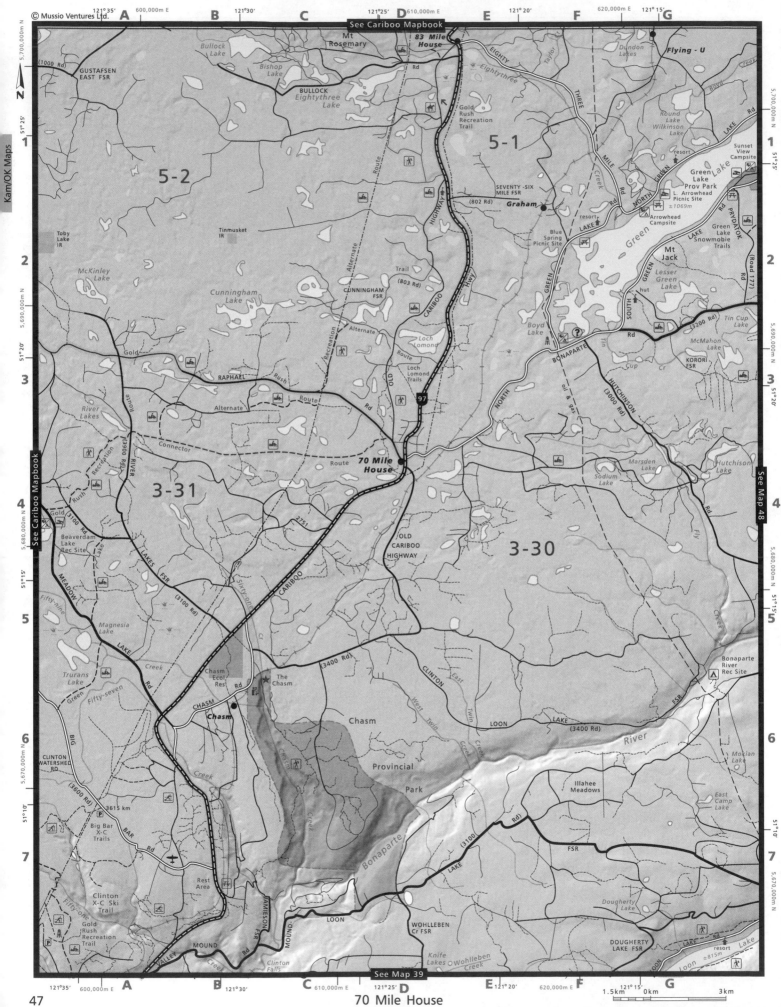

83 Mile House

Kam/OK Maps

5-2

5-1

5-1

3-31

3-30

Flying - U

N

70 Mile House

70 Mile House

Chasm

Chasm Provincial Park

Bonaparte River Rec Site

1.5km   0km   3km

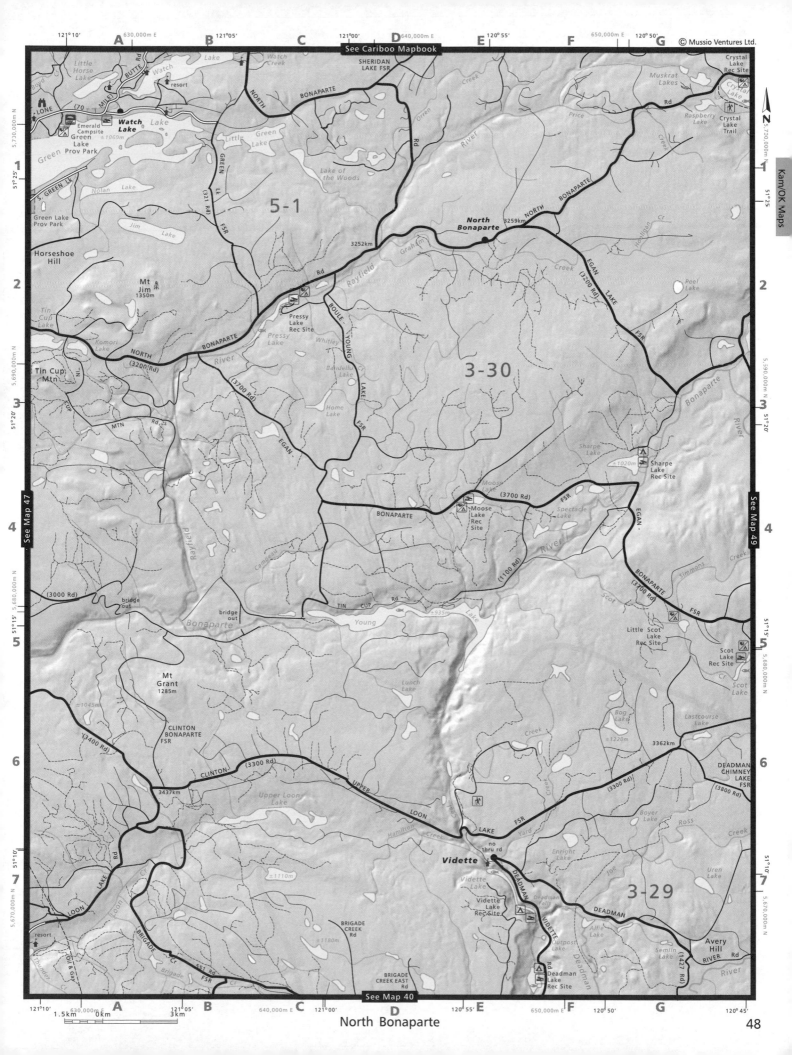

Kam/OK Maps

See Map 47

See Map 49

5-1

3-30

3-29

See Map 40

North Bonaparte

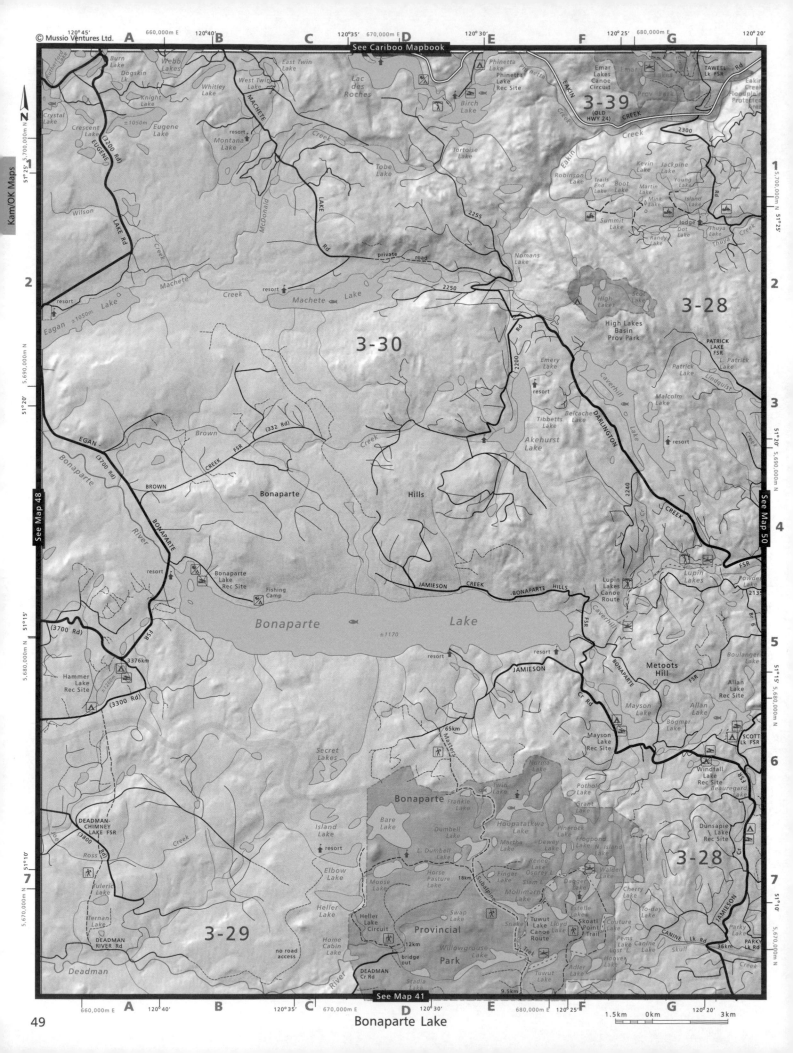

Bonaparte Lake

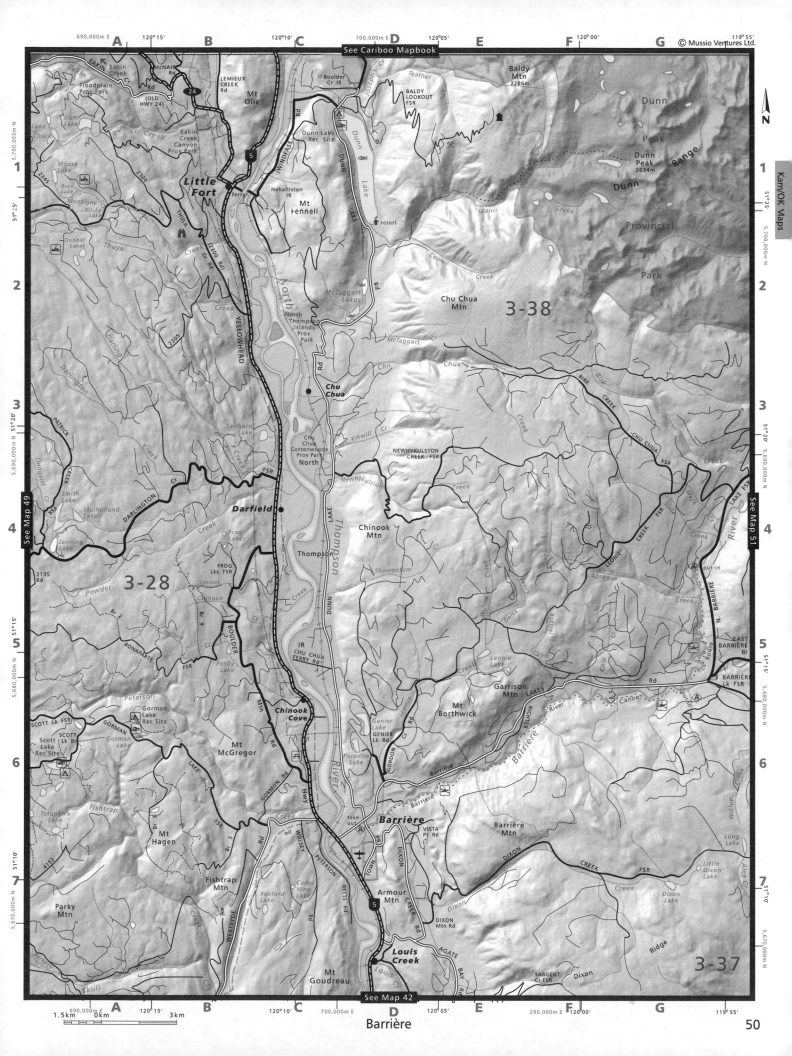

See Cariboo Mapbook

Kam/OK Maps

Baldy Mtn 2286m

Dunn Peak Range

Dunn Peak 2634m

BALDY LOOKOUT FSR

Teather

Eakin Cr

McNAIR Rd

24

LEMIEUX CREEK Rd

Mt Olie

Boulder Cr IR

Joseph

Floodplain Prov Park

Dum Lake

Eakin Creek

(OLD HWY 24)

Eakin Creek Canyon Prov Park

Dunn Lake Rec Site

Dunn Lake

Dum Cr

Luke Chuck

5

Moose Lake

Buck Lake

2345

2320

Little Fort

ferry

5

Nehalliston IR

Mt Fennell

resort

Dunn Creek

Chu Chua Mtn

3-38

Montigny Birch Lake

Dunbar Lakes

THULA

Thuya

2300 Rd

YELLOWHEAD

2305

North Thompson

McTaggart Lakes

McTaggart Cr

DUNN LAKE Rd

Cowell Creek

Chua

Dunbar Lakes

Janning Lake

PATRICK

Darlington Creek

Sanborn Lake

Chu Chua

BIRK CREEK

See Map 49

Lindquist Lake

Smith Lake

Mulholland Lake

DARLINGTON

FSR

Chu Chua Cottonwoods Prov Park North

Kikwill Cr

NEWHYKULSTON CREEK FSR

Newhykulsion

CHU CHUA FSR

Slate Creek

Mack Creek

RIVER LAKE FSR

See Map 51

2135 Rd

Powder

3-28

Frog Lakes

FROG Lks FSR

Darfield

Frog Cr

Chinook Mtn

Thompson

Skowootum

LEONIE CREEK

Sprague Creek

put-in

N. BARRIÈRE

Janning Lake

Ipsoot

Chinook

Br 9

Br 2

Nelson

BONAPARTE

Posby Lake

BOULDER FSR

IR CHU CHUA FERRY Rd

Willow Creek

Leonie Lake

Delta Cr

Bottrel Cr

Ehip Cr

RICHTER Rd

Route

EAST BARRIÈRE Br

S BARRIÈRE Lk FSR

Peterson Creek

Gorman Lake Rec Site

Gorman Lake

GORMAN

Mt McGregor

Chinook Cove

Genier Lake

GENIER Lake Rd

Mt Borthwick

Garrison Mtn

LAKES

LEOTIE

Leonie Cr

GORDON Cr Rd

Canoe River

Barrière River

SCOTT Lk FSR

Scott Lake Rec Site

SCOTT Lk Br

GORMAN LAKE

Mt Hagen

Fishtrap Mtn

Totunkwa Lake

Fishtrap

Rexford Lake

Camp Nine Lake

Paradise Lake

Barrière River

Barrière

take-out

Barrière Mtn

DIXON CREEK

Wikiuri Creek

Long Lake

4152

Parky Mtn

Skull Cr

Fishtrap Mtn

WESTSYDE Rd

WOLSEY

oil

PETERSON Rd

BETTS Rd

TOWN

HWY

VISTA Pt Rd

DIXON

DIXON CREEK

FSR

Little Dixon Lake

Dixon Lake

Mt Goudreau

5

Armour Mtn

Louis Creek

AGATE

BAY Rd

Louis Cr

DIXON Mtn Rd

SARGENT Cr FSR

Dixon Ridge

3-37

See Map 42

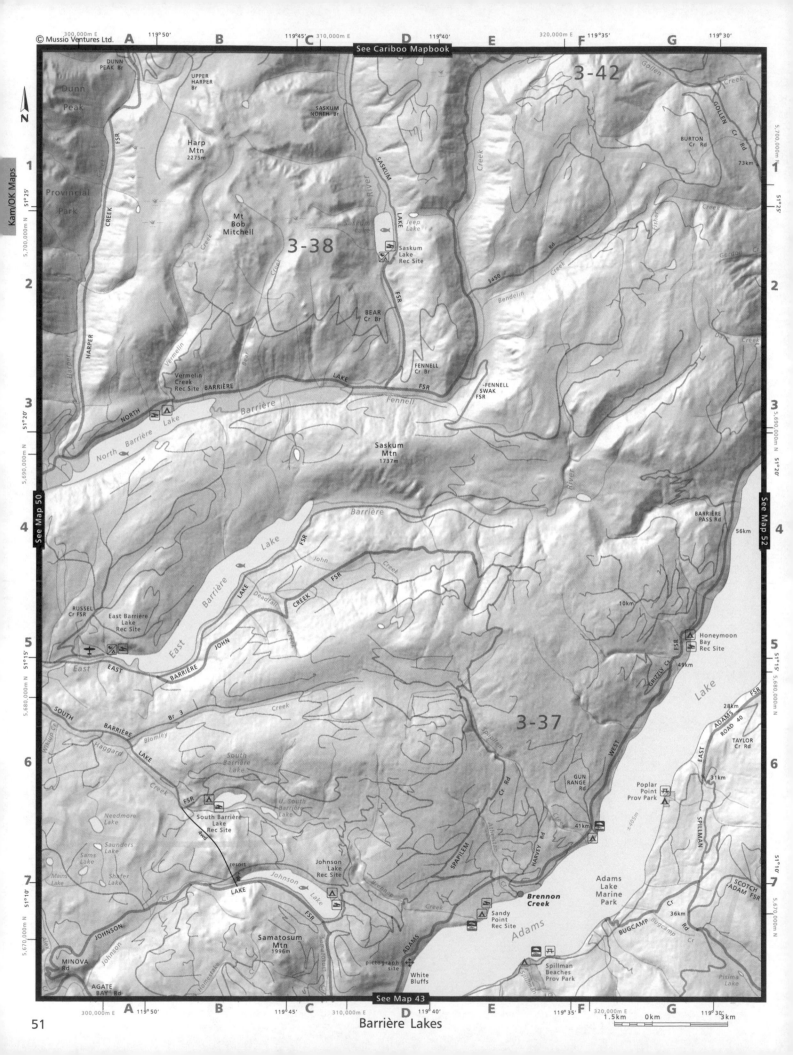

© Mussio Ventures Ltd.

A 119°50' B 119°45' C 310,000m E D 119°40' E 320,000m E F 119°35' G 119°30'

Kam/OK Maps

N

300,000m E

51°25'

Dunn Peak
Provincial Park

DUNN PEAK Br
UPPER HARPER Br

Harp Mtn
2275m

SASKUM NORTH Br

3-42

BURTON Cr Rd
73km

5,700,000m N

51°25'

Mt Bob Mitchell

3-38

Saskum Lake

Jeep Lake

Saskum Lake Rec Site

3450

Bendelin

BEAR Cr Br

Vermelin Creek Rec Site

BARRIÈRE

FENNELL Cr Br

-FENNELL SWAK FSR

NORTH

North Barrière Lake

Barrière Lake

Barrière

LAKE

Fennell

Saskum Mtn
1737m

5,690,000m N

51°20'

BARRIÈRE PASS Rd
56km

Barrière

Lake

River

See Map 50   See Map 52

FSR

John

Creek

East Barrière Lake

RUSSEL Cr FSR

East Barrière Lake Rec Site

JOHN

LAKE

CREEK

Deadfall

Creek

10km

BARRIÈRE

East

EAST

Honeymoon Bay Rec Site

FSR

49km

East Barrière Lake

SOUTH

BARRIÈRE

LAKE

Blomley

Br 3

Creek

3-37

Lake

28km

ADAMS ROAD 40

TAYLOR Cr Rd

5,680,000m N

51°15'

Wilhup Cr

Haggard

Creek

South Barrière Lake

U. South Barrière Lake

Spapilem

GUN RANGE Rd

WEST

31km

Poplar Point Prov Park

SPILLMAN

Needmore Lake

FSR

4wd

South Barrière Lake Rec Site

Cr Rd

41km

5,670,000m N

51°10'

Saunders Lake

Sams Lake

Mains Lake

Shafer Lake

resort

Johnson LAKE

Johnson Lake Rec Site

Johnson Lake

FSR

Athelstan

Cr Rd

SPAPILEM

HARVEY Rd

Brennon Creek

Sandy Point Rec Site

Adams Lake Marine Park

36km

SCOTCH ADAM FSR

MINOVA Rd

JOHNSON

Johnson

Samatosum Mtn
1996m

Homestake

Umagorges

ADAMS

pictograph site

White Bluffs

Adams

Creek

Spillman

BUGCAMP

Bugcamp Cr Rd

Pisima Lake

AGATE BAY Rd

Spillman Beaches Prov Park

300,000m E A 119°50' B 119°45' C 310,000m E D 119°40' E 320,000m E F 119°35' G 119°30'

See Map 43

51

Barrière Lakes

1.5km   0km   3km

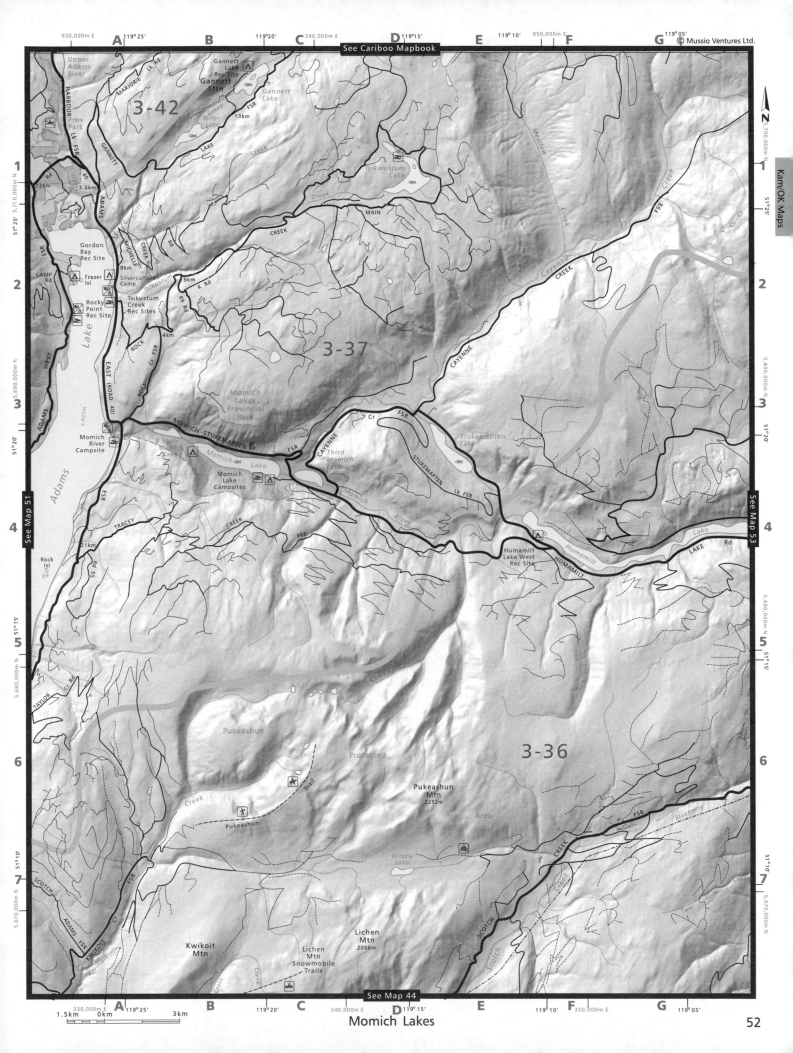

© Mussio Ventures Ltd.

3-42

3-37

3-36

Upper Adams River

HARBOUR Lk FSR

MARJORIE Lk Rd

Gannett Lake Rec Site

Gannett Mtn

Gannett Lake

Telfer Lake

13km

GANNETT

ADAMS

3.5km

72km

40

MICHELLE CREEK

Gordon Bay Rec Site

8km

Silverculture Camp

Fraser Isl

CAMP Rd

Rocky Point Rec Site

Tsikustum Creek Rec Sites

Deve Cr

WEST

ADAMS

Lake

EAST (ROAD 40)

ROCK

ROCK Cr FSR

±405m

Momich River Campsite

4km

9km

K Rd

49 Rd

Tsikustum

Michael Rd

Tsikwustum Lake

MAIN CREEK

Creek

CAYENNE

CAYENNE CREEK

Meadow Creek

Scotch Creek

FSR

MOWICH-STUKEMAPTEN FSR

Little Momich Lakes

Momich Lake

Momich Lake Campsites

Third Momich Lake

CAYENNE Cr FSR

STUKEMAPTEN Lk FSR

Stukemapten Lake

See Map 51

Adams Lake

TRACEY

21km

Rd 55

Rock Isl

Momich Lake

CREEK

Momich River

Humamilt Lake West Rec Site

HUMAMILT

Humamilt Lake

LAKE Rd

See Map 53

TAYLOR Cr Rd

Celista

Creek

Pukeashun

Pukeashun Trail

Pukeashun

Protected

Pukeashun Mtn 2252m

Area

Grizzly Lake

SCOTCH CREEK

Blueberry

Two Mile Creek

SCOTCH

ADAMS FSR

KWIKOIT

Kwikoit Ct

FSR

Kwikoit Mtn

Gross Creek

Lichen Mtn Snowmobile Trails

Creek

Lichen Mtn 2088m

SCOTCH

1.5km   0km   3km

330,000m E
340,000m E
350,000m E

119°25'   119°20'   119°15'   119°10'   119°05'

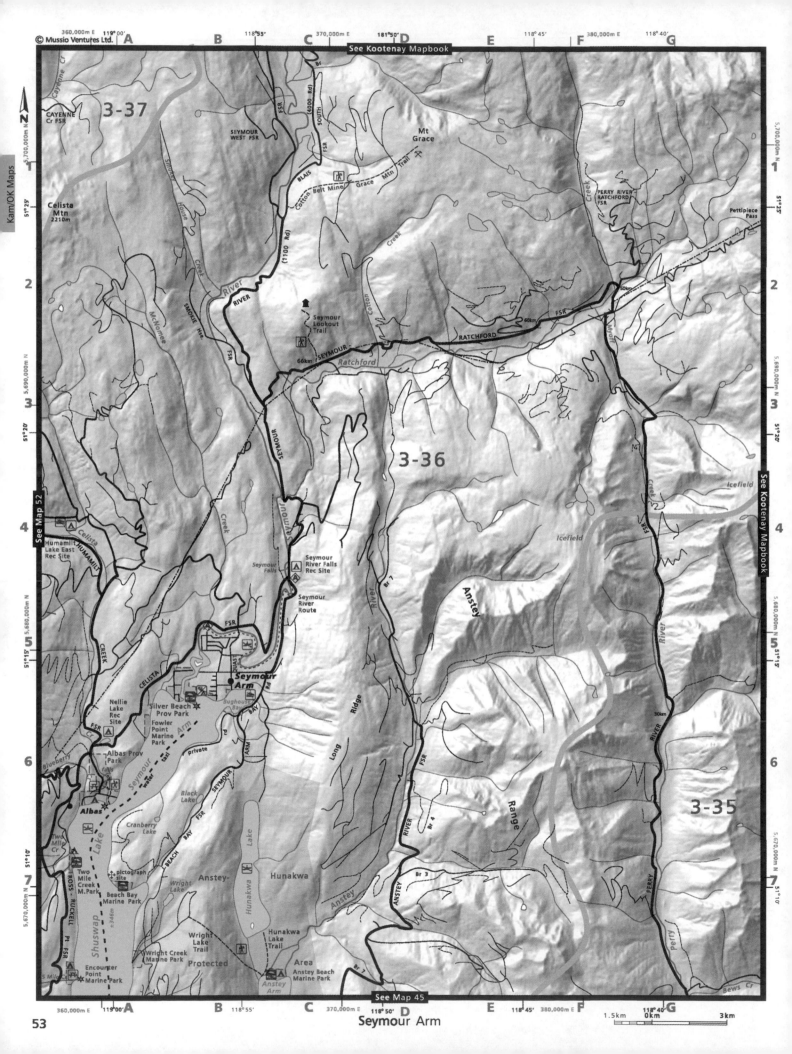

Kam/OK Maps

3-37

Celista
Mtn
2210m

CAYENNE
Cr FSR

SEYMOUR
WEST FSR

Mt
Grace

Cotton Belt Mine

Grace Mtn Trail

PERRY RIVER
RATCHFORD
FSR

Pettipiece
Pass

50km

Seymour
Lookout
Trail

66km SEYMOUR

Ratchford

RATCHFORD

60km

See Map 52

Humamilt
Lake East
Rec Site

3-36

Icefield

Seymour
Falls

Seymour River Falls
Rec Site

Icefield

Seymour
River
Route

Anstey

Br 7

Nellie Lake
Rec Site

Seymour
Arm

Silver Beach
Prov Park

Fowler
Point
Marine
Park

Bughouse
Bay

Long Ridge

FSR

Albas Prov
Park

Black
Lake

Br 4

3-35

Albas

Range

Cranberry
Lake

Two
Mile
Cr

Two
Mile Creek
M.Park

pictograph
site

Beach Bay
Marine Park

Anstey-

Hunakwa

Br 3

Wright
Lake

Wright Creek
Marine Park

Wright
Lake Trail

Hunakwa
Lake Trail

Protected

Area

Anstey Beach
Marine Park

Encounter
Point
Marine Park

Br 7

See Map 45

53

Seymour Arm

1.5km   0km   3km

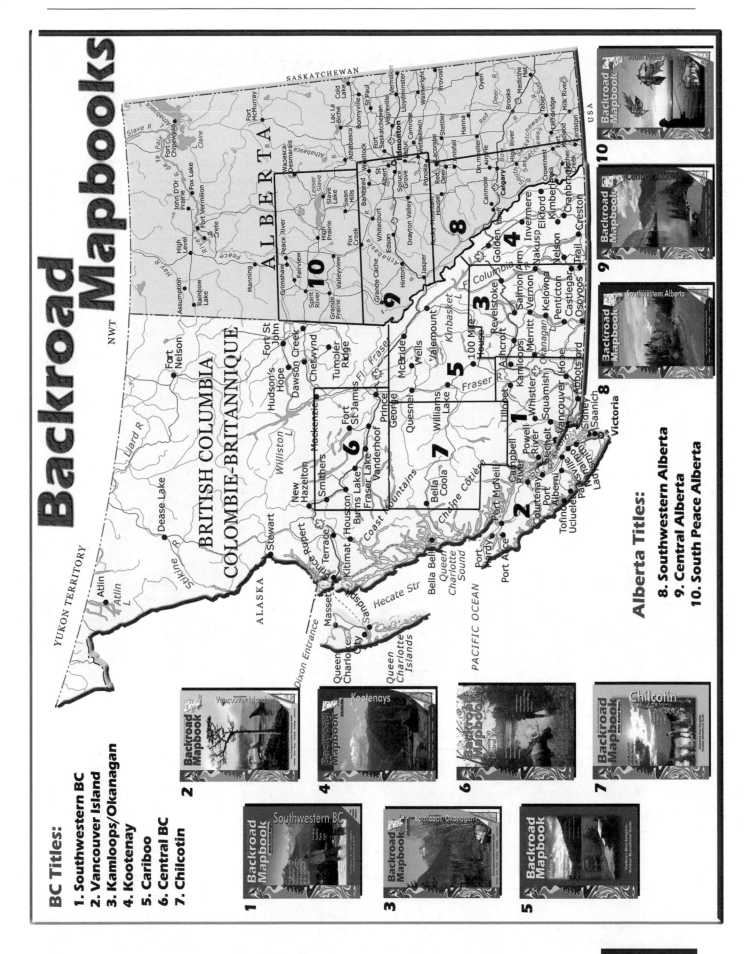

Backroad Mapbooks

BC Titles:

1. Southwestern BC
2. Vancouver Island
3. Kamloops/Okanagan
4. Kootenay
5. Cariboo
6. Central BC
7. Chilcotin

Alberta Titles:

8. Southwestern Alberta
9. Central Alberta
10. South Peace Alberta

Service Providers

Accommodations

Acacia Grove R.V. Park & Cabins

1block off Hwy. 1 in Spences Bridge.

Thompson River steelhead angling, rafting, full hookups, cabins, laundromat, store, payphones/modem.

1-800-833-7508

Fax: 250-458-2227

www.acacia-rvpark-cabins.com

Alpine Wilderness Retreat

Located in Bonaparte Park. Our resort access is mostly by helicopter with foot access through the park. Advance notice is required for hike-ins. Open from June to mid-September.

#20-1755 Ord Rd.
Kamloops, B.C V2B 7V5
1-888-668-1615
Fax: 1-780-962-4237

www.AlpineWildernessRetreat.com

Ashcroft Legacy Park

Full service RV park, tenting, picnic, sani-dump & showers. Open May1 to October 15. Located next to the river downtown Ashcroft.

P.O. Box 183
Ashcroft, BC V0K 1A0
T/F: 250-453-2642
www.village.ashcroft.bc.ca

Email: ashchamber@goldcountry.bc.ca

Brookside Campsite

Tenting, RV sites, group sites, pool, laundry, free showers, no trains

1621 East Trans Canada Hwy #1
Cache Creek, B.C.
1 km East of Junction of #97 & #1

1-250-457-6633

www.brooksidecampsite.com

Email: brooksidecampsite@hotmail.com

Campers Beach Cabins

Rustic cabin rentals on private beach across from Kelowna B.C; on Okanagan Lake; ten minutes to downtown.

3392 E. Boundary Rd. Westbank B.C. V4T 2H4
250-768-7592
Email: campersbeach@shaw.ca

http://members.shaw.ca/campersbeach/

Cascade Cove R.V. Park

April 1 - Oct 31. Fully Serviced Sites

Showers, tenting, hiking, swimming at the foot of Cascade Falls.

1211 River Road, Christina Lake, BC
V0H 1E0

1-250-447-6662

Fax: 1-250-447-6163

Cathedral Lakes Lodge

AT 2000 MTS CANADA'S HIGHEST FULL SERVICE RESORT

Stay in a comfortable lodge, cabins or campgrounds to enjoy the spectacular hiking and fishing in CATHEDRAL PROVINCIAL PARK.

1-888-255-4453

www. cathedral-lakes-lodge.com

Eco-Heritage Campground

Pristine camping, historical surroundings, abundant recreational opportunities, minutes away from downtown Grand Forks. Free "ionized water" for our guests. To insure a site call in advance.

P.O. Box 2593
Grand Forks, BC V0H 1H0
1-250-442-3153
Email: pod@sunshinecable.com
www.ecoheritagecampground.com

Elk Ridge Outdoors

Clean, private, wilderness, riverfront chalet, accommodates up to 6, 14 large riverfront campsites, 1 group site.

Visa/Mastercard accepted
250-295-6229

P.O. Box 1274
14 km. W. Princeton, B.C.
V0X 1W0

Email: elkridgeoutdoor@uniserve.com

Goldpanner Campground and Cafe

Located in the Monashee Mountains

Gold Panning, hiking, fishing, serviced RV sites, tenting year round cabins. Home cooking in the Cafe.

423 Highway 6
Cherryville B.C. V0E 2G3

1-250-547-2025

Highland Cabins and Tours

Lodging and adventure on the K.V.R. with all-season access to the Okanagan Highlands.

P.O. Box 191
Beaverdell, BC V0H 1A0

250-484-5505

Email: highlandcabins@msn.com

Johnson Lake Resort

Beautiful crystal clear waters.

Cabins, campsites, open year round.

A peaceful retreat for the whole family.

P.O. Box 78, RR1
Louis Creek, BC V0E 2E0
1-250-672-1008
Email: info@johnsonlakeresort.com

www.johnsonlakeresort.com

Knouff Lake Resort

Your Year Round Vacation Spot.

P.O. Box 158
Heffley Creek, BC V0E 1Z0
P: 250-578-8155
F: 250-578-8683
www.knoufflake.com
Email: knoufflake@telus.net

Logan Lake Lodge

Full service lodge with restaurant and pub.
Country hospitality & reasonable prices. World
class fly fishing, golf, x-country skiing, snowmobiling and ice-fishing.

111 Chartrand Avenue
Logan Lake, BC V0K 1W0

www.loganlake.com

Mabel Lake Resort & Air Park

35km East of Enderby. Open April-October.
90 RV Sites, Cabin Rentals, Boat Rentals, Store,
Liquor Store. 2900 ft airstrip.

3514 Mabel Lake Road
Enderby, BC
V0E 1V5
250-838-6234
www.mabellakeresort.com

Nicklen Lake Resort

Open all year. Fishing, hiking,
ice-fishing, skating &
snowmobiling nearby.

P.O. Box 28025
Lavington, BC V1B 3L9
Cell (250) 549-0290
www.nicklenlake.com

Othello Tunnels Campground & RV Park

Open all year. Full, Partial H/ups & Tent Sites.

67851 Othello Rd
Hope, BC V0X 1L1

P: 1-877-869-0543

www.othellotunnels.com

Peach Orchard Campground

Located 1km east off Hwy 97 on Peach
Orchard Road , Summerland, B.C.

RV and tenting; grass sites with shade;
the soothing sounds of nearby creek; clean
washrooms and showers, convenience store,
tennis courts, close to city center and more.

1-250-494-9649

Email: peachorchard@telus.net

www.peachorhard.net

Princeton Castle Resort

Log Lodge - Jacuzzi tubs
Log Chalets - Hot Tubs or 2 people Jacuzzi Tubs
Cabin/Sleeping Cabana's/Tipi's/RV Park/Tenting
Located on the Trans Canada Trail/125 acres of
Natural Beauty
Reservations **1-888-228-8881**

Email: info@castleresort.com
www.castleresort.com

Riviera R.V. Park & Campground

Located on banks of Kettle River
Close to Trans-Canada Trail section
running from Grand Fortks to Christina Lake.

6331 Hwy. 3 East
Grand Forks, BC V0H 1H9

www.sunshinecable.com/~riviera

Spruce Wilderness Lodge

Situated on beautiful Bonaparte Lake, offers
an ideal setting for a relaxing outdoor vacation. The accommodations provide you with
first class comfort, while the licensed lounge is
a great place to socialize. A wide range of
activities ensure an enjoyable holiday for every
member of your party.

PO Box 119 Kamloops, BC V2C 5K9

250-706-9111
www.sprucewildernesslodge.ca

Wonderful Waterworld RV Park

Free evening watersliding July and Auguest.
Full hook up and tenting sites.
Family oriented.

185 Yorkton Avenue
Penticton, BC V2A 3V3
250-492-4255
www.pentictonwaterslides.com
waterworld@shaw.ca

Tours & Guides

Keith Martin

Private & Group GPS Training

3175 Webber Road
Westbank, BC
V4T 1E8
**Res: 1-250-768-9817 or
(250) 596-9709
Cell: (250) 869-9340**

Email: learn-gps@canada.com

Monashee Adventure Tours

Bike, hike or snowshoe along the historic Kettle Valley Railway's Myra Canyon & the TCT. Half to 8 day tours.

470 Cawston Ave
Kelowna, BC V1Y 9V8
1-888-76C-YCLE (2-9253)

www.monasheeadventuretours.com

Reel Fishing Adventures

Fishing B.C's Big Interior Lakes

Located in Sicamous, we fish beautiful Shuswap Lake and several other big lakes in the area. Half or full day guided fishing trips for huge rainbow and lake trout!

Sicamous, B.C
1-250-309-1361

www.reelfishingadventures.net

Important Numbers

GENERAL

Fish and Wildlife Conservation 1-800-663-9453
....http://www.sportfishing.bc.ca
Highways Report 1-800-550-4997
To Report Forest Fires........................... 1-800-663-5555
....*5555 (cellular phones)
Tourism BC 1-800-435-5622
....www.hellobc.com
Updates............................ www.backroadmapbooks.com

BC FOREST SERVICE (ROAD & TRAIL CONDITIONS)

Ministry of Forests......................http://www.gov.bc.ca/for/
    100 Mile House .... (250) 395-7800
    Arrow Forest District .... (250) 365-8600
    Cascades Forest District .... (250) 378-8400
    Kamloops Forest District .... (250) 371-6500
    Okanagan Shuswap Forest District . (250) 558-1700

PARKS

BC Parks...... http://wlapwww.gov.bc.ca/bcparks/index.htm
    Okanagan District Office .... (250) 494-6500
    Park Reservations........................... (604) 689-9025
    1-800-689-9025
    .... www.discovercamping.ca
    Thompson River District.................. (250) 851-3000

Other Numbers

BC Hydro .... www.bchydro.bc.ca/environment

---

Pictures Wanted!

Backroad Mapbooks is looking for pictures and stories on areas people visit. We also appreciate any feedback on road/trail systems, fishing holes or anything you think we could add to the book.

Backroad Mapbooks

Mail to: 5811 Beresford St, Burnaby, BC, V5J 1K1
Email: info@backroadmapbooks.com
toll free: 1-877-520-5670
phone:604-438-FISH (3474)
www.backroadmapbooks.com

Index